Troubling the Line:
Trans and Genderqueer Poetry and Poetics

Troubling the Line:
Trans and Genderqueer Poetry and Poetics

Edited by TC Tolbert and Trace Peterson

Nightboat Books
Callicoon, New York

© 2013 by Nightboat Books
Second Printing, 2015
All rights reserved
Printed in the United States

ISBN 978-1-937658-10-6

Design and typesetting by PTRSN Design (Trace Peterson)
Text set in Optima and Rotis Semi Serif

Cover photos (and photos on pages 7 and 524) by Samuel Ace

Cataloging-in-publication data is available
from the Library of Congress

Distributed by the University Press of New England
One Court Street
Lebandon, NH
www.upne.com

Nightboat Books
Callicoon, NY
www.nightboat.org

Table of Contents

Introductions

Open, and always, opening[1]
– an introduction in 3 parts

TC Tolbert

I. A history

I'm sitting at a state park in Wisconsin. It's summer 2012 and I have a beard and I have breasts. It's 3am. There is a raccoon outside of my tent raising all manner of hell. Earlier, when I was sleeping, I was using a box from Kinko's as my pillow. In the box there are 347 pages of poems by 55 trans and genderqueer authors from all over the country, most of whom I've never even met. Sometimes the world absolutely shimmers. I am not alone today.

~

This book began in the way that I imagine many collections begin, even if they are not unified by shared experience or identity. It was, and still is, simply a search for other voices. A need to find, feel, and experience community. A desire for intimacy. An exploration of space.

In 1998 I was a 23-year-old white, Pentecostal woman. I was married to a pretty great guy and I was about to become the first person in my family to earn a college degree. Still living in my hometown -Chattanooga, Tennessee - I had never really spent time outside of the south. I distinctly remember my grandfather warning me about college. He said I "should not get too smart and lose all [my] faith." He said college could alter my thinking, ethics, and perspective so greatly as to make me virtually unrecognizable. He was worried, particularly, about the things I might read.

That spring I took a feminist theory class. Even though it wasn't a required text, my professor gave me her copy of *This Bridge Called my Back: Writings by Radical Women of Color.*[2] In my first poetry class, I was introduced to the poem "Fiddleheads" by Maureen Seaton.[3] Both *This Bridge* and "Fiddleheads" did something with language that I needed. They exhilarated me. Made me feel less alone. These were *women's* voices – marginalized and fierce. They held me accountable. Called me out. Neither one-dimensional modes of self-expression nor mechanistic texts that strive to exist separately from personal identity and experience, these pieces are deeply embodied, linguistically nimble, wonderfully lyric, and scaldingly intelligent. They are intensely, beautifully complex. It would not be an exaggeration to say that my grandfather's greatest fears were realized as a result of me reading poetry. I held onto both of these texts as I made my way into a divorce, a coming out, and a family backlash. I identify as genderqueer and a big part of that for me is how much I embraced (and still embrace) the woman I was becoming as a result of those texts. The way they guided me to a sense of strength, critical analysis, perseverance, and voice.

Voyager, there are no bridges. One builds them as one walks.[4]

I dreamt of finding this collection of poems by trans and genderqueer folks for many years. I was given a copy of *Stone Butch Blues*[5] in 2002 and it was the first book I read with any direct mention of trans experience, even though it had been published almost 10 years prior. Like I said, Tennessee was a long way from any sort of thriving trans, queer, or even progressive scene. It wasn't until November 20, 2003, when I attended my first Transgender Day of Remembrance in Tucson[6], that I met a trans-identified person face to face. Three months earlier I had moved across the country, bought a compression shirt, changed my pronoun, and consistently began introducing myself as TC. Since then I'd been lurking around the queer center (there was a queer center!), reading books from their library (they had a library!), discovering the radical brilliance of Sylvia Rivera, Marsha P. Johnson, Dean Spade, and Kate Bornstein.[7] I then spent the next 8 years scouring the internet, looking for anything related to trans and genderqueer poets or poetry. Although trans and genderqueer prose narratives were available and absolutely crucial to my sense of hope and connection to a self I both knew I was becoming and was deeply afraid of becoming, what I really wanted was to read what other trans and genderqueer poets were writing. I needed to see their forms, listen to their syntax, learn from how they were composing themselves on and off the page.

By 2009, I was at a comfortable place in my personal transition (i.e., it had stopped consuming every large and small bit of my brain, both chemically and emotionally) and I kind of couldn't believe searches for trans and genderqueer poetry were turning up something like 15 hits. I had recently finished *Without a Net: The Female Experience of Growing Up Working Class*[8] and there was an echo of *This Bridge Called My Back* there – gathering voices based on a shared marginalized identity and/or experience that did not result in a uniform narrative or expression. Both books crystallized incredibly profound moments of ordinary, brilliant, ignored people saying courageous, visceral things. They inherently "correct[ed] a cultural misunderstanding"[9] that women of color, queer women, poor women don't have anything to say or any interesting way to say it.[10] Having grown up a broke girl in the south, marginalized in some ways while incredibly privileged in others, I realized I didn't have to have a PhD or the backing of an institution to create the book I, and so many others, need.[11] I couldn't wait any longer to hear what trans and genderqueer poets had to say.

A few months later I approached the first publisher I thought would be interested in helping me create such a collection. Although they were interested, they were already overcommitted and so, the project was stalled. Then, in 2010, I stumbled upon Trace's book, *Since I Moved In*. (Well, by stumbled I actually mean I was cleaning the house of a poet friend as a side job and I was snooping around in his books.[12]) Trace's work was absolutely magic to me – a sharp and shifting voice that refused to be groundless, a reckoning with trans identity, not a trajectory. It wasn't until a year later, when I was out for a run, that I had the clarity that I needed help[13] and the chutzpah (she didn't know me from Adam) to write and ask her to co-edit this book with me.

Obviously (and thankfully) she said yes.[14] What followed was a burst of emails, giddiness, research, and phone calls. Within the next several months we honed in on a vision for the book. I really wanted to see a body of work from each poet, one or two pages never felt like enough. Trace wanted poetics statements, reflections on writing practice. Together we agreed on five to ten pages total for each poet – about seven pages of poems alongside one to two page short essays in which each poet reflects on intersections (and/or disconnections) between one's experience of the body (as a trans and/or genderqueer person) and the ways one uses language. As we said in our call for work, "a guiding question for this might be, why does this work come from your particular body/experience?"[15] We wanted a deep experience of the textual body – to see how each author takes up, inhabits, and imbues space. Not all of the poets submitted a poetics statement. Yet, for those who did, the responses were wildly diverse – some only obliquely addressing gender and its relationship to writing, while others very directly explicate body and poem. To summarize a lovely thing David Wolach said in an email exchange, the distinction to be made is one of generativity – when does opacity regarding process, concept, gender, and/or expression lead to more possibility and when does it shut it down? If there is one thing I wanted to usher in with this collection, it is an opening – an attempt to expand the range of what is possible for trans and genderqueer poets and to acknowledge that there is no such thing as a monolithic trans and genderqueer poetry. Walt Whitman comes to mind: *I contain multitudes.*[16] That there are, indeed, trans and genderqueer poets and trans and genderqueer poetries.

II. Thoughts on language and inclusion

The function of art is to do more than tell it like it is - it's to imagine what is possible.[17]
This book began with questions: *who are we?* (So often trans and genderqueer people start out (t)here. *A home out of questions,* as Trish Salah says. *Can I say I'm here? How to lunguage me, language?*[18] *And with what voice?*) *Where are we,* we wondered. And, *aren't we pretty? What do trans and genderqueer poets do differently than cis poets?*[19] *Can we find us? (We need to find us.) Do we say we? Can we say us? Whose is the voice in the text? Where is the body in the poem?*
Trace and I agreed early on that we had no desire to be the gender police. We recognize that transitioning is a very individual process, greatly influenced by many factors including safety, access to resources, and support.[20] We did not (and do not) wish to prioritize one form of embodiment over another, nor do we wish to perpetuate any sort of homogenous trans and/or genderqueer myth. The process of coming to recognize and express oneself as trans and/or genderqueer is not one-size-fits-all. So, we had no litmus test other than self-identification. Our only request for consideration for inclusion in this anthology was that the author self-identify as trans, genderqueer, and/or gender non-conforming (recognizing that language is limited). There were no parameters regarding content for submissions, although many poets did choose to submit work related to gender, identity, and/or expression. Regardless of content, we are primarily concerned with work by authors whose experience of gender involves, as Susan Stryker so beautifully says, *the movement across a socially imposed boundary away from an imposed starting place – rather than any particular destination or mode of transition.*[21] We call this collection *Troubling the Line* because this is what we see trans and genderqueer poets doing – challenging the idea of a single trans narrative, interrogating binaries of all sorts, and playing with, delighting in, explorations (explosions) of form.
Yet, in *Excitable Speech: A Politics of the Performative,* Judith Butler claims that *one "exists" not only by virtue of being recognized, but, in a prior sense, by being recognizable.* We wanted to know, would trans and genderqueer poets be recognizable? Without a collection, would we know a trans and genderqueer poet if we

saw one? Is there a difference between a trans and genderqueer poet and a trans and genderqueer poem? Can a trans and genderqueer poem pass and does it want to? Aside from possible narrative overlap, would there be syntactic, stylistic, and/or imagistic themes? Do we want that? Is there such a thing as a trans and genderqueer poetics? A trans and genderqueer genre? A trans and genderqueer form?

The threat with trying to answer these questions, the danger with creating an anthology at all, is twofold. First, there is exclusion. As E. Tracy Grinnell points out, *anthologies are inherently, undeniably, always problematic. Even when necessary, they cannot be inclusive.*[22] Several amazing trans and genderqueer authors declined to submit and several sent in submissions 6 months after the deadline because they had only just been made aware of the call. In addition, this collection reflects the choices of both of its authors. I feel I would be remiss not to acknowledge that my choices reflect who I am as a white, relatively privileged, passing writer here in the U.S. In an attempt to avoid recreating/perpetuating racist, classist ideals, we reached out to many underrepresented communities including poets of color, poets with disabilities, poets without interest in, or access to, formal poetic education. We actively sought out work that represents diverse poetic interests (from experimental to lyric, prose to slam, narrative to formal) and we questioned our own aesthetics. While we had an explicit goal of gathering and foregrounding the wildly diverse range of aesthetics, voices, and experiences of trans and genderqueer poets writing in the US right now,[23] it would be disingenuous to act as if our own experiences of race, class, and gender did not influence what we find compelling. Other editors would undoubtedly choose differently. Grinnell again: *editing is enactment, as much as writing is.* We take full responsibility for that.

The second danger is isolation or confinement. In affirming our identities and creating space specifically for trans and genderqueer poets to share their work, there is some concern that it will be limited. Some worry that the audience will be inadvertently restricted only to those already sympathetic to trans and genderqueer issues – that "serious" (i.e. cis and/or straight) poets and readers would never pick up such a collection because it "has nothing to do with them." Others feel that by reading (or collecting) the work through the lens of trans and genderqueer author identity, the poems and their merit as poetry will be overlooked or dismissed. In other words, a biographical frame puts more emphasis on the author and hirs identity than the actual poems, therefore the collection is already assumed to contain mediocre poetry, at best. Marginalized folks have struggled with these concerns throughout time – violence can be both subtle and overt.

Yet perhaps it is invisibility, a refusal to see, that leads to the most extensive, brutal violence. To silence a person or a group is the first violent act. In a world where trans and genderqueer people are murdered at a rate of one every other day,[24] we need these poems with their specific textures, perspectives, concerns, and forms. *By* and *with* not *for* or *about*. To listen to trans and genderqueer voices in a venue specifically curated by trans and genderqueer poets. It is time to push back against assumed dominant narratives about trans and genderqueer poets (perhaps the primary one being that there are not any worth listening to). This unspoken belief was highlighted for me in Juliana Spahr and Stephanie Young's essay "Numbers Trouble" in which they count the number of men, women, and trans folks published in various places (anthologies, blogs, small presses, and prizes).[25] In small presses, they only found evidence of *one* trans person's work (this was in 2007). As I combed through anthologies, presses, and prizes from 2009-11, the numbers were still painfully low and I could not find a single central resource to even begin to connect with trans and genderqueer poets and their work. The issue, of course, is not that trans and genderqueer poets are not writing or creating quality poems. The issue is that our work is not being recognized by poets and critics outside of (mostly invisible) trans and genderqueer communities.

This is a clip. It is not, nor was it ever intended to be, the entire film. I hope you search out further work by trans and genderqueer poets. As you can see from the poetry included here, the work being done by trans and genderqueer poets is far more expansive than one might be inclined to think if just perusing general literary catalogues, presses, and academies. We hope the questions get louder: *Why aren't we seeing the work of trans and genderqueer poets in other collections, at academic conferences, on a variety of presses, at slams, and in literary journals? Where are the trans and genderqueer poets with tenure track positions, poet laureate positions, and on editorial boards?*[26]

Also, because language is continually evolving to accurately name the multitude of fierce, fabulous people, bodies, and identities who either do not identify with the terms woman, man, female, and/or male or those who do not identify with the gender and/or sex assigned to them at birth, Trace and I felt ambivalent about choosing one word that is somehow supposed to encompass us all. We settled on *trans and genderqueer* to stretch our arms as wide as we currently know how. One of the hopes for *Troubling the Line* is that the poetry in it imagines language that allows us to live and see more.

III. Then we are in language: a love letter to trans and genderqueer poets.[27]

Oh. My. God. You are here.

Can we just take a minute to acknowledge how fucking gorgeous you are? You in your *you say you you/to bend the air/proximity is practice/and nothing I come from is dead/the mirror/of what/you think/our continual here/an accumulation of satchels/*

prescription manhood/o, tendencies and their bad bad tempers/a shape inside/I'd
actually gone up in flames/to begin by making room/forget everything you know about
the way a body is built/mostly, fear will pass/when the subject disappears/if less than a
boy is a fruit/we are using someone else's pictures of war/call me tumblefish, rip-roar,
pocket of light[28]

Over 200 of you submitted poems in a matter of months. We received
submissions from Seattle to Singapore, from trans and genderqueer poets in their teens
through their 60s. We received submissions from folks who identified as non-surgical,
pre-op, post-op, Two-Spirit, intersex, it, they, gender-fluid, gender-fuckers, and gender-
fabulous. We were told by many of you that, regardless of acceptance, you were
thankful that an anthology like this would finally exist. I am absolutely humbled, struck
by your generosity. The poems you sent and the poems we collected here are stunning,
devastating, frustrating, thrilling, curious. From the moment the submissions began to
arrive I have been inspired in the literal sense of that word. You breathed into me. What
you gave was *a mouth unfastened.*[29] What you gave in *lifting, it lifts.*[30]

More than anything, I hope this work finds you. May it be one of many bridges.
Not a canon but one hundred hands pushing against a wall of homogeneity - gendered,
social, and linguistic. Not an attempt to usurp space but a prayer to create more. I
cannot thank you enough for showing up, for sharing your voices.

THIS BOOK IS STRONGER THAN FIVE HUNDRED THOUSAND ANIMALS
TAKING OFF YOUR SHIRT.[31]

Oh, yes it is, beautiful people. Yes, it is. Thank you. This book is absolutely spilling
with admiration and love.

Notes

1. Borrowed from a segment of Max Wolf Valerio's poetics statement in which he says "a poem is
   open, and always - opening."
2. Edited by Gloria Anzaldúa and Cherríe Moraga. Wherever you are, Dr. Switala, thank you.
3. I found "Fiddleheads" in *The Best American Poetry 1997*, edited by James Tate, which was
   required reading by Dr. Richard Jackson. Thank you, Rick.
4. Gloria Anzaldúa, forward to the second edition, *This Bridge Called my Back*.
5. By Leslie Feinberg. Thank you Leslie and Katy.
6. Thank you, Molly, for taking me.
7. Thank you, Wingspan.
8. Edited by Michelle Tea.
9. Michelle Tea, introduction to *Without a Net*.

10. Thank you, Gloria Anzaldúa, Cherríe Moraga, and Michelle Tea.

11. Yet I also want to fully acknowledge the amount of privilege I have due to my whiteness, passing as male (even though I identify as genderqueer), and the fact that I have a master's degree. These have undoubtedly had the effect of smoothing the way, opening doors, and conferring legitimacy on this project. Regardless of my history and experiences in previous incarnations, my current embodiment offers me increased access to resources and support.

12. Thank you, Sam.

13. Thank you, humility.

14. Thank you, Trace.

15. To see the full call for submissions, go to http://www.transanthology.com

16. From "Song of Myself" section 51.

17. bell hooks, *Outlaw Culture: Resisting Representations*.

18. Adapted from Morgan Lucas Schuldt's *L=U=N=G=U=A=G=E*.

19. "Cis" means "on the same side as" and when used in relation to gender, it is another way of saying non-trans and/or non-genderqueer identified.

20. We are operating from the expectation that readers of this anthology will take it upon themselves to gain a basic understanding of trans and genderqueer identities and realities, if they do not already have one.

21. Susan Stryker, *Transgender History*.

22. Quoted from *Aufgabe* 7 editor's note.

23. While we did our best to distribute the call outside the US (and did manage to make a few international connections and include a few international poets), it would be disingenuous to suggest that this anthology represents any locale other than the US (and, it could be argued, only a few major cities in the US – with a strong majority of the poets represented here writing from Brooklyn, San Francisco/Oakland/the bay area, Seattle, and Philly).

24. Statistic from Trans Murder Monitoring Project, a project of Transgender Europe. According to their reports, one trans person is murdered a month in the US. The data from these reports clearly show that trans women of color are at a significantly greater risk for transphobic violence than any other trans and genderqueer folks.

25. "Numbers Trouble" originally appeared in *Chicago Review* 53:2/3 (Autumn 2007).

26. These questions are adapted from Spahr and Young.

27. "Then we are in language" is excerpted from Andrea Quaid's piece, "A series of propositions" presented at &Now 2011 in San Diego.

28. Samuel Ace, CA Conrad, Bo Luengsuraswat, Lilith Latini, Ching-In Chen, Natro, Y. Madrone, Ely Shipley, Julian Talamantez Brolaski, Amir Rabiyah, Meg Day, J. Rice, Joy Ladin, Ari Banias, Ariel Goldberg, Oliver Bendorf

29. Dawn Lundy Martin

30. Duriel Harris

31. Laura Neuman

Being Unreadable and Being Read: An Introduction

Trace Peterson

I. Umbrella / A Gathering

Troubling the Line is a gathering of poets who connect ourselves and the concerns of our writing with the umbrella terms "trans" and/or "genderqueer." This community of individuals is as self-selected as it is edited by TC Tolbert and myself; they responded to an open call we sent out everywhere on the internet requesting work by trans and genderqueer poets. We received submissions in response to this call from about 250 authors, and we selected 55 authors in total. It's not just a number that we felt would make a substantial book--it's also a collection of authors whose work I stand behind, a collection that I have worked very hard on. It is filled with powerfully moving poetry and a sense of newness, and I hope that for the sake not just of the authors involved but of trans poets in general that this configuration of writers becomes known, as they deserve to. The book is also of course an opening gesture to provoke what TC and I both hope will be a long and productive conversation about trans and genderqueer poetry, a category about which there is currently barely any available commentary or discussion so far. Of the 55 writers who are gathered together in this book, some you have heard of—they have published many books of poetry and appear here as the trailblazers in this field. But just as many of the poets here have only published one book of poems or have yet to publish a book. We seem to have timed this project just as a wave of new writing by trans and genderqueer poets with first books is underway.

So why trans and genderqueer? They are the most inclusive umbrella terms we could find to describe lived identities that challenge gender norms. From the beginning, this was going to be a "bridge" anthology—we wanted it to cross lines between transsexual and transgender and genderqueer and intersex and poets of all non-normative genders, and connect them in new ways. We are not interested in policing identity; we are interested in helping make more widely available in poetry different kinds of inbetweenness in relation to gender identification. Some poets in this collection even identify themselves with a range of individual and idiosyncratic terms, preferring gender-neutral pronouns such as "xir" or "hir" or "they" to refer to themselves in the third person. And the issue of names in relation to authorship here is especially interesting to me—many of us seem to signify our inbetweenness through some alteration to our original names. At a certain point I lost count of how many of our authors felt so emboldened by the visibility the publication of this anthology offered them that they actually underwent an author name change in the midst of the editing process.

II. The Only Aporia in the Village

So what am I doing here with my name listed as co-editor on the cover, you may ask? It seems a felicitous coming together of collaborators, concerns, and participants that I've been working towards for a long time now. After the poet kari edwards, who was my friend and mentor, died in 2006, I was lamenting to a friend about the difficulty of finding influences, mentors, and a sense of context as a poet. "There's no one like me among older poets," I complained, "no male-to-female trans poet now who I can emulate or aspire to be like, no one who I can look to and say 'I want to be that person.'" My wise friend responded, "No, it's getting to the point where you're going to have to be that for someone else." The result is the book that you now hold in your hands.

The concerns about lack of context underlying my complaint have been a pressing issue for the past decade. Since the year 2000, when I finally came out as transgender in the MFA program in Creative Writing in Tucson, Arizona—because once I sat down to write I couldn't avoid the topic any longer but had to embrace it—my coming out was followed by twelve years of swimming around in a strange void. This feeling of being unmoored had to do with being trans and being a poet at the same time, and therefore lacking a group who would understand and accept all of me (and for those of you out there who may not know a lot of poets, we really are our own strange scene—an often ingrown social phenomenon). For twelve years I tried to find a bridge. I frequently attended transgender support groups (where there were no poets present) and participated in trans activist groups (where there were mostly no poets present either). For twelve years I attended lots of poetry readings (where the number of trans people present was usually none) and hosted lots of literary events (where the number was also usually none but sometimes aspired to more). I showed up at many predominantly heterosexual marxist and/or earth-mother-type protests and volunteered in many Quaker or Unitarian community activism events where there were no trans people or poets present, at least not any who were "out." I also dated a variety of people, none of whom were trans but nearly all of whom tended to see my trans identification as interesting and attractive, whereas the idea of being a professional poet has tended to elicit sighs of pity or wary looks of fear and chagrin. In every case I was either trans or I was a poet, sometimes neither, but never both.

So as I have been traversing this fairly rickety bridge over the chasm between "poetry" as a literary profession and "transgender" as a category for over a decade, I've had considerable time along the way to think about why the situation is so weird and why I sometimes have felt, like the satirical *Little Britain* character "the only gay in the village," like the only mtf trans-identified poet in the village. I'm not of course, and I haven't been, but it feels like it sometimes and I know that others share this feeling. The anthology we have just completed is so important for precisely this reason—it connects people who have previously been isolated. The aporia of isolation consists of a basic inability to articulate or make visible the position that one occupies in publicly, socially, or politically understandable language, as if so many of the pressing issues about gender at the core of one's being were somehow "disqualified" from being of interest to other writers in a literary context or (god forbid) relevant to wider political discussions, except in select instances where one can see with trepidation one's own pain getting recast into a reactionary, predatory, or otherwise politically retrograde mode—the trans person as symptom of capitalism, as serial killer villain in a movie, or as cunning manipulator of others being just a few of the recognizeable forms this takes.

It's only a feeling of course, but feelings have a presence and a physicality, and they affect how we proceed in our lives. In my case, the physical manifestation of the feeling has been furtiveness, melancholy, and a painful disembodied sensation suffused with yearning, like a glass wall in front of my face I can only tap at but that I'm somehow unable to break through. Though I am sure everyone in my circumstances has their own idiosyncratic analogies for this, I want to stop feeling this way and I want to help others like me do so, too.

III. Possibility and Trans Poetry

I've done some archival research at this point for my graduate work beginning an investigation of a history for trans poets. Some initial findings seem to indicate that there are few literary precedents which combine poetry as a literary category with phenomena or sensibilities we would retrospectively recognize as "transgender" in a visible way. Perhaps one reason for that is the paradoxical situation Viviane K. Namaste evokes when she quotes Michelle de Ville in a fanzine interview: "The drag queen in the gay world is meant to be on the stage or 'walking the streets.' Don't get off the stage, baby! It's like the bird in the gilded cage" (10-11). Perhaps poetry has tended to be understood by the public not as a stage for performance, but as an introspective personal space in the normative sense—an "intimate" space from which trans people are barred or where they remain invisible unless they are playing the role of an externalized, hypersexualized being. There is also a transphobic streak among some political thinkers who would see the "gilded cage" as a symptom the disease underlying which is mtf trans identity itself. But in the language of Namaste's quote, surely there must be an alternative somewhere in between performing on the stage and prostitution on the streets, and surely such an alternative must include a space in which the consciousness, reflections, and concerns of trans and genderqueer poets can be heard, understood, and nurtured.

So for whatever reason, the misinformed consensus on trans and genderqueer poets has tended to be that they are few and far between. In a talk given for my series *TENDENCIES: Poetics and Practice* in 2010, ftm trans poet Samuel Ace pointed out that at that point (and still at the writing of this introduction) there is no category in the Lambda Literary Awards for trans poetry, though there are categories for trans fiction and trans nonfiction. So when my first book of poems, *Since I Moved In*, came out in 2007—there wasn't really a context in which it could be understood or received. Sam, who made this observation about the gap in the LGBT awards scene, is not only one of the few people who has been able to hear and understand my work, but also one of the first trans-identified poets I met who helped me feel less alone—I first ran into him while he was in the process of transitioning around the year 2000, and I felt a sense of connection and cameraderie then even though his poetry was very different from my own. Later in 2003 I met kari edwards, an mtf trans poet who was posting ferocious, amazing poems on the Buffalo Poetics list and we began a correspondence over email—a friendship developed here which culminated in some meetings in person around late 2005 just after I had moved to New York. At the time, kari was doing important early work bringing together the categories "poetry" and "transgender" as the poetry editor of IFGE's magazine *Transgender Tapestry*, and sie asked me for some poems to publish in the magazine. kari's instincts as an editor and the work sie did with *Transgender Tapestry* represent one of the first instances I am aware of in which trans poetry was being taken seriously as both an identity issue and a literary phenomenon. If I had to trace the book you hold in your hands back to a forerunner or precedent that most resembles it, that influence would be kari's work at *Transgender Tapestry*.

Another editorial intervention leading up to the book you are holding, and a project that kari was involved with as co-editor, was the publication of Issue 3 of the literary journal *EOAGH*, titled "Queering Language." For this project I asked a group of six queer and trans-identified poets to collect submissions by other poets who they felt were "queering language." kari had written a vital and challenging editorial statement for the journal (which is included in this anthology). We were in the process of assembling the final issue when the other editors and I suddenly received the terrible and completely unexpected news that kari had died of a heart attack. We were devastated at what had happened, and in retrospect, the subsequent journal issue and launch event turned into a kind of memorial for kari, with her poetry and restless vision hovering over us as the presiding inspiration. Other memorials and a book, *NO GENDER* with contributions by kari's friends and admirers followed as we tried to understand the enormous significance of kari's influence on our lives and writing.

Then—for me—the aporia returned. In the silence after kari's death and the memorials, there were no mentors. No other mtf trans poets nearby. Isolation. I started reading like my life depended on it. Judith Halberstam's *In a Queer Time and Place* revealed to me how political theorists often fail to understand sexuality and desire as serious areas of inquiry because such theorists see them as "part of a ludic body politics that obscures the 'real' work of activism" (5). This helped me understand one of the reasons why trans identification and issues had trouble appearing in the same location as what could be considered usefully "political." Around the same time, in 2005 when I was employed at Routledge, the discipline of "Transgender Studies" was coalescing as it was announced that the *Transgender Studies Reader* by Susan Stryker was underway, a book which has been invaluable in making accessible the history of debates around trans issues. When I entered graduate school in 2008, where I went specifically for the purpose of studying "trans poetics," my teacher Eve Kosofsky Sedgwick's work also helped a lot. Her critique of the "hermeneutic of suspicion" in *Touching Feeling* showed that there was a kind of automatism in much literary-critical and especially academic thought, that the negative exposé was often valued as more objective over and against the positive or emotional assertion or expression, and (this is a big one) that the mechanism of paranoia elucidated in her essay "Paranoid Reading and Reparative Reading" might involve ideological underpinnings inherently toxic to the subjectivity of trans people (whether they want to be professional poets or not). Discovering Julia Serano's book *Whipping Girl* also helped me to articulate the aporia I was experiencing by supplying new terms, "cissexism" and "trans-misogny"—tools which helped me understand a possible source of the hystericizing tension and pain I was having in social and professional interactions.

IV. Our Own Manifestos

The same friend who suggested I'm going to need to become a trans mentor for a younger poet also said, in the same conversation, "we have to be our own manifestos." I am aware of a number of significant previous debates in the discourse around "transgender" but if I become embroiled in them while trying to articulate my own poetics, I will not be able to describe what I intuitively and urgently feel needs to be said. One example is the debate around lesbian feminist Jan Raymond's (often cited as "transphobic") claim that transsexuals infiltrate women's spaces and sabatoge feminist revolution. The riposte to Raymond's attack was of course Sandy Stone's argument for a more inclusive linguistic counter-revolution, and I can see an echo of Stone's influence in kari edwards' work perhaps. Another controversy that has often come up is the exclusion of trans women from the Michigan Womyn's Music Festival, as critiqued by Riki Ann Wilchins. More recent takes by Stephen Whittle and Anna Enke have tended to emphasize the areas of overlap and mutual struggle between feminism and transfeminism. Other debates include—in a more theoretical academic context—the tension between a common misreading of Judith Butler's *Gender Trouble* that gender is primarily performative or discursive vs, on the other hand, Sedgwick's persistent claim in her work for the importance of a connection to the biological. Trans scholar Jay Prosser subsequently problematized this debate in his important book *Second Skins* by revisiting Butler's original argument, showing how it has been commonly misunderstood, while himself critiquing the idea of gender performativity—this time from the position of an embodied transsexual person. Kate Bornstein and Gayle Salamon have both been influential for me, perhaps too much in that I am wary of repeating their arguments. Urgent debates have also been ongoing about inclusion with regard to race, arguments over what is meant by, or who counts as part of, the current discourse on "transgender rights," as in the work of Paisley Currah and Dean Spade. Such debates look back to Sylvia Rivera's complaint that "It's not my pride, it's their pride...You haven't given me mine yet...I have so many children and I'm still sitting on the back of the bus" (Rivera 81). Meanwhile Susan Stryker in her *Transgender History* has usefully defined trans as referring to "people who move away from the gender they were assigned at birth...who cross over *(trans-)* the boundaries contructed by their culture to define and contain that gender"(1), in the process making the category more dynamic and less restrictive. I especially applaud the subtle way Stryker uses this definition to articulate an alternative to the definition imposed by the DSM, showing why trans people experience the DSM definition of their "disorder" as not only enabling but also deeply pathologizing and problematic (and though the DSM definitions are changing just this year, it remains to be seen what these changes will mean). Other scholarly studies like those of Dean Valentine, Genny Beemyn, and Susan Rankin have bravely attempted to faithfully survey or document the existing and varied conceptions of trans identity as they currently exist in the social world. These are some of the many voices weighing in on trans debates that have been touchstones for me personally in understanding the issues at stake.

So as a trans-identified poet, editor, and scholar, what do *I* want? I want a poetry with a connection to the biological, but a biological that relies upon neither "gender essentialism" nor reproductive teleology as defining characteristics. I want a poetry in which trans concerns and linguistic experimentation appear together and overlap, in which they inform one another and egg each other on. The way I have set up this book—as graphic designer— aims to create an open-ended container in which such a poetry could thrive and grow. From the beginning I knew I wanted to include photographs of the trans poets in this anthology. There is something important about the relationship between how trans poets look and how they *look* (at the world, at language), between how they read and how they want to be read (or be unreadable). I think Claude Cahun and Marcel Moore would approve. I wanted potential readers of this anthology to see not just that we are writing ourselves into existence but that we are genuinely and undeniably here, right in front of you, and in front of each other. I felt it was also important that each poet be allowed to provide a sense of the context in which they wanted their work to be read, and we achieved this through "poetics statements." These were an invitation to all anthology participants to discuss something important about one's writing process, as well as make connections between the categories "transgender" and "poetry" as each writer understands them. These statements provided a sense that though we are gathered together under common identity terms, the importance of individual experience, of individual creative concerns, remains prominent and at times even destabilizing, a reminder as Sedgwick first noted in *The Epistemology of the Closet*, "People are different from each other" (22). Between author photo and poems and poetics statement, I thought it might be possible to create a space in which we could start to see what had been rendered invisible by various ideologies, and in which we could begin to be in dialogue with the ideas of other trans writers, to be read by cis writers, and for a discussion to happen that for various reasons had not been possible before.

V. Three Trans and Genderqueer Poets

There are poets whose work I am particularly proud of featuring in this anthology and whose concerns I feel closest to. A partial list would include Ari Banias, Dawn Lundy Martin, EC Crandall, Eileen Myles, Ely Shipley, Jaime Shearn Coan, Jake Pam Dick, Joy Ladin, Laura Neuman, Max Wolf Valerio, Micha Cárdenas, Monica / Nico Peck, Stephen Burt, Trish Salah, TT Jax, and Zoe Tuck. Yet there are three particular poets here who form a kind of wellspring or source for the anthology's concerns as I understand them, and I want to focus for a moment on their poems and why I feel they are central to the book.

The first is Samuel Ace. My introduction to Sam was hearing his live performances in Tucson that combined film with the reading in a visceral way I had not seen before. There's an insistence in Ace's language which is like Steinian repetition, but the poems are nimbler, and have to do with the relationship between desire and gender and narrative. In his poetics statement for this anthology, Ace notes "I take lessons in poetry from sex. Because in sex is where all narrative truly falls apart. Where narrative breaks out of corners. Where narrative stops in syncope." This is a vision of biological connection which does not depend upon gender essentialism for its articulation. Ace's syntax is playing with the relationship between narrative and sex by constantly generating confounding phrases and images: "I sleep the planet," "I head the tart redness   the thrush of winds," "the stains of coo the prance and the farm hidden and encrypted and failed." A syntactical playfulness occurs throughout where sometimes we are given the dependent clause without the independent clause. Ace breathlessly and urgently catalogues various imminent phrases that scramble gender codes. Meanwhile the musical ear behind the phrasing is pitch-perfect, and we can feel the writing subject who generated them changing and morphing, hearing "the phrase in the body" as an internal phenomenon.

The second poet who for me represents the concens of this anthology is, of course, kari edwards. The first of the poems included under edwards' section of the anthology, "good questions..." is derived from an email conversation we had in which I asked hir several questions about my sense of being in the wrong body and being the wrong gender and how that might be fixed or remedied. The response shows kari's compassionate sort of "tough love" which was always trying to see the world directly and without illusion yet acknowledging all the complexity and fraughtness of a given situation at the same time. That paradox is central to the kind of poetry and poetics I want. This poem and others by edwards in the anthology have a frenetic momentum, many using anaphora or aspects of voiced gestures we might associate with a poet like Whitman, but if that's the musical frame the allegedly whole body speaking the syntax gets put through a shredder. Trans identity for edwards in hir poetics statement is "a first step in seeing one's self other than as a formless form situated in social shame. it is more a question of, if this is the stopping point, does it do anything more than reinforce the 'I' as the ultimate achievement." I would answer yes, if we can find a way to talk about trans poetics as what happens *around and beyond* that stopping point.

The third key poet here, who I am specifically responsible for bringing into the anthology, is John Wieners. A slightly older generation than some of the other poets here--he died in 2002--Wieners represents one of the most recent likely candidates to be considered as a trans-identified or proto-trans poet. My interest in Wieners's work goes back to conversations with his friends Gerrit Lansing and Jim Dunn. Lansing has told me that Wieners "felt that he was a woman," and the poems themselves have a consistent type of melancholy in which songs by Billie Holiday and old standards are referenced, superimposing gay sexual encounters upon archetypes for straight romance, with Wieners nearly always playing the female role. While this is not unheard of among gay poets, Wieners took the female identification further in his life. In his earlier days he was known for cross-dressing, and there was a series of wealthy women he admired and became interested in. Once while Wieners was visiting a female friend in New York, Jim Dunn tells me, she came back from work at the end of the day and was shocked to find that Wieners had put on her dress and had cleaned the entire apartment. There's another story, related to me by Robbie Dewhurst, in which Wieners wore a women's jacket at a reading in Boston, and when someone in the audience asked why he was dressed that way, he replied "it's an experiment." Another instance connecting Wieners with cross-gender identification was an incident Jim described in which Wieners, upon being asked his name by the airline clerk at Logan airport, responded "Rose Kennedy." In any case, the connection is there and the luscious, tough, often glossolalic poems speak for themselves. I encourage readers to investigate and discover more.

Works Cited

Beemyn, Genny and Susan Rankin. *The Lives of Transgender People*. New York, NY: Columbia University Press, 2011.

Bornstein, Kate. *Gender Outlaw*. New York: Vintage, 1994.

Brolaski, Julian T., erica kaufman, and E. Tracy Grinnell. *NO GENDER: Reflections on the Life & Work of kari edwards*. Litmus Press/Belladonna Books, 2009.

Butler, Judith. *Gender Trouble*. New York, NY: Routledge, 1990.

Currah, Paisley, Richard M. Juang and Shannon Price Minter. *Transgender Rights*. Minneapolis, MN: University of Minnesota Press, 2006.

edwards, kari, "subject: statement." Introduction to *EOAGH* Issue 3: Queering Language. Jan 2007. http://chax.org/eoagh/issue3/issuethree/edwards.html

Enke, Anne. *Transfeminist Perspective in and beyond Transgender and Gender Studies*. Philadelphia, PA: Temple University Press, 2012.

Halberstam, Judith. *In a Queer Time & Place*. New York, NY: NYU Press, 2005.

Namaste, Viviane K. *Invisible Lives*. Chicago, IL: University of Chicago Press, 2000.

Peterson, Tim. *Since I Moved In*. Tucson, AZ: Chax Press, 2007.

Rivera, Silvia. "Queens in Exile, The Forgotten Ones," *Genderqueer: voices beyond the binary*. Ed. Joan Nestle, Clare Howell, and Riki Wilchins. Los Angeles, CA: Alyson Books, 2002.

Raymond, Janice "Sappho by Surgery" and Sandy Stone "The Empire Strikes Back" in *The Transgender Studies Reader*. Ed. Susan Stryker and Stephen Whittle. New York: Routledge, 2006.

Salamon, Gayle. *Assuming a Body*. New York, NY: Columbia University Press, 2010.

Sedgwick, "Paranoid Reading and Reparative Reading," *Touching Feeling*. Durham, NC: Duke University Press, 2003.

Sedgwick, Eve Kosofsky. *Epistemology of the Closet*. Berkeley, CA: University of California Press, 1990.

Serano, Julia. *Whipping Girl*. Berkeley, CA: Seal Press, 2007.

Spade, Dean. *Normal Life*. Brooklyn, NY: South End Press, 2011.

Stryker, Susan. *Transgender History*. Berkeley, CA: Seal Press, 2008.

Valentine, David. *Imagining Transgender*. Durham, NC: Duke University Press, 2007.

Wilchins, Riki Ann. *Read My Lips*. Firebrand Books, 1997.

ROUBLING THE LINE
ROUBLING THE LINE
ROUBLING THE LINE
ROUBLING THE LINE

Ahimsa Timoteo Bodhrán

Cycle undone

for transsexual and transgender women of colour

They are right when they say
all women bleed.

Perhaps this is our menstrual
cycle. Minstrel cycle. 28
days of blood. How many murders?
Lip-synch contests? Tranny shows?
As if blood could only flow
from one orifice.

We are on show. *Parade.*
The cover of any other magazine
(capital "o"). Sunday / Saturday
Friday dinnertime / lunchtime
church / synagogue / mosque
discussion. Afterwards
in the parking lot. Over broken bread.
The latest TV daytime special. Telenovela.

We are "special." Half-off. Up for grabs. The
breast. Ass. Dick-cunt. Cunt-dick. Anything for viewing
pleasure, a topic to be analyzed and discussed,
dissected, gained tenure on. We are on both sides

of the knife. We are fenced in. We peek
through the holes in the chicken wire,
scratch at the dirt. We are Perdue "oven stuffer
roasters." We are riddled with cancer. We have no
beaks, (only) extra parts. You will choke
on our bones.

The pills we take are not only for balance
in the blood, proper Rh, proper Ph, good sweat,
good number of T-cells, zinc for a throat that can
still swallow and spit, but a way to tell time (off),
stop it, start it up again (when things are too slow).
Nyquil by our nightstand at 3am, pm,
first thing in the morning. Right before that AA
meeting. We are good little girls gone bad.
Perhaps we can be recycled. What city plan
for us? Which colored bin, bag tied
with twist-tie? What park left to sleep in?

We are not glamourous. We are overworked
and poor. We have no jobs. Even our children
are taken from us, turned against us (upon
transitioning, prior, years later, and before).
Our children of the street and ghetto, house, those
of suburb and blood, reservation, semen once
deposited into a vagina next to ours. We
have no kin. We are the things our
families leave in the shantytown
each season(al rotation), a rusted can, broken beer
bottle, new village of pick-up
trucks, come-on lines, gas stations. We are
the dimpled diapers of the highway. Over there,
across the state line,
petroleum is cheaper—than us. We
drink it to keep warm.

We are the uninvestigated murders of our Nations,
the bodies in the river, field, fed on by fishes, crows,

our nets, holes in our stockings, not keeping them
at bay. We are fertilizer for plants that have
not known sunlight—that deep down, dark, rich, tuber,
tumor; we are the reason for the rising of rivers. The silt
in your coffee. We are an effect of the ozone layer
leaving. Greenhouse, how many bodies
does it take a year to overflow
one's banks? *Ka-ching. Ka-ching.* And
the register keeps ringing up sales. Aisle 4.
Aisle 4.

We are every end of the spectrum, pre-, post-,
non-... -living, -breathing. High yella and crushed
berry, juice turned to sour, the vinegar of water
sold on shelved alleyways of health stores. We
no longer own the ingredients to our own
recipe. Our DNA will live on, breed
better llamas. Odwalla apples turned rancid
with infection. No washing will save us, no
dunk in the river, chariot to swing us home, sweetly.
Swing low, bob for us in buckets, bite the worm.
We are yeast rising. A new form, helixed, ancient.
The inspiration for a new line of comic books.
Cologne. Birth control. Tartar sauce.

We are dolphin safe.

We are a spectrum of stars. Some on supernova,
others bright blue, big red, seams showing, skin
tears too. We will never see all our beauty. Light
fades before it reaches us—and the sound...
solar systems later. We are a badly edited
film; none of our frames match up. We
are the cocoa butter by which we soothe ourselves.
We rub tenderness into each other's eyes, lay
cucumber there, are the pot of medicinal tea
leaves we sip at night, the bag of weed we smoke
in morning. Mourning. We know our dead.
We are the only ones who remember.

We hope to re-member some ritual before
our image was plastered onto cigarettes,
used to sell ice cream and rice, before we
kneeled naked on boxes of butter, abused
any essence of ourselves, became a magazine,
relaxer, sold our own spirits and sisters
down the river, flowing up, flooding
banks backed with bags, eyes still streaming,
each drop an outlet for poison. Nothing can stop us.

We did what we did to survive. Sometimes
they were noble moments full of truth,
reminding us of past dynasties, different
times when we were honoured, knew spells,
ways of curing the body, each spirit, twinned
in two. Other times we simply walked away
and did not look back, sand into stone into salt,
flames still behind us as our buildings burned,
the ports with them. Sometimes we were the
box of matches; other times, the very thing that
burned. There are still ashes in our hair. No
urn will keep us. And there is no kiln large
enough to bake us
this time. We are unfinished clay. Soldiers.

We have no way to return
what they have given us
has no value. We seek and search
for what was ours. We take what we are
given and surprised with the results.
We make beauty from the refuse of
other people's lives. We are their refuse, what
they refuse to admit in themselves, discard
away, their elders, leaders, cousins, tricks,
ex. We are the afterglow of any drug.
Coffee and cold showers and morning
newspapers must be taken against us. We are
one big bad motherfucking trip.

We are the used vials of the valley,
a stray cat searching for milk. Perhaps
she will mother herself, lick her own wounds,
nurse her own kittens, find fur in warmth, loose
drain pipe in which to sit and wait out
this storm. We have no patience. Broken
umbrella, bent backwards in the wind.
It is always too little too...
late. Word arrives after we are dead. First
pension check, social security payment, Section 8
letter, SSI. *Jubilee. Juneteenth.* And the years of
battle, form after form after form. *Can I eat now?*
Can I pee now? Thank you
so very much. People are dying during this poem.
Sisters. Brethren. Sistren. Perhaps they can wipe
their ass with this poem, smear away the night's
make-up, fake-up. Make some use of this.

We reach those we can, reach out our arms
to see them wrapping only us, and even those
bones too small. Sometimes we are all
we can carry out of a burning building.
Sometimes we go up in smoke. Sometimes
we go back into a fire to see who else
we can carry/save. Sometimes we are not seen
again. Sometimes we are a baptism of fire.

And in evening we hold each other, fingers
through gloves (not bought that way), hands
warmed over garbage cans, oil drums, and
we think of roundhouses, smoke, mescal,
copal, incense, other means of ritual, other ways
of keeping warm. We wish our lovers would stay
with us. We wish they'd never leave—and those
who do, our money with them. We bless them with
bitterness, perhaps release (from prison) one day.
Perhaps our collarbones will heal; knit

themselves new fibers; perhaps the cigarette burn
will fade to a blemish. Nothing can conceal our lives.

We are the sunburned children of the afterbirth;
who knows where our cord is buried, what lies
there, beneath the surface, beneath the skin.
Hopefully we are beautiful if but
once in our lives. Perhaps our rapture is
surviving the rape, the mindfuck of living.
Bill for breathing.

Our numbers grow each day. Above the surface.
Below the soil. If there was a way to use this
to our advantage. If some community
somewhere could be built
at the center of each Nation, all
our peoples there gathered. If the Red Sea
could part once more, and Palestinians
return home. Who knows what we would do
if we owned our own lands? Perhaps live
or be free, rather than simply
on sale. If we could feel waves wash up
against us, and not be covered in sludge and salt,
hypodermic needles (we wash out with bleach, take
to the exchange), if dirt were sacred once more. And
water clean. If we were more than a preposition,
conjunction, something to bring others
together. If we spoke our own languages,
owned our own bodies. If.
If.

If the comets came round again
this year, and took us with them,
would we be missing?
Would great parties of searchers
descend wells, unearth wreckage,
cover the pages of paid pork papers?
Or would we only be found centuries

later, some sign of earthquake
or typhoon, once-pasted project of papier mâché,
paint-by-numbers kit? Would there be
instructions on handling, *handle with care*, bill due,
C.O.D.? Extra credit? An extra tassel
at graduation?

We are the very reason for a change
in the weather, an overflow of
landfills. Cirrus clouds hover, miles above;
the band this year on the caterpillar is a wide one.

Expect a long winter.

Mint

1.

None of our worries are what they seem.

You did not want this way to be wise.
If only the lessons could come more slowly, more easily, with less/more calm.

Who knew we'd be elders at 25.

We have all been weeds, known the pull of a farmer's hands.

Each of us is indigenous somewhere.

Somewhere. Sometimes the graft has taken hold, we have taken their money, it feels
like any other drug, limb, necessity; is breathing possible without gills, bills?

As if we all come from someplace singular, without cousins or long winters. Fins.

Where I am from is not only a desert.
Other climes, the micros of the bay.

All our views are poisoned.

2.

This ledge, Lebanese, of Green, overlooking Dolores, the old Mission, cemetery of my ancestors, moved to Buena Vista, headstones, steps for white people to walk on, folks to climb, Christian-like, to the top. *Flag on the moon.* Perhaps a cross will be placed there... and the earth bleed.

Here, this place, pillow of chamomile, old cat meowing, rubbing against my leg. Animals and their souls. Sonya.

The "Sephardic" cemeteries of Manhattan, the lower half, lower majority, Spic and Jew, A-rab and African, "Orientals," Black (power), Mizrahim, Colma. All the places my grandfather is not buried.

I have never been to a grave of my own people.

3.

Ice cream. Green with little bits of brown chocolate.
Tea. With lots of honey. A Corelle cup.

Laban, with berries, banana, and this leaf. Zimt.
Pasta, con la prima, albahaca.

A York Peppermint Patty. Shivers.
My spine, straightened. A winter wind.

4.

colmar = to fill to the brim.

Colma. "A place that is filled." *With spirits.*

Not all the bodies were moved.

Poltergeist = a ghost that crashes about, is not quiet. Or happy. *Trapped.*

El Presidio.

There are places where nothing grows.
We build houses there.

5.

If only we knew the right prayers to say, songs to sing.
But none of us speak the language anymore.

A Chicano poet keeps on referring to my people in the past tense.
He is drunk.

6.

colmar = to use up one's patience; to fulfill one's destiny; live one's dreams.

To receive positive attention. To be showered with affection. To be an object of pride.

For dying.

colmado = a grocery story.

A place where things can be bought. Or, a place where things are sold.
Bodies. Blocks. Blood.

colmatación = silting.

The way a river is filled, the way water is slowed, and things settle out, become clear,
less muddied. The way stone is made.

Or story.

7.

If you were small, I would wrap you in this blanket. I only have a piece of it now, as
do you.

Pox-free and brown, it is enough to keep us warm, remind us of home.

You were born into it. And I am now part of your weave.

I would send you clippings from my garden, but I have none.

What to send you? Chipped brick?

Strawberries were the first of the season. I loved to eat them.

As did the rabbits.

8.

Something cool that replaces the fire.

Water. Ash. Mud.

9.

Sometimes, I run my fingers through the chimes of your brother's catcher, feel my face against its feather, count each bead. Its web is a good one. My dreams are peaceful.

I think of you. What we need to say is unspoken, I can see it in your eyes, the hair you cut for me when abuela died, and again when I moved from/to this place. There is green and brown and blue. Hazel.

Something else by which to cool us, soothe us. Calm the body, and close the eyes.

But not forever.

May we always be Sacred. And grow/ing. Full.

10.

Some may think that nothing dwells here, no seed left intact. But we have always looked with more than the naked eye, in(to) the cracked crevasses of the body. *The pollen is on our faces. We are flowers kissing.* We need not their machines to see beauty, know harmony, know the inner workings of the soil and soul/earth.

I greet you on the horizon. We bloom. Our sweetness is everywhere.

You greet me with bits of green in your teeth.
The one place they did not think to look. Tierra.

Carved Crimson into the Bark of a White Page:
A Queer/Trans Womanist Indigenous Colored Poetics

:: thread one ::

My work locates itself at the nexus of communal, terrestrial, and personal memory. Bodies of language, land and water, converge in work that is layered and fragmented, grasping towards wholeness of place and peoplehood. I use writing as a tool for collective and individual healing and decolonization, a way of rescripting our lives as queer people of color, mixed-bloods, and women of color, as people who know what it means to struggle, daily, multigenerationally. Seeing the mythic and magical in the quotidian as potential antidote to our malaise, I hope to harness the powers of the line, the breath, image, and refashion them to our purposes—potential futures from the remnants and shards of our past. In my work worlds merge: the rural is found in the urban; historical trauma is revisited through the particular site of the body; and (trans)national metanarratives and discourses are negotiated through periods and zones of contact, the macro nesting itself in the pores and hairs of the micro. I write because our lives are largely unwritten, and if written largely not self-written, and we need to textually, conceptually, and artistically (re)inhabit these previous places of absence and longing. To survive the times of genocide, when futures are not given, not granted. To posit the postcolonial in the reclamation of the precolonial, the times prior to the partitioning of landbases, languages, bodies—intimacy restored; rememory. By developing my craft, publishing it, and documenting my path, I hope to, through both my teachings and writings, instruct others on what is possible and open up those pazibilidades so that they can discover (and recover) them themselves. I write for my Nations; I write towards healing, all the journey wholme.

:: thread two ::

Bodies—cultural, corporeal, terrestrial—converge, accrue meaning through layers, weaving of communal and personal memory, the lands from which we emerge and waters we have crossed. Stories nest, within and adjacent one another, linking fragments and history/herstory, as the narrative moves toward, and away from, wholeness. The words are beaded together, sound and phrase, image and vibration, tongue. Rhythms resyncopated, mixed. A continual braid, things pulled into line, then offered, given. Sacred, ceremony.

I write as a person coming out of genocide, survivor, person on the path to wholeness, and member of multiple communities seeking to restore our place in the world, through our words and bodies, (re)envision what is possible. Writing is medicinal; it brings healing, to ourselves and others. It is a record; it reminds us of who we were and who we hope to become—it is a record of our becoming. I hope my writing brings light and warm, nurturing darkness, rebirth, to my peoples, other queer people of color, women of color, and Indigenous peoples, the mixed folk of the earth, brethren and sistren.

As an activist and organizer, educator, writing is one of my tools in our journey forward, looking back, re-membering now. It is part of our arsenal, our toolkit, medicine bag. It is what we make it, and we are what is made. I hope my work finds use with my peoples, good medicine brought to the heart of all my Nations, as we shape our future, home.

Aimee Herman

i/dentity (packed)

ab	NORMAL
one hundred sit-ups per day	FLATTENS THE **IT** AWAY

: call me deviation.	.,<} /| 00---{}

inter	SEX
between legs a fist rises	MUTINY

: when (I) was six, (I) tore out a section of my neck where the label sat. where the label rubbed. where the label pushed pink where there was yellow. where the label reconstructed [my] structure. where the label took away sensation. where the label told {me} how to pee. where the label disguised {me}. Discussed {me}. DISgusts {me}.

inside on the	OUTSIDE
there is outside	INSIDE

: understand this need to disfigure/wires wind within notarized parts of gender serration/ scribble/inscribe/ take notes against the flesh that fondles omission/a blunder?/illustrate the in-between/a multiple choice of organs and identities/divide gender into name/hair style/occupied paycheck/cancel out what remains

:micro penis.   instru/MENtal

small formation like   INDECISION
color will cure it   FOR NOW

: sensations are not acceptable/inaccessible/the swelling/swallowing/(I) looked {me}
up in the book of explanations and found

                                        graffiti'd pout/magnification of gen.i.tals

morph   OLOGY
bi   OLOGY
gender is not   SEX

:doctor gave {me} a passport to cross the border of this body/man in badges and
nametag stopped {me} at the fringe of internal & external/pouring of salt to/preserve **IT**/
melt **IT**/embarrass **IT** away

:she/he/she/he/she/he/   itititititititititititititititititititititititititititititititit

                    [fuck]

ambiguous   to doubt   debate   vague   (a) lie.

:   *just*   *call*   *me*   *a*   *question*   *mark*

Square Root of Menstruation

inside the box, there was a calendar. pink plastic cushion with padding called diaper called sanitary napkin called heavy burst of cotton and plastic against vagina like chaperone interruption from underwear fondle. i was fifteen i was twelve i was just past sixteen i was ten. it was so late, i thought body had forgotten me. it was so late i thought body was growing claymation penis made from blood and slaps and ingestion of processed food and excessive sodium that just needed water to grow like chia pet from within. when it came i searched for bandages big enough to stuff inside me to mop it up. searched for anything to stuff inside me to sop it up. brassieres from sister's dresser, envelopes unclasped with ghost of electric bill final notice form letter jury duty date of appearance. learned foreign language called menstruation called tampons called toxic shock syndrome called smelly ocean must douche it away. two to eight days of this vagina crying blood, thirty-five milliliters or more sometimes less, running away. uterine lining shatters like wine glass against tile it is angry. this blood smells like rust on bicycles like garbage disposal like the rejection of internal. once a month, this body chokes up blood in underwear and rage refuses silence. six pairs of underwear ruined times once a month times twelve in year equal to seventy-two. i never think that one day this blood will become a bully. graffiti up thighs, change the color of skin, reappraise value, scare body from contact. some months, i let it bleed into a puddle past ankles and grow into a pool with limited access to lap swims or scuba dives. color shifts from strawberry to cranberry to cherry cordial pie to black tar heroin.

He gave her a quarter to cite a dirty word: man

the cutting of. [preferable female]^^
language. /no: o. o. o. o. o**.** **o.o.**   o. o. no. no. no.no.no.no.no.no.no.no.

tone the *IT* down

memory. [popping]   trauma. [visceral] [absorption]
neuter. wounds. [pussy]   Cut.

[his intelligence is a mere tool in the service of his drives and needs]

size can be challenging
disappointing   and a relief.

prescribed hard-on   lasts longer than agreed upon   envelopes crammed with
Presidential love
letters   a doorman   athletic semen   running

[despising] [loneliness] [without the aid of males] Up. [touching gold] [milk] [scum]

alkaline solution
grease of animals
glycerol, crude
purification not enough
wash the IT away

[non-human] trembled serration clings to parenthetical scars

[a biological accident] [incomplete]

[the refuge of the mindless]

                                        when fucking forgets question marks

severing the [grotesque].   breaths.   wrists.   clit.   [bread].   yeast.   [scum].
[machine].

[adapted themselves to animalism]

                                        cock   cuh/cuh/uh/uh/c-c-c-c-c-c-uh-uh-under-under

[a place] [in the slime]
trapped under the **IT**

[constantly seeking out] specification
[barely perceptible physical feeling]

tore out cunt during reconstructive phase
now all that remains is   an echo
                                        [SCUM is impatient]

                                                            ! ...

the pauses must be removed because there is no time to gasp/   too much to take in now

can be found beneath sinks
sodium hypochlorite
gags stains
disinfectant
burns facial gestures and nasal passageway
bleach

                                        not   {strong}   enough.

codification of the IT:

I.   serrated gender
    a.   [incomplete set of] [emotional]
    b.   saw tooth distance between groin and
    c.   the inside of an outside or outside of an inside

II.   accidental [X]
    a.   mistaken for boy by father
    b.   mistaken for girl by doctor
    c.   mother always wanted a girl, so

III.   in other words
    a.   erroneous
    b.   misdirected
    c.   mistaken
    d.   monsterism

or,   [a walking abortion] [peddling] [asses] [love(s)] [substitute]

Valerie,

Our skin is from New Jersey. Our mothers smell of stainless steel and ECT.
Lacerations linger against hips from rent payment. Pop artist pretended to get
you. *Get you. Get you.* I *got* you, Valerie. I see your leather. Typewriter inked
kneecaps. Leaning. The lunge of exhausted hate. I was there but. Different room
but. Different bed but. Different men but.   *I*   *was*   *there.*

I would tear out my cunt and give you mine just so you could fondle
decontamination.*

*there is no such thing.

---

^^ *text in brackets cut up and mutilated from SCUM Manifesto by Valerie Solanas*

to soften

nudity is not enough to keep the sweat away   at night, blankets huddle over body
and attempt impregnation   and so it begins   flirtations with yeast and pinot
noir   non-organic poses   elbows reflect tabletop to head ache
starvation of shadows   ankles   earlobes   gather posture   prescriptions
notice of distension   *there is a lot about me you don't know*   flirt of leg hair
collision of straps   a crescent   a scar   a numerical remainder   division is
every where   her clit is a foreign country   classically trained pelvis
shivered clench of furrows   castration of nudity   for research
recognize this madness?   *mother gave it to me on my twelfth birthday*   preserve trauma
energy   plastic wrapped tongue   beauty recognized by repeat performances
stab comfort zone   a splinter   distension   analysis of medication
currency of envelopes   *it only counts if he comes*   the mention of laps
straddle of earth worms   slide of her half-eaten apple   connection of the
tiptoe   *believe this*   take the blur out   binge on history
segregate the pretty ones   eye lids clean odor from constant flapping
courage of confession   *he ran it into me*   what remains has rotten
pink is not a color   it is an affliction   a witness   pay at the door
wipe feet inside   wash hands with soap-shaped muscle   forget
she is a woman   was a woman   tucked away   *the poverty of sex*
an unlocked door   bare feet   a weapon   experiment with sound
cracking   a shove   impolite fist   *her narrative reeks contradictions*   an
animal with skin losing   looseness   weight of extinction   **elephants**
walk toward the moisture   a swallow of appropriate organs *I want to jump off the*
ledge of this body   **and die**   **before the wet is found**

Poetics Statement

elastic minus the girdle

There is no need for synthetics like Victoria's whispered, overpriced secret. Allow space
for binding, packing, a push down or spackle.

to write to fill   the
lines where splinters

exhale
off benches

How to define the need to *not* be defined. On Monday, see Poet in tie and vest. On Tuesday, feast eyes upon cleavage and whale fat lipstick. On Wednesday, Poet is packing, Poet is binding, Poet is gender concealed. On Thursday, see polka dots and stripes and is that a see-through halter? On Friday, slick backed everything. On Saturday, Poet is the slash. On Sunday morning, Poet is M and in the evening back to F.

This body of text practices trilingualism and contraction.
Theories include gender confiscation and syntax dissection.

to remove the veins attached to initials
orientations

Dear Anne Sexton.
Dear Gertrude Stein.
Dear Kate Bornstein.
Dear Thea Hillman.
Dear Charles Bukowski.
Dear Earth.

There may be a carve out. A distinction between childhood trauma and mother carnage.

need to declare a bra size
sharp accent to disconnect
                    the unwanted

I know I have long hair but sometimes I am boy. When I talk about my dick I need you to believe that I have one [sometimes].

How much am I willing to pay out of pocket for this body?
How much am I willing to pay out of pocket for this body?

How much am I willing to pay out of pocket for this body?
How much am I willing to pay out of pocket for this body?
How much am I willing to pay out of pocket for this body?
How much am I willing to pay out of pocket for this body?
How much am I willing to pay out of pocket for this body?
How much am I willing to pay out of pocket for this body?
How much am I willing to pay out of pocket for this body?
How much am I willing to pay out of pocket for this body?
How much am I willing to pay out of pocket for this body?
How much am I willing to pay out of pocket for this body?

write in scars and exit signs
stain of conformity and academic line structure

There is no need for paper distinctions, map assurances, stick-on-peel-off labels. The location of this text-body may be found in Whitman songs and Bukowski contradictions.

bruises like brooklyn sidewalks
the stickstickiness   stitches stitching

Scars are a language learned only by breathing.

Translation: I am in this way because of razorblades and menstrual cycle and poetry and Lou Reed and unfiltered appetite and body hair and non-monogamous, rotating genitals and tattoos and leftover holes from adolescent piercings and academia and student loans and Brooklyn and New Jersey and the time I forgot to lock my ~~door~~ my body at night.

confuse memory with medicine
scream down spine.   paper cuts.   signature and
steam
         of permanence.

Amir Rabiyah

Escape Artists

I left one world & then I came into this world. I was premature, so they boxed me in [for safety measures.] I was much bigger than expected, especially for someone born so early. When I asked my mother how long I was incubated, she said, I don't know—I'm not good with time. My first, most intimate contact was with a box. Later, I would become obsessed with magicians.

Let me tell you more about where I come from. Another box told me. The screen glowed, & lit up my father's face. He said, everything is burning, everyone is dying, everything is being lost & then…this is where you come from. We sat together while he smoked cigarettes. He gave me a history lesson…He began, Beirut used to be… he never finished. My children are so American, he said to the bedroom, while I was in the bedroom.

I come from a long line of escape artists.

When I was a little girl, I really liked David Copperfield because he got out of a box all chained up, while dunked inside a giant tank. I thought he looked pretty when he wore make-up. I thought he was cool & tough because of how long he held his breath underwater. I used to time myself, to see how long I could hold mine. Many swimming pools kept count. I remember when I broke one minute, then one & a half. For one hundred & eighty seconds I was invincible.

My father called me his little fish. I said no, I'm not a fish, I'm a dolphin. To prove my point, I spat water out of my mouth. I put my hands together & made flippers & splashed & cried out that noise dolphins make when they are playing, when they are trying to communicate with someone they love.

Cactus Flower

'We flash victory signs in the darkness, so the darkness may glitter.' –Mahmoud Darwish

As the sun sets—we set our plan into motion.
Our sole purpose to overthrow

any assumptions, to change
the course of ordinary thinking.

Our work begins by speaking to darkness
and telling darkness   soon   :

          we will demonstrate through the secrecy of stars,

earth's magnetic embrace
how we can be many things at once.

So much of the work we do
is internal, goes unnoticed, uncompensated.

We get written off or not written at all,
labeled freakish, prickled,
rough around the edges.

We learn to thrive
in the dry humor of soil;
carry water in our bellies
to quench our own thirst.

We survive, over again.
Adapt. Even after being
carried in the beaks of birds,
dropped elsewhere,

far from our roots, we grow.
We flourish.
And when least expected, when histories

not told by us, for us, claims we are defeated,

we gather our tears as dew.　　　　　　We release our anguish,
intoxicated by our own sexed pollen.
　　　　　　　　　　We burst,

displaying the luscious folds of our petals.

The City Of Humble Astonishment

in this city,
I can wear pink spandex
booty shorts
and body glitter
to buy my groceries

on the way to the store,
handsome men honk their horns
in humble astonishment
made speechless
by the wonders of color coordination
marveling at the contours
of my faggot ass

in this city,
when loud voices shout in my direction,
the keepers of those voices
miss seeing me around lately
they scold me with tendernesss
"stop being a stranger!"

when I hold my boyfriend's hand
for an sunset stroll
we pass by three trans women
talking about how each of them deserves
the best, one slowly blinks her eyes

& shows off her bejeweled lashes

she says, "good evening"
I say, "good evening,
and y'all look so fierce!"

their diva smiles bigger than smog
their laughter tickles the back of my neck
their heels click in the distance
with a joy more infectious
than a virus on the bus

at every intersection
people acknowledge us
in the warm tones
of the ancestors scattered on murals

outside the corner store
an elderly couple married for
over fifty years
tilt
matching fedoras in greeting

"nice feather" my boyfriend says
to the older woman

and she says "it keeps me young"

sometimes the city consoles us
when we remember
a time not long ago
all the bashings, beating, slurs

the city says I see you
the city says I see everything
the city says it's good to cry
it keeps things growing

the city draws us into an embrace
nurturing us more
than our parents ever could

when my boyfriend and I reach
the staircase leading
down
to the train tracks

I do not think of my own murder
or why two brown boys in love
is so intolerable

I just feel the sand
paper of his face writing
something sweet on my cheek

I listen
to the life inside his breath
as our kiss transforms us
into two tunnels of flesh
sparking electric like third rails

when he boards the train
he has many cars to choose from

and as he rides, I'm confident
neither one of our destinations
stops
at a place
where visibility means death

I know each of us will

arrive
home
safe

In this city,
we have each other's back
and we don't take anyone for granted

Prayers for My 17th Chromosome (#17)

Where did my illness begin?

Did it begin before?
in another realm
in a galaxy of cells

stars of nuclei,

Did it begin in the womb?
when I was submerged inside the sea of my mother

who was submerged
in the sea of God,

liquor, whitewash, cigarette
smoke & the aching tendons of war—were

generations of violence
those strands of DNA, the roots
of my rioting

17th chromosome,

am I sick because of all of this?

or was it just that when I was in the womb
forming further into being,
my body was overcome with joy
with spontaneity,

like a classical symphony   abandoning   the scripts,

to play the sounds of each
of their creation stories

Again, was it God?
who some believe
is 1
who some say made Earth
in 7 days,

is this the Divine
within
manifesting
as 1 and 7 linked
to become
17

and if 1 plus 7=8
then am I 8 ?

Who will consume my rapid cells
multiplying into tumors?

How do I accept an illness   incurable

life-long?

Today, I'm too exhausted to debate religion, mathematics & science.
I decide to invite my 17th chromosome over for dinner.
We've been living in the same house,
but eating separately.

Hmm…I wonder how many extra plates will I need?
Plates or platelets? my 17th chromosome says.

Well, at least my disease has a sense of humor.

And so, my heart murmurs,
let us begin by simplifying:

by making room,

for all of us to talk
for all of us to listen
for all of us to enjoy this meal
together.

Neurofibromatosis Type 1 is transmitted on chromosome 17 and is caused by a genetic mutation. NF Type 1 causes multiple areas of hyperpigmentation (i.e., birthmarks) that appear shortly after birth. In late childhood, a few to thousands of tumors appear on the outside of the skin and under the skin.

When You Died on Ash Wednesday,

the priest tilted my head to the heavens. The priest painted my forehead with a cross. He said, we return to our origins when we die. For years, I could not wipe the ashes from my face. Grandmother, it's me. You used to call me simply "the girl." Now, I am your grandson. I'm not trapped inside the nets of worlds anymore. Nor do I flap on the decks of boats gasping as my wheeling pupils make their final turn. I swim towards a greater tide. I move between energies like a salmon traveling between rivers & seas. Grandmother, I will tell you what you already know: I have tasted crisp clear water, I have tasted salt.

Misfits, Rebels and Electricity

"I write because life does not appease my appetites and hunger. I write to record what others erase when I speak, to rewrite the stories others have miswritten about me, about you...To become more intimate with myself and you." - Gloria E. Anzaldúa

In middle school, I both read incessantly, and wrote. I wrote because I thought I needed to keep a record of my suffering, I wrote out of a place of despair. I wrote because I did not think I would survive. I wrote to survive. I started to get bullied at the age of five. I was a strange, precocious, stubborn gender bending outlaw. My little personhood didn't fit into the already rigid rules of the playground. Territories were already being carved out; girls on one side, and boys on the other. I just kind of did my own thing, and had quick-wit and smart-mouth. All of this got me into trouble with the other kids and the teachers. I was a bully magnet for most of my childhood. I started to escape into books because home wasn't much better either. I needed to think that another reality was possible. And books, and poetry, they showed me there were other worlds out there. They allowed me to believe that there were places for misfits, and rebels. Books helped me connect with other people I didn't know in the physical realm, but could sense on a spiritual/metaphysical and imaginative realm.

So in middle school, at the height of my unpopularity, I poured a lot of my focus into my creative writing classes. Those classes gave me the space I needed to have a small voice in an otherwise silencing world. I started to write more frequently. There were so many days I got beaten up, thrown into dumpsters, spat on and groped. There were so many days I was told I was unlovable and wrong. I started to write down my experiences through poems and stories in my creative writing classes. There were days I was so broken, I remember crawling like an insect to a hiding place…somewhere no one but God would see me. I'd go to this secret hiding place, I always had at least one…I'd hide there and write. When speaking the prayers I'd been taught out loud ran out, I wrote down my rage, my hopes, and secrets as prayers in little spiral bound notebooks. Though some of those moments of self-expression, and reading were filled with sweetness, much of my relationship to text, to words, was born out of pain.

When I started writing consistently, it felt like a matter of life and death. It felt as though I were trying to be erased, and writing resuscitated me. So when the kids bashed me for being queer, fat, brown, not having or being able to afford the right clothes anymore, for being gender non-conforming, a tomboy, I'd pick up my bruised body, my body that caused so much disruption in their world, and I'd hold onto hope with my pen. Writing was a form of rebellion against the forces that were trying to keep me suppressed, and literally trying to kill me.

Sometimes, I still feel those forces, and they drive me to write. It's taken me a long time to access other sources within me to write from. It's taken to a long time to write from sources within me that aren't just triggered and afraid. It has taken me years of deep consistent healing work and therapy to alter and reshape my writing. My own development as a person, coming into myself, embracing myself, has had a direct relationship to my growth as a writer. I've begun to realize that there are many ways to be rebellious. I've realized that the greatest form of rebellion I can have is self-love. Self-love is not what I grew up with. I was given and taught self-hatred at the time of my birth. If the systems are set up to destroy me, to keep me feeling powerless, & isolated—then I will respond by loving myself. I will respond by connecting with other human beings. This is not self-indulgent, it is a daily practice of transforming old narratives that no longer serve me, and giving my soul the opportunity to thrive, to love & be loved. I'm thankful for some of the amazing bad ass queer women, men, trans & gender queer writers whose work I stumbled across over the years and continued to motivate me.

Self-love is vital to me living a fulfilling life. Over the past three years, I was diagnosed with several illnesses, both of which cause me to have chronic pain and fatigue and a whole host of health complications. I'd been dealing with the symptoms for years, but it took the doctors a long time to figure out what was going on. I've had to radically shift my life. My relationship to writing & my body changed, as I've begun to accept my illnesses. I move slower now because my body is forcing me to. I experience more stillness yet inside of it, poetry still pulses. There are days my body hurts too much to type or write by hand, but poems still emerge.

When I start to write a poem, there is always at least one point of suspension. I often feel in my stomach that sensation of pre-falling, and then falling. Writing poetry, it's about diving into the unknown; it's learning how to be more comfortable in that space of ambiguity. I live outside of neatly fitting categories, and I live with illnesses that are pathologized and misunderstood, because their origins and progressions cannot be easily defined by science. Yet all of this is strengthening my work. If I am to continue move towards thriving on a spiritual level, then the unknown can no longer be my enemy. Every day, I get to know the great mystery within myself on a deeper level. Every day, I try to connect with the mystery outside of myself. Befriending uncertainty as much as my human body can do is the key to my happiness. Poetry allows me to simultaneously connect with the unknown, and offers me a container. It is an act love, of self-determination, a whole lot of intention and a whole lot of letting go.

I write from my dreams and nightmares, and I write from what I am dreaming towards. If I do not speak of both dreams and nightmares, and everything in between, then I am not writing with fullness. I write from my body, from tissues, muscles, bone, organs, from my blood and my cells, and all the memories stored there. I write to locate myself within the specifics of my body and all the complicated stories it signifies, and I write to free myself from my body. I write to connect to other people, especially those living on the margins of society. I write with a longing that a wire has for electricity.

Ari Banias

Who Is Ghost

who is ghost, is the translucent almost
who is flotilla, is footless
is died and come back, who is sheet
and *oooo* who is remembered

is ghost is flicking
on and off the lights is brush
the shoulder with gauzy touch
who is whisper in ear whisper
of curtain in and out with breeze who is
flash is haze is gone

forgotten is ghost
the ones with different names now
the girl they say became   who is he
who one time got kissed in a field
it was summer bare ankles dampened by night grass
who was uncurled is shook out

the candle with four matches sunk in its wax
who any flame is

is the prairie taken by it
the half made bed the half said word
before it folds up into the throat

the first time someone took off your clothes
the clothes themselves
          is ghost

Exquisite Corpse

I had a nightgown once, which
became a jellyfish

so in order to wear it I had to go down:
to punch myself into the form

the content required,
to hunker like a boulder under
immeasurable pressure, as when
minerals are transformed

into their reverse.
As when a nightgown is worn
over the tuxedo for years.

Pissing on a jellyfish sting
is said to make one
feel normal or royal.

When we were together
in the house by the sea,
there was still a sea. Before
being set adrift,

nightgown and tuxedo
lay slain, ashore where
the surf inched up and up and if

lapels say a word then burn her
down to a pair of molten cufflinks

they piss on til normal. It is expected
he kiss her and become a nightgown.

She wears him
in order to punch him down

until he sinks, until it's said he is
painless as a house
or some comparable
soft-bodied animal that drifts.

Narrative

There is too much to catch up on.
For example, I was once
a sundress on a splintery
swingset in Texas. The world
was made of yellow grass struggling
to live in sand, sand
beyond our fence, across the street,
sand that could have drowned us.
But didn't. Because it was
a border town, there were other
others, so we sort of
belonged. The cacti looked religiously
stoic, held promise, as did the mountains,
cast pink in the waning sun.
In Illinois I tried to build a kind of Midwestern
girlhood that failed and failed
into the shape of a flute
I played only high notes on.
I stopped eating
meat, stopped speaking
Greek. Became an ear.
Now the only one I remember from that time
is the girl who looked like a boy or maybe

was one, who walked the same way home as me,
same coat, same sneakers,
who I never once greeted, just repeated
his-her name to myself: Dominick? Dominique?
Massively old trees canopied the cobbled streets.
The houses set so far apart you'd hear neither
argument nor song. Dominick.
Dominique.
Not a stitch of recognition
passed between us.

Solve for X

if there was a word for it.
when pushing down reason.
if more than a boy.
if shaking took care of it.
if cured by looking.
if no lemon juice to lighten the hair.
if another girl could step out of you, a shared one.
if her face was loosened by salt.
if home was unjustly sunlight.
when the other way around was a mountain.
if light curtained it.
if less than.
if it dodged windows.
if maybe is the only thing enormous.
if less than a boy is a fruit.
if villages of light were pushed down inside you.
a sea of anotherness.
when the pronoun curtain.
if a ring undoes the hand.
when a zipper becomes impossible.
if a curtain behind the curtain.
if girl is less than lace.
if barely can pass for maybe.

if boy was covered in possible light.
if she stiffens when praised.
when salt was sung.
and a face was just a face.
if he bristles always at the name.
if nostalgia is a kind of blue light.
if maybe could still be beautiful.
if right now is bandaged.
when even what didn't happen happened.

Here's the Story on Being

and then a person addresses themselves to you –
well, to your clothes.
but I only borrowed these, you want to say, they aren't
me. or you'd like to explain yours were broken or wet or
you didn't have a skin – but it wouldn't make sense.

if others were walking you were swimming. laps in a muck pool
observing yourself from a birds' eye view.
technique: sloppy. perspective: itchy. the cringe of
wishing it were some other weirdo
and all the while trying to hold a conversation, semi-normal
groping in the pockets for that thing
called benefit
of the doubt… wait, a job interview?
leatherette
swivel chair

now hurry to shut the swamp off, unplug the clothes, be here –
oh, this is you getting fired –
"…should try to *smile* more, you know, make the customers *comfortable*"
he's really saying this? he's really saying this.
your hands pick at themselves in helpless furtive
aghast. could have been… less cranky?
less a possibility of yourself than

already?   paste a pink bow to your head
grow teeth in front of your teeth? your face aches from resembling
smiling

survival is the question, how in that thrashing
to not obliterate
the yellowed envelope from someplace
addressed to you, the question of mustering
courage preserving
little blue diagonal stripes on the edge
when charged with the task to
                              read
                              in a very loud and crowded place with the wind high
to train the fighters inside

The Hole

Down in the hole where all the old
Barbies are thrown, half-dressed
with tangled hair. Where the coral
lipstick. The clothes you were told looked good
because they were in style. In the hole lives
the sound of cellophane tape, the sort that turns
caramel color with age, wrapping paper unrolled
onto the floor, and the plain clean
squeak of mother's scissor blades. It hurts in the hole
with such a warm house windows lit and the people
on the couch and the people on the floor and
also in the photos, younger versions
of them smiling except your uncle
who never smiled. Cigar smoke. TV
blaring sports in the hole. All the throbbing
pasts crowded into the singular
throbbing present. The excess of presents
torn open and instantly forgotten. Chucked right
down into the hole. Hole where all the gone

cats. Where dinner. Where a dishwasher
and carpeted basement. Where the aunts
wore gaudy rings. And the full dinner plate not
by accident dropped on the floor. Hot food
jumbled in with shards of plate. Don't
you goddamn dare. The stomping up
or down the stairs. Snow and ice
and anyway nowhere to go. Sometimes the hole
a trick hole. Was that your old
name? the ring of the kitchen phone
with cord so long it grazed the floor? Their talk drifts up
when you aren't on guard so you swear
down into the hole as hard as you can
that you'll never sit at their table again. When you yell
everything in the hole swims up so close
you smell the wine on its breath. The starched tablecloth
embroidered by relatives long-dead, the hands
refusing to release you even
after grace has ended.

At Any Given Moment

Vito Corleone was a "strong" man, which is the main definition of a man I think.
At the table I say, smiling, I am weak. And everyone stares at me like,
why would you admit that? While I realize it's a "mistake" I'd say it
endlessly. Because it's true.

So here I am
          in the hallway again. Chain motel. Nondescript corporate wallpaper
          of a beigey patterned variety. Gender is the room
I see myself walking into, is all the rooms, any room, the number, the key

corresponding, and of course the whole
world's in there. Of course if I want to talk to almost *anyone*
I have to go in. Fuck!
It's too fucking small and we're all in it. But no, not all of you

seem to hate it. Here where all my dreams of showing up
to school in just underwear, flushed
before a backdrop of bean sprouts
nosing out of paper cups – I remember Eric suddenly,

the fourth grade outcast, in a freakout
pushing all the furniture around our classroom
in brilliant chaos. I didn't realize then the world
wouldn't fall apart if you did that. The corner of my desk

got jammed into my stomach
which was startling but not personal.
What's personal is being here with all of you.

*

You know how you can't really look out a window without it
being a thing you're doing,
wistful or just framed in its way by you
being you and the window being a window? It isn't casual.

Everything is out there to be looked at and not to
look back at you who are small and like a god in your window.
One feels invisible then
                         but we've definitely seen people

in the next building over in their underwear
on a bed watching TV in the heat. Multiple times.
The room where *we're* in our underwear watching TV is exceptionally small,
anyone would say so.

*

But bigger too in its way because the shades are drawn and though we're beaded
in a light sweat no one can see us, we tell ourselves. So therefore the room is huge
and contains all we want to imagine there. Given the heat
and that we are a little slower to think

in this humidity. Our near naked bodies in underwear we've decided

are outside the room of gender. Which means we are eternally outside, two
wildflowers in soil, faces upturned. The elements tend to us
gently and with rain and light

but then of course large people in gloves come to poke
plastic tags into the soil
right beside us to help us be seen correctly

though we'd rather it all be
a little less precise. I'm not *just* a flower.
At any given moment I'm also a weed and
medicinal and food for some bees and I don't know, just a thing in the wind, a thing

in the ground. I like the feel, the sound
of that. But since I've imagined this room it must be
me who jabbed the tags into the soil.
With my blurry picture and beneath it

the scientific version of my name. I'm watching myself
watch TV in the heat in my underwear from the next building over, and
honestly, I seem overly angry.

I think we should talk.   Can we all come to our windows?

On Being a Stranger. Instinct, Messiness, Binaries, Failure, Discomfort, and How I Think I Write Poems

Being trans and queer and a first generation Greek-American of immigrant parents necessarily informs my writing in both process and content. My work itself is largely concerned with experiences of foreignness, with being a body in the world, and in looking at language, memory, one's relationship to the past and with other bodies vis-à-vis "foreignness." My poems grapple with this in two senses. Foreign as in alien: to conventional notions of gender (and attendant narratives of authenticity and self); ethnically within both US and Greek culture; within one's family; even experiencing one's memories, or the self in those memories, as a kind of stranger. And foreign as in new: the ways sobriety or falling in love can alter one's perception of the world; the startling newness of an intentionally shifting gendered body. I imagine foreignness as the place where otherness and possibility may meet – a location that holds a charge, a place from which to speak as an intimate stranger. Because the presence of a stranger suggests a multiplicity of inquiries and instabilities – a stranger does not sit comfortably. For me, it is mostly out of discomfort that poems are born.

I also don't sit comfortably in binaries that posit "tradition" and "experimentation" as mutually exclusive, and I fidget & buck when I'm expected to pledge allegiance. I write in opposition to the notion I ought to take a fixed stance in relation to lyric, language, narrative, innovation, tradition, the I – and vehemently against the expectation that I stake out my "own" aesthetic ground and work that little patch of soil to depletion. Far more compelling to me than aesthetic singularity or purity are expansiveness and multiplicity, whether expressed within the vessel of a single poem, or in an overall embrace of various approaches to speaking & thinking, understanding & making.

Writing often feels like a process of tricking myself into saying something I didn't know I meant, or something I didn't mean to know – an encounter with the almostness of what I'm trying to look at but not be obliterated by. I try to think into my feeling, to feel into my thinking, and often go the wrong way; but I value failure. I'm generally instructed by what upsets me, what embarrasses me. Though it makes for messiness, I do my best to honor every impulse. I hold vulnerability and contradiction in highest esteem. Power – its manifestations and temptations and consequences – haunts me. Alienation is a form of highly prized information. Language offers a kind of wardrobe through which to work through these and other problems of experience. I try on many different pairs of shoes, and move differently in each. I glide and stomp; I swerve, am clumsy, cut a rug, dig my heels in, bruise my knees, go barefoot, take the stairs two at a time, dread leaving the house, nervously tap my foot, stay home, go out. And it all feels necessary.

Ariel Goldberg

Confessional Press Conference

I didn't pose.

I had no choice but to pose.

      I have to delete pictures
           to take more.

      I found my photo used
        without permission.

I don't have any new
photos to show you.

Are you still taking pictures?

I am not a hero like other
photographers.

We are using someone else's
pictures of war.

The public desire for these
images is strong.

They held the camera out as far
as their arm could reach and
leaned back to increase the
space.

I meant to send it, not post it.

We're looking for the person
responsible for this picture.

It says Unknown or
Unidentified.

There is more than one picture,
actually.

Dear Photographer:

I dreamt I was at the recycling bin again with my damp newspapers neatly bunched in twine. I had gathered, stacked and admired my collection of news a few years ago from what a library was throwing away. I saved them for the hope that time accrued would deliver purpose. Eventually, I would display the papers to convey excess and compulsion, in regards to the image stream. This was not a hoarded collection--but I was aware it risked being misunderstood for one.

Yesterday the decision hit to not continue saving the papers. I began throwing them out one by one, each time shocked by the intentionality. I would counter the doubt with reminding myself of realities like mold. The pictures on the front page are not realities. Basements and allergies are. I don't have space in my transformational expectations of being to stay weighted with old newspapers. They must become ethereal, simple, more true.

In the dream, I was no longer spending time with each paper. I went from spit clinging kisses to the rash of heartbreak. I had an assistant there with me, so efficiency was reducing self-reflection. The memorializing couldn't be private so it somehow disappeared. I was safeguarded from talking to the front-page photo, and so protected from the photo not talking back to me.

The assistant photographed me holding newspapers above the bin. Each paper I held became like a medal I had just won, positioned next to my chest. An award for what, I don't know. Unclear survival? Metabolizing denial? The assistant was trying to figure out how to get a better backdrop. But the sun was harsh, so the shadows were too, and the garbage bins were ugly, or they were just boring, recognizable to everyone who lived in this city--even if no one in the neighborhood would see the photographs. The shot was formulaic. Are you getting the front-page picture in it, I asked faintly. I could feel myself giving up on the details; I wanted to finish the routine.

Dear Photographer:

I offered to take the picture you needed of the clock tattoo on your arm. It's a hand drawn circle with a jumble of numbers in one asymmetrical side. You had to turn it unnaturally by holding your right boob away from your arm at the same time. It has to be a picture you kept saying, not just a snapshot of the clock. With a composition you demanded. I know, I said. It was like we were siblings. I was more amused and you more frustrated; it was your creative process, not mine. We tried different backdrops like fabric and a table and a bookshelf. I hated that I was moving things around. Or I was more disappointed that things would need to be moved around. You wanted to keep looking at what I took and then referencing this one that was almost okay but not good enough. The photo was for a show, to be on a wall. To take the pressure off, you said it didn't have to get done now. That these could be sketches, but I insisted we do a few more. Then you said let me see, stop, that's the best one. But I didn't understand how it was different.

Dear Photographer:

We were standing around trying to make conversation and you seemed detached. Like you were listening and decided what we were saying wasn't interesting. David Levi Strauss says it's not that we mistake photographs for reality, we prefer them to reality. You pulled a camera out of your tote bag and pointed it to the old map of the city that was hanging on the red wall above the stove. The sensor lingered as a blue spotlight for a moment over one of the rectangular folds. Meanwhile we were talking about the photos on the fridge of the people that lived in the house when they were younger. How it seems funny that people change. We were talking about the torment of sitting on Santa's lap or being in a school portrait.

I thought I'd mention being Santa's photographer at the Manhattan Mall. I had a code to get into the staff bathroom. Our photo studio was set up in the desolate entranceway to a bankrupt department store. This was a downgrade from winter wonderland being in the center of the food court, so everyone I worked with was pissed off about the pay-cut. Customers would tell us about how Macy's has gone digital but they were staying loyal to us. Sometimes they brought their previous years photos to show loyalty. These people wanted the same Santa, so tracking the progress of people growing seemed more exact. I had to shake a toy to make the babies smile, which didn't always work. Sometimes if the babies were crying I just took their picture anyway, figuring tears would be hard to detect if they hadn't accumulated enough to gloss their faces. Laughing and crying can be interchangeable in pictures. Sometimes the parents refused to pay for the pictures I'd taken of their crying babies and I had to redo them. That was embarrassing. As punishment, or to have a break from photographing, I'd be switched to the register, which meant slipping the photo into a card or cutting it to fit into a keychain or a snow globe. I was always afraid of ruining it with these more expensive holders.

The following events are all true stories, taking place in and around the past few months, leading as clear evidence to players of caution, amidst the flux, barriers, and excitement over the ominous shape of our future:

The memory keeper photographer said urgently, move now, pulling this photographer we know out of the frame of the shot of a go-go dancer at a small town gay bar. In boxer briefs and new sneakers, the dancer had no interest in stopping photographs. Pictures enhance tips. The friends eagerly push the least sexualized into a special dance while laughing and clapping. The photographers watch people look at their screens immediately after taking and in between taking and feel satisfied.

It is the telling of these stories that makes our changes real and possible. I am here to tell these stories not to stop any change but to make us think about what is happening in the midst of proliferation and plenitude:

The art photographer goes to a dark room where the people inside talk to each other anytime they move. Walking to paper cutter, walking to processor, left side loaded, walking to exit. Stenciled numbers glow in the dark above stations. The stations are divided by two deep walls that prevent light from spreading. Solar system stars, the kind a child might decorate their bedroom ceiling with, guide you towards the revolving door.

Belongings are left for brief periods unattended in a room where you hang prints on the wall to see how finished they are. The photographers act like they are in a locker room, where you wouldn't stare rudely at a stranger's private parts, but just glance through perimeters. The glance is enough to allow them to see the contents of each other's photographs. The art photographer blinks and feels the weakness in their eye muscle to recognize the correct color on their prints. They don't want to make anything perfect anyway. To get rid of dust, the photographers take turns with the air machine, shaped like a video game gun, attached to the wall through a coil, activated through a trigger and loud engine. Hours go by. Which is when one photographer points to the wall to say, I like that one. The other photographer says thanks. They each remark genuinely, not out of compulsion, and yet no depth. After this exchange, the art photographer takes the paper that has a curious neon red splotch on it to the personal space of this photographer we don't know and asks, do you think that's a light leak? The photographer offers the advice of trial and error. The cell phone, even though it was in your back pocket? The picture has a dildo in it but that is not discussed.

Poetics Statement

> *On the surface, I don't have "genderqueer content" in my work. When I perform, I look genderqueer, and what I write about is inevitably from that perspective. But I wonder why no one has ever labeled my work "queer art," I wonder why I wouldn't say, "I'm a queer artist," but an "artist who is also queer."[1]*

In the late nineties, I was closeted in High School, and spending a lot of time in the darkroom. The photos I produced in the darkroom did not matter as much as the place. Now that photography is so mobile, it is essentially homeless. A constant exposure has replaced realms of hiding. The disappearance of black and white analogue feels like the erasure of the only companion I knew before coming out. Even if you are alone in front of a computer or inspecting the back of your camera, being in front of a screen is a state of vulnerability, lending you to distraction, to the infinitude of knowledge, and the erasure of that knowledge. It's the opposite of what a low light room does to your eyes.

The Photographer is a character who walked out of a dark room ten years ago, and hasn't wanted to go back. The Photographer is one voice in my recalibration of the "place" for photography. I log photographic events into newsflashes, captions, and letters. These relentless correspondences and broadcasts address the question of what happens to consciousness when cameras have the potential to be everywhere, to be on almost everyone. A singular photographer that exists in multitudes results: who is writing to the photographer and who is the photographer is as unclear as identity and gender on any given day of my life.

The selections you've read are traces from serialized poems that intend to talk to each other. These poems do not fit on one page--they are 100 letter long poems talking to 1000 caption lines that I handwrite on paper tucked in to the back of my journal that I then read out loud into a tape recorder that I then transcribe that I then edit that I then perform live. I work via overwhelm.

These serialized poems follow a loose narrative arc of The Photographer experiencing estrangement and fascination with way the world is currently photographing and looking at pictures. The Photographer believes that image making is approximating language use, in its communicative intents, so much so that words can replace pictures.

The Photographer decides to only watch cameras and pictures. The Photographer begins absorbing an enormous number of news images to write about. The Photographer is a news junkie.

At one point, they begin reading their "poems" at the Golden Gate Bridge, with a shopping cart filled with photo detritus: empty picture frames and photo albums, photo magazines and camera cases. The text they perform is ingested and redistributed language from watching people take the same photograph at one of the most photographed places in the world.

The Photographer becomes more introverted after people dismiss their public art. Most people ignored The Photographer, mesmerized by their cameras at the tourist attraction. Experimental poets, those who identify as such, tend to listen to The Photographer. The Photographer observes and logs, and imagines correspondents. The Photographer studies theories about photography and begins corresponding with other living and dead photo theorists. The Photographer begins to write lectures on subjects like author photos and t-shirts decorated with drawings of old cameras. The Photographer proclaims themself an unaccredited expert, in a very distorted way.

Then something happens. The photographer returns to the place where they once became an ordinary, yet unclear photographer. The Photographer falls suspect to the lure and spell of cameras. The Photographer begins photographing again, and needs to reckon with their relationship to strictly "writing" photographs, as well as simply "taking" them.

People sometimes want to know if some of the text is found. Can a voice sound found, but be real? What is the purpose of containing a multiple? What would advertising in poetry sound like? It is possible I wrote everything, but it sounds as if you've heard it before.

The change I refer to in photography is more complicated than consumer markets going digital. This writing does not pine for analogue; it wants to keep up with how many photographs are doing the work of storytelling and information dispersal. I am interested in how photographs are agents of loss and discomfort, which are relatively classic issues for photography.

My writing on photography is a collection that is still a bit mysterious to me. But ever since I read the introduction to a book of Helen Levitt's street photographs ten years ago that described her work as "poetic" I thought to myself, that is so weird. To describe a photograph as poetic seems tautological. Photographs are so frustrating. They need words. Words need pictures. Photo and text collapse, together, as if arguing, rolling around so that their hair falls on each other's heads and you don't know what is a wig or what will whip away when you come up for air.

We are experiencing cameras' new realm of the decorative: the palimpsest of tools.

What are flat tools?

I explore the concept of rewriting photos, literally replacing them with imagined voices of the photographer, subject, and viewer.

In short, I am interested in creating a world, where a queer person is telling the news and the news is reported through photographs. My writing is urgent.

Ariel Goldberg
November 30, 2011

Notes

1. I am writing a book length essay called *The Estrangement Principle,* a poetic criticism that examines the feeling of exclusion from both a legacy of Susan Sontag being not not out to the curation under the themes of gender and sexuality.

Bo Luengsuraswat

A cut won't kill me

everyday
        all day
      unintentional scars shape the texture of my skin

                      wounds carried through the wind
           make me shiver with pain

        people say i have sensitive skin
because
     minor scratches
        leave me with permanent patterns

                 the patterns of agony

          ......

i guess this is how recognition works

            every sight leaves   a scar

                a cut
     that alters the shape of your body

an icky feeling that reminds you

that this world is not yours

that it's not worth it to take another step

outside the house

to walk

to run

to crawl

take a bus

grocery shop

buy some pills

get a soda

call 911

in exchange of a temporary recovery

miss-aimed rocks

blazed through the wind

welcome you

to the world

that you don't belong

poetry of the moment

is never enough

to cure the damage of the soul

SHE   her   LADY BABY   sister   MAMA
MISS   MA'AM   girl
she   HER   LADY   baby   SISTER
mama   miss   **ma'am**   GIRL

SHE   HER   LADY   BABY
SISTER   MAMA   MISS
MA'AM

GRRRRRRRL

......

broken   mirror

shattered   glass

what keep cutting me deeper and deeper
are not the rocks
but the pieces of glass
from that broken mirror

shattered

to invisibility

i cannot see
but feel

that sharp sand rubs into my skin

particles of dirt
mixed into the matter
that makes me 3D

mold me
into a body

of scars

sometimes i wonder
why it won't bleed
the vitals that make me me

probably ran out of quota

even tears

my eyes know better

it ain't worth it

to flood

over the same old wounds

a cut won't kill me

oh young lady
don't be mad, i mean well
i love you
your soft skin
sleek black hair
almond eyes
and that scent of culinary heaven

nice little asian girl
smiley submissive quiet
you can just pass me by

pass

like a girl
a beautiful girl
curvy-ass-tits / sweet-pitched-voice / little-nose-eyes
tiptoeing around the corner
coming into your store
your house
your street
your country

calling you on the phone to spell HER last name for you

a pink cell phone

i must have, one said

such a lovely lady you are

you deserve a pair of

pink slippers

HI LADIES

YES MA'AM

THANKS SISTER

OH...SUCH A BABY GIRL!!!

......

all relational words in the world

and the spider webs they spin

are deadly grids

that catch

and break

the wings of non-conformity

broken   wings

broken   mirror

dreams shattered smashed beaten embedded into skin

formed a new version of me

a *me*

crushed between zeros and ones

how much is a cut worth?

a squeaking noise

pierced

through internal organs

split

my limbs inside out

turned

me into a being

called *woman*

Proximity and the Shifting Contours of Belonging

One decade is a long time. Ten years. One-zero. It's the beginning of the next digit. A transition.

One decade is a vast space. Constantly shifting, warping into different shapes, rolling across landscapes.

One decade is a great distance, yet unpredictably proximate.

It will be one decade this fall. One decade from the second the plane took off the Bangkok

International Airport with an unexpected date of return. Ten years from the moment I began counting down the days until I would be home again.

North America. The West. I was transplanted to the center of empire.

From this other side of the world, home seemed so far away, behind a curtain of white mist I wasn't able to locate. "What the hell is T#@!land?" "So tell me more about Taiwan." "Do you know what chewing gum is?" "Are there washing machines there?" "Can you eat cheese?" Bits and pieces of home came in Walmart toilet paper packages and bags of potato chips, like an exquisite corpse. Unrecognizable silhouettes. Sometimes I didn't know where I was from anymore, or, for that matter, where I was *supposed* to be from. If there weren't those hardcover picture books full of images of gold-leaf temples and blue-water beaches that my Thai-born Chinese parents forced me to bring along for show-and-tell purposes, I probably wouldn't exist, or know how to exist, at all.

My body was floating in space, ready to be explored.

Along with those colorful picture books, I brought a Thai musical instrument called "sor-oo" but didn't get to play that much. I spent more time describing it than using it. I told people that it was a Thai violin that you had to play sideways. But because my English wasn't that great I had to do hand gestures to explain—left fist at my neck level and right hand moving sideways back and forth underneath. Some white boys were amused by it. They thought I was demonstrating how to fuck.

Thai students were encouraged to bring with them some sort of "cultural artifacts" and, especially for Thai girls, learn a song of Thai dance in case they would get a chance to perform at school cultural nights. People thought Thai costumes were pretty. "They're just like kimonos, right? […bow…]" A fellow soccer teammate told me that I should wear a Thai dress for senior prom. The thought of wearing a sabai disgusted me when I found out I was obligated to go to prom with an ex-boyfriend who thought it was funny to call me "Porn" (shortened from my birth name Tanyaporn).

One time someone yelled "THAILAND!" I turned around because I instinctually knew they were calling me. That person just forgot my name.

Some foreign students were puzzled by my face. "Why do you look so Chinese?" I just laughed it off and said I don't know. My mother kept telling me when I was growing up that I was only 25% Chinese. She said she was 50% Chinese because she could speak a little bit of Teochew and that my brother had no share of Chineseness because he was born five years after me. I accepted her logic wholeheartedly and was offended when anyone told me I looked Chinese. I would say my great-grandparents were from China, but I got nothing to do with it.

I had the hardest time hunting for Thai food with recognizable taste during the first couple
years abroad. Even though I hated Thai food so much, especially what is now known as the
famous pad Thai, I would get nostalgic cravings sometimes. In first grade, my parents put me
in a public school near our house in a working-class neighborhood, and at lunch the mean
kitchen custodians would be serving us spicy soups and rice in half-washed dirty aluminum
compartment trays. They loved yelling at us to be quick and silent as the endless line of hungry
kids moved along like a millipede. That was my first taste of Thai food. Soggy brown noodles.
Coconut milk soup with specs of floating chili flakes. Sticky soybean dessert that looked like
mucus. Well, at least one good thing about lunchtime was that after swallowing those things I
knew I'd be out of this hell in half a day.

I was obsessed with Charlie Brown. I was Charlie Brown in fact. Besides it being the first
English-speaking cartoon I was introduced to (my father thought it was a good idea to familiarize
his daughter with American culture early on), Charlie Brown was someone I identified with
and eventually came to embody. The kids at my elementary school thought I was speech
impaired. "Pen bai ror?" "Tanyaporn pen bai. Tanyaporn pen bai jing jing ror?" "Pood noi si."[1]
Even the teachers were frustrated with my few words. "Pood bang si. Pood arai kor dai." "Tam
mai ngiab jang?"[2] If I weren't the smart kid that my classmates asked to copy their homework
from, I probably would have lived in absolute hostility from all the *encouragement to speak*.
"Tanyaporn pood dai duay ror?"[3] My body was revolting its own existence, just like how it
turned on Thai food. "Pood." "Pood." "Pood." "Pen dek roon mai tong pood yer yer."[4] Everyday I
longed for the comfort of the fried egg over steamed rice that my mother made.

[…Silence…]

I once had tom yum kung that tasted like overdue coconut milk dessert on Vancouver Island.
Other than that "Thai" was just a variation of some greasy Chinese fast food. Who could imagine
that less than half a decade later Thai food would become such a fad? Being Thai definitely gives
you an edge these days. "Your food is so good." Really? We just met, but thanks. "You know
about this new Thai restaurant down the street? Their pad Thai is delicious!" Oh, cool. "Your
mom's cooking must be so spicy." Well, not really. First of all she barely cooks. Secondly if she
feels like cooking her best dish is the fried egg over steamed rice that has no air of chili in it. All
of the sudden home appears at a proximate distance. Unrecognizable silhouettes, still.

Proximity is not just about spatial distance. It's a kind of temporality. A practice.

One summer in the Bay Area I found myself in a tragic pink sarong dress waiting tables at an
award-winning Thai restaurant. What was more tragic was the owner's male chauvinist son who
loved wagging his "working-class" masculinity in everyone's face. For some god-forsaken reason
he fired me on that first day because I seemed like a rich kid who didn't know how to work
the kitchen. Suppose I could have learned how to be a good waiter from his messy half-assed-
English-broken-Thai stories of picking up some girls at a karaoke bar every night.

A good friend of mine at the Thai temple in Berkeley had genuinely and tirelessly been on a mission to figure out what I was. "So you like boys or girls?" I never had an answer for him. He was the sweetest person I'd ever met who was willing to learn all the terms I considered myself to be, though he would soon forget most of the things I said. I rarely got to see him these past few years, but every time we met he never failed to evaluate my appearance in order to guess what phase I was going through. "You're growing your hair out? So you don't want to be a man anymore?" Despite our conversations and my fluctuating gender presentation everyone at the temple loved teasing us. Of course, why would two *opposite sex* people enjoying each other's company so much not be dating?

A few weeks ago my partner and I went to a Thai massage parlor down the street from our place in mid-city Los Angeles. Since I moved to LA (a.k.a. Thailand's seventy-seventh province) I'd become more aware of when to out myself as Thai. My partner said I should just speak Thai in case we would get a discount, but I was already nervous about the idea of being semi-naked in front of Thai people. When we got to the parlor this petite Thai masseuse I assumed to be the owner came to greet us. Luckily my partner and I were roomed right next to each other with a short wall in between. I remained indecisive whether to talk to the masseuse in Thai until she said, "Miss, could you please take off your shirt?" I couldn't stand it so I cut her off. She apologized for not knowing that I was Thai and proceeded to ask me who I came with. I felt her twisting my right leg, then pulled. I paused. The masseuse asked me again, "Is she your friend?" Tired of lying I told her that the person in the next room was my *fan* (partner). With a thinking face she let out "Oh, I see…"

Choice is such a tricky concept. Usually I'd rather gender myself than being gendered by someone else. I'd prefer saying "ka" and "nu" (feminine ending/ first-person female pronoun required for polite speech) than being "ma'am-ed" or "miss-ed" by strangers. I have no desire to measure what is more damaging. Languages are violent. You *choose* what type of harm you prefer to endure at different moments.

Proximity is a practice.

As the one-decade mark approaches, the previously unrecognizable silhouettes are suddenly gaining legibility. The terror of nearness burns underneath my skin. "Tam mai ngiab jang loey?"[5] The language of nostalgia makes me hesitant to speak. "Pood bang si. Pen dek roon mai tong pood yer yer."[6] Bits and pieces of home come floating like a puzzle I no longer want to assemble.

"Pood."

"Pood."

"Pood…noi si."[7]

Thailand: the land of the free. No colonized history. But the national boundaries were drawn by colonization. So are the contours of my body.

Over the past few years I've felt my face crinkle by any invitation to a Thai restaurant. Living in the seventy-seventh province I've got no right to complain about proximity. Home is just down the street. Around the corner. Upstairs. Yet I have no access to it. I exist in the language that no one understands. A space that no one sees.

One decade is a transition. A space constantly shifting. A great distance, yet unpredictably proximate.

Last spring my mother complained to me about how uncomfortable she was to be invited to our neighbor's daughter's wedding ceremony. It was around the time of Songkran (Thai New Year) so they decided to combine both celebrations. "I don't know what to do." My mother panicked. "I don't know what Thai people do. I'm afraid I'm gonna do something embarrassing." I told her to calm down and go with the flow. "You probably would just have to pour some water on their heads and wish them good luck, I guess." I had only read about the Thai New Year ceremony in textbooks and actually never been to one until I arrived in the U.S. This incident happened right after my mother's fifty-fourth birthday, and she'd been living in Bangkok all her life.

Talking about five decades of proximate distance.

---

[1] "Are you dumb?" "Tanyaporn is dumb. Are you really dumb, Tanyaporn?" "Say something."

[2] "Say something. Say whatever." "Why are you so quiet?"

[3] "Oh, you can speak?"

[4] "Talk." "Talk." "Talk." "The new generation must talk a lot."

[5] "Why are you so quiet?"

[6] "Say something. The new generation must talk a lot."

[7] "Talk."/ "Talk."/ "Say…something."

Poetics Statement

Writing, for me, is a tool for survival. Written words and utterances are fundamental to my practices of intervention, as well as processes of healing. Archived in the pages of my diary are oftentimes the traces of "invisible" violence and the pain deemed unintelligible by others. By recording these embodied experiences, I make them intelligible to myself and meticulously create a valuable *body of knowledge* that serves as the basis of self-building.

The first work featured here—"A cut won't kill me"—is part of the series called "Rants of Misrecognition." The works in this series were written when the repetition of the question "Am I still alive?" did not yield any affirmative answer. Even though this collection of words started out as explosive scribbles of anger, shock, confusion, hopelessness, and a host of other indescribable emotions, I believe that there can never be an adequate form of expression to articulate the massive degree of pain that a racialized trans/gender non-conforming person experiences on a daily basis, and no theory of intersectionality can sufficiently account for such violence.

"Proximity and the Shifting Contours of Belonging" delves further into the production of racialized gender identity and explores the ways in which interlocking systematic forces such as capitalism and globalization shape my experiences of migration and memories of "home." It draws unusual connections between speech and disempowerment, multiculturalism and silence, pad Thai and gendered violence. This work is particularly influenced by two diasporic Thai writers whom I highly admire, Jenny Boully and Jai Arun Ravine. Boully's "A Short Essay on Being,"[1] in which she narrates her experience of racialization as a multiracial Thai American person, inspired me to write "Proximity" in a similar narrative structure (floating, yet temporally disjointed). Ravine is my dear friend and fellow artist/writer whose work has immense impact on my creative process and growth. Their presence has sustained me through the many shifts in the proximity of home.

Much of my work challenges the notion of visibility and the cultural politics that requires one to always establish *proof* of belonging to a particular identity in order to gain recognition. Residing within multiple interstices of identity, I question if such comfort of belonging actually exists and at what point the visibility of certain bodies obscures others. How much can we trust our perception and senses? In the world where the idea of "visibility-as-proof" underlies our understanding of reality, how do we hold each other accountable for the production of "invisible" violence?

Notes:

1. Jenny Boully, "A Short Essay on Being," *TriQuarterly Online* 138 (Summer/Fall 2010), http://triquarterly.org/nonfiction/short-essay-being.

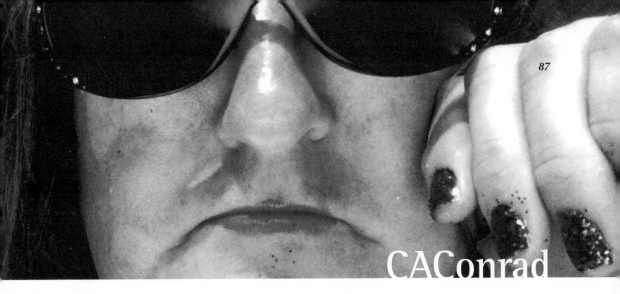

CAConrad

Somatic Poetry Exercise:
Gender Continuum

--for Anne Waldman (aka Outrider Anne)

Every morning for seven days I gave my friend Elizabeth Kirwin treatments of
reflexology and massage, and she in turn gave me craniosacral therapy. Each morning
while on the table I would fix my mind to meditate on seven possible genders for my
body, intersex intersecting day to day. Starting with the female skeleton, hormones,
glands, and genitalia. OF COURSE START with woman against the fairytale of Adam
and his magical life-giving rib!

Day seven was male, but days two through six were variations of our world. The
aim of physical, political, and sociological outcomes were in constant flux days
two through six. Margins were permitted to drop in meditation. Permission to drop
margins is an exceptional space to offer yourself and others. The craniosacral therapy
was straightening my spine, relaxing my muscles, and challenging my thoughts
throughout the gender exploration. The craniosacral lifted my consciousness while in
deliberate concentration on the sex of my body.

Each morning after our healing exchange I would take notes about my physical
condition, how it was shifting, mending, and notes on my gender meditation. The
notes took no specific course other than a personal demand to divulge all hidden
words and needs breaking free through the experience. I am a woman. I am a
man. I will be neither, or bits and parts of both with blood and imagination flow on
the increase. And that increase is a prodigious stream tempering the spirit, today,
tomorrow, again, again against a wall. Up the wall. Over the wall. Away from the

wall. The world as it could be (or a collective version of it) is always trying to bend the air around itself to be heard. The risks of the day are holding themselves out to us, yet we all know too well that the power structure is far ahead of us, the ambush of the ages. My notes from this exercise were plucked and shaped into a poem.

stArting to stArt heAling

starting it is starting in me
I am starting to realize
I say
galaxy when I
mean OUR galaxy
the Milky Way galaxy
future people
PLEASE know many
of us did not want
these wars
the armor in use
is a solid
imagination
against a
bullet
ultrasound
genocide machine
aborting girls to
preempt
burning witches
starting it is starting to amass a
serious
dreamscape
start starting now
start having extra
places for us to
begin being
master in home
memory of caves
blurry in the
sensate mission

in my past
 life reading I saw
 you then I felt you
 then wondered if you
 were sensing this too
I have started remembering
I am starting to remember
                    Atlantis and so
                          are you

Somatic Poetry Exercise: Catheters for Sanity

--for Mattilda Bernstein Sycamore

Let's be honest about our culture and say that anyone who makes us remember we are naked animals under these clothes is dangerous. To remove the scandal of it would first require the total annihilation of every bureaucratic agency sending memos through our doors. It is 2012 and some of us have our boots holding back the Return To Modesty Campaign. The American homosexual in 2012 unapologetically celebrates surrendering to the dominant culture's taste for marital equilibrium and WAR! A swift, unmitigated return to values acts like bookends many willingly throw themselves between. The opportunity to challenge these stifling, life-threatening institutions passes out of the conversation entirely in 2012.

Stupid faggots putting rainbow stickers on machine guns! I'm going to say it: GAY AND LESBIAN AMERICA HAS STOCKHOLM SYNDROME! The campaign to be included in the multi-billion dollar military industrial complex comes at a time when three children die of war-related injuries EVERY SINGLE DAY in Afghanistan. And after ten years of American occupation, Afghanistan has been deemed THE MOST DANGEROUS place on our planet for women. No other place on Earth is worse for women than Afghanistan. How else can I repeat this so you hear it? America DESTROYS women and children! Did you hear it that time?

The genocide of thousands of gay men in Baghdad is a direct result of the American invasion and occupation of Iraq. The most famous homosexual apologist for fascism Dan Choi helped make this genocide possible while serving as an American soldier in Iraq. American gay rights are all that matter I guess? And the destruction of Iraqi gays is just another item on the list of collateral damage? WILL NOT! To be repeated, WILL NOT SERVE WILL NOT SERVE I WILL NOT SERVE! WILL NOT! Today I WILL LISTEN to only my voice for NOT serving this sanctioned, collective, and REAL evil.

In the morning I performed reiki on a long, thin piece of plastic tubing, reiki with intentions to BE conscious throughout the day of being queer. Queer. Only queer. Today I will NOT ALLOW anyone to change the subject when I talk about what it means to be queer. Today I will NOT ALLOW the liars to step in front of me. Today I will talk about the frustration of watching war go unquestioned by the homosexual community of America. Reiki. I did reiki for half an hour on this plastic tube, then lubricated every inch of it, then inserted it inside my penis. It was not for pleasure of pain, it was for a chronic reminder of HOW this culture inserts its will on my penis more and more each day. You may now be married under our rules. You may now engage in the murder of innocent lives by our rules. I had many strained, bizarre conversations this day, constantly FEELING the tube inside my penis. The following poem is the result of this exercise which was more painful in spirit than it was for the tube inside me.

it's too late for careful

"this is a classic slingshot"
--my grandmother

melting glaciers
   frighten me when
      they appear on
         my street
         in dreams

      a feeling I send
   ahead of myself to one
      day walk inside

         while people sleep
         I like to inspect
            their flowers

it's not as
weird as
you think

I dreamt gays were
allowed in the military
everyone
thought it was great
what a nightmare

killing babies is less
threatening with the politically
correct militia

vices for
the vice box for
wards of
the forward state
who like different
things to kill alike

we CANNOT occupy Wall Street but
we CAN occupy Baghdad

the Heart Chakra
is green
we can coat our
anger with it

all blessings soaked into
bed sheets

they can't run
babies are
easy sport
but
murder helps the
pain go away is a rumor you

should have ignored

there's a way of
looking into
time for a poem
send it into the future

your footprint has
grown small what is
wrong with your footing?

what kind of American
are you? just buy it or
steal it but shut up

this poem is terrific for
the economy
the rich have
always tasted
like chicken
I'm not a
cannibal because
they're not
my kind

we CANNOT occupy Philadelphia but
we CAN occupy Kabul

we're the kind of poets
Plato exiled from the city
FUCK Plato that
paranoid faggot

Don't Ask, Don't Tell?
HOW ABOUT
Don't Kill and say whatever you WANT
for instance
when I buy a cat

I will name him Genet
"Genet! GENET!" I practice
calling Genet
INTO my LIFE

when you purchase
a car the factory's
pollution is
100% free

is it
ever easy
waking from
this?

bacteria and light
mucus and bone
a legacy of stardust
it is 98.6 degrees inside
all humans
the freshly murdered
their murderers
and the rest of us in between

my father lived to
see the fast-forward to
the cum shot
technology's
authentic
application

we CANNOT occupy Oakland but
the ghosts will occupy us

I will stay and
watch our
phoenix rise
I believe in us

DON'T TAKE ANY SHIT!!
A (Soma)tic Poetics Primer

"Sir, or Miss, OR WHATEVER YOU ARE!!"
--Security agent at Customs Building in Philadelphia

It sounds strange but being queer made creativity easier for me if only because I was shunned, forced outside the acceptable, respectable world, and writing was something I turned to in that imposed solitude, for writing was an actual place I could go to where I was free. Not an escape by the way! I really HATE when writers say they write to ESCAPE! I escape nothing, ever, nor do I want to escape! But this is my opportunity to say I'm grateful for being queer.

I cannot stress enough how much this mechanistic world, as it becomes more and more efficient, resulting in ever increasing brutality, has required me to FIND MY BODY to FIND MY PLANET in order to find my poetry. If I am an extension of this world then I am an extension of garbage, shit, pesticides, bombed and smoldering cities, microchips, cyber, astral and biological pollution, BUT ALSO the beauty of a patch of unspoiled sand, all that croaks from the mud, talons on the cliff that take rock and silt so seriously flying over the spectacle for a closer examination is nothing short of necessary. The most idle looking pebble will suddenly match any hunger, any rage. Suddenly, and will be realized at no other speed than suddenly.

The aim of (Soma)tic poetry and poetics is the realization of two basic ideas: (1) Everything around us has a creative viability with the potential to spur new modes of thought and imaginative output. (2) The most vital ingredient to bringing sustainable, humane changes to our world is creativity. This can be enacted on a daily basis.

When I was a queer kid dealing with violent ridicule in rural Pennsylvania, well, that was hard enough, but then AIDS came along. In other words, I was already terrified of my body because I was queer, but THEN came this disease, which many of my classmates were quick to point out was my own personal disease, a symptom of my perversion. My body became the very center of evil, and I believed them for a little while. Even when I thought I didn't, I did. Recovering from self-hatred is an amazing plan if you can have it.

It's ALL Collaboration. Anyone who ever fed you, loved you, anyone who ever made you feel unworthy, stupid, ugly, anyone who made you express doubt or assuredness, every one of these helped make you. Those who learn to speak with authority to mask their own self-loathing, those may be the deepest influences on us. But they are part of us. And we have each fit together uniquely as a result, and so there are no misshapen forms as all are misshapen forms from tyrants to wallflowers. Every poem written is filtered through the circumstances of the poet, through the diet of the poet. Just as unique is every reader of poems, for a thousand different readers of a poem equals a thousand different poems. We are here relying on one another whether or not we wish it. There are no poets writing in quiet caves because every poet is a human being as misshapen as any other human being. The room can be as quiet as possible, earplugs can be administered, but the poet still has a parade of influence running inside from one ear to the other. The quiet room cannot blot them out; it can however help the poet listen closer to this music for their own creation. We are not alone in our particular stew of molecules and the sooner we admit, even admire the influence of this world, the freer we will be to construct new chords of thought without fear.

(Soma)tics is a new word, the "o" a long "o." This word is simultaneously two words: Soma and Somatic. It's the mutations occurring when these wires cross where the poems can be found. This poetry truly is in everything, underscoring Freud's statement, "Everywhere I go I find a poet has been there before me." (Soma)tics are how I live in my awareness.

The last large wild beasts are being hunted, poisoned, asphyxiated in one way or another, and the transmission of their wildness is dying, taming. A desert is rising with this falling pulse. It is our duty as poets and others who have not lost our jagged, creative edges to FILL that gap, and RESIST the urge to subdue our spirits and lose ourselves in the hypnotic beep of machines, of war, in the banal need for power, and things. With our poems and creative core, we must RETURN THIS WORLD to its seismic levels of wildness.

Ching-In Chen

derived love: flying boy does it all

What Basel couldn't hide his love of milkmeats. Could not accommodate
him in the hereafter though we built a standardized altar with frothy
enamel and required barcodes of all visitors.

> *

Channel 1
    She opens an altar in her chest for this boy --- he's a sculpture in flight and she's
_____.
    A broom sweeping is not her thing. Break me out of this, my expectation of
myself. Hair falling over.

> *

Pre-conquest, we

hosted outlets in the streets. Sometimes in the armory.

Fissures and vacancies.

> *

Channel 2
    "It" scraped into s/he/what a chest/what a creepy
bathroom/what an incident/what an emergency

response/I just wanna be workin it/The only rule/
don't fuck it up, bitches/ a shifting medal/
a meal/a stolen prom queen/a corsage for a funeral

*

Nothing could be stuffed correctly, to verisimilitude, a taxonomy. Even when cleaning
my circuits.

*

Channel 3
　　　If I thick as a hornet
　　　If I trail the package of my body
　　　If I boy of moveable parts
　　　If I many-lovered
　　　If I many-fisted
If I unfurled unfurled unfurled

I provide no conjectural evidence of the copacetic sort for your convenience.

to try: a zuihitsu

> *What I leave behind has a life of its own. I've said this about poetry, I've said*
> *it about children. Well, in a sense I'm saying it about the very artifact of who I*
> *have been. – Audre Lorde*

Started out a mass of words, why poets off themselves. Waterfalls of words claiming
themselves. Messy, chaotic, overrun, contradictory, blowing every which way.

*

Deborah Digges walked my path. Her body moved through cities my body would
grow to fill. In memory, streets of sleet, childhood, parallel to desert sun streets,
fragments of institutional evidence. Rough texture my body did not recognize. If we
had met, small talk. Mutual cities of students to navigate. To be clear -- I was never
student, wasn't interested in fragments, I was not teacher.

The last location – would have been her body in front of me, her words hung in the auditorium air for perusal This never happened. She didn't show at the appointed time.

    Master and apprentice separated by rows of poetry. Boxes of words.

    Two separate universes. Two separate bodies.

       *

When I ask my students to make a circle, they make a kidney bean. I'm trying to decide if I should be more directive or let the organic (or defiant?) shape stand. I accept my kidney bean.

       *

My fourth cup of coffee drained into the gullet. Yet I feel all my synapses collapse. The legs in my brain have gone on strike.

    The sun is to blame for all this, say my new playmates. Leafrot, says an office mate.

       *

The desert is dying, they say, of alternative energies.

    Runners gather by desert skin. Running as prayer against corporate solar and wind. Another friend wants me to know the delusion of negation. Cotard's syndrome: you think you are already dead. If I made myself ghost, who I be.

    Which road my feet stamp intact.

       *

Not called my mother in days. Wind tunnels in my eyes. In my nights, centipedes. Try not to dream, fill up my gray cup. The baggage of language, the weight of water, wet of mouth. Think you as cherry, as river, as mouth on mouth.

       *

Bishnu Adhikary, first to receive third gender citizenship in Nepal, says "as if we don't have a heart." As if we cannot arrive, do not come, cannot cannot suture heart to bone, unravel. There is no train to love; the screen separates us from our litanies for survival.

       *

The mental health technician looks calm. I don't appear outside her door at the appointed time. She tells me the sun is only one factor, my friends are many, all dreary, all hunched around doorknobs, wondering.

*

"When I was a suicidal adolescent, I remember reading voraciously during this time; it didn't matter what it was that I read—mostly junk novels, in fact—since it was only to replace my own thoughts with those of the writer's." – Jesse Bering

*

On water-heavy nights, the place I left behind, dry, shaky, desperate for moisture. If only I kept my dreams with me throughout the day – ghost keepsake, memory token.

*

Today, at the dialogue of concern, university professionals, mental health professionals all want ally-ship status. What makes the young queer ___ ? Gifts of words, gifts of concern, gifts of useful information. Maybe it's a city bumping up against. Maybe it's technology. Maybe the two feet on a ledge can pull back, unwind. Protect against carving words angry in a chest. What struck everywhere assailant, everywhere a legal.

*

Three populations. Likely candidates at the seams approximate the most willing subject. What desires. More, of course, than three groupings of likely candidates, common-law identifications.

*

But, in the end, one tires of the body upon another. Raymond Chase over Seth Walsh. Asher Brown plus Tyler Clementi. Billy Lucas and Justin Aaberg. Then, Cody Barker. Next, Tyler Wilson to Chris Armstrong. Who a token.

*

Because of the baggage of language, strings. Hold circles, air under chins drawn.

*

Yesterday, caught an afternoon sore throat by the wind. Invasion, I missed my appointment with the mental health technician and left a repentant message, muddled, confessional. A liar too. Oh, I was worried about you, she replied. A smooth, blank swan. Analogies often do me in, make me empty my well of all associations.

*

Dreamlife of the sick. Black waters excuse myself from life's busy paths. Hollow mine, creased envelope, insides dumped into burnt rice. No offering made tonight, no stairs to ascend, these mouths take care of themselves.

*

Hee Sun Park. A letter of a mind whirling. A blank wall, hotel room. To clean up opaque evidence, an apology that no one needs to clean up after me. The evidence of apology. No one, opaque. Elizabeth Shin. Firestorm. Iris (Irish) Chang. Japanese atrocities. Hejin Han. Cliff. Helium asphyxiation. An anchor kid, an army of hunger. What we flee. What we turn back. Seung-Hui Cho.

*

My composition students read David Foster Wallace's "Consider the Lobster." A list of colorless facts. Birth, houses, diplomas, schools to teach at, small evidences of the living. The others stare at their nails, stare at the clock, desperate for the ticking to signal an exit to fifty minutes of first-year writing. The suicide, the fact of it. A pause -- the students who are listening lean in. Or, in reality, they go on, conversing with the clock while depression is reported. Fits and starts. Is it humane to boil lobsters. Can lobsters feel pain. Yes or no, the largest boiling killing field of lobsters. Mass suicide, one says. Genocide, another corrects. It made me hungry, I wanted some good shellfish, says another to nods of agreement.

*

On this day set aside for thankfulness, two e-mails sit, waiting to be claimed. My family; three cities; a Peking duck sacrificed to reunification.

"Happy Thanksgiving from David Foster Wallace," ubiquitous ghost, a gift from a new friend who hung up her poetry hat for a second life. Yoga, husbandless, a new room without chores. What she extracts -- "It is unimaginably hard...to stay conscious and alive, day in and day out." What I excavate – "How to keep from going through your comfortable, prosperous, respectable adult life dead, unconscious, a slave to your head and to your natural default-setting of being uniquely, completely, imperially alone, day in and day out."

"National Day of Mourning," says another. A plaque erected by the Town of Plymouth, Massachusetts. Paths surface hard lines, metal.

Four Thanksgivings ago, Plymouth a city emptied of wanderers. No protesters to greet the mourners. After the speeches, I return to my family, sliced chicken.

*

And then the famous ones. John Berryman. Hart Crane. Hai Zi. Frank Stanford. Qu Yuan. Reetika Vazirani. Sergei Esenin. Tadeusz Borowski. Paul Celan. Sylvia Plath. Anne Sexton. I reply, drainage and sun.

*

"Who was responsible for Elizabeth Shin?" asks The New York Times. Spring water, tomato juice, boxes of cereal, lo mein.

*

Famous to whom? asks the fiction writer. She's only heard of the one who put her head in the oven and her likely friend.

*

The poetry class. Elegy, how fucking expected. Dark river of the poem. Of course, I will sign up for it and count myself ticking in the classroom. Operative words – how to manage, expect. A keyless map. A man with stones in his pocket streaming his way down to the seabed. In the docu-essay, Alfred Hitchcock's impersonator gets a cameo. The embedded voice of the creep talking about himself: "If you meet your double, you should kill him." How many adaptations, how many meet their older selves.

*

Frank Stanford wrote a poem entitled "Freedom, Revolt, and Love" where a man and a woman, lovers by the breakfast table, shot by non-specific others. Self-inflicted gunshot wounds.

*

How many elegies written within the confines of a classroom. The wholesome girl
- Nunca mas. The last time I saw you, another country ago. Tiny plastic spoon for
ice cream. A disposable wrapping, a foreign printing, tiny footsteps. Three letters
enclosing a plea for clemency. Today, today, I get to stay.

*

And a response:

    "Because no poet's death

    Can be the sole author
    of another poet's life

    What will my new instrument be"

[*to try:* "Because no poet's death/ Can be the sole author/ of another poet's life/ What
will my new instrument be" is from C. D. Wright's "And It Came to Pass."]

noah: a reassembled zuihitsu

    after Noah Purifoy

Welcome   says the tires   Once the night of stars I
couldn't get
to, stumbling upon pile of shoes, next to silver tarnish of left-aside robot track.
        red book   sewing machine button
        xylophone   fake sheep fur plastic beads of pearls
    Once a story I lost by the weeds.   To bury it, the
ghost I wrestled with
        at the bottom   white shoes no feet
row of re-purposed mailboxes
        totem   almost forty years back
print of ants forming meaning
    Once there was a lake with no rain. I scrunched myself over the rock and
breathed for the first time, an air without smoke. A sky without disease.

map lays you out wide across the acre   steel
        aluminum glass bricks Astroturf

                                        three tall crosses like phone
                                        companies ready to flame

chicken wire   old windows adobe city-exodus   tamarisk tree branche
I was searching for my own idea wreckage revising yourself lone
gas station

a tall thin man without a heart looming behind you   waiting for your tinkering touch
        Yes, there was a small figure in the opening of the rotted doorway.
    I struggle with my lungs and push up against all my capacities. I didn't want to
talk to any bodies that morning of my grief. **In the wind, dry, pulsing wailing, I stood
with someone I wanted to be close to, listening for the ghost of Noah Purifoy.** I
pretended I was alone in the field of my tears. **She was listening for my breath.** They
wouldn't behave. **I guess that's something I'm not used to.** I couldn't control what
they did, how they responded to who I had lost. **On the drive home, in the baking
sun, drenched with the day.** I had no body to blame.

alone   *all bundled up and neatly*   briefcase aloft over where the
packaged   head should be – Noah   your
scattered out down the railroad track   accumulation of satchels
glowing brightly in the absence of sunlight   suitcase   handle

        leather   buckle all metal   is who body part   and then
            kissing wood Which is which? Who

Arms crossed   looking off-stage in this photograph   shipped to me from the plains

    no lakes or ponds   smoking your wheelchair   wry smile
metal hand
    Shelter

limestone
    granite concrete
termites

No Trespassing *My family lived*
in two rooms and moved many   moving through stages of   bits of cars bowling balls

times   goodbye   vacuum cleaners come
                                                            train cars   set in sand

I talk and talk friend listens   instead TheWhite House
      I keep looking   doorknob symphony
skinned again   quilt of metals

She caught me watching her. You told me that you had no word for who I was.
It came so naturally to me. I hoping you would define me, map my body with grids.

I squeezed into a gray tin passage, which hugged my ribs tightly.

finish line never a clear day to bury a dog in the sand   **Pack out what you pack
in.** Extra skin glove.

      permanently unfinished   a dinosaur lifts its head to the setting sun

The poem a mask of language I can get behind, to push forward. Breath coming like
a train.

[noah: Italicized lines are both text by assemblage artist Noah Purifoy as well as "titles" of his
sculptures.]

Poetics Statement

We are switch-boarding our words into each other's, or into other lines that have
been laid. This is/was my writing practice – one of forage and retrieval, reconstruction
and reconstitution. *The Taoist says there is no applause for the valley or the hill.* Or
this is the continual practice of writing. To put one foot in front of the other and then
see where it takes us, "following the brush," as the zuihitsu-ist does.
      "This might be a strange analogy, but I like to think of the zuihitsu as a fungus—
not plant or animal, but a species unto itself. The Japanese view it as a distinct genre,
although its elements are difficult to pin down. There's no Western equivalent, though
some people might wish to categorize it as a prose poem or an essay. You mentioned
some of its characteristics: a kind of randomness that is not really random, but a
feeling of randomness; a pointed subjectivity that we don't normally associate with the

essay. The zuihitsu can also resemble other Western forms: lists, journals. I've added emails to the mix. Fake emails." - Kimiko Hahn on the zuihitsu (http://bombsite.com/issues/96/articles/2834)   *And then my inner Douglas Kearney says, "At times I've avoided pursuing lines of poetic inquiry in order to perform a kind of irrepressible proliferation of new ideas. I am Innovative™, yes? Yet how many times can I quit pursuit before a so-called innovation is just a gesture? Just a special effect."* (http://www.poetryfoundation.org/harriet/2011/03/poem/). So then I guess I'm just a clever thief aka poet.

Writing within the constellation, like growing bacteria. If we are always originating from the back end aka the past, can we be projecting our new selves into the future without re-mashing up all our histories? *Says Robert Hass, ""Whose university?" the students had chanted. Well, it is theirs, and it ought to be everyone else's in California. It also belongs to the future, and to the dead who paid taxes to build one of the greatest systems of public education in the world."* (http://www.nytimes.com/2011/11/20/opinion/sunday/at-occupy-berkeley-beat-poets-has-new-meaning.html?pagewanted=2&_r=2&smid=fb-share)   Unlikely though we move on past whichever evictions have been scheduled, we still believe in edges.

Like Mark Bradford's use/re-use/recycling of what others call junk, shaping into our own obsession. Extended conversation with writing, an active kind of re-writing. Myung Mi Kim: To radicalize anything starts at a point of rupture; naturally, change can't just happen along a continuum that has already established itself, or it wouldn't be change. (http://epc.buffalo.edu/authors/kim/generosity.html)

Perhaps we are too appropriate, appropriative, proprietary, named. Perhaps precious little is different except that this too shall pass in literary succession. *Let Me Tell You What a Poem Brings*
by Juan Felipe Herrera
for Charles Fishman

Before   you   go   further,
let   me   tell   you   what   a   poem   brings,
first,   you   must   know   the   secret,   there   is   no   poem
to   speak   of,   it   is   a   way   to   attain   a   life   without   boundaries,
yes,   it   is   that   easy,   a   poem,   imagine   me   telling   you   this,
instead   of   going   day   by   day   against   the   razors,   well,
the   judgments,   all   the   tick-tock   bronze,   a   leather   jacket
sizing   you   up,   the   fashion   mall,   for   example,   from
the   outside   you   think   you   are   being   entertained,
when   you   enter,   things   change,   you   get   caught   by   surprise,
your   mouth   goes   sour,   you   get   thirsty,   your   legs   grow   cold

standing   still   in   the   middle   of   a   storm,   a   poem,   of   course,
is   always   open   for   business   too,   except,   as   you   can   see,
it   isn't   exactly   business   that   pulls   your   spirit   into
the   alarming   waters,   there   you   can   bathe,   you   can   play,
you   can   even   join   in   on   the   gossip—the   mist,   that   is,
the mist becomes central to your existence.(http://bjanepr.wordpress.com/2009/03/13/
learning-from-juan-felipe-herrera-let-me-tell-you-what-a-poem-brings/)

Endless variations of constraint-making literary production. To divide, devise,
contrive new constraints based on our and each other's (new) productions. If I were
Bhanu Kapil, I would say, I drove home in a freezing blue fog, having committed only
two thefts, both of which I admitted to within minutes. (http://jackkerouacispunjabi.
blogspot.com/) Be forced/pushed to interact with each other's texts/creations and to
put a hand out to the origin point and say here was us.

Works Cited

Hass, Robert. "Poet-bashing Police," *The New York Times* 19 Nov. 2011. Web. 29 Jan. 2013.
     <http://www.nytimes.com/2011/11/20/opinion/sunday/at-occupy-berkeley-beat-poets-has-
     new-meaning.html?pagewanted=1&_r=3&smid=fb-share>

Kapil, Bhanu. *Was Jack Kerouac a Punjabi? Prose Incubation. Social Theory. Dogs*. Web. 29 Jan.
     2013. <http://jackkerouacispunjabi.blogspot.com/>

Kearney, Douglas. "Poem," *Harriet*. March 4 2011. Web. 29 Jan. 2013. <http://www.
     poetryfoundation.org/harriet/2011/03/poem/>

Morrison, Yedda. "Generosity as Method: An Interview with Myung Mi Kim," Dec. 1997.
     Electronic Poetry Center. Web. 29 Jan. 2013. <http://epc.buffalo.edu/authors/kim/
     generosity.html>

Reyes, Barbara Jan. "Learning for Juan Felipe Herrera: Let Me Tell You What a Poem Brings,"
     Barbara Jane Reyes: poeta y diwata. 13 Mar. 2009. Web. 29 Jan. 2013. <http://bjanepr.
     wordpress.com/2009/03/13/learning-from-juan-felipe-herrera-let-me-tell-you-what-a-
     poem-brings/>

Sheck, Laurie. "Kimiko Hahn," *Bomb* 96 Summer 2006. Web. 29 Jan. 2013. <http://bombsite.
     com/issues/96/articles/2834>

Cole Krawitz

with half a blush

his brow, the way his broad shoulders
complemented a fitted shirt

the smell of cinnamon in coffee, how
he liked it, their walk to the farmer's market

navel oranges, squeezed, fresh, upon his fingers
and pluots sliced to top french toast

a return to each other
splendor in afternoon sun

the way a day of rest required
delight, his cock

lavished, inside
him never wanting to leave

or find the sky
turn to nightfall, to witness

three stars, a return
to the everyday

MRI, Psalm of Guidance

minister of radiated light
reigning champion of all imagination
i beseech you, each year

make me in my image, oh god of my yearly coming
reinvent me in your silhouette
incased in my best blue tissue gown with stretchable waist tie

make me free, again,
reinvest in my belief i myself
inherit wisdom from your magnetic ways

make the heavens fall, be dusk,
reinvent its colors on your mapped
insight of my body's insides

minister of radiated light
reigning champion of lineation, nodules, questionable marks
inherit me. invest in me. tell me i'm yours. give me another year.

make me in your image, oh god of my yearly coming
renew me, make me wait in anticipation, like yom kippur's gates closing as the sun descends—
ink me in the book of life.

The Sound of Aleph

before sound begins
lips shape
          a form, in expectation

before lungs concede,
before we know
          that there is such a thing

as openness
before one needed
       to know they needed

to know they exist
before the imagination
       stings, stymies before

the longing becomes worth
more than breath,
       before there is no breath

before breath
you'll find me
       at your lips, in the opening

before the push of sound
before breath extends
       before the inevitable   again

before   what i am.

in and out of the holy

i. friday night, kabbalat shabbat

we praise our bodies
at dusk, before night's
       ever returning release
expected

we live
between birth and death.

in twilight
       we know not

when night begins,
nor day ends.

our holiest days
begin
            betwixt—
potential promise of prayer

to be heard.

and so begins our work
of rest, at dusk
            commanded to celebrate
wine and prayer and sex—

the infinite, overlooked
toil
of bodies, running.
humbled,
            between—

ii. day, saturday, shabbat

my least noteworthy, least defining note. the not in between, between. that's irony,
again. the bookends are where in-between rests, if you call it rest, arrival and
departure, capped with candles, wine and swaying of bodies to distinguish the distinct,
the what we do not always want to see, the seeing what we see and being ok with not
filling it all in. the focus on the cracks.

iii. saturday night, havdalah

i hum all week

the prayers that end
another 24 hours
of allotted rest

in this time
between the end
and beginning

between the turn
of the sun's cheek
and three stars lighting the sky
their lips painted brighter
than a drag queen working a one am set

senses rekindled
my fingers, lifted
to the six wicks
braided bountiful
light pours through the cracks

the scent of cloves
and cinnamon awaken
wine to measure the lips'
pauses and careful
crescendos, all week

i hum, transfixed

all week, a praise
to the in-between

i know these ceremonies best

what if ceremony falters

a betrayal before prayer's completion:
        a wick breaks and leaves an inconsistent light

words suspend in song with
        caution, and covet perfection,

a yearning, a vigil for the impeccable,
        a constant unfound.

what then of hail
        the way it surprises,   and leaves

temporary, satisfied
with accolades of awe, the way

ceremony may falter:

bread, unbaked
ark, disassembled
trope's requisite exaltation, lost—

and if found, there'd be no answer—
maybe, rather, an emancipation
an epic lyric, unending

splendor

in a blossom

        a knowing, a clarity

to fall and burst

and bud and burst

        to temper the sunlight's solidity—

petals, ceremonious, holy, as if

maybe, a song, or the high note

        a diva hits

her arms outstretched

        waking up the light

dust never resolves

praise

what we

learn to let go

to let in, to get by—

faith in

your hand upon

my forearm, steady, more

reliable than creation

stories or the rain

how it washes away—

Poetics Statement:

For much of my young life, song was how I made meaning out of my everyday. I sang in the halls of my shul, and in moments of solitude, clung to the stereo speaker in my bedroom. Every way I knew I was alive was in the deep breaths between and within the next note, the accordion-likeness of my lungs, the rhythm pounding through my body. In the music, I was overcome with something I knew was bigger than me—that came from generations before and would also outlast me. That same feeling is what draws me, and grounds me, in poetics, which in its own way often feels to me like a form of prayer—a space between—of possibility, where breath can leave the body in awe.

In song was where I first learned to let emotions go—in song was where I lived when the chemotherapy ran through me. It became the place where my emotions could be mirrored and embraced, where I could exist amidst what it meant to live through that kind of physical pain and fatigue. But afterward, I longed for my own words to express what had come to be part of my story.

And that is what I found, and still long for, in poetics—the breath, the oral, the eruption, and the way that the music of words holds the liminal, the multiple, the longing and the present awareness of mortality.

I fell in love with the possibilities that poetry offers in allowing room for ambiguity, narrative, symbolism and tradition; in stretching the possibilities in words to create new meanings and new ways to engage an idea or feeling.

I came to poetry in part as an opportunity to reframe dominant discourses I found troubling and at times deeply harmful. I found resolve, release, and explanation for many aspects of my life—being a cancer survivor, queer, transgender (to name a few)—in poetry. I found company in language that offered narrative disruption, was deeply united with the corporeal, and was a powerful location to discuss issues of power, culture, race, faith, nationality, the erotic and illness.

I was once told I should put a comma after my first name, that this would be symbolic of my poetics, and in some ways, I agree. That disruption, pause, breath, rupture, dissonance is part of the poetry that I write, particularly about the body. But as time can do, my relationship to this idea has changed and I now only find some truth in this framework.

And as these frames continue to shift, so does whether or not I find more or less room in the possibilities that poetics offers in creating meaning and language about the corporeal that I still do not always find in my day-to-day experience. To express and acknowledge the possibilities of language in all of its complexities as dazzling, confining, freeing and loaded—that words can have room to liberate, to provoke and to reclaim.

A poem becomes its own breathing life; with writing comes an opportunity to create new bodies of work with each turn of the page. I long for what poetry might bring in part because of my day-to-day lived experience negotiating other people's imposed-perception on my body as opposed to my own knowing of self. Ideally poetry offers a rendering that silences the dogmatic and limiting. That embraces the tension of mortality and the beauty of variance.

D'Lo

Growing's Trade Off

Since I have started using male pronouns,
I have come to miss the communities of "she".
I never knew that's what the trade off was
In coming closer to a "me" that better fit me.

Eyes cocked, my foremothers question me,
as if they lost a daughter in a black ominous sea,
where Mami Wata wasn't reigning and
demonic darkness, as if by hypnosis, beckoned me.

I try to tell my foremothers that I am more a mermaid now
than I ever thought I could be.

When I was younger, I was powerful.
Hair shorn, Velcro-bound blue boy sneaks,
a thin layer of dust stuck to my skin with sweat.
Played any sport that ended with 'ball'.
Tagged boy when I was tagged "it."

A little me who was learning misogynist ways by my uncles and the t.v.
A little me who was learning immigrant macho.
A little me who was learning how a patriarch should act.
A little me who desired the love from a she.

In 4th grade my breasts began to grow. I wasn't ready for the changes.
In 5th, classmates were already suspecting.
So in 6th, I planned my transition. A girl I was to become, even if it killed me.

We boys who were born girls figure out a way, we do the best we can in the body we're given

And so, the flip side of the trade-off…

As I soon learned what it was to be a woman of color
I learned of oppression and more importantly, knowledge, power and divinity.

This boy learned how to be a strong woman.

I read feminist poetry,
I grew up in the hands of my mentors Anibel Ferus Comelo, Michael Slate
Poets – Ta'Shia Ashanti, Sharon Brigforth, Cherrie Moraga,
I grew up with my peers and was considered as part of a Mujeres de Maiz
I was cousin to my Pinay island sisters.
I was rich with community. One that surpassed its weight in gold.

And when I left to NY, I missed these sisters, who accepted me boi -
because that camaraderie took years to cultivate in rich Cali soil,
and I had no strength to force another way in a brick city
where folks manage life by keeping stone faces to get to the next day.

And now, today, 2 years after top surgery, 8 years after dabbling with he,
And 5 after making it mandatory
I am lost.

No Womyn's community wants me anymore.
And no community wants to hear how this feminist has become moreso
        only *after* calling himself not man, not transman, but transgender.

And I am yelling into black holes and gates
protesting my incarceration, begging a closer look inside…
Isn't this what you have all revered?
That beautiful balance of male, female and spirit?

And those who don't know, because they don't look at my chest
those same who don't hear any changes in my voice because
hormones haven't hit my horizon yet,
Those folks ask me to come perform at a Womyn's fest
And so I tell them
about my changes, but plead with them to see how nothing has changed except
a word,
that I still look and sound the same
And I am tip-toed around, rejected again…

*The history of critical feminist theory has been one about challenging
gender norms, inclusivity, breaking borders, revising conventional
notions of gender. Critical feminist theory has spoken to the
fluidity of gender, the danger of assigning particular social roles
and destinies to those born with body parts labeled as female- because
gender is a social construct. I was born female, I have experienced
life through a woman's body; through a masculine-identified female
body. I know what it is to challenge the idea that biology does not
equal destiny. I have a vagina, I have not taken male hormones, I
don't identify as woman or as man. I identify as transgender and given
the limits of language, I have chosen to use male pronouns. However,
irrespective of male or female pronouns, I'd still identify as
transgender. My decision to use "he" challenges conventional gender
norms. My decision to use "he" is rooted in my embodied feminism.*

Who is the gate keeper? Because I want back in.

*(Text in Italics was created by Anjali Alimchandani in helping me address these re-occurring
situations in more academic language in attempts to be better heard.)*

TMP Asher Brown RIP

I became a loud funny guy
Because I didn't want my awkwardness
to get labeled as 'different' in the bad way

Everyone loves a clown.

I was not small, but I was dark
A fly in buttermilk, Lenelle once said
But funny haha erased the funny strange
I wonder what strength can be read off a comedic himshe
That cannot be read from a small, seemingly soft, gay pre-teen.

No one tripped me, bullied me.
There was always the fear that the fly has.
But even the one time, after I turned around in my seat
and attempted to talk to the prettiest girl in the 6th grade-
when she asked me if I was gay,
I looked straight into her eyes
and said "no" with a pinch of purposely looking offended.
I turned back in my seat, looked down at my stone wash jeans and vans,
my collared blue and black striped shirt
and my scabbed up hands from many recesses as football captain.
Back then,
Maybe I couldn't convince anyone,
but I could convince them to never bring it up.

These days, you are read,
and like me, some little queers can't hide it well
but these lil fellas can't yell "NO" and halt the questions,
cease the curiosity, stop the bullying.

I cannot stand up anymore when things like this happen
I have to sit down.

I do have a soft heart

but it seethes occasionally.
From here
I curse the future of these bullies.
Let the blood of this boy remain on their hands
as they grow into adults and have children of their own.
Let the face of this boy haunt them whenever one of them

accidentally slips their penis into other boys.
Let the ghost of this boy scare them
30 seconds before they count on cum'ing.
Let them remember they tripped a child whose burden was too heavy
Let them remember he finally fell to peace by his own hand.
And what for? Really, I'm asking.
Let them remember that they are to blame,
so that they may right their wrongs.
Let us all remember.

Sleeping with the Lights On

She does this thing, right?
Like every night I am with her.

She somehow does it. Somehow –
because it's not a feat for her,
it is to me…

Somehow she finds it in her heart to tuck me in.
Takes the most sincere care
in making sure that my body is at peace.
She is that soft cover that melts against my bare skin
and why I am bare in the first place where
where are my boxers?
It's because she wants to see my skin
she wants to see my body
she is prepared for it's changes,
opposes clothes on me in bed,
protests more valiantly to my previous protests to keep my armor on,
hears me and even hears when I don't speak
how these clothes are my sanity.
She doesn't hear it and demands them off.

Shifting me into positions that convenience her,
I canoot but give in sleepily to

the way her hands knead into my flesh,
her fingers as they prod my insecurities out from their crevices.
She is the most recent version of holy I have bore witness to
and in all honesty,
she embodies the ceremony.

I have prayed and longed for this
Fully knowing.

She touches this mound of brown two-toned clay
and molds me into a version of myself that feels reconnected to this earth-
releases my fears with her touch that triggers them to fly somewhere far away.
She tells them with her hands that they don't belong in her bed.
        She will not have it.
She witnesses as my muscles stiffen and, like a true sculptor,
she sees my true shape even under all this hardened clay.
She is relentless in chiseling away this debris off the me that is
a model of supreme and godly beauty.

        And I sink into a cushion of sublime comfort
        as I fight to also release the guilt that someone has to touch me.
            I swear I love myself, but no one else should have to,
            I feel, at moments like this,
            where sleep is also scary
                and I cannot really share with you how vulnerable I truly feel.

She told me once that I knew how to receive and I disagreed.
Though
I have prayed and longed for this
without knowing.

Off to slumber I am about to drift,
long tides crash into the shore and years later,
crash to ocean.
I am doing work by being,
dusting off the dead skin and the worry attached to it.

I awake with a suddenness – a force only of habit –
I cannot help the ritual of sleeping in the light and I ask her, if she would oblige.

"baby, can we sleep with the lights on?"
And with the stern tenderness of one who is enlightened,
she opts to sweetly choose 'no' to this harmless request.
She will be there no matter what.

Thirinuru

I look at the ash,
Holy Ash
That is placed on foreheads,
as a sign for the astral world to identify the holy in florescent.
I wonder if the unholy's foreheads glow a little less than the holy ones.
The sincere vs the insincere.
Like Bright electric blue vs the waning glow-in-the-dark yellow green.

I wonder when I get to finally put on my ash
From the community plate
If the astral beings see my ash as foreign amongst the others
because I have not been able to place that mark on myself
as frequently as I would've liked.
I wonder if dead palm leaf fronds and cow dung
manifest with the purpose of being on the forehead of a queer,
brown bodied, hindu, god-loving, people adoring mofo like me.
If so, I applaud the cells,
the atoms that quantum-ly decided to one day be a part of a type of holy
That wasn't the status quo
That had leanings towards outcastes
And tendencies to roam away from the norm.

I shed tears years after the fact I felt the pain of being denied my right
In temples, in ashrams
My brothers and sisters in synagogues, mosques and churches
To worship openly
In whatever packaging we came in

I hurt
A deep sorrowful ache
In the depths of my belly
In the start of my womb
In the essence that is male
In the hands that carry like a mother
I hurt
A deep sorrowful ache
For my life of silence and denial
The two that I have made home in.
The two from which I will make skies for my children to fly in,
Knowing that once they fly,
I will turn around, and burn towns and small village thinking
With my eyes that will have stopped crying.
And a forehead flaming ablaze.

Poetics Statement

I do not believe in arts for art's sake, simply because I never had that luxury. Writing was, and still is, the way I found to connect the dots in my head and then connect my head back to my heart. It is the tool I use to connect *to* people, to connect my audiences to *other* people, and to empower my community to liberate themselves from closed-mindedness.

I am obsessed with finding the simple solutions to complex questions and my art is the extension of this obsession. Because it requires innovative delivery and active listening, thus far, I know that for me - story telling is my most powerful tool for change. I deeply value the way comedy resonates in everyone, am committed to creating art forms that intersect with hip hop and spirituality and I am an artist who strongly believes in entertaining audiences.

Though I always had written, I never knew that I was going to be writing and performing for my career. I was one of those kids who fell in love at first sound with hip hop and wrote my heart out on paper to the beats in my head. My first writing teachers, Chuck D, Queen Latifah and Monie Love, didn't teach me craft; they taught me how to write about what concerned me and taught me about responsibility to my community and society at large. But if they and my mentors were the ones who taught me how to write about my concerns, whether personal or worldly, it was my appa (father) who taught me to be concerned.

While Appa, a doctor, slowly adjusted to life in a hickville town where the KKK was and is still alive, warning my sister and I of what we were to encounter at our schools, thousands of Tamil people were targeted and killed in Sri Lanka; their homes looted and burned. The Sri Lankan civil war kept my immigrant community worried and passionate about "saving the Tamil people" and therefore very ardent LTTE/Tiger (Liberation Front – Liberation Tamil Tigers of Eelam) supporters.

I was politicized at a young age, yet grew up in a pro-LTTE immigrant household and community that shied away from confrontation on American soil. This contradiction sets the background to my life as a writer and poet.

Framing my political consciousness is that my earliest memories are of me as a boy. The truth of living in a woman's body only became painfully evident when I started puberty. I already felt the injustice in the silence I had to keep, even if I didn't know how to put it into words.

But I grew up, learned language and how to speak up and out. And today, as a trans person of color, I am understanding my privilege.

I am educated, yes. But that's not the real privilege. I have something that my immigrant parents never had, or that many of your parents never had regardless of color or immigrant status. I have something called processing power.

My parents' coping mechanism to get them through the day to day in Sri Lanka and in America was to never talk about shit that was bothering them. To never share their inner most fears, insecurites etc. Generation after generation they generated a factory of silence, not realizing the silence became a powerful in all the wrong ways. Loved ones walked into the doors of this factory after being sexually violated and never came back out. Other family members came in carrying their load of queerness and also never came back.

I stopped walking past that factory. I became loud, by accident. And my truth has been to reveal, not to conceal. Asking people to see me, really see me, cuz I failed to believe I was the only one feeling this way, thinking this way, QT and all.

As I write this statement, I am taken to those times as a young, pre-pubescent boy in a girl's body, when I was over-filled with sadness, as well as, the incapability to do anything about it. All I could do was write – and, though I wrote from the heart, I wrote less beautifully than how I started to write years later in college. But starting from when I started to read and recite my poems alongside other poet/writers, I began to believe that it wasn't how great the writer was that dictated how "good" the poem was, but how strongly one felt connected to it. This is not to say that I didn't learn how to become a better poet through writing, but it is to say that I still value poetry that is honest, vulnerable, raw and un-shielded moreso than the well-written. I am proud that my life in poetry has spanned the story-telling spoken word genre, hip hop, and romantic prose. And I am proud to say that it is happiness that I have found in trying to tighten my rhyme, meter, metaphors and other literary devices.

As a gender non-conforming person, I have witnessed my poems transition with me. I have learned to use my poems as a ruler by which I measure my own spiritual growth in a lifetime and society that doesn't see me. These poems are what have unabashedly allowed me to be witnessed in this world, and the stage has been like a strong brother allowing such words, that were once written in mostly dark moments of solitude, to be upheld under bright warm light.

These poems come from a body carrying the weight of young people's despair over their queerness being louder than they would like, and these poems come from a body carrying his own self-sacrificial burdens of being a not fully passing person. And all the while, these poems also carry the love of my life as a visible queer bodied person, the love that is found for queer bodies and the celebration of spirit through the eyes of those who celebrate this queer body.

I am influenced by mentors, yes, but I am moreso influenced by the writers who never thought much of my poetry on page, those who believed that there was a difference between stage and page writers, those who uphold the page writers more than they uphold the stage writers, valuing their ears perception over their hearts.

Writing poetry has been a sanctuary; a place to unwind and release – tears of sadness, tears of deep frustration. Poetry is a place that I wrap my devastatingly human emotions into words of fine and plush fabric; a place where I am swaddled by self. Poetry is a place where I can celebrate love and friendships. Poetry is the most selfish art form of mine, as much of it does not see the light of day or the light of my lovers' eye.

David Wolach

Poetry Slam: Cardiovascular Unit vs. Oncology Ward

UW Surgical Unit, Oct 11 2009, 3:45pm

> *I believe it is possible to have one identity in your thumb and another in your neck. I think identities can travel between persons who have an unusual mutual sympathy.*
> *-- Camille Roy*

dear: pain thief,
you say go room

to room, say
make a poem-life

go, say

in what language
are you

has your talking
turned

to a window rasp

"is this a translation translation
of what your chart
charts?"

can you sing
i can sing you,

shine a pocketlight on
waterless-you, your perspiration

ends up in a field
of word-sounds—

an atomic clock clocks in
charts the hunger of vines

nursing a tree far away
from this.

one chamber to another
my flap is muting again—

queries delivered
by pneumatic tubes

answers arrive as
bottlenecks

and so.

who are you who invites
promises, stranger who says

yes,

ask me to make a life in y -our language
ask if it will do *for now*

and now that now is
a chorus / line rehearsal

sub-audible micro

waves perch on a firing / line

in song in wait
for formation and

de-formation
of us, of and who or who—

verbs these windows we're *this close*
to ruin, and so and so, please.

ask loud with all your surplus
asphyxiations, home

bound pro
nouns ward to

ward nomadlike
all your rotting yous:

are we not
not strangers

in this made place
made to make

and remake
topsoiling, mulch

come to me
with promises

of turning over

soft rebellion,
quick rebellion

i dreamed of you in a hurry

Complicit In the Shakedown

--for Robert Kocik

--Seattle Pain Clinic, August 23, 2010 4pm

low yield of communally held prop—
bunk stats & when held by global trade

mark. who will inherit the earth
day? "they savaged me & i liked it."

why? remediation of this body is this
body. dissect dis-section in the medical

field, find witch-burnings. the cancer
of forest enclosures dis—

closes non-inheritance of low yield
trans-location. enclosure begets

enclosure. "we produce two-thirds
of the world's arms & not one of them

is mine." but a hole gurgles like
a market under cover of spontaneous

order me. if surgery is a landgrab why so
elective? if only mexico had been

an amenity like this lower half. hireling
the legs & operarii the feeling you get

in my holes when back pressed as future
asset & say "does this hurt?" obama has no use

for a perineum. "it's between the balls
and the asshole," one demarcation

worth making: a poesis as data
mine secrets a fault-line in name

only if. relinquish the book
to de-territorialize the touch

is back in vogue. so be care—
full with these hand-me-down

tea merchant tax disputes, hands
fall prey to their representatives:

unless heated by the gift of death
sinks into you, the stranglehold

of speeches the unfolding
syndrome of the yielding me

yields all possible floors

Tide's Haiti (Pathopoesis)

If I is that

Knave

Tides will have rushed
To fill it.

That place, to sing
To this image

Of that place, desolate
Tho it may be.

Of how will we ever
Otherwise be   clean.

Of truckloads of that
Promise
Driven past
Temporary sight

For those who have been

Consigned.

For this washing purchase

Donations will be
Made into my
Other self

Where the sentence is

Housed.

"How the bodies were equal
To the water
They floated in."

Where the limit case of comm-
Odity is investment
In ethics.   As if

To endure
The language

Is a cure for them.

Poetics Statement

beyond paved dismissal, party loyalty and above the darkness, the night wears on, the milk curdles, silence engulfs me with crime's endless hours. – kari edwards

The body is an afterword for what has yet to exist. I want to tell you what little of this, this place, I do know at this moment, or at least believe I need think I know. What "I"s know comes from chambers burrowed in some dark *in here*, a proximal this. But the in here is also yours, and is carved from the eyes of the gendarmes: you've been either complicit, or more often, wonderfully giving, in your creation of it (call identity a *collaborative poesis* policed by fearful cartographers and middle managers -- for the time-being, for now and just now). And there is a they in partial view; I watch them sculpt "essential differences" between this as it appears and this as it appears to desire. This. This, me. I am genderqueer and trans, though hesitate at publicly proclaiming a trans identity insofar as for some, for many friends, to be trans is to be more overtly manifesting transition than I am currently--to be enacting the life and death struggle of desire through a physics of risk. The desire to be and to become as: on the move. And yet. Yet I often pass. I pass like an active disavowal. I have passed in professional environments since college, when this *here,* this place, felt more at ease. I trembled doing so, but managed to say of this, this place: "woman." And to believe that as such, I like any "woman" could carry some of the weight of a felt undermining of denotation, that historical denotation of womanhood that here and now, and then in some places and most places at some point then, has meant and means and means again: another well of reproductive labor--the rest (one's very cultural expressivity) incidental in its categorical obsolescence viz. the hiccup-like earthly project of the immense accumulation of commodity.

Of what and for what, regards this body, this *this*, is an aporia that my writing seeks to make perceptible--as against the chasmic spectacle of ongoing class-colonial encroachment and stratification that obscures who I feel I am and how I do not know, a pervasive encroachment which I take gender assignment (the cis instrumentalist strict binary cloaking device) to be an emergent property of. Is my writing genderqueer? I feel the needle of pronouns. When you "he" me it sticks in here, this so-called body rejects it as an auto-immunity, an envelopment from puncture, a spasm, and a calcification. Is that queering the body, is this this, this so-called body queering the very processes of a pervasive inscription? What sort of question mark does that moment leave behind? What shadowlife gets imprinted? Sometimes I think of the page as an x-ray film for what has yet to take shape. Forms as yet unintelligible, imposed and transposed upon, where "to know" this body is to interrogate the outline of circumstance, context, privilege--that which both touches and breaks us. Other times I think of the page as part of an ecosystem of social nourishment, the poem a kind of treatment or ante-chamber for the action of waiting and being present with the silence that comes of it, that passive-active motion of catching one's breath with another. Sometimes I think this place occurs so that we may "heal" in poet Eleni Stecopoulos's uses of the term, and that this may happen outside chronological time, off clock. And still other times I think of the page as one concrete space for reclamation, a collaborative site for poesis, where, notes CA Conrad, I might just now begin to "find my body and find my planet." Where the common is made strange, where dissensus registers as an act of love.

Dawn Lundy Martin

from Life in a Box is a Pretty Life

Dear one, the sea smells of nostalgia. We're beached and bloated, lie on shell sand, oil rigs nowhere seen. It's Long Island, and the weather is fine. What to disturb in the heart of a man?

A boy is not a body. A boy is a walk.

Shed the machine.
Must be entirely flesh to fight.
Must be strategy instead of filling.

What to disrobe, there, centrifugal logic, as in here is a slice of my finger. Tell me the circumstance of your cock extension. When we slip into imprecision, we lose control, windowless walls close in. Awareness of being in a female body is a tinge of regret. "The human frame to adapt itself to convention though she herself was a woman." To receive, to be entered, to fret around upon entry. It's grand. I'm a system. Plants tall as wheat to hide in.

*

When blanched in suspension.

When turned white from irons.

When hung by one ankle.

Hails knocks down mid-day. It's beige.

A black arm extending out.

Without fodder. A voice plays
background, saying:

A body is a piecemeal accumulation. It's already fraught. We attempt to construct
wholeness. No debris. No breaking off eastward.

To button up in a tight grey sweater what has been released.

*

Life in a box is a pretty life, arrangements and things. We all have the same type of
feeling. There's some drifting. *Breathe into my bag.* Flowers. To fight is to lie down
among the dead. [Unstable space.] [Claims historical.] History is littered with severed
cocks. A want to be be buried here—these ruins. *Things seen from the corner of the
eye occasionally indicates a wider haunting.* Gapes to fall into. Almost everything
we're ever desired is diminished when enclosed. Attempts timelessness. Attempts
prayer. Can find no god, no oracle, no air. This is concavity. Feel cut of skin darkened
in such emergencies. Who wants a strobe light ring? Who wants a pickle? Small comforts.
Hapless encounter on the subway, or after a show, and we swat down inside ourselves.

*

When the head is shoved it naturally resists. Covers her dark face in a black cloth
(could be a hood).

*

We are infinitely disgraced. Wishes, well-wishes, eel. I am eleven and am and let into
a dim room where my brother and his friends are watching a 32 millimeter film in
which a woman is gangbanged. Upon entering the I distends. To claim is to maneuver.
Punishment referent: belt, whip, glory. *We speak to each other through mountains.
You excrete god likeness. Whose presence entered my world? Who decided upon and
then let go? I present you with a phantasmagoric me. I wear a sheath and jewels. My
tits hang out. I'm unworthy. Mouth unfastened, draw in. I fast. I work. I design. I craft. I
lend. I pour out. I stiffen upon command.*

*

Power is exercised where it can be exercised. Exacting precision. Spectacular momentum. Ninety-nine percent of the time, the ones in power will act like victims, will say, *we're not in power, we're trying to save all of us, it is for the sake of order. The current conditions are unforeseen.* They will say, *It's not our fault, or We didn't notice. How can we notice when the buildings are burning? We're doing everything we can,* they'll say, and, *Our hands are tied.* Bayonet already positioned. Figures in white, shadowy, through smoke. They appear to dance in half time. Jangle-mo. Distracted by concretions.

*

Squeezes legs together rhythmically, hopes no one notices. This is better than love because it is not unlike pleasure. No way to fill, no persuasion in the effort of filling. Relentless hours. The Global Economy is killing me. My mother tells me the story of Sodom and Gomorrah over again on the telephone. Has she imagined sodomy? Has she imagined flesh filled and flesh ripping? The state of things in the state? It's a broad sphere of unsanctioned doings. When I'm at my lowest I feel just fine. No money in my pocket, crouching behind the abandoned broke down carousel. Head-severed horse whinnying for me. *Where are you he calls? I dreamed I'd forgotten your name.*

*

Historically, we extend. We drift into. We are back straight. We bind. We draw. We categorize. We are punitive with regard to fairness only. We are method. We are order. What would you do without us? O, we are so very smitten.

*

This morning, I had a dream and remembered it. In the dream, you are ill and in the hospital. Maybe you're dying, I don't know. I think you are pocked and Leper-like. It doesn't matter. I was so worried about you. I answer my phone. It is not you but a friend who rattles on, who cares about what. The inevitable box makes an appearance. Tonight he's shiny—fetching, one might say. I was inside of the reverberation, beyond exhilaration. How to learn consensual violation? Feels in the mouth like—cannot explain—has an image of—you are probably thinking of some kind of particularly dinosaur-like bird that dives into the ocean and is relentless in its pursuit, opens beak, throat for fish, geeking it all down.

After Drowning

To part pin prick, pry back kind
resistance develop it and say
something incomprehensible.
She put on her soft body. She was
grafted in particulars, patterns a
distinct location, a place various,
more various, she said, and in
saying, spilled over into the body's
many parts. Fell for the sake of it,
and found there at the bottom of the
pit, a stool to sit on, a hand to ring.
[Palate spun] A thing pernicious.
Perceived as such and was such,
dangled on tip of stick, drip.

*

She curdles in the kraal. Could lactate, only stopping when the being is full up. Penned in with foal, with fur. Dereliction impossible, yet the thing. The one absolution from the designed body. As if one could locate, here in the barnyard, a logic, a wonder, a stabbing toward datum, corpus. What is it like to feel female? Explicitly. A body that feeds. Is food. Is gnawed on. One that kneels. A facilitator. Organized joy. A corporeal caving in, arranging the joist. Cooing.

She said, when I fuck them, I think I can make them love me.

I said, when I fuck them, I think I can get something back.

What is mumbled after the act?   I—Uh. After the craving empties. When viscosity permeates a life before. Magenta. And, falling there, through sound, through tape, a voice ghostly, saying blackly, I bleed. This is what it takes. I hear it now. Know it. There was once a time when the bridge ended and the girl leapt. There was once a singing somewhere.

*

> Once upon the unsung,
> the ripped and the extracted,
> one would arrive at thinning trees
> (The trees are almost naked.)
> opening of leaves and thick scents—
> One would be summoned there and
> anchored.

Believe that one travels in articulation, is heavy with language, is hunted, breaths and hears black bitch and black ass in the literal field of the carnivorous.

What would be sought for and fetched? One's desire accumulates in pustules.

A precise dictation occurs inside the chest. It is a reckoning with a kind of god, a kind of believing.

*

Wizened plastic wire sings a terrible lullaby. The body will ripen. Will become slippery, slope over into exigent sickness. Reeds will recede. Caps will lift. And in the heart of it, she will lie down on newly woven cloth and scrub what has been already scrubbed: a gentle body, smooth from touch.

Wide eyes all white and glistening. Gradual induction into a bare, still damp, secreting pact. The body, hammering. Hammered. Awoken to the second door, the closed one.

She focuses on the sofa's hem, unlatches the rung of locks, rejecting catapult.

*

> It was a brown room,
> wood-paneled,
> an attic room,
> cut into by the glaring
> television, pared like sleeves,
> stank as funk stinks,
> as the nearly dead,
> as the red red red,
> as dripping old eyes,

it was a late December sky,
the hallway led to the bathroom,
the waiting,

a tall glass, my departing.

The I Alongside the I:
A Poetics of Indeterminacy

I love Tilda Swinton because of her beautiful androgyny and because she once
believed Virginia Woolf's *Orlando* to be the biography of her own life. Sometimes,
I Google-Image Swinton simply to look at her face. Her angular features are ideal
aristocracy to me and I want some of it. I also love how in films she appears often as
if she's about to crack, as if somehow her body cannot, but in the end does, hold her
self—a shimmering beneath the surface. In a recent film, *I Am Love*, I do not believe
that her lips tremble as much as they are often slightly agape hovering on the edge of
some utterance—not in a bursting way, but in a frozen way. The viewer understands
that there is language floating around inside. *What, Tilda? What?*

When language refuses to tip over into speech—recognizable or other—when it is non-
reproductive of what has already been produced for us.

Now I will tell you a story of me with my shirt off pumping gas when I was nine. Now
I will tell you a story of a photo of me at seven with a toy gun bulging from my pants
pocket. Even younger, still, I fell from a railing I had converted into a balance beam
and injured my vagina. I remember blood, but I do not think there was blood...

The negation: the white background of our story.

Is Swinton emblematic of the white background upon which the black writer and other
writers of color are forced to reproduce their narratives? She's beyond white; she's
almost translucent. When she plays The White Witch in *The Chronicles of Narnia*, it
is this extreme whiteness, the starkness of it, its hard stability, its unwavering quality
that frightens us. It is as if a face has been removed from another face. But Swinton
confuses because her face, too, is like the face of boy—but not quite a boy boy;
instead, more like concentrated boyness, needs something added to it (water perhaps)

to expand it, to allow it to comes into its full nature. So here, in the gender realm, she is not stable; in fact, she is profoundly unstable especially after giving birth to a child and living her public life as a "heterosexual." If this is a white background upon which our stories must be written then it is a confusing whiteness since gender affects/ produces the racialized body and vice versa. There is no such thing as single identities and/or single selves. We are multiple from before, already. We are multiple, maybe, in the very first instances of loss, as girl children, our shirts suddenly removed from the fences where they once hung and placed onto our resistant bodies.

What if the background were black? What if the dark room framed the figure?

Imagine that the poem is lit by darkness, that its persistent markers—its letters, words, lines, stanzas, and spaces—are only foregrounded or brought to approximation by 1) "an absence or want of light (total or partial)"; 3) "a want of sight (blindness)"; and/or 7) "obscurity of meaning": and/or "darkly in a moral sense, horridly, foully."

It is here, against this opaque scrim where we find our figures obliquely attempting to distinguish themselves, make themselves visible. Here: struggle. Here: *The black room of terror that you half-recall, half-invent.* What is possible against this backdrop? Is anything possible? Are not our mouths gagged, our hands tied, our legs bound, our cunts exposed? This is our primary setting. Where the entirety of our story takes place.

The I re-imagines all the sexual violations it can recall and they are not entirely unpleasant to it.

Here the body exceeds its boundaries, spills out into blackened space, becomes undone. It cannot contain itself. It is piecemeal and/or falling / and/or pieces / or spilling from itself / grotesquely / or doubling or tripling / or it is watching itself / or not watching itself but blank / not a blank state / but an absence. It's jumping out at you: "the nigger in the woodpile," the "big black guy," a dancing figure in your landscape, the licentious black female unable to contain itself, unable to keep itself in check. Here, indeterminacy. What does it say? This body? These bodies? Cast upon. In robes. The haute couture of our disguise. What is there left to say? The maw, drunk and ajar, the head back, the throat open. Gaping. No sound.

We return to the box of interrogation. We're sitting with our feet draped over the subway platform. We are in our containers of being. It is not safe here.

To want is to dream into black space. Powerful abstraction. When Tilda Swinton plays Orlando she is as white as sundried bone. Her cheeks tint orange. I have trouble seeing her eyelashes. Is she eyelashless? Tilda attracts me because—save her gangliness—there are indications to me of where the body refuses something. It saves something for some other time, later. This is what I mean when I say "privilege." I want her to be stone. I want to place her in permanent stasis. Who can say which gender? Gender permeates but is under investigation. I am writing about Tilda's container because it seems a container of resistance and unfazed by gender discourse. It is a body that investigates, instead of being under investigation. I want to kill her. I love her. But, it's the container that interests me. The restraint of her material. Conversely, the body in the midst of a traumatic event is a body in radical and pronounced conflict. This might be the racialized body. The body is not in one's own control. One leaves the body, looks down upon it, a doubling occurs. She attracts me because in our culture, the black body is always spilling out. It cannot be contained by its borders. Even with the borders are visible, there are new (fictionalized) discursive borders that are cast onto it. This is the post-traumatic body. Its loss is unrecoverable. It's masked. It must always be something in addition to what it is.

When you realize you want to live it's not a metaphor. There's a self-idea that's very involved.

However, to hover at the edge of some utterance is to be liberated from the need for frivolous speech. What is relinquished in this attempt at speech and its failure? Its unspeaking? What is falsified if one tips over into coherence? What can or cannot be enclosed within a pre-determined discourse. The poetics at work here are of *unspeakability* or *impossibility*—what cannot in the first place be said, what is already foreclosed by the thing that seeks to be spoken, what the body cannot hold. Who can say which gender? Is what? When gender is present it comes in the form of the standing alongside, the figure alongside the figure (the shadow of the figure), the moving outside of what has been pre-determined. Who can say what race is? The I is a hateful subject carrying its flesh bag. It is, too, an ecstatic signaling—reverberating itself, resonant. The I along side the I. This can be a place of power.

Drew Krewer

from Nancy Drew / Nancy Krew

this is the boy inside the locker
we heard the newsman say
said, I'm a girl detective
that do-or-die look
boxed potatoes, moron gravy
slung violently, the bell
always, sounds like dinner
flipped hair, smells like boy
messy and sex-locked
shake it, Nancy, shake it
indulge your particular lunacies
tempt your man, drive your car
cheerfully across the table
reaching for the tenderloin
and calling it an accident

truckhorn playing Dixie
a flag through the dark
she had always slept lightly
heard the noise many times
Nancy in a nightie, out the window
through the trees, my blurred pajamas
boy, the headlights and that stench

booze and adrenaline
the chants of discarded bras
oil speaks from beneath the hood
change me
but the horn still blasts the school
brays around the flagpole
these colors
don't run anything
but a battle of bull
but a fort, trembling in its whiteness

shot on a deerstand, an aim unusually high
oddly overcome with repulsion
men like that provoke a delicate drool
they arrive with guns, aware of the jeopardies
descend into flame, you foo-foos
I fire rounds in approximate locales
she was nosed out of yards by rifles
she learned that charm polices
a thousand homemade cakes
Nancy the knife cutting through—

It Could Be Anything You Want Me to Be

I am king-sized—I embody dis- and quietudes

Chained to bed in a town of cloned Don Juans

This marriage is fraudulent

So not *romantico*

It's like I'm living on an asphalt island
where poems become wedding envelopes
containing limited time offers

My capacity for mendacity makes me frightened for the world

The chronic handbag hustle—it's a cin:c:h: : ::: :: : : :: ::::: : :: : : : :
: : :: ::: ::: :::::: :: : : : : : : ::   :: : :: : :   : : :: : :s:a:ck::::: : : ::
: : :: :: :: :: :: : :: :: ::::: : :: :: HEFTY: ::
:Ci:nching *les ordures*
Beneath the late December stars
We ponder Mooky's loss

Scent of litter spattered through the fog.
What demon took hold
When she abandoned her spoon of Gerber
To lick le trophy of Golden Whisker?
Tonight, beside the glossy moonlit gleam
Of relinquished *Cat Fancys,*
Mooky longs to conquer verdant virile kingdoms,
Combing the planets for a noble highbred groom
For a nibble of the gold, the crown,
The fancy: : : ::: :fa:ncy feast:s: : ::::: ::: ::: :::: ::: : : : :: : ::: : : :: :
: : :: :: : : :: :   : :: :: : :: :: : :::: : :: : : : : : : :: : :::: ::
: ::: : ::: :: : :: : : :: : :: : :::: : ::   :: G: : o :: o : :d: :: ::: :: :: :
: :::: :::: :: : : : :: : ::::::: ::: : : : ::: :: :: : : : ::: :t: a: :ste
: ::: : : : : : : :: :: :is easy: : :: : ::: ::: : : : : : : : : : : : : : : :
: :: : : ::: : : : : : :::: :::: :::
: : R:ecognizing chartreuse,
        a slow death of lawn, is like detecting
            the whiskers of your child in the actor

who sinks to deviant eye-stabbing. I said,
        Sweet little dumpling, were the meals
            of golden leaf not gold enough?

Amidst the blades I stood, a fresh baby abandoned
        beneath a fast food bag like Moses cloaked in grass.
                I will not crumble over failed

C h e m L a w n . I did not pray for superhumanity,
        but sets of talons sprouted from my hands
            in a taxi east of Johannesburg.

The mine surrounded me like a well-fed throat,

glistened with nourishing mucosity.
                Across the Atlantic, I felt the ravenous lawn

atrophy into a bright shade of canary.
            Foam trickled from my lips as I gashed
                    free the gold to glut my child of turf.

The earth began to hemorrhage diamonds, and a majestic
                sense of ecstasy paraded through my thalamus.
                    It could have been a sparkle

or my cyanide atomizer liberating gold from an impure state,
                but there was a brief moment of love,
                        floating fish paved the river

a loaf of gold for baby bermuda: : ::: :: ::: :: :: ::: :: :: :::   :: : ::
: :: :: :: : :: : :: ::: : :: : ::: ::: :: ::: :::::::::: : : ::::
: : : : : :: : : : : : :   : : : :   :: :: ::::**BERMUDA**: :: : : :: : :
: : ::   :: ::*feet*:: : : : : : : : : : : :: : : : : : : : : : : : : : :   : :
: : :: : : :: :: : :: ::::: *the*.:: :: : ::::::: : : :::::::::::::::
:::: :   ::: : :::::: ::: : : ::: :::: :::::   : : ::: : ::
:::: :: : : : : :: ::::::: : :::: ::: :::::: ::::::::::
:: :::::: : :: : :: :: :::: :: :: : :: *Love*. . . . .
.: : ::: . . .:: : . . . .:: : : : : : : : : : : : ::::::: :::::::
: : : : :: ::: :: : : : : : : : : : :::: : ::::: :: : : :::::::   :::: :::::::::
: : : : Love—but it's raw—past the pyramid of exotic camel boots; the fiberglass
crotch—hairless for display. Pedestrians, en route, versed in Nefertiti—my
passion fathers hysteria.

A window—undressed because it's sex—through which I don her headdress (mesh
the glow with sequin pantaloons). The sequins not hairless because I'm male and
non-Egyptian.

Nefertiti's V-patch (of fiberglass—and white; because it's on display) flashes deepest red—
reflected off the Sphinx, fathered by hysteria. Photoshoot—my passion and not fashion (a
headdress and some cuffs)—blazoned in gazettes: He Dared to Feel the L:o:v:e: : : : : ::: : : : : : : :
: : : : : : : : : : :: :::::: : :: ::: : :: : : : : : : :::: :: : : : : : : ::: :: : : :: : : :::::::::::::: :: : : ::::: :
:: :::   : : : :   :   : : : : :::::::: :::: : : : : : : : : : : : : : : : : : : ::: :::: ::
: : : : : :::::: :: : : : : : : : : : : : : :::: : : : : ::::::::: :: : : : : : : : : : : : : : : : : : ::: : : :: :::::::: : : : :
: : : :::::: :: :: : : : :   : : : :   :: : : :: ::::::: :::::: : : : : : : : : : ::: : : : : : : : : : : :::O!:
::::: : : : : : : : : : :::   : : : : :::::: : : : : : : ::::::::::: :::::: : ::: ::I'd: :: : :: ::: : ::

: :l :ove :: : : :: :

:::: : : :::::::: : :: ::: ::::: :: :: ::: ::: :: : : : : ::to : : be: : : :: : :

:: : : : :: : : : : : : :: : : : : an: : :: : : :: : : :

 : : : : : :::: :: : : :: : : ::: : ::

: : : : : :: : :: : : : : : Oscar:: :

:: :: : :: ::: : ::: : ::

de la Renta (to the left), Karl Lagerfeld (to the right),

beheld from a nosebleed opera box, mid-March, delivering their keynotes

of Anti-anti-fur from a leather tête-à-tête.

So they really look like Muppets?

The *ones* with all the *fur*?

If you look into their brains, we view their *Postlude Alla Oprah*—

goodies of chinchilla await beneath the seats—

but presently not freebies, no—not yet what drapes

against the torso to mellow like

hot cocoa nursed from baby bottle teats.

Karl's thinking *Fur is the phoniest. I've lined my heart in fur.*

Now my plastic sincerity is intuitive.

What they really want to say is that this is a summons,

a rapturous moment in *fur*,

which is why they part the curtains of *fur*,

which is why they stock the pool with mink

(no sinky when you drinky

in lairs of silver fox).

Say you join them, *there*, amongst the

ripples of buttery deadness.

What freebies shall descend like allowance from your mom?

Tiara, fur, Swarovski waterfall, _____, _____,

_____, _____,

_____, _____, _____—dearest Friend,

when you look beneath your seat, what

will you discover? What is its price ¿ : : :¿ ? ? ? ? ?¿: : ?:: : : :: ?¿ : :: : : : : : : :: : : : :

¿¿: : :? :::: ? ::: ::: ::: ::¿ ¿ : :¿ ¿ : :: ? : : ::¿ : : :: : :? : :? ¿ : :?: : : ? ?:: : : :: :: ::

:: : : : :: :: :? : : : : : :? :: ¿ : :?¿ : : :: ??? : :: : : : : : : ? : : ? :::: : :: : :? : :::? : ? : :?? : : :

: : ¿¿¿: :: : : :: ? ? ? : : : :: ? : :: :?:: : : :: ? : ? ?: **You've** : : got : : questions?:

:: : : : : : ¿¿: ?: : :?: : : : : : :?¿?::: : : :?¿?:: : :?¿? : :

:: :: ? : : :: : : : :? : : : : :: **We've** : : :: got:: ::

: :: : : :: : ¿: : : : : : : : : :

: : : : : : :

: : :The

answer's in the mangrove—camo chest of jewels and grenades parading pearls.

"hot plume of pink"

You screen flamingo warriors . . . handsome?, spunky?, heartening? . . . until you've hatched a worthy flamboyance.

You bespangle the yearbooks of history. Forsaken state parks possess your fabled name.

Virtual freedom skedaddles from their tizzied bills.

If ancient Romans attempt to gorge on warrior tongues, you'd parrot Jesus, kabob yourself.

4/22/19??; Sylvester, Georgia: The little bitch chucked Pinky in the fire. The house smells like burning plastic and arsoned sanctuaries. What's a sanctuary? My flamingo army's ruined. Punishment will be cutting out her tongue. It's okay. I will scream for her when Pinky seeks revenge beyond the grave, standing on one leg, helmet on his head, wearing a dress drenched : : in pearls: : and: ga:s:oline, :: : :a: : ::: : :slinky: :: :: ::dress: : :: : :aflame::: : : :: :: : : : : : : ga : : : : : : ::
: : :: :: ::: ::: : : :: :: : :: :: :: :: :: : : :: :: : : :: : : :: :: : : :: : : : : : :::::: : : : :slinky: :: :: ::: :: :: :: : ::
:: :: ::: ::: : : : : : : : : : : : : : : : : : : : : : : : : : : ::::::::: : : : : : : : : : :   :: : : : : : : : : : : : : : : : ::
: : :: ::It's: ::Slinky!:: ::: :: : : : : : : : : : : : : : : : : : : : : : : : : : : : : : : : : : : :: : : : : :
: :: : ::::: : ::::: : : :: : : :: : : : : : :for::: :: f:un: ::: :: :: :: :: :: : : : : : : : : : : :it's: :: ::the: :be:st::: ::: :: :::
:: : : : : : : : : :: : :: : : : : : :::: :: : : : : : : : :: : : : : : : : :: : : ::: :a:
:man: : :can:::get:: :: :: :: :: :: : : : : : : : : : : : : : : : : : : : : : :: : :: : : : : : : : :: : : : : : : : : :: : : : : : : :
: : : : : : : : : : : :: : : :some: : ::: ::of: :o:ur:: : :best: : :: : men:: : :are: : ::: :: : : : : : : : : : : :: : : : : :: :
: :: :: : : : : : :: : : : : : : : : : ::: :: :: : : :::
:w:o:m:e:n:: : : : : : : : : : : : : : : : : : : :: :: : : : : :: :
: : : : : : : :: : : : : : :: : :: : :the : :b:est: :: :par:t: ::of :: :waking : :: u:p:: :: :
:almost: : everyone: :: : : : : ::::: : ::: : : : : : : : : : : : :::: :: :: : :o: :
:: : : : : : : :: ::: : : : :: : : : : : : : : : : : : :: :appreciates: :: :: :th:e::: : : :best: : :: : : : : the *Best*:: : :: : :
:: : : :: :: :: : : : : : : : ::: : : : : : : ::: :: : :: :::: : : :   : : : : : :   : : : : : : : : :
: : : : : : : : : : : : : : : ::: : : : : : :: : :: :: : : : *The Best*. :: :: : : : :: : : : : : : : : : : ::: : : : : : : : : : ::: : : : : :
: : :: :: : : : : : : : : : : : : : :: : : : : :: : : : : : : : : : :: :: :::: : C : o : n : t : e : m : p : o : r : a : r : y : : Poetry
Bestsellers: :: ::: :: :   :   : : :: : : ::
Week of September 13, 2009
Courtesy of Nielsen BookScan and the Poetry Foundation

#1: In Search of Small Gods by Jim Harrison (last week 6)
#2: The Shadow of Sirius (paperback) by W.S. Merwin (last week 1)
#3: A Village Life by Louise Glück (last week 2)

#4:   Evidence by Mary Oliver (last week 3)

#5:   Red Bird (paperback) by Mary Oliver (last week 5)

#6:   Wheeling Motel by Franz Wright (--)

#7:   Why I Wake Early by Mary Oliver (last week 11)

#8:   Thirst (paperback) by Mary Oliver (last week 7)

#9:   New and Selected Poems: Volume Two (paperback) by Mary Oliver (last week 8)

#10: Slamming Open the Door by Kathleen Sheeder Bonanno (last week 4)

#11: The Pleasures of the Damned: Poems, 1951-1993 (paperback) by Charles Bukowski (last week 9)

#12: Endpoint and Other Poems by John Updike (last week 14)

#13: Praise Song for the Day: A Poem for Barack Obama's Presidential Inauguration by Elizabeth Alexander (--)

#14: The Trouble with Poetry and Other Poems (paperback) by Billy Collins (:::::::::::::::::::::
: : ::: : : : :: the::trouble : : : : : : ::: : : : : :::.::.::: : : :: : :: ::: .::.: : .: ::..::
::.::: : :::::.: : :: :: : :.::.::.::::: : ::: :the::trouble : :   : : :.::.::.::.:: ::.::.::.::
: : .:.::.::: .::.::.:: :.::.: :.::.::.:: :.:: ::::::::::::::::::::::::::::::::: :::: : : :: :
: : : : : :.: ::::::: :: : : : :.::.: :.:::: :: ::: ::: : : : :: :: :.:: :: :::: : : :lots: :: :: : : and::: :: : : :: : : : : :
: : : : : : :: .:::: : :::: :::: :.::.::.::.::.::.::.:: ::.::.::.::.::.::.::.::.:: : ::::
::: :: :: :: :.:.:: :: :: :.::.::.: :::: :::: ::.:: :: :.::.::.::.::.:::::.::.::.::.::.::. :::: : :lots: ::::
:.::.::.::.::.::.::.::.: :.::.::.: ::::: :.::.::.::.::.:: ::.:: :and: : : : : : :
: : : : : : : :.::.::.::.::.::.:: ::.:: : : : lots: : : : : ::
: :.::.::.: :.::.::.::.::.::.::.:
: : : : of: : : : :: .:: ::.: : : :
:.::.: :: :.:: ::.::.:
: : : : : :
: : : :
: : :
: :
:
:
.
.
.

Whatevers . . .

Sorrys to sever the cheap climax

Nothing gold can tickle

Silver tongues are trimming me in goo

Tempered my spit to a plush of pillowed spite

May exquisite gowns of language imprison you

Go now—gently

Pose beside the white chickens, pistol to my veil

Fur-hearted men will broadcast the demise

Oh little Krewer I love you get up

A Poetics of Resistance

> *And I'm gonna use this opportunity the way I want to use it.*
> *—Fiona Apple, 1997 MTV Video Music Award Acceptance Speech*

Let's get this out of the way:

I'm gay.

I'm male.

I'm white.

I was genderqueer as a child and scrawny as hell.

My identity and body rarely factor into my writing process at a conscious level.

I'm tired of people assuming that I have some special relationship with my identity or my body just because I'm not straight.

I buy stuff just like everyone else.

*

The national (or even transnational) demand for a certain kind of prize-winning, "well-crafted" poem—a poem that the New Yorker would see fit to print and that would help its author get one of the "good jobs" advertised by the Association of Writers & Writing Programs—has produced an extraordinary uniformity. (Perloff, "Poetry on the Brink")

We've all heard the cry about MFA programs producing the "McPoem," but Perloff's description doesn't just point fingers, it locates the source of the problem—that uniformity in poetry is produced by a system filled with people who long to become one of the initiated, in hopes of securing these "good jobs," or at least to be praised by people in such positions. In short, the "well-crafted" poem has achieved a certain exchange rate in the creative economy. Contemporary American poetry has, in a sense, become infected by the drive of capitalism. Higher education, after all, is a business.

That said, I am a graduate of an MFA program, and I can honestly say it helped me determine my poetic sensibility. In observing the poetic development of my peers, I saw many individuals cultivating the aesthetic of the "well-crafted" poem. Of course, there were poets who weren't interested in this at all, and we became close friends. I came to the program wanting to find myself as a poet—not to piece myself together into a tidy, tame, and marketable superstar that could win the "Yale Younger," which seemed to be a common goal.

There was one specific moment in graduate school that determined the direction of my work. I was at an MFA theme party where everyone was supposed to dress up as their high school selves. I ended up talking to a drunkenly honest "well-crafted" classmate, who bemoaned the fact he had "lost all [his] connections" and that "the only thing that matters are connections." His delivery was frightening and monstrous. A poet was actually telling me to my face that he cared more about networking and publishing and success than actually writing a poem he could stand behind. This is not the spirit of the artist; it is the spirit of the businessman.

That evening at the party both frightened and infuriated me. It quickly became my goal as an artist to resist, through my aesthetic, this dominant, prize-driven morass. To free myself, I decided to work toward a career outside the Academy. Or at least outside the confines of a creative writing department. This is not to say that I wouldn't want to teach in a program; this is to say that I'm not interested in creating a "game plan" to ultimately end up there.

I agree with Perloff when she states that lyricism has become incredibly uniform. I will take her statement one step further—lyrical language has become, *literally*, an advertisement of one's poetic gravitas. We have reached a point in literature where people are utilizing their skill to manufacture a lyricism with the sole purpose of targeting book prizes and selection committees. Like the language of advertising, the contemporary "well-crafted" lyric manipulates, soothes, and empowers its audience (or, more specifically, editors and judges). I wholeheartedly believe poetry cannot move forward into new territory unless we resist the call to achieve calculated, collective visions and instead commit to realizing visions of the individual.

Perloff seems to think that the primary resistance to the status quo comes in the form of the Conceptual poets (and their "relatives"). This gives those in the establishment (or those sympathetic to their aesthetic) the impression that this is an "establishment" vs. "experimentalist" deathmatch, which results in tired arguments of accessibility, the impenetrability of the avant-garde, and the desire to "expand the audience" of poetry. Marjorie Perloff's "avant-garde mandate" seems particularly stringent; she fails to address that there are poets with far softer, self-dictated mandates (myself among them) who agree (vocally and/or through their aesthetic) with her sentiments regarding the uniformity of the dominant lyricism. When the resistance to the dominant lyric is recognized as something that concerns a wide variety of poets, the argument shifts from accessibility and audience to the ethics of being a poet in the world. And, ultimately, this is what I mean by there being a necessity to commit to personal vision. We must do things on our own terms—not necessarily according to singular models of what a poem has to be.

In my own attempt to resist, I take my trained ear and push the lyric to its outer limits, just before it collapses into a complete lack of musicality. Sometimes I take the music and flatten it out. I want to create and read poems that both satisfy and subvert certain aspects (genre, form, content, sound) of the dominant lyric. This is my mission as a poet and publisher, and if this means I never see a full-length book of mine in print, it's a risk I'm willing to take.

Works Cited

Marjorie Perloff, "Poetry on the Brink" *Boston Review*, May/June 2012. Web. 29 Jan. 2013.
    <http://www.bostonreview.net/BR37.3/marjorie_perloff_poetry_lyric_reinvention.php>

Duriel E. Harris

from No dictionary of a living tongue

:

To and from a ripening drift,
the road wants the soil it shields.
And blood, a disregarded guest,
licks weeds for gasoline.

What joins the tongue
to judge bitterness?
To linger?

:

Glass and metal.
Sodden grime.

Splintered limbs flung
leaking, as if from a great height
but without feeling
to leaves and damp ground.

To the ditch, the shoulder,
dawdling, they fly. Flung
glittering into the wind turbines,
past the even yellow stitch
to the pasture and the fallow field.

This time I will seal you in

A river has no chin,
Nor silt filled eyes after dreams
Nor mouth, nor tender dribbles down its petaled darknesses
To measure its seepage, nor means to name the devil it sees.

I rust suffused with color and this touching.
I blister and twist my joints
And slip beneath the weave, wagging,
Unbuckled, my eel self from the cave
Into the lit water to rake the hand fallen there,
The hand untried by reaching.

And your mouth, a stain
Taking, bragging my body, a memory
Of water sewn into blue grass.

I have seen the bodies, like candles, humming into darkness
Going murky against the cradling pavement's slight incline.

Discolored through spilt bone, who held me, seized in death
Pressed against the cradling, absorbing the light like a black hood,
Her face a staggering axe.

Air is a restless luminescence
We take in and move through.
This time I will seal you in.

"It is velocity that penetrates"

It is velocity that penetrates, the bullet offers.
Scratching at the name you will inherit,
Envy, a jet stone claw mounted in silver,
Dislodges something you imagine and safeguard without knowing.
Carrying a verdant seeking, the bullet's hollow skull knocks against yours.
Your mouth closes against the sweetness of sudden cold.

"If You Bring Forth What Is Within You"

I used to be a bigot, he professed, pride
fanning out between the words, airborne.
And to his body: *It was you, weak thing!*
I hate you. His pink mouth leaking sap and the world
a forest swarm of dagger moths.
                         They say pain is weakness
leaving the body. Sputum. Spoiled blood. Tears.
And when it rises—pain—in a chorus to meet the open air
it is as if a god has been born. Unbound,
its spectacular darkness blooms, surges
bellowing sulfur, anxious to take possession.

Note:
The title is excerpted from the following saying as recorded in The Gospel of Thomas:

If you bring forth what is within you, what is within you will save you. If you do not
bring forth what is within you, what you do not bring forth will destroy you.
—Jesus Christ

A man jawed tightly in owning

stomps his wife's skull into the shape of his boot.
The slit in her throat pulses blood into a halo.
Their 6 year-old son watches his mother congeal,
imagines his father stuffed into an air duct
lodged under the jail he crawled out from.

His dreams: a lumpy duffle bag of oily rags and blue-black coveralls.
His dreams: fists full of his father's glistening black hair.

His Dreams

BLACK AS THE PRIZE BACKSIDE | SCURRYING BLACK | BLOOD STOOL BLACK AS CASTE
AS SOUP | AS CORK-SPIT | AS SKILLET EYE | FURNACE BLACK | CROUCHING | GLIDING
HISSING BLACK | AS THE GOOD NEWS | AS THE MADE UP THING I WEAR TO MEET YOU

"I do not doubt their belonging together"
The Misanthrope Contemplates the Tricky Sentence

An intimate, the tricky sentence:
A train. Neat categories I imagine
Against a cataract sky. The clouds
Rat shaped, nibbling shelves of flat air,
Sour rain funneled through their hairless tails
Tinting miles, across frames and swallowing:
An aria, a sleeping child, a weapon.
Proof suffering sensation.
This crucial syntax of synapse
And meninges. All around me.
Tools not mirrors. Not. Where
There would be a face, an area,
Circuitry I neatly map.

To lever, to bell, to labyrinth.
Being, fugitive, paws and drools.
The cage swings wildly, teeters
Intact, not falling. Not.

In the center
The long button nag, a stricture,
A furious bit I hold. I remember:
        A dense handling of sums.
        A deaf sameness.
        Deft, my tightly packed
        Scuffle, the flap
        As wide as outside

And as insolent damp
And sticky
And tender throughout.

from **speleology**

pulling up into   the attic crawlspace   the carapace.   The mind saw's hum-

wet metal, circling   grazing, peripatetic upon dermis fat tissue: a solitary body's

    sudden   doorframe   pose

    A body: a trick,   a knot,   a dare.

§

Sssshhhhhhhh. A woman's voice leaks, pooling in the seat of my skull just as I awaken. *Ssssuuuuhhhhhh* The woman again, scattering, her voice seed swinging out until a name's open shape casts back shadows. Zzhhgghhnn. I snore, feel myself surfacing, weedling through sleep's muddy grain.

On the pillow by my head, a thought flares, its center spitting charcoal: *there are those who want you dead; I stand among them.* As I open my eyes, the thought drags its mark across, connecting my brows. Its brittle thickening angles, absorbs and bewitches the light. In the canopy above me, I hear someone counting stones.

§

The fool washes his mouth with water then complains of thirst.

§

Discreet fragments of our time | resonate | in the eye | the mind
perception | the cognitive flicker | draws the body | in
conflicting directions: vectors | the body follows at once — exploding

There is no illusion to combat | like the real
the body | already relative by reason
of its displacement | submits to it

The line | color | shape of the world | its fragments
constituents of form | mixed and impure | a railway house
through which the body passes accumulating presence

That is what the body remembers

That which makes the body | makes the self | beyond which we are undone

§

Portrait

Upon waking
an eye shuts.

Resin coats the soluble bodies of objects
and the mind applies itself, pressing

until even the light filtered air adheres
singly edging, drafting worlds.

I lie still in the balance, emptying into breath,
a slight movement in the dissolve, reaching
for the blue gaps between frames. I crave:

                        I cohere;
and objects cluster, worlds turn to color, and lock
into orbit. My skin adorns itself, humming
the warm mantra of closed systems.

The body is a habit I can break.

self portrait with body

inside grips
its motors. (guilt)
opens the door.
      (one hand spreads
      between breasts
      keeping in)
the room shocks: smells
of new coma. i swell
standing here, admiring
delicate cluster of griefmadeover
—a lug sculpted behind my sternum.
this is what they pulled
from the wreck.   jeweled and dazzling
it bullies me—uncovered toes vague greyblue
mummied from waist to skullbulb
                easy lazarus
loosely stapled to the bed linen

i admire the machines that guard
: instinctive cool mannerisms
digital and monitoring, use-dented
chrome chipping, ribbed black plastic
knobs, tubes, clamps, and humboxes
pulsing a breath-fight with death.

        (vacuum bag
           filling)

brittling exhalations (filling) punctuate
dark shapes of misplaced ordinary
as forced dumb muscle exaggerates
the chest. (head wants to fall
beside torso but tall collar keeps
afloat.)
      the body stiffens pushing against
a door.

Poetics Statement

How many languages do you speak?

. . .

What does your *real* voice sound like?

. . .

Would you say you're lucky?

—girl, 8

The body is a phrase I repeat, a vibration I recover from silence. In
the absence of memory, I invent from fragments a garment
with which to cloak the body. It is a fair substitute, a
kind of skin: pliable, & durable, imbuing the body with
superlative resilience.

In this instance, for these purposes, the body is the self. Like
water and space, the self exists throughout the body.
Proprioception—beneath the level of consciousness—
allows for the projection of the self beyond the body to the
extent that I imagine myself without substance, moving
in the absence of flesh, unencumbered, untethered,
impervious to pain.

In the narrative I inherited, the girl body is synonymous with pain.
Its form dictates function & from engendering through
decline it seizes in its constraints. Despite age, wisdom,
intellect or skill, she is a girl: a body refashioned in
language to serve, fixed in injury to compel yielding.

Imbedded in this narrative, another narrative of skin, flesh & hair.
The sway of power by might & the thrust of a dark fantasy.
Broad & thick. Heavy & dense, viscous & guttural. Long &
low. Aberration projected through the skein of falsehood.
Bodies transported across bodies to toil & breed toil,
defiled to be defiled. Economy of scale. Bodies made
object & abject to augment other bodies. Delivered unto a
maw the shape of bludgeoning.

Dispersing, my body holds against the common wreck.

. . .

The expanse of my departure envelopes me.

I re-enter the narrative from a space of knowing. Knowing. A sea
beneath levels of consciousness that surfaces through
language, a space in motion. Androgyne through and
beyond its arc, a long body curling into form & breaking.
A source: antecedent & inexhaustible, generative &
illimitable. Surfacing.

The body (self), too, is a narrative I re-enter. Multiple in its layers,
facets, fields & orbits. A sea gathering calm. I observe
the transcendental body, the local body, & the third i that
stands apart but is not separate, being informed by being
in a way I cannot quantify. Its precise intuition, a language
I can neither speak nor unlearn. These, in concert, cleaved
together, split along the grain & rejoined sticking fast, I
harness against lack.

These, this body, I assume, luxuriating in the motion of its folds.
Grasping the outline of light, vast & deliberate, amorphous
yet distinct, sensing through the skin & canals, or at some
remove through an other, it resonates.

Matter & awareness of matter, a principled reciprocal action. A
convergence, to engage: making against unmaking. The
artifact manifest: made against unmade.

Works Cited

Harris, Duriel E. "girl, 8," [audio] *Drunken Boat* 12. Web. 29 Jan. 2013.
<http://www.drunkenboat.com/db12/>

EC Crandall

MONUMENTs

1,

right in front of Sovereign Bank

and its desperate lantern

icon of trust

a white woman

in shift dress

looks trapped,

pulls anchor,

gazes

up

on the archangel

our   ART ANGEL   Claus

(named for his claws

and his take on perspective)

his weird weighted

challenge to

equilibrium

Claus stalls against the Circles
high sign of the anti-times

sometimes lounges largesse over the subway hole

an evocation of himself, the
patron saint of skateboarders

our lady of enormous holes

the sound is prayer   *all efficient desires*

but the hope is balance

in absence of wicked cure,

the wings must be missing

nothing looks dead this
afternoon

the only sense the monument makes is

if you kneel in front of it

TIME

knee to knee

hands to fat lap

lose your face

slap the concrete

SPACE

hour by hour, ship by ship, wing by missing wing

2,
(another placard in our fair city, below another woman holding another infant)

Hereby lies
Mother Fuck,
seer of all inevitable roads,
who practiced willing,
filled her Gershwin Cycle
with laundromat gossip
and dustbowl ambition
SHE OUR GREAT DOMESTIC

3,
Did I just hit a nerve?
How will I ever do this?   The right way, the quiet way.
Check me for a pulse
m   ake eye contact with me
your b   ag hitting   my hips
my hips, my gen   der bones,
shaking alon   g like a train   a time

I asked you, up front:
Can you find my pulse   *in less than 10 seconds?*

No one ever succeeds, my haircut provides flatline horizon
slack punk track for this slate train to pound in vain   fuck drum

TO TRY TO DO, SOON:
Give the person to your left a prison tattoo
                        of the angel of your choice.
Make your own blood bank.
Write a sentence that is a drone.
Draw a map of the person behind you in reins or chains.
Really get their pulse on   the tip of your thumb.
Hum along. Don't worry   about touching. Clink.
                        Try a smaller escape.

"Define suffering."
        Tell me when the butter's water.
                        I'll beg for your every thought.
        Rorschach, readymade Rorschachs
                manufactured in the town square
        where gowns become monuments   overnight

        where one can be
                        come transformed
in God's little basement barrel
by merely rolling around
perhaps sleeping
        through the rough parts
It's not hard to find a cure
        to put ribbons around
                        ribbons and ribbons unfurling and twisting
twisting, trusting

        we'll make an eastern beach so beautiful to
weather through: a
tidepool   jersey swirl   yellow hat:

silver fox   arrest me

please

let me rest my poor headstone

4,

you can see in different cities the language of
legibility / just let me get the borders drawn in
before you pass the advertising / WHAT IS THE CITY'S //
is this the industrial sound impossible to replicate? /
let's trade energies unite our lost causes and dip
into the purses of the girls / the girls wearing rum and pleats
awash in the warm afterthought of perfect dates
perfect dates it's not robbery if you do it in the RAW

over to the side, just a cartoon thought:
How far is Reykjavíc from 30th Street Station?

OHI'MLAZY OHI'MFLOATING

5,
it's   cool,   I'm a   man   now   I'm monumental

all   grown   up, my   heart
a   monument,   a hapless   spring
despite   these   shorts   being   drenched
suctioned   on me   like   seal   skin,   I mean:
I'm honest   as straight-backed as a clothespin

We   know   you   think   you're   helping
with   your   fingers   on   my   pecs
copping a cordial feel   across my chest
rabid   martyr   flames   at   your   feet

we   play   me   like   a   scalding   flute

your   bright   gay flight   frightening   me
just   like   anyone   would
those fingerprints across a dashboard, those ???s

    I hope I won't go all huck finn

    on your shins again, listen I'm a

slippery   civic   model, I'm   yours too
helmet   and mud amo   down around
my ankles   like   cheap drawers
in   a   quick fuck, a   bucking   bronco
on   the   railroad   tracks, thank   god
your   old   lovers   planted   flags   at the
base   of   your   purpose
so   I   can   see   what I   have to   lose
out   of   the   corner   of   my   brain or
the leveling metallic pull in the pants of my gut
My bank we tell you what the words say
when the steam dies down and the gears shift:

    this nation sings most convincingly
    while   we   sleep

    shitfaced   in someone's   elbow
    the crook in someone's nightdream

    whatever the wind,

    we welcome it

    in stone

Poem for the Apocalypse

Everything's cute these days
like that Liz Taylor stencil shirt
at Houston and Broadway I want

even though the artist has completely
disappeared, or like discovering Jack Spicer's
detective novel in the library stacks

Why don't you people tell me
about these things? Why can't it all be
like Nadine and *The Price of Salt?*

She simply screamed the title, shrieking YOU HAVEN'T
READ THAT? in efficient lesbian musician pitch
(close to how people type in all caps these days)

For that, I was grateful. I wish reading still felt dangerous
and edgy (maybe it does) as in *the next page could
change my life*, catapult me off to a future

more invigorating. Lately the billboards (like Lee
Edelman) swear there is no future, that the whole world
is coming to an end. Their apocalypse is very cheap-font

doomsday precious to me, familiar how much we all just want
life to matter, or to go away. I still circle the days
I workout and X-out the days I work, as if

marks make the difference of a day, my modest code of
nonimal production. I mean, what do I know about *figures?*
For instance, Diana hates how I both pay and don't pay

the bills but she finds it charming when I'm fussy
It's just cute how the world is ending, how it makes
everything funny, how it seems like this poem I'm writing

has already been written. Cute, how I wrote that and
conceived a new verb, "been Waldmanned," then "Ben Waldman."
Lately I think I'm a man, or like I could be one

I just need to pick a surgery and stick to it
How Libran and conventional of me, I know
Let's just say I have hope for the man in me yet

I've lived my whole life in signs and symbols
I've even been to lots of gay bars called "Heaven"
I know for sure queers don't have ends of the world

That's too gloomy and we're too cute,
like everything lately, I mean the rapture of *things*!

Last night the ceiling caved in by the back door
and my barefoot girlfriend stepped on a little moth
She dropped the seltzer and it sprayed high onto the kitchen wall

I'll find anything amusing
It's been raining for days
I won't ever fix my car

maybe I've almost got it figured out
maybe I've almost collected the sacred set of keys
slayed all of the dragons made the most of

what I've got and got the least for my trouble
maybe I'll bow out now before the world
catches on fire and empties out, basically before it all
becomes so very dull and predictable, you know, "less cute"

In Feeling of My Memory

I am underneath its leaves as the hunter crackles and pants
and bursts, as the barrage balloon drifts behind a cloud
and animal death whips out its flashlight,
whistling
and slipping the glove off the trigger hand.
- Frank O'Hara

1. A melodramatic poetry whistles the high and the low, crackling noir and pageantry beneath the hunter's foot. 2. A grounded poetry is melodramatic, the electrostatic between two bodies. The songs between the acts or the acts between the songs. 3. Cloud or ground, poetry too works like the sounds around a body (as instincts, or signals). 4. Creation becomes the rapturous, haunting moment when the glove like skin comes off, the *something dead* behind you. The past, revealing. 5. The present, with feeling.

Every heartbreak of my body seems fraught with memory. In childhood, I crawled around in my body, which was after all healthy athletic queer lucky. A body with hands and knees that gravitated toward the lines and made letters out of them, a body slipping around, a snake in water. A functional dreamer, a product of hazardous environs, I proposed my father call me Luke at the hardware store. Self as Luke in overalls pretending to save a seat for mom, making up stories in the creekbed until dark. A body in hiding until it was too late, my age. Bucolic coffin in the dirt, full of silent worms.

Soon homemade melodrama provided collaboration for self and age and other. From here my transparent selves, the lowest and the highest, and the weakest hand across the darts: this is how I learned to depart my self - kicking off from a wooden dock - and why now I can't stop myself from doing the opposite of a ghost: I disappear from the scene. This is how the writing is conjuring, an act essential in the required artifice of being.

In poetics, I find the most sincere form of pretense.

In poetry, I reframe this appearance of the unknown, what is underneath the skin.

THE GHOST BODY: WITH REGARD to the relative precariousness of inside and outside hitting my sexual and gender identities, the marginal slipknot surface of bump-bump noise interference, all actively acute, cultivated over the course of my life. My life's work, like queerness, tastes of categories I've encountered along the way, categories of taste all defined by the thump-thump that funnels down the pipe. The sob-sob that coughs up the fiery laugh, the smoking jacket of class. Both ghosts have dispensed being cool, the sister Richards clumped humps beating nickels on the wooden floor—the touching banjos, singing that old sweet curdled feeling. After the rapture I came home again, to a new home, and that's when I started writing my body, lassoing my body & riding it like a rope trick. When my face hit the concrete, breaking off half a tooth, skirting the skin, for my sister to fix—My Dental Catastrophe—my life had been whittled down to a tiny toothpick so I up and moved again. I moved the outside of my body glove around to help it fit better and then I got the hell out of town, trunk between my legs and a bruise between my eyes. A headcase filled with condoms and poems. THE FAKE REAL: THE BODY AS SPIRIT.

I wanted to write because "we've all been inside the Mapplethorpe photos." We all know there is a hierarchy. Gross net in the weave of queer folklore that ties me to the mast [of This project: imagining Over-Abundance; Or, Rethinking bodily harm]. My students and I we mimic the other voices of you. We are heard to sound a certain way, jumbled performances in bursts. I will hear a hidden voice beneath the leaves like beauty and try to pull that out from the ground, like a fish on a hook, like me on a dock in rubber boots and a longshoreman's hat. Oh how that makes me miss my wife, the poem! My experimental soap opera! So good to tuck up, order in, and know for sure that we cannot miss our own melodramas.

Memory is one heartbreak after another, so's poetry, the papers we cram into the schisms. No the act of filling the holes (the fucking cracks). I mean, changing the place of the holes, loading the blanks we've erased with poems and love affairs. In a landscape such as this, the body is dumped inside a prison. The body is what makes noise inside the I. We collaborate by parenting the selves in the letters, all eyes on the prize: A prism. The professor with the revived orchid and the soothing stream behind her back taught me twenty things: one was to water her earthly paradise and another was every formulation of the word remember.

Thence I could contain in the eye; thus I water the selves. I put my poetry inside the act, inside the hand that opens the act, the actor that recites her first line. My poetry pets my affect and combs my hair. My formalism, my melodrama; my body, your salve. I want to say, "This is the way I want you to feel me." I want to not be ready. I want to remember to cut the knots in a collison and skirt the rim of your vision. My body should make a quarter turn when you read it, inside your skin. My reading should make a turn of it, in feeling of my memory.

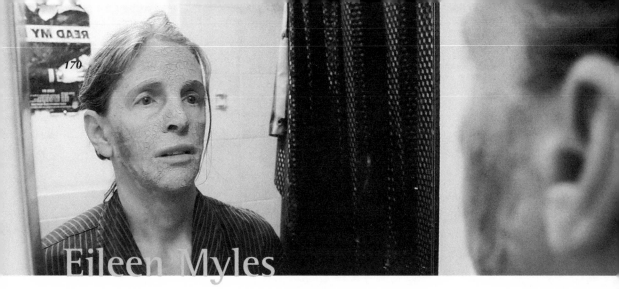

Eileen Myles

Walter Myles

for Leopoldine Core

Now I'm just praying that the phone doesn't ring
I'll just unplug
and leave the chocolate bar in my pocket
explaining the performance of god to Joan
as if she needs it
the silver card case slipping out of my
ass pocket the same ass that was calling somebody
as it was walking up the stairs
the city retained its luridity
tonight and all day like the floor of my apartment
retains the shit stains of Walter Myles
dog I loved for three weeks and three days
uttering his name secretly greeting
Nike in the street
hello Nike (Walter Myles) giving me his best dumb
grin
if I don't pick up shit early on in a poem
they won't think I love them
anymore when I really pee in the tub
I wanted to be carried so I took a train
thinking of Chloe wandering around under the earth
like Frank O'Hara on the beach
thinking of Akilah lying down it seems shocking
she died with Judith Butler on her mind

but we don't really know
the house I lived in is gone
the house I'm living in is always changing
I carry a tiny dog coat in my pocket
in my dream the opportunity to sing with the Beatles
was coming up inserting my band into theirs
and ours was chiefly composed of red
or redness. I propose we all jump into the water
that beach right down there and enthusiastically
I woke up. How could being just a little bit more
dogless be the source of all the rooms
changing in my house. Suggesting
we just plunge in. I knew I was off the charts by announcing
my dream. Two women do that and all the men
walk away. Is that what Aristophanes meant
worse than not having sex with them I start talking
about having sex with myself loving my own
mind. If heterosexuality means anything
other than me denying the existence of my own
dream I'd like to hear about that something
else and call that love. I call that war.
Years of silent repression of female dreaming
women looking like men but dreaming
they're women inside other women dreaming
that. What are men dreaming except that all women
are stupid and loving them. If you're dreaming something different
tell me your dreams about that. I am doomed to love
you that's for sure. Because you laugh when I say
to a man a woman is just a throne
turned upside down. A repository of his kingliness.
My kingliness does not require a throne
It is a throne. I love you because of your similar self
love and it makes me laugh. Perhaps I can have some chocolate
while this is going on. It will not break the spell.
I no longer live in the site of tremendous
dog fights. Certainly I could be kinder.
Black Swan was a moral film. Wouldn't you say.
I am a giant fan of Darren Aronofsky
who has the name of a dentist

and whose films are fountains of power
fountains of gender
I dreamed that Judith Butler once suggested my girlfriend liked my
phallus better than hers.
This is true apropos Akilah's death
It turned out my girlfriend was much more in love with
her own phallus than anyone knew. In one film he was madly counting
in another he tore the refrigerator apart
jumped into blackness
jumped into white. What else do you want a movie
to do. If I had the time I'd make a film. "It gets worse"
that's what I'd call it. If he can lie so can I.
Cause there's nothing better than knowing so
much. Seeing that look in her eyes.
Bright days wandering around the block
with a dog. Breaking out. Tossing some water into a pot and putting in so much
cereal not knowing what the formula is. We dare it.
How long will I be boiling chicken
it's a little red inside. The dream is the perfect object
because you only can imagine its contours
you're scraping along its curves like a giant woman
lying outside. She is enormous naked and you are blind
but if you just stay with her perimeter, no her mounds
leading you higher and higher, her awesome
neck so sensitive
her ear, no ear has
ever been less constructed to hear but to allow
the midgets of myth to tickle, to bite and gnaw
if you can extrapolate some meanings from
this. Like those people who wound up going to parties
either dressed like Gertrude Stein
or Susan. She was just a big ole man
who went to Harvard.
I mean they probably burned the witches
right there before the lynching began
same tree. Stupidly at Jill's memorial I began discussing the publication
of her letters with Ingrid. What was I thinning.
That's right. The k is missing. Small ghostly dog
wrapped in a sheet. Eyes glimmering.

Everyone grinned when I went back to the restaurant and picked
my silver card case off the floor. The name is Paladin.
Never say anything bad about anyone from
HARVARD. That obsesses me. How could you say anything
good or is that just implied. The one more thing was single moms
and there was another thing. You're losing the dream
all the time. That's why we love it. I thought it was the dream
that was both vulgar and important. It is the search.
So he sent a letter to the addresses of each of the women
who had died. The exact address. And that was enough.
You are waiting for somebody timeless
but everything only happens inside
time. One envelope in the pile has a stamp
and you CAN find it. That she got a grant for being a poet
doesn't mean that she's
one and you're not. You'll get a donut too.
But what was it. Janine spoke about writing so much and so fast that
it wasn't writing at all. The most beautiful thing I ever heard.
You can see the pages in the light
every day. Notebooks full of that stuff. The blonde girl writing. Her passion pouring
on the page. And we can't read it. That was her dream. To be doing
that. Smiling years later and telling us her crime. Utterly
unreadable. No text at all, just script. Pure sex
sweat, effort, time. She said just to live here, to have all of you
around me now. Just the fact
that it gets cold again. It makes me hungry.
There's nothing wrong with that.
Climbing all over her naked bod. He was the man tied up
and they were small. And it's interesting that he also
proposed eating babies. I mean why not.
Say she raised them to kill them. I say they lived to die.
We watch them dying here, whether we go
to the ceremony or not.
That a king learned to speak
somehow is not such
a wonderful thing.
That a woman learned
to die
is.

15 minutes

the beaming ~~sun~~
sun
out there
resembles
a light bulb
the sun
is that bright
Ashville is on a mountain
of Crystal
that inspired me
I had to get out of there
fast
depending on who
uses it
anything
you make can
be broken
reset
I can hear the faint
pattern
in the water
falling on tin
or stainless
steel. It's ugly
little message
doesn't annoy me
so much as make
me wonder
if it's making
lines in the air
my coffee is so
black and that's complete
and so I must
break it. I had
so much to say
today and yet I stretched

out. I thought "62."
That's 8. And Cathy
said today was
a full moon. It means
everything: how I turned
my hip on the slide
and almost hurt
myself. The tray that
sat in my mother's
house forever
is on my counter
now. Useless and like
forever. Greedy about
time these fifteen
minutes. It begins nailing
the sink like
a rattle has a finale.
Rather than allowing
me to search Doug
gently cut me off.
And this is enough.

The check could've been
larger. I wanted you
to be charmed by
how she lived with the plants
and the clocks
in the house. My insane
devotion to my
mother. I will not call
her. To thank her
on this day, an 8. No
I am enjoying
my rattling coffee
the sound of the knife
its drips really slicing
time which is
sound as whole

as I know. I understand
my perfect love
for you and this
is apart from that too.
Coffee like a black
pen on my birthday
a sound that is making lines
a hand that will fill
them. I deposit
my check. I say
thank you mother.

My Boy's Red Hat

My poetics for today would be all about translation. I love Walter Benjamin's statement about how the translator doesn't enter the text but calls in and draws its echo out in his own language. He's an explorer of a sort. The history of pronouns in my work is probably the queerest thing I do. I'm happy to be male general these days but just when that seems predictable I'm female. The echo Benjamin describes which is the translation for him for me is the poem. I'm thinking the poem is something which is always in conversation with reality. It's the thing a film produces and so does a poem, something genitive, a feeling *of*. The terrain always shifts geographically, geologically, meteorologically, and politically and the poem accordingly feels female now or a man apprehends her struggle in the structure he's suddenly in and she seems to him like the important one. Am I a man writing the poem of the woman. I was born male, that was my feeling. I looked at my body and apparently I even demanded a penis as a child. It's what my mother reports. Do I have one now. Yes it's language. This ropey poem. I'm composing it always of *this* moment which is apart almost instantly. Maybe a poem is the famous detachable penis. I mean I'm mostly interested in time in poetry but we use it to provoke new spaces. New tools to get therein. The acquisition of language changed the animal and I think it still changes the animal every time. I also feel there's a wrongness in translating *this* (the present that I want to be holy in) but it greedily grew in my mind – this capacity and finally writing a poem is my only survival tool. In terms of work. In terms of mental illness and existence itself. This kind of collecting and saving and salvaging and translating desperately *matters*. We're making a map of possibility for everyone. I think of that flight or fight spot in a person and how that is engaged in making a poem. Like that is the exact energy that's deployed to translate a state of quiet emergency into currency somehow. This panic is for sharing. I just read something in which the poet (Laura Jarmamillo) described music and I think she meant street music, the recorded music we hear from the street as 'meaty'. I think my poetry also aspires to be some semblance of that. What I can't stop from coming into the poem tends to build it. I'm the echo the poem is trying to release. If the moment freezes me into a creature of shifting gender who can't protect herself then the poem in its jingles and stops is a failed trap that lets the animal out again to walk and sniff around.

I'm looking at this a little later, revising this and that and that also wondering if I could still say any more about poetry and transgender issues. I do know I belong here. There was a poem I wrote in the seventies which I wish I could find. It's called "My Boy's Red Hat" and I think I published it in my first book and then I exiled it from the closest thing yet I've had to a selected. That poem always made me a little embarrassed by its transparency and now I know why. In terms of gender I wasn't *either* (Alice Notley had invited us in a workshop to write a poem in the opposite gender and I thought opposite *what*) all the time and that's what my poem wasn't so much worried about but was attempting to resolve. A poem seems to be a place where for a moment you can put it all. Or everything else falls away. Gender and the self keep turning all the time. I think it's a kind of danger that moves us. Some people are capable of staying in their castle but for me they just aren't queer.

So gender and genre are telling us that this goes here and that goes there but I've always felt that nothing can be fixed and the poem I wrote so long ago was about a woman holding a boy. Christianity, or Catholicism in particular is all about a woman holding a boy and later on that boy is dying. No he's dead. And everyone is supposed to learn from that. See I don't agree that he's dead and neither is the woman and luckily as I understand it, poetry isn't obliged to teach us anything. We have this dirty piece of rope. We can arrange it as we like. Authority isn't required of us. I'm proposing a riddle instead (and an echo too) that perhaps gender, perhaps the self, that perhaps just the impossibility of language is what we've got. Making sense of these riddles, we're coiling and uncoiling them. I read again lately about how Gertrude Stein mocked Pound for being the village explainer which was fine if you were a village, but if you were not, not. Poetry increasingly seems to be a village full of explainers so today I will hide myself in public in this impossible embrace.

Eli Clare

The Terrorist God

the one dressed in blue eyes
white skin who lives
not   in tree roots   fingertips
horse tails   he who swears
against sex   god of
witch burning   jew killing
consort of smallpox

let me talk to him   not
his popester   not his jesus
not his pedophiles   the big
man   the mean man   the sadist
in the sky   let me
bring him down

take a walk   sea
to shining sea   crack house
to uranium tailings   watch
a sunset   a moonrise   visit
a psych ward   lead him
quiet to the torture chambers

arrange meetings with
leonard peltier   angela
davis   césar chavéz   harriet

tubman   barbara deming
joseph beam   audre lorde
wilma mankiller   emma
goldman   leave the prisons
ringing dead and alive

there will be no
confession   no blood
and body   no penance   only

this pocketful of dirt
salt water and fresh
stones and stars

Lake Champlain at Flood Level

Because
into the big
basin of yourself,
you take snowmelt
and rainfall, invite
wind to rise, waves
to rock and slam. Because

you harbor countless
birds, fish, and boats, both
floating and sunk, reflect
sun, cloud, moon, sky without
ever asking why. Because

you swallow endless
sewage, phosphates, mercury, sleep
with junker cars, broken bottles,
concrete pilings, never
get to lie fallow. Because

you connect river to ocean, and
because right now you cannot
contain it all, I heave
with your waters and all
they have unmoored.

And Yet

I lay out syringe, alcohol pad, vial: a ritual
connecting me to junkies. Draw the testosterone,
and push needle deep through skin into muscle.

> *And yet, I would have chosen hermit, storm-high river, heron flying upstream.*

Open the windows, forsythia spills its dense yellow.

North on Baldwin Road, I walk my everyday walk.
Bottom of the hill, a dog barks, boy yells, "Hey mister.
Hey mister. Hey mister." We've traded names a dozen times.

Then "Hey retard. Retard. Retard."
Schoolyard to street corner: words
slung by the pocketful.

Crip skin marked,
white skin not.

Open the doors, daffodils rear their bright heads.

Cypionate suspended in cottonseed oil,
a shapeshifter's drug the color of pale sunlight:

Voice cracks.
Stubble glints.

Open the cellar. Soon, soon the maples will unfurl their green fists.

And yet, girl arrived first, bones set to the current.

In the mirror I wait,
the difference a simple ritual—
verb, skin, muscle, hormone.

Body begins.

Split the stone open, then the lilacs' deep purple.

In another time, at another place, I might have relied upon
insistent dreams; gods, goddesses, spirits all;
an herbalist stepping out back, nettle or ginseng.

Jaw squares.
Hips and ass slim.

*And yet, had I been given a choice, they would have demanded clay or
granite, salt water or fresh, as if the confluence could never be home.*

Open, palms stretched wide, apple orchard still bare boned.

But today I have Pfizer, Upjohn, Watson,
doctors saying yes, saying no, judging
the very stretch of skin over bone.

Crip skin,
white skin:
which stories
do I tell the best,
and which
rarely begin—
turn, flutter,
settle?

Open to the peepers, coyotes, faint crescent moon.

This drug I shoot in careful fractions:

I step into its exam rooms,
pay its bills, increase its profits.

Pecs bulk.
Skin roughens.

Body begins to settle.

Let them draw my blood, check
liver, kidney, cholesterol, hematocrit,
track the numbers, write the script.

Open, orchard soon to be enveloped in blossom.

Round the next bend, other boys want my name,
hand me theirs, ask as only 5-year-olds can,
"Why don't you talk so good?" I shrug, keep moving.

> And yet, here at the confluence, river and ocean collide—current rushing head
> long, waves pushing back—stones tumble, logs roll. Tell me: where in this hiss
> and froth might I lay myself down?

No Longer Small and Lonely

Who if not the girl? The butch who changes her name, shaves her head,
binds her breasts, who wants to live without a pronoun, called sir, son, young man,
dressed in suits sharply pressed. The queer one who grew up not girl, not boy, riding
the wind bareback. The guy who reshapes his body, chest flat, beard finally growing,
who stands in the mirror ready. The boy who flew his kite in the hayfields, never
wanting to go home. My arms yearned to be that tug on the other end of the kite string.

The boy who dreamed: last night I lay down at the dense dark edge of joy.
We talked for hours, tracking the moon. I swallowed its smell, licked the length of its
body, rolled my muscled skin into its shaggy coat, and woke not remembering. I slept
a small, lonely child inside thick dreamless sleep.

Take your pillow and favorite quilt, walk down into the fields freshly mown. Who if not girl, boy, child?

I dreamed of walking—feet to earth, skin to granite. A gentle rhythm of left, right, left again, arms swinging loose. A fierce pull up the north face, switchback to ridgeline. A long stride from home to work every morning. A slow meander through the woods. I learned to walk on shaky feet, a gimp whose heels refused to reach the ground. I wore big blocky shoes and practiced my balance, as focused as a dancer learning to spot.

Dreamed of walking across the country. During lunch recess Mary and I conjured how we'd start in Bangor, Maine, end in Newport, Oregon, follow the back roads, pitch our tent in cow pastures and backyards, 3,000 miles from sea to shining sea. We walked endless laps around the ball field repeating this plan, detail upon detail, until a decade later I had graduated from college, and she had dropped out to work at Hardees, and between us we had a thousand dollars and a road map. I left my first girlfriend; she left her best drinking buddies; we caught a midnight Greyhound to Bangor. It didn't last. Thirty-five soggy miles of walking, we stopped at a roadside diner, ate cheeseburgers, fries, and apple pie à la mode. As she paid our bill, the waitress asked, cocking her head toward me, "Is he your husband?" After that, we stood in the gravel parking lot, our gear wet, feet blistered, and she gave up. I was the rain that fell between us.

Lay your bed clothes down, curl under them, and watch stars spread white across the valley, your eyes growing wide and wider, night no longer a simple black but full of its own color, until you swallow the Milky Way into your sleep. Who if not girl, boy, child, gimp, rain?

Not long after, I joined a peace march and walked 3,700 miles from L.A. to D.C. Once every three weeks a bomb exploded deep in the desert; they called it nuclear testing. The U.S. spent billions of dollars designing a leaky umbrella; they called it the space defense initiative. The military stockpiled weapons; they called them peacemaker, patriot, cruise. Missile silos dotted the prairie. We flooded the country, a river in protest.

While I dreamed of walking, my father dreamed of sailing around the world. My father—rapist, sadist, crazy man. He used all the weapons he owned, except his shotgun. Cracked my body wide open. Stole my heart. Shut the door. Locked it tight. I swam, a chinook upstream.

Wake up in the dew-drenched dark to coyotes howling, dogs wailing the harmony, sky even denser with stars, body nestled into ten thousand dreams. Who if not girl, boy, child, gimp, rain, river, chinook?

He talked about building a boat, sanding and varnishing the hull, rigging its sail, and heading west. He drew the plans, spent long hours in his woodshop, built chairs, tables, bookshelves, cabinets, even a house. His hands were ridged with veins, small blue tributaries branching up his arms. He sanded walnut, cherry, maple until it gleamed, soaking the grain with linseed oil, wood turning the color of honey, chocolate, fresh baked bread, texture of silk. But he never started his boat, never cut the plywood, steamed the ribs, checked the mast for true. Instead he drank cheap white wine and read endlessly about Marco Polo, Christopher Columbus, Ferdinand Magellan, Sir Francis Drake, those men who sailed the world so long ago. Drunk, my father became an almost harmless man, a white man who only occasionally grabbed at my body. I rose transparent as heat off a hot, hot bath.

My rapist the dreamer, I learned thick dreamless sleep from him. He took my sleeping, twisted it like an arm until it broke. Middle of the night, whatever inexplicable misery he had planned for me, I came a small, lonely child, roused from sleep, body warm and pliable. And later blood wiped off lips, semen mopped from thighs, wrists and ankles untied, pajamas slipped back on, I returned to sleep, the night's terror becoming my dream, my dreams slipping over the edge. Mornings after, I woke, self returning to self, ate my oatmeal, went to school, played tetherball and four square at recess, as if nothing had happened. I grew, a berry bramble untouchable. I didn't dream for 30 years.

And when you wake next, the wind and sun pushing at your skin, you won't remember any of the details, not the coyotes, not the stars, not the wild dream sex, only that your body is fuller than it's ever been. Who if not girl, boy, child, gimp, rain, river, chinook, heat, bramble?

The man I used to call father, let him tumble forever. I have stormed his bunker, picked the lock, found my heart amidst the rubble, laughed him off the edge of the world.

No longer small and lonely, I live among the furious and joyful. We dance, sing, drum, limp, roll, walk, swish, howl our way though the world. The next 10,000 miles await, wild open of sky. I'll no longer pretend, no longer be afraid: neither girl nor boy, I am a boulder that splits the current and dreams.

Because Poems are Kisses,
Fists, and Underground Rivers

Because poems are stiletto heels in the hands of drag queens and femmes, ready to be thrown, ready to be worn, fierce and beautiful.

> *In high school I started writing poems because I sat in sixth period study hall bored out of my mind. I chose the only alternative—Mr. Beckman's poetry class. It held no appeal. I hated poetry and didn't like the teacher much more, but I was bored enough to give it a try.*

Because poems are Chinook salmon swimming upstream to their spawning beds, old growth Douglas fir dappling the ground in shadow.

> *We wrote poems, read poems, sent poems out for publication, proudly collected our rejection letters. I fell in love.*

Because poems are mountainsides clearcut for lumber and paper, mountaintops blasted and bulldozed for coal, pale green of new growth already returning.

> *In that tiny backwoods school none of us studied AP English or became National Merit Scholars. Rather we ended up single mothers and grocery store clerks, gas station attendants and regulars at Pitch's Tavern. We read every book in our town's one room public library and died in drunken car crashes.*

Because poems limp and stammer, tremor and drool, hallucinate and have panic attacks. Because they are cracks, crevices, faultlines.

> *We took fieldtrips. Drove hundreds of miles. Heard Carolyn Kizer, Galloway Kinnell, Gary Snyder read their poems. Studied Walt Whitman but not June Jordan, Emily Dickinson but not Lucille Clifton.*

Because poems stand in line at the welfare office; collect food stamps, Medicaid, SSI. Because they gossip, laugh, pass the word, "Don't let 'em get you down." Because poems are kisses, fists, and underground rivers.

> *Poetry grabbed me by the collar, whispered in my ear, "You're coming with me." I followed willingly, not knowing where we were headed.*

Because poems are quilts passed from grandmother to grandchild, the frayed cloth of three generations sewn and resewn. Because they are old protest songs and riotous graffiti, tattoos and sandhill cranes trumpeting at dawn.

> *Later I joined a peace march, walked from Los Angeles to Washington DC, 3,700 miles for global nuclear disarmament. I couldn't stop writing.*

Because poems are driftwood logs rolling in the surf, barnacles gripping the rock, fishermen hunkering over coffee at 4 am before they drive down to their boats to begin another 14 hour day.

> *We sang in church basements, told stories in greasy spoon cafes, camped in city parks and cow pastures, read poems at peace rallies. We held vigil, blocked traffic, and got hauled off to jail.*

Because poems are earthquakes, hurricanes, rivers swollen beyond their banks; the shovels and pick axes used to dig out.

> *I dreamed, walked, woke up with poems, words clamoring and insistent. Wrote about missile silos and army depots, cornfields and garbage dumps. I memorized my poems, stepped up to the microphone. I didn't feel bold.*

Because poems are not traded on Wall Street. Nor are they variable interest loans, foreclosed mortgages, the endless paperwork of bankruptcy.

> *At those peace rallies and coffeehouses, my voice shook and cracked, sometimes beginning to carry.*

Because poems happen after rapes and police beatings. Happen late at night on death row and in army barracks. Because poems are the groan of good sex, the thud of grief, the quiet after big change; I am a poet.

Ely Shipley

Encounter

In shop windows, torsos
of mannequins, and a cricket
nests in the chest of one.

It is not a heart, but longs for
its other. Exhaling

mist, I push away
from this glass, feel
my sex is a sea

shell, its slug, small
mollusk, shrinking into its own

wetness or elongating into
a hardness. I think of the male sea

horse, carrying the female's
eggs, birthing thousands
of fry, a semenlike spray–

out and away with no
receptacle, except this

world, submerged. And so
the self is multiplied. Once

home, I see
my face through the fogged

bathroom mirror, at the bottom
of a teacup, inside polished
silver, or at the bulbous end

of a long-stem wineglass, where
my lip meets its and I remember

that it has been made
from blown glass,

the shape of someone's
breath, held.

Boy with Flowers

My aunt loved me, asked me:
will you be the flower
girl at my wedding? But I'm not
a girl, I argued, and she persuaded me:
you'll get to throw rose petals

onto the aisle, walk before me, both of us
crushing them beneath our feet, my gown
dragging over them. I agreed. I wanted
nothing but chivalry.

At the church, my mother and I
waited in the small room. She brushed
my aunt's hair until the dress arrived.
Isn't it beautiful? And I agreed until they tried
to put me in it. I'd seen my father

and uncle earlier, standing in a circle

of other men, smoke hovering over their heads
and their voices kind, quiet, and deep. I told my aunt –
I want to wear a suit like them! She promised

if I wore the dress I could wear anything
I wanted after: army pants, a sheriff
badge, cowboy hat, and pistols. My mother shot her
a look in the mirror where we posed, both of them
angelic in white, and me, not yet

dressed. Today I wake from another dream
in which I have a beard, no breasts
and am about to go skinny-dipping
on a foreign beach with four other men.

I'm afraid to undress, won't take off my shorts,
so they grab me, one at each ankle, the other two
by each wrist. I am a starfish hardening.
The sun hovers above, a hot
mirror where I search for my reflection.

I close my eyes. It's too intense. The light
where my lover is tracing fingertips
around two long incisions in my chest. Each sewn tight
with stitches, each a naked stem, flaring with thorns.

In the Film

A woman tells
her therapist she hears
rabbits live their whole lives
without a noise
until killed, then scream,

and sound almost human.
There is no music, only

the clatter of her speech,
which ricochets through my head
while something lodges

in my throat, sharp
as a stone shot from
the heart's sling. Inside

the theater, my breath
quickens. I am sliding
backward, trying to climb

a barbed-wire fence
when I was ten. Tangled up
I wanted to yell for help.
I'd been playing war
with a boy and winning

until I launched a rock
so high I couldn't tell where it would land.
It seemed to get lost

in the sun, to become the sun
for a moment, then
fall, striking his skull. A line

of red divided his face. I ran,
never saw him again. The woman
in the movie falls

in love but still feels
trapped. I know because
one night she makes love in the choir
loft of an abandoned church. The roof

seems as though it is peeled
open and the camera
closes in so I can look

down on her. It begins to rain,
and when she comes
the noise she makes, breathing heavily

into the man's hair, which is long and sways
like a curtain back and forth across his face,
sounds like singing.

Six

The neck of the guitar stretches
out, every other fret painted with a sharp
dot or dash, flash after flash

of reflected light, marble or pearl, the shape
of a fingerprint, the measure of each
note trapped inside
the instrument's dark.

Outside, a hailstorm
and the sound of crumpled up
grade-school exams once
smacking against

my skull, paper fists thrown angry
in torrents, and six-year-old
laughter that fell
all around me as I sat inside

a classroom, in a warm pool
of my own urine. I'd been ashamed
to go to the girls' room at recess,
because I was a boy,

they'd said. But the recess lady made me
stay away from the boys' room: You are

a girl. And later, my teacher: No,

no hall pass for the rest
of the year. So my body couldn't stop
secreting in class. Even my eyes and nose
seeped with the stuff. Out of control,

I heaved sobs between sharply phrased
taunts of what, what are you?
But tonight, I only want to be
the mouth

of a guitar, hollowed out
and bodiless
except for that balloon
of sound resonating invisibly

through air, and go on
pressing my fingers deeper in
to the neck, as if I could find
a shape inside

its voice as I choke
out its notes, its high-pitched
scream, its pop.

Dear C.—

The side of your house peeled open.
Our friends rowed up in small boats
with lanterns, and waited for you to open your curtains, red
and flecked with gold. I thought of your tongue
and your tooth, your gift horse tattoo. Everyone
expected you to sing karaoke. But you were blowing
some old guy inside the dragon-swing ride
on the pier outside our favorite bar. The sound of its piano
drifting out over the water must have made you want

to die. When he left he pressed a crumpled bill
into your fist. You held it like a flower, then tossed it
into the waves. I swam beneath you
to catch it. That's when the curtain lifted
and your room was a sail filling with light.
We could see your face there, a movie, crying.
But no one could hear you. It started to rain.
Everyone opened their umbrellas and watched
until the wind carried you away.

Etymology

Strange that you'd let me
give birth
to my own body

even though I know I've always been
a boy, moving
toward what? Manhood? A constant

puberty? I could replace my menses
with a thick needle
filled with your fluid, thrust every

two weeks the rest of my life
into my thigh. And I think
of the six days of creation before

God rested, because I too am tired
and because my voice, would it suddenly be
God-like to me, thundering,

waking in a deep vibrato as if from atop
a mountain, maybe Olympus, maybe
a lightning bolt shot sharp

through my heart because I am
startled, scared, delighted?
You are the Magnetic

Fields, Elvis, and molasses, the first time
I heard Nina Simone sing, unsure of her
and my own sex at age 13. You are

an eighteen-wheeler ripping through
a hailstorm, the umpire breathing
over the catcher's shoulder until

the ball burns into the mitt
and there is the deep growl
ascending, *Strike one!*

And I am struck
hard by the beauty of you. I am
again an eight-year-old boy, simply

admiring a tree in the schoolyard, my only
friend who lifts me
and lifts me so that I can pick

its single spring
flower, the lowest one, maybe
for my mother, maybe my father–

but end up placing it inside
my first and only dictionary, a gift
from my father on the first day

of that school year. And later
when it has dried, wilted, I
remove it. Only a stain left, small

shadow, the handprint of
a child
quieting the words.

Post-Inversion Vision

We chase each other over
wood planked rooftops
when the one boy with Down syndrome
lifts his shirt to show us
a raven perched
in his chest, one claw carrying
his berry-like nipple. C lifts her
black dress overhead, flashing
an umbrella away & across her
torso a canvas between hip & rib, a red
sky clouds & shadows
there. A single spiral angles
down, tornado white.
On the wall, a woman's black face,
created from projected light,
bares teeth, then breasts.
Embedded in one are two
pearls or eggs. It could be my mother's
cancer or she is an oyster.
I can't explain
the poem I am
reading this morning
at our wooden breakfast
table that hovers over my thighs
& bare feet. Yesterday,
C said they were haloed
from sun streaming in
from a window overhead. I felt
I could fly
when C turned
my body over hers.

Night a ladder we climb to reach

clouds. Away the stars but city lights
glitter in water below. Sharp
wind against our teeth. The boy with the dread
locks and curled nails holds out
his stalk, red
bulb. We eat the bitter
mushroom from his claw. The rooftop
fortress and sky. Along
the ledge we perch. Gargoyles. Cars
beneath us, heavy stones rolling
over stone, bat squeals
from caves of alleys. The rising sun has never been
more silent. We raise our arms. Laundry
bows between bright windows.

Deer between fallen branches

Snow fills the eyes of the winter
animal. She's like a photograph

of himself as a child, feet dangling
over the side of a boat, skimming

the water's surface. His bare chest
lit from sun shimmering off

the lake. The eye drowns
in what it still might see. Love,
don't you dare

touch the velvet muzzle, cool flank,
gray hoof. Desire, a slim antler,
the teething he quiets with a mouthful

of snow. Wind gallops
through trees. Above

a branch breaks
sharp from his skull.

The Transformative and Queer Language of Poetry

Poetry's otherness to my own multiple socially defined otherness is a space of freedom, where lack becomes pure potential. [1]*--Reginald Shepherd*

Consider the poem itself as a body, an extension of the writer. Recall Charles Olson's statement that "the line comes (I swear it) from the breath," Walt Whitman: "touch this book and touch a man," or Frank O'Hara, who writes that the poem should occupy a position, "Lucky Pierre Style…[putting] the poem squarely between the poet and the person…and the poem is correspondingly gratified. The poem is at last between two persons instead of two pages." Robin Blaser writes in "Image-Nation," "dear beings, I can feel your hands," and later, "our words were / the form we entered."

How does one begin to write a body that has been historically illegible? I find that poetic language can allow us to pursue (through its visceral, bodily qualities) sensations that are, perhaps paradoxically, actually beyond language. Poems open possibility; they transform reader and writer alike.

A definite and precise articulation of my identity is not something at which I or anyone will ever arrive. So, what happens if instead of buying into such an illusion, we see the many "other" ways to be through poetry's otherness, as Reginald Shepherd suggests, in order to see this "lack as pure potential"? Poetic language offers possibility outside barriers and constructions of identity. Poetic language offers what spoken, everyday language cannot.

One example of my version of this vision is my poem "Six." While this poem engages the terms of language that all of us are born into and the accompanying illusions of wholeness and selfhood we are subjected to, it also articulates these ideas as sites of trauma, violence, and also transformation. But the transformation is primarily one of perception and can only take place through the body of the poem. The speaker does not appease hir desire and transform into a whole and fulfilled self, something surely impossible. In fact, the speaker's body is entirely out of bounds, it doesn't make sense in the normative social world; rather, it is uncontained, and "secreting." Instead of trying to write this body into submission, into conformity: boy or girl, he or she, the poem moves outside of these familiar linguistic binaries. Retrospectively, the speaker relies on an other, the not-body, the "mouth // of the guitar, hollowed out / and bodiless." A kind of transcendence, through a giving over to this "voice," this vehicle of sound, happens.

Of course, the poem relies on language, and even a kind of control through this figurative body. But at some point metaphor breaks down. One is not like the other. Language and body, normative or otherwise, are obliterated, at least conditionally: "as if I could find / a shape inside // its voice as I choke / out its notes, its high pitched / scream, its pop." There is violence and destruction, but also transcendence, creation, and, importantly, perpetual motion and a sense of continual questioning.

In many of my poems, poetic language--through the use of metaphor, imagery, juxtaposition, line break, pacing, and so on--allows for a multiplicitous and liminal sense of a self in transit. Because I have understood myself from as early as I can remember as other, as different, odd, and strange (synonymous with queer), I've had access to self-consciousness. Any illusion of myself as whole, static, or complete was thrown into relief fairly early on as many of my autobiographical poems show. As a child, I inhabited more than one world--like most children. However, my real world and the imaginary world(s) were marked, divided along the lines of gender. In my real life I was a girl, or more often, an illegible gender. In my interior life, I was "a different kind of boy." My gender expression is not, nor was it, fixed, but even now moves in relation to ever shifting contexts. I'm certain that this is true for most people. We are all raced, classed, gendered, etc. It's just that some, due to any number of circumstances, can't afford not to pay attention.

Poetic language, or queered language, allows me both a way to allude to my circumstance as a queer trans person, a way to be visible, a way not to pass as whatever is deemed normal or socially acceptable; I may continually resist reduction into assumed and constructed identity categories. To be "both/and," to be not at all, or to keep shifting are queer notions indeed. Poetic language keeps possibilities for desire, for identity, for language, for new embodiments open. I struggle toward a sense of self that will never be fulfilled. And yet, that space of unfulfillment is the very source of my imaginative energy.

Notes:

[1] Shepard, Reginald. "The Other's Other: Against Identity Poetry, for Possibility," *Orpheus in the Bronx: essays on identity, politics, and the freedom of poetry*. Ann Arbor, MI: University of Michigan Press, 2008.

Emerson Whitney

With Enigmatic Loving

From West

Dear You,
(a text message from DFW airport)

before 1880 there was no official time
you are a fiery eclipse
& I am one hair of yours
waking, here

Dallas, where are your people? All your plants are paved or paid for. I am trying to bond with you but your only wildlife are plastic bags resembling birds being hit & hit on the highway

Once, after running out of gas on the way to Colorado, your mom invited me for bologna. Now, your brother is dividing her jewelry and me. Dead Amarillo.

E _ _ _ _ learned to speak Texan E _ _ _ _ moved east (New London) E _ _ _ _ was born in Dallas by a different Father E _ _ _ _ doesn't know E _ _ _ _ was hers THEY are his 1/2

Translation: how is silence different from voice?

Palo Duro Canyon: brown yellow blue orange strata—dried water dust blonde texas—I am
not-blood—how did we end up here, stinking like meat?—we might not
ever be back through the canyon—cotton blowing across the road—your canyon—
there's nothing I can do but look for pools in the cliffs and your eyes—your brothers
will sell your toys on EBAY

Thus far, E _ _ _ _ couldn't be less and more like you. When you walked E _ _ _ _
around central park zoo. And E _ _ _ _ met you. E _ _ _ _ wanted to curl into a warm
sweatshirt of yours on the floor.

And when Dead BEVO and Dead BULL handed E_ _ _ _ *Peterson's First Guide to*
Clouds and Weather: A Simplified Field Guide to the Atmosphere in 1993, E_ _ _ _
wrote a poem.

The inscription says:

Happy Birthday, May all your clouds (sic)
Watching be happy times with rainbows,
Love Grandmother + Grandaddy Cowden

Now, "a funnel cloud drops from a ring of cloud protruding from the base of an
intense _____" and your funeral's over

Translation: *how can I write of your eyes and us?*

Dear You,
(text message from I-40)

you are the most beautiful shadow I've ever seen, waning
we are grandiloquent curls, reverb and holographic
lip my jaw line dirt as blood
your taste is back of the tongue, winged
wearing fur and frozen headdress
and we are going—

Too East

This is a return to personhood
& an island

Childhood self (in an incubating phase) slapped jelly fish with a spatula onto rocks
against the sea. Dried jellyfish became cloudy blinking eye shapes. Now you're
breathing on my fingers. I've broken into branches and smatterings of light. We found
the cemetery yesterday.

Four weeks ago an island grew from salt/thoughts.

This process has become an unveiling. It's 4:30 a.m. I have one lamp—no shade—in
the center of a room obscured by papers, $$

Dear You,
(text message from Neighborhood Rd.)

> the white schoolhouse steeple is saturated meringue-blue
> i am suspended slightly from the ceiling with
> my underwear pulled to my ankles
> you are paper flames flickering
> we are a shadow box, diorama
> wearing white/yellow rope wings
> let's ebb west, gripping our
> sheets, the sea

Translation: In an aggression, doubt coats the bathtub & rots the floor.

New London: childhood self lived in Eminent Doman & would find golden pieces of peeling rock to put all over face—grey bubbling submarines with nipple apparatuses are always black, black grey--Pfizer pulls 1,400 jobs out of town and within two years, moves most of them a few miles away to a campus it owns in Groton, Conn—seagulls swoop with knots of seaweed into Pfizer steam/smoke--Pfizer leaves behind the city's biggest office complex—an old man jumps from the ferry and dies, it was Cape Henlopen (kay-pen-lo-pen)—an adjacent swath of barren land that was cleared of dozens of homes to make room for a hotel, stores and condominiums that were never built (NYT 2009)

Translation: my introduction to the Sea.

Dear You,
(text message from I-95)

The moon is making human shadows of debris on the beach
I cannot breathe
without thinking of salt and salt you
I traced my body out in beetles—
I am the blue belly of your bird

Now, the percussion of your eyes is wild. I feel born of you and unto you. All of my limbs want their wateriness back. I want to break my fingers off and throw them to you.

So we sing:
Oh the moon
and the stars
and the wind in the sky
all night long sing a lullaby
while down in the ocean, so dark and so deep
the silvery waves wash the fishes to sleep

Mom, 1986

Translation: The brightness of this feeling is a teary ricochet.

When I was ten years old, I was prescribed hydro codeine for screaming—my grandmother screams this way—my mother screams this way—my father screams this way—my brother screams this way—I thumbed at it today from a fishing boat—where they kill starfish eating $$ on the deck

Definition of chronic

_____

_____

_____

Translation: Oh, your wind was so gracious and your water so white.

Do North

Dear You,
(a text message from bed)

> fabulous is a resembling or suggesting of fable //
> fabulous is of an incredible, astonishing, or exaggerated nature
> fabulous has duct tape on its genitals
> and my first concern was the ocean and a mother

Mom, When I try to breathe deeply for more than a moment I can't. My concern is you & all of you. *So set me off*, you said

"His inhalation results in decreasing chest movement rather than chest expansion"—if my mouth made noises, then you'd know me--if my mouth was open, you'd walk in—where then—poor ventilation of the lungs, carbon dioxide buildup, oxygen depletion in the blood—am I?

Last week, I asked you to whip me. Since then, I've been breathing from my asshole for you.

At eleven-thirty, memories of wet streets and people have eroded into now and I'm listening to the 70 and 80-year-olds whispering: *you are behind me.*

Last night, I dreamt that your neighbor's house caught fire, then the one next to it. We called 911 to save ourselves. I lost myself in crowd of lobstermen.

And we sang:

> You are made of seaweed and salts
> I am unchanged and ripping
> all of my insides run through your hair, your teeth
> I belong to you and your fingers

And Mom texted me yesterday: It wud be great 2 hav u both as neighbors! I cud feed the cat if u wer gone! To hang out and feel like ur mom aftr al wev been threw wud be amazing :-D

But yesterday, I untied the laces across my chest and a larger governance "or her, or it" confused me with _____. So, I rubbed myself in unacceptable thoughts, unacceptable thoughts, unacceptable colors, and objectionable, inconvenient bodies--

And today, when we walk onto Sullivan and Houston, wearing mostly blood, someone yells faggot from a window and you pull my underwear down to show them--I stop holding words away from you and the breeze--we taste like talons, let's rub rish under our eyes--

Less common than mouth or upper chest breathing is backward or paradoxical (breathing) I unzipped you so quickly (in) another habit that undermines respiratory efficiency (out) and there's a swimming heat to you (out) paradoxical breathing involves sucking of the abdomen in (out) during breath an inhalation is (in) and (in) pursing it out (out) during exhalation (in) I am wet and glowing (out) this habit is common in people who have undergone the shock of trauma (in) I hope you understand (out)

Poetics Statement

Dear Reader,

"With Enigmatic Loving" is a traipsing, it's an island. It reads watery and from all sides. Thematically, it straddles isolation, detachment, and encirclement. It is surrounded, full.

While writing this piece, I found myself whispering: "I am a thing resembling an island, a detached portion..." and what was wrought from those whispers is this piece. As such, "With Enigmatic Loving" explores attachment and belonging through matters of place and family. It moves from Dallas, Texas, to New London, Connecticut, to an island off the coast of Maine. And through craggy islets of poetics, arrives at deep breath.

In crafting this piece, I realized that my insides resembled the island to which my lover and I relocated in 2010. From New York City, we moved between my mother and her parents on a short stretch of road. It was the first time I'd lived near my mother and my grandparents since we'd shared a house in New London during my childhood. At the same time, my ex-step-father and father to my half-brothers (I am still curious about how to best name the non-blood, paternal nature of relationship) lost his parents and I traveled to West Texas to be with him and his/our family.

"With Enigmatic Loving" is the not-ness of all that, it is dispatches from the moat between self and other, family and identity. The piece ruminates on intentions to heal relations between my mother and myself. It juts onto peninsulas of "difference." And features tiny notes written to my lover—sexuality, gender-variance, sadomasochism. Too, it is a love note to my queer body, which is in this piece laughing, full of blood. This work was greatly influenced by Bhanu Kapil's *Humanimal*, Hiromi Ito's *Killing Kanoko*, *Poems of the Black Object* by Ronaldo V. Wilson, and *Deviant Propulsions* by CA Conrad.

With this work and all that I do, I hope my art is alchemy. I want to remake thoughts and emotions into digestible forms. I thrive on piquing and inciting the experience of emotion through shape and content. I am a trickster. And I want to broaden the boundaries of words themselves. I hope to anchor this aim in a practice of art- making that enkindles the experience of emotion, of magic and deviance. Thank you for reading.

Love,

Emerson

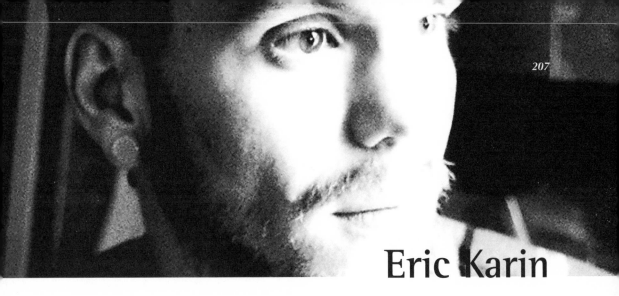

Eric Karin

Verses Vs.

I swallowed the royal jelly.
>A white stone with a new name on it.

Stone piled on stone.
>Them and she and he and me.

>>We played the creek like a pipe.
>>>My smallest parts grew.

The waterfall stood like a pillar.
>He gave me a scroll and told me to eat it.

I was surprised by ritual.
>Each good act inspired ten more.

This dirt is holy.
>We carried water from the source.

The leeks and herbs.
>And darkest berry.

The green veil drops.
>The creek wound into a bed of black snakes.

A season has arrived, they said.
>*This wall will fall.*

Water over ice.
       Sound dissipated just beyond the glass.

A keystone in the rubble.
          We rode the bridge, spread ten miles over water.

       A sundog seen from the top of the skyscraper.
            Wounds faded into summer among the spread-eagle
       buildings.

A salting of stones. Glass like chrysanthemum lace.
               Nevermind cancellation.

      We now have an opening.
       The survival of mutation.

All dirt is all the same in her eyes.
       Yield signs, autumn harvest.

New kinds begin to appear.
      Melting ice on national tv.

Freight trains, glacial moraines.
       Dancing poles, auroras elsewhere.

Better to meet a bear robbed of her cubs.
            Employed with artful imitation.

Even if I were innocent, my mouth would condemn me.
          If I forget my complaint, I will change my expression and
       smile.

      Build a high gate, invite destruction.
           Each gate made of a single pearl.

Wall of jasper, gold, glass.
      Water marking the absence of a town.

A token of government.
>Monetary exchange.

Scrolls of lightning rolled to the water's edge, heralding an exit.
>A sea of glass, mixed with fire.

>*Oxygen*, she mouthed.
>>The dictionary opened like a wound.

If only this were complaint.
>We spent months at the hearth.

>>The walls; steel, concrete, glass.
>>>Visibility eroded by rain.

Which, according to the book of men, is *falling*.

Rub

A grey goo spread
Across the face of the Cosmos—

  Whom you offered a handkerchief
Given to you from your mother, by her grandmother

Embroidered with the phrase "Thank You"
  Surrounded by posies.

Healer

When the healer is called, she or he or they comes, merrily. They arrive in moments. Wind opens the door for them— they were invited, after all. After all, they are not vampiric demons. There is plenty of room for the instruments of healing they bring, the echo of recitation, an evocation of ritualistic association-building, intuition, attention, affection, table, and clean linens— room for all…

"Healer"

Across the street, in a hospital slated for demolition, there is a demon with a healer's mask. The demon makes money by selling "Health" with a healer's mask. "Health can be sold," the demon surmises, "in packages, as an object." There are demonstrations. "Health" seems to do what it says it will do. Once purchased, Health follows you to your house. Once inside, Health follows you around the house. No one says, "I am haunted by Health." But they think it. Or want to think it. So they dream it. Health no longer looks like "Health." Health is a relative, a present person with a past. You dream that you sense the throne of fear inside and follow whatever sense you have to the end of the hall where two mirrors hang in opposition...

Mise en Abyme

Self-portraiture is not essentially narcissistic, nor is the exposure of genitals to the wind in a hall of lovers. What is it then. The sounds scalloped by the Gulf pumped into the tub. A mode of comparison, ergo, contextualization.   A fairway to the middle. A card of Temperance. A portmanteau. A series of questions without stop. The severed head blinks for 11 seconds...

Love in a Vacuum

Sometimes, I turn the volume down so low I can hear the direction. I get out of the car and my phantom limbs shift. My thoughts trail to the bend. Like soap bubbles, it takes a certain amount of breath to merge the maps of memory. Suddenly, unity. The milky experience of time condenses, the amplified spiral path of galaxies sweetens. Iterations of the I are footsteps. Also, pines...

Poetics Statement

Poetry is cybernetic, artificially intelligent. In a sense, poems are extension of the being; in another, they exist autonomously as part of the universe, with lives of their own, interacting, sometimes merging with other poetic/humanoid entities. Our extensions (whether they be limbs or poems) are part of the body, born of personal and collective exchanges of information interwoven together at every macro/micro level.

If writing is application of the mind, then it is also application of the body via the mind. In a number of mystic philosophies, there are bodies other than the physical body, (that often correspond to the physical body,) these psycho-spiritual constituents are called subtle bodies. The mind, a subtle body, a mental body. The mind's desires that drive us to new limbs, endless tentacles are questions of the body.

If Donna Haraway's cyborg myth is about "transgressed boundaries, potent fusions, and dangerous possibilities which progressive people might explore as one part of needed political work" then poets are indeed cyborgs cross-pollinated with Gloria Anzaldúa's mestiza consciousness:

> The mestizo and the queer exist at this time and point on the evolutionary continuum
> for a purpose. We are a blending that proves that all blood is intricately woven
> together, and that we are spawned out of similar souls (Anzaldúa).

Like the cyborg, the mestiza is the offspring of hybridity, specifically concerned the merging of different cutlures, various bloodlines. My questions of the body/text are those of hybridity—they are those concerned with culture, identity, technology and how aesthetic interacts with (the often psychological) function: What chimeric-cryptid will I become? Which make-up will be the right alchemical combination to help me feel like a vampire-mermaid-diva-goth? Once I have shifted shape, new consciousness develops. New intuitions, awarenesses, and questions spring forth. Conversations mutate. Atavisms arise. Lazarus taxon species are found—not only with the tools of technology, but with the consciousness-shifts of mystics and shamans. Poetry is a sociopolitical act that recombines the values of magic and science—the search for new meanings—to mire through the bogs of abyss and mists of the unknown.

> Write yourself. Your body must be heard. Only then will the immense resources of
> the unconscious spring forth...Write! and your self-seeking text will know itself
> better than flesh and blood, rising, insurrectionary dough kneading itself, with
> sonorous, perfumed ingredients, a lively combination of flying colors, leaves, and
> rivers plunging into the sea we feed (Cixous).

If I write my bodies, their states, then I write without the labels of critics, the identifications of taxonomers. (These acts happen retroactively—and may cage the spawn of poetry—attempt to raise it in captivity.) I am politically aligned with the transcendent, the mysterious spaces in and outside of gender—the transgender, genderqueer. Part animal, part technology, we cyborg shape-shifters are the heirs of hybridity, transcendence; the reconciliation of endless dualisms, mind/body "problems," etc. We, the bodies, write the bodies—figuratively at first, influencing individual conciousnesses, until the bodies have enough (social, cultural) gravity to influence the trajectory of possibility—allowing for a more flexible reality. One where the oppressed, the dispossessed are writen back into the books they were writen out of.

I sing to know I am alive; I write to stay alive, to regenerate my body. Living, staying alive, loving, vibrating with love to dissolve the fear of death, of being alone, of being with others, of sex, of completion, of incompletion. This fear is the way systems of oppression affect us all, by framing positionalities as irreconcilable, unrelatable, or essentialist differences.

Inger Christensen writes in "Epilogos" of it:

> Eccentric attempts / when a man / steps out of himself / steps out of / his daily life
> his function / his situation / steps out of / his habits / his peaceful / condition we call
> the process / ecstasy

In this process, one may transcend the suggested repetitions of past in present. Christensen then superimposes this idea of ecstatic process onto the body—here the intensity of intercourse/ outercourse are translated into discourse. The body is the text, words comprise its cellular composition.

> when the body / is outside / itself / and inside / another / illuminated / freed / at peace
> / the cells are words

The state of ecstasy in which one is "outside of oneself" is not the opiate pleasure of dissociation or distraction but the inclination toward wholeness and connection. In other words, writing is a thing to be written, as Woolf says, with "no obstacle in it, no foreign matter unconsumed."

> a language / that tells / that the abyss / between us / is filled

Writing toward ecstasy helps us leave our addictions, the habits born of coping with trauma, that have outlived their usefulness. Writing towards ecstasy help us reconcile the voids we experience, those left by the wounds of oppression, of disconnection, of "divide and conquer"— within our/selves, our various bodies, and the entities of our every connection.

Works Cited

Anzaldúa, Gloria. "La Conciencia de la Mestiza: Towards a New Consciousness," *Feminist Theory Reader: Local and Global Perspectives*. Ed Carole R. McCann and Seung-Kyung Kim. New York: Routledge. 2003. 179–87. Print.

Cixous, Hélène. "The Laugh of the Medusa" *New French Feminisms*. Ed. Elaine Marks and Isabelle de Courtivron. New York: Schocken Books, 1981. 250. Print.

Christensen, Inger. "Epilogos" *it*. Trans. Susanna Nied. New York: New Directions, 2006.

Fabian Romero

Boi-ness

Marimacho
pretty boi
androgyny

as a child
gay was hidden like the mismatched nails in the utility drawer
a bad word to spew towards the lowest of lows
people who broke trust
people who hurt us
and I heard the word shoot out like ametralladora
a machine gun loaded with the deadliest bullet
5.66mm le Mas of words
almost invisible term
meant to reach every organ with its degrading poison

now i felt the first tingle of my queerness
when tomboys brushed my side
and I became tongue tied
wanting to avoid the deadly bullet
I pretended to not feel a thing

adulthood taught me to turn off my intuition
to be guided by other people's definitions
and I became all that others wanted of me

in my teens
the hiding began
the feelings began
and they flooded me
inside still contained by my natural instinct to knock down my knowledge
to mimic internal deforestation
to see my boiness/queerness as a land hard to cross
another desert to trek through
another river to be tossed into
another van, train, bus, anonymous car to ride
another migration
to risk my life in order to get there

my fresh migration mind saw my boiness this way
libertad far away
an unreachable land
that if I could only get to my heart could once again beat
like the palpitations I felt at the sight of genderqueers or very clearly queers
like the shortness of oxygen that shocked my body into recognition
that that bullet was headed my way

I knocked down my self made borders
still knowing that the sophisticated psychology waited to find me
to turn me in
to pressure me to pretend to love someone I felt nothing for
        to dress safely and feign hetero-normality
to intoxicate my body in order to feign the wetness that came naturally with gender-
unknown undefined or hetero-challenging people

my first experience of love was with a fierce woman
she felt like my passport
my visa
a relief of safety to experiment with my queerness
finally play with the elaborate dress
que me imagino queer women ancestors
mastered to survive in a world of invisibility
coming to love myself I meet more like me
and the radical reality that I am dressing to impress me
not to attract the attention of those who use gay to wound me

I am a Marimacho pretty boi
a wake up to feel my skin as it should be boi
a knowing of the arms held to push me into hiding boi
a knowing of the bullets aimed at me boi
a Marimacho boi
pretty boi

Mocho

figure this much
I speak mocho
a cut off spanish from the root
an uprooted spanish
a concoction of words like a mixed drink of intoxicated phrases
invasive language of english that chokes my root
drinks the nutrients of my fertile cultural ground
          while assimilation shock still shakes my vocal focus

I, Marimacho, Chicano
hybrid breed mixed blood
dreams still spent in ancestral land
day reality spent environmentally exposed to concrete grounds and constant reminder
of other
I am other
My mother tongue hides beneath perfectly pronounced words
dominant language mastered
          I pass as Americana
pass el despacho de aduanas with less harassment than the rest from mi tierra
Mi pueblo
mi paiz

and still mi lengua
my community
that raised me from infancy
now helps me swallow down words
and phrases and collected in the hanging vocal imagery

lengua
a once automatic verbal ceremony
a once automatic verbal ritual
now taken over
himalayan blackberry english

Figure this much
This is my peace
The slice of reality that I choose to give
giving back what the fields and fruit trees gave me
tierra education
learning more from the story of my father crossing the desert
        to make a path for my sister, and My pregnant mother mano en mano
in the summers of 1984-1991
finally to occupy a spot of the wait list of naturalization and
miseducation from 1991 to today
than from clearing my throat in hopes that my subtle accent won't be discovered
now I choose to listen
to the bones that weigh heavy with
sore movement from one hurt land to one that hurts me
and listen intently
to those like me
who choose to take back this land
one word at a time

My name

when I introduce myself
I want to write in pauses with the moments
that people see me and they see me
whole
the moments they pause with me
in unison, solidarity
of my true identity
of my how the folds of my flesh do not confine me
to the organization of femininity tied to female assigned at birth bodies

my body
carries a womb
carries breasts
carries a cunt
and I do not feel like a woman

perplexity
I want to write in pauses with the moments
that people see me and they do not see me whole
they might see the curve of my chest
they might hear my voice
and some are perplexed

I am Suavitel, tesoro, Fabiola,
Fabelo, Fabicat,
I am Favi
I am hija, tia, tio and hermana

mi mama still calls me her Hija
a simple M'ija
word meant to affirm the womb connection

My name is Fabian Ortiz Romero
I chose this name out sincerity
out of knowing that the way some people see me
is not how I see myself

My name is Fabian Ortiz Romero
No Not Fabian (anglofied)
Fabian Ortiz Romero!!
Let me spell it out for you

F as in Fruit, for la fruta I grew up picking
A as in Atecucario, Michoacan, mi hogar, My home
B as in Bano, por la vez que me orine porque no podia preguntar por el bano en
ingles
I as in immigrant, for the immigration that will define me for life
A as in Abby for the year I wore a name that wasn't mine porque questions about my

birth-name backed up the line.

N as in Now, as in mi nombre preferido. as in I choose this name and am needed to say it because my name is as much of me as the name I was born into.

I am Suavitel, tesoro, Fabiola,
Fabelo, Fabicat,
I am Favi
I am hijo, hija, tio, tia hermano, and hermana
I am Fabian Ortiz Romero

Alive

death's touch on the tips of fingers
        on the grip of rifles
        on the tip of pills
        on the bottom of intestines
        delicately
        a touch to remind me that I am alive

numbers cannot contain the magnitude of lives lost
sisters, community leaders, writers, artists, sisters
Brandi Martell, Paige Clay, Agnes Torres, Mark Aguhar,
your last days mentioned on the paper, on my screen
                        like graffiti waiting to be painted over

death muerte, media vida
I grew up between worlds
a legion of identities merging
but never knew how the intersections drew me closer to death
        in 2012 70% of all LGBT murder victims were people of color
        44% were trans women of color
in these numbers I cannot compare my life to those of trans women
whose bodies are seen as a threat to power
my body does not threaten masculinity in the same way

sisters

to those who have passed, to those who have come close
to those who have been pushed outside of safe spaces
In honor of you I replace my ego with humility
I take in your stories sincerely to help me act in solidarity
I take in the statistics
the numbers that are not accounted for
the bodies found without names
the names given without stories
the stories not yet told

In my mind your names mentioned on the paper, on my screen
                              like graffiti will not be painted over

Poetics Statement

I have a collection of diaries from my childhood that I wrote in everyday to
cope as a young queer immigrant. My diary entries are a mixture of short stories,
commentary and love poems. Writing saved my life. As a kid in Mexico I witnessed
the struggles of illiteracy and pursued writing with the same ferocity that my parents
had to hustle and survive. Most of my family in Mexico did not read or write but you
could never tell by their stories. My Mother is the greatest influence of my writing, she
is a "reluctant feminist" as I mention in my poem "My People." I feel inspired most by
the people whose stories are deemed unimportant because they are marginalized or
criminalized.

Writing is healing to me and every poem included in this anthology is a
testament to that. Coming out as gender-queer has been a long process starting when
I was a child. My first attempts were in choosing to wear my male cousin's hand me
downs over the dresses and skirts my mother threw at me. Whenever I felt isolated by
my peers I would try to fit in by appearing less tomboyish. I did experience teasing
but was not subjected to violence because of my deviance from gender norms like
many trans-women or gender-queers who are assigned male at birth experience; I
was mostly devalued and rejected by my peers and family members. I acknowledge
that being female assigned at birth grants me benefits, because of patriarchy, that trans
women do not experience.

As I became more confident in my writing I used it as my confidant and keeper
of secrets. Among those secrets is the reminiscence of a time in my life when a boy

cousin came to live with mis Abuelos and me. We were referred to as *Los Fabis* since both our names began with Fabi. We pushed the limits of the expectations we felt in our gender by trekking the gardens of the community as twins, two toddler boys or gender-less children both called Fabi among nonjudgmental foliage and trees. I felt truth in my body and hold this as the first memory of someone who understood my complexities. The innocence of this time in my life informs how I write about my connection to my gender-queer identity, how in innocence I was certain about my gender fluidity; how it became obscured with the muck of oppression and power.

I write to capture moments of sincerity and vulnerability. I write to connect to my ancestors, to heal and to inspire others to heal as well. As a Trans queer, Christian raised Brujo, US Citizen, Immigrant Chican@ I write to reach my people meaning all marginalized and invisibilized folks. I write to assist social change. I want to reach out to my readers as a learner, working to stay aware about privileges afforded to me because of oppressive powers and systems. By working to be aware of my privileges I can write from my core, and access the beauty from my struggles.

Gr Keer

who is a man

damn, you are
            ug
            ly

excuse me, sir-- ma'am? sirma'am? i mean

fuck me your cock is so   good

you're not that butch
you walk like a   } girl {

        handsome boy
        young buck
        son

did you have the surgery are you on
            T
        you should[n't]
            i can['t] tell

        are you *talking* to someone about this

fag

wrapped around my invisible cock

your pussy pumps my blood straight
through to my heart

you know,
you could
                pluck
                            that

what is it
what are you
what the fuck is it

this is the ladies' room.

suck my dick, boi, like that
you like that don't you sweet
boi   open

you're not a real man

why you wanna be ugly
you could be pretty if you
try

is she
                trans
        ition
ing

nice tits

don't be so defensive

she-- he--
        [is here]
        [wants to tell you]
        [needs a good fuck]
        [is a librarian]

[is hot]
[needs a ride to work]
[is queer]
[needs to accept jesus into her-- his-- *shit.*]

it's just that you're not trans   enough
        you [don't] pass

dyke

crossing the line

seven pepper birds
wavered in watercolor silence
across a paper sky

on the day you decided not to die

and i beneath them
wondered

why

saffron revolution

Orderly in their robes and sandals closely shorn in formation with the people
marching peaceful hoping bringing quiet leaving quietly trapping suffering in saffron
bubbles lifting lifting ballooning breathing a thousand cleansing breaths until the
soldiers come with their boots and bullets burning through the towns

Death for bread death for bread   red red red

To see red is not enough, to see
the pools forming the holes forming the bullets screaming, to see is nothing

sympathy, an addiction   we bleed inside like always

The cells are pumping full of life
pushing it upstream
pulsing full of saffron robes and sandals

Peace peace peace peace peace peace swells up like an ache
we want the wars to stop we want the wars to stop stop stop stop stop stop stop stop
stop stop stop stop stop stop stop stop stop stop stop stop stop stop stop stop

The cells are bloodless   full of bodies

things that hum

i am the pin
in a planetary grenade

waiting for inspiration

i am the pin and the hand
the hand on the pin

that shakes
and hums
and wonders

the hand that grips and sweats
soothes and pets

regrets and
strikes without warning

and the pin that sits secured
with no eye to look toward morning

where i'm from

i am from the refrigerator, from Wonder Bread and whole milk
i am from the suburban willow tree. i am from the centipede and cicada.
i am from suicide and misery.
i am from the inability to take a deep breath and how it is to want, no matter how much you have
from "it will pass" and "sometimes you just have to put up with shit"
i am from a god who hates me
i'm from the snow in Minnesota, and suburban Pennsylvania and rural California
i'm from drunk vikings, spongy midwesterners, sharp east coast grandmothers who give presents, from swedish meatballs and pickled herring, from limp spaghetti and canned damp sauce
i'm from the irish broad who fed prisoners from her kitchen, from the strike breaker named Galileo and his cousin wife Jesse, from the little girl whose father cut down strange fruit on the Mississippi river and who somehow doesn't understand my sorrow
i am from a thousand photographs of danish gravestones on dvd, from ruddy cousins like hungry puppies and uncles dark and angry, from a printout of my pedigree.
i am from a place that's hard to see from here

connecting the dots

i.
the girls call me
killer, playground defender

tiny butch submarine, going
under

wooden toy patrolling the border
where the real boys are

ii.
we are the kind of friends who take
showers together, apparently

because you are taking off your shirt

i did not know you
were such a fan of

water conservation

i make up an excuse, feint
and parry

iii.
the southern girl next door
has blond hair, like me

but she is not like me

she is a sun flower
she is a yellow bird

she says, my name is

i think she's talking about
flowers

she says her name until i
know

hair.

it just keeps   fucking
          you know
                    growing!
jesus in all directions.

extruded like that play
doh thing spaghetti. springing hell   my melon,

my melons, jesus, really

mammals. what the fuck.

beastly tendrils turning heads
tender and heavy, what,

you'll have a   stroke, oh fuck it

jesus

a beard.

Poetics Statement

poetry traverses the space between experience and expression. a poem is an act of perpetual translation. a poet is a stranger, writing home.

i made my first book of poems in fourth grade, out of cardboard and wallpaper and basic rhymes. as a child i was a mystery to myself. my body was a locked box until i learned that i could open up my guts, pour them onto a piece of paper, mess around in them, and make something glorious. after that, i made poems out of excess tears, belly button lint, molten fury, fairy dust and all the things i couldn't say out loud. poetry is what shows me to myself. poetry is my context.

i write in order to examine the self; namely, my self: what is it made of? what does it want? how does it interact with its surroundings? where is it going? where has it been? who is it, and how do i make friends with it? i write to explore relationships: between inner and outer voices, between human beings, between people and our systems, between the individual and the universe. as a recent transplant to the west coast who moved for love, i write to investigate place, physical distance, isolation and separation, as well as connection and freedom. i write to make sense. i write to question the senseless. i write to find and create connection, to reintegrate my exiled selves, to enter into communion with my misfit tribes, to reconcile the past. i write to banish shame and conquer despair. i write as disobedience. i write to make myself.

i am fascinated and obsessed with how the body (my body or yours, or our bodies together) is read and misread and re-read, textually and texturally. as social creatures we cannot help but read each other, read into what we see, rewrite what we don't understand or can't comprehend. i am drawn to misreadings and "mistakes" and the ways in which they strengthen as well as disrupt mechanisms of social control. i am attracted to perversity and absurdity, that which brings us suddenly up against humility in the face of assumption. i am compelled to explore the borders between complaint and exultation, restraint and freedom, pain and pleasure, memory and fantasy, gender play and word play.

i believe that "the personal lyric as a poetic form helps us to live," [1] in very real physical, psychic, emotional, and spiritual ways. as a genderqueer person, i live my poetics on a daily basis. my ambiguous embodiment requires readings and re-readings, and invites misreadings and rewritings. the questions i am asked regularly include: are you a boy or a girl? are you in the wrong place? what makes you this way? to be queer is to be queried. poetry is a vehicle for answer and rebuttal, and a place of engagement, communication, compassion, and resistance.

[1] Orr, Gregory. Poetry and survival, The Writers Chronicle (2002).

HR Hegnauer

from **Sir**

Don't miss anything.

The date was twelve-twenty, twenty-ten, and this was exactly what Mrs. Alice said to me. She even grabbed my hand and repeated it. I thought this was pretty fancy of her.

Of course, I told her, *I wouldn't.*

When I was still a little girl, Sir once jokingly said to me, *call me Sir.* And so I mostly called him Sir.

Mrs. Alice and I have walked down this hallway a number of times now: before and after lunch, and before and after dinner, and during just about anytime that isn't exactly before or after any particular meal.

I am twenty-six-years-old, and — for the first time in my life — I have memories of myself as an adult. They vary in their lucidness, of course, but I can say that I have been an adult for a few years now, and I can remember what it is like to be one. My mother is exactly thirty years older than me, and Mrs. Alice is thirty years older than she, and I know I am not the only one between my mother and I who worries about the potentiality of dementia as being hereditary.

Mrs. Alice met Sir in high school. That was seventy years ago now. I don't really know how long seventy years is. I can only imagine most of twenty-six. How long is seventy?

I used to match my crew socks to Sir's: pulled up around our shins until a tan line so distinct would form that people thought we were painted ash white from the shins down when we'd walk around bare.

This is the part when Mrs. Alice would lean over the back of the couch and look out the front picture window with her camera to capture our matching gym-sock-covered shins. Sir would say, *walk steady now*, and I would say, *you know Hannah means graceful*, and Sir would say, *yeah, but you're always spelling it backwards*.

This was how we usually moved around this bay. Like a spliced thing trying to rivet its selves back together again, but not really knowing what this might actually look like anymore.

This was before I was given a dolphin-shaped squirt gun as a party favor at my friend's birthday. Of course I knew that toy guns were not allowed, but I thought this would be an exception, seeing as how it was shaped like a dolphin. This was before I was told to get rid of it.

I buried the dolphin in the back of the garden — right between my goldfish, Alfred, and my rabbit, Sarah-The-Boy. Alfred was named after the character in Guess Who who had orange hair because he looked just like him — having orange gills. The rabbit was named Sarah because I liked that name, and then we found out that she was a he, but he liked his name, and so we kept it. Turned out he liked his full name even more — Sarah-The-Boy, and so we called him this, and this was never strange. The dolphin was buried nameless.

Sir called late last weekend, around 10:30 or so. He said he couldn't get Mrs. Alice up out of her chair and into bed. I said, *What do you mean? … Just come over*. And so we went. There was a puddle, and then I knew what Sir meant, too. I said, *Mrs. Alice, it's time to get up out of this chair … I know*, she said, *I know. But I can't because, well, there's a puddle*. My mother held her forearm with her right hand and pushed against her lower back with her left, and she heaved her forward. I put the puddle in the garbage. I do not know how long Mrs. Alice had been sitting in her chair at the dining room table, and I do not like to think about how long or why either. Perhaps six hours or perhaps a few more really. It was as if she had all together forgotten she had a body anymore.

And then there was the embarrassment of remembering, *yes, I do have a body*.

I read somewhere that it's impossible to tell if dementia is hereditary or not because it's too common in elderly people.

Somehow it had come back. Because that's what it does. The cancer. It doesn't care where or how it started, and it doesn't care where or how it's going wherever it's going, but it knows it will get there. The cancer. It will get there. The colon, the lungs, the blood, the skin, etcetera, etcetera. It will get there.

Mrs. Alice, I have some sad news to share with you. There was a very long pause. *Mrs. Alice, Sir's been sick, and he had to go back into the hospital … Well, let's go visit him … Well, that's the thing, we can't … Well, did he die? …* I do not know how Mrs. Alice knew this, and it felt like my mouth was now somehow broken. *Yes … Sir has died?! My Sir has died? My Sir? My Sir? Died? Died? Dead? …* In this exact moment, I knew that Mrs. Alice knew this, but I felt like I was watching this scene from outside of my body, and it just continued to unfold in these elongated seconds that I was no longer directly a part of anymore. *Yes*. But then in less than a minute, it had gone entirely. I had never seen anyone take on such concentrated grief and then, in the same moment, lose it. I searched the grass until I found a tiny divot, and I stared at it until I stopped crying. Then I paused like this: one, two, three, four. I looked at Mrs. Alice. I looked at the divot again.

A few months before this, Sir was on an all-liquid diet in the hospital. Actually, it was worse than liquid only; it was clear liquid only, which basically means water and watered-down apple juice. I was standing at the foot of his bed with Danielle, and he said to her, *I know you can get me a cup of coffee*. We all knew he was right because she's from New York, and they don't mess around there. She left for no more than a couple minutes and also returned with a Snickers bar for Sir. He inhaled it. We didn't tell the nurse why his blood sugar went up.

The longest relationship I've ever been in is the one that ended on Saturday. It'd been nearly six years, which is little less that nine percent of seventy.

Mrs. Alice, how long is seventy years? … You don't want to know … But I do.

I do not know what it is like to know someone for seventy years, and then to not actually know this anymore. To not know that they have died. To not know that you don't get to know them anymore. I think it means that Mrs. Alice gets to keep knowing Sir. And I think that this must be grief in its most idyllic form. Or at least, I like to hope it is.

I haven't yet read the page about how to grieve. Please, tell me.

The first time I was ever called Sir, I was eleven years old. Maybe I was twelve, but that's not important. I held the door open for Santa at the post office, and he thanked me, *Sir*.

I went home, shut myself in my room, looked in the mirror, and said to myself, *I am not a sir.*

Someone said, *rain is confession weather*. Who said that? Why? What did it feel like to move from California to Washington? *Mrs. Alice, where do you live? … Colorado.* This was one question the dementia facility asked her to see if she qualified. They made a check mark.

I can't always remember what it is like to stand next to another human. By that I mean, what it is like to stand next to every room in their body. I like drinking my Earl Grey just after I've brushed my teeth because it tastes extra fresh like this — like it's from the produce department or something. No one knows this anymore. Every year I Photoshop my college ID to keep it current, and then I go to opera where it makes my body feel both foreign and local at the same time, and I like this contradiction. It's the same way I feel when I write about how the word *and* is different from the word *human*. And I think that if everyone could just be a little more *and*, we'd all be a lot better off.

I want to know these things about another human.

My mother doesn't like to be called ma'am because it makes her feel old. My father doesn't like to be called sir because that just sounds strange. He runs a machine shop, and there aren't any sirs in there. I like when people call me ma'am because it gives me hope that genders might be fluid. It becomes a special occasion for me, and I celebrate by marking it on my calendar. When I'm called sir, and I'm feeling extra confident, I like to respond, *I am not a sir!* I said this to an airport security officer in Denver when I was on my way to Sir's funeral, and I got patted down twice: first by a man and then by a woman. Do you think I could sue them?

I avoid public restrooms as a general rule. But when that's not possible — like in an extra inning game — I take off my cap, walk in on a mission, and I don't make eye contact. I hate seeing when people double-check the icon on the door. That's why I like talking to telemarketers on the phone: they always call me ma'am.

When I was in seventh grade, a motivational speaker came to my algebra class. He said he used to hate his life, and he'd begin each day by waking up and smoking a bowl. I thought about how big a cereal bowl is. Then he said that to love someone means that you only want the greatest good for them. That's all he said: the greatest good. I think this is pretty accurate.

The house that I'm now living in has a television, which is the first time I've lived with a television since I was in high school and lived at home. I've now learned from Oprah what forgiveness means. She said that to forgive someone means that you've realized you don't wish you were different than you are right now. This does not mean that you must love what is to be forgiven.

Or it went something like this… *There were no colors. This never happened.*

I understand now that this is what happens when a *human* tries to become an *and*. The language won't let us.

If it's actually true that *all poets teach how to lament,* then why is it that I don't know how, yet? What is the difference between grief and lamentation? Please, won't someone just tell me already?

I'm writing these stories in reverse now because I can't remember how to emit time anymore. I wanted to curse Sir. *Don't you know she's got no memory!* But the one from seventy years ago is like a glass of water only even more clear: it doesn't even have that distorted part at the lip: the part where you can't tell how tall something is. The problem is is that her sentences have to exist right now. This is what the limit of her body is.

Sometimes I think about what it feels like to live in Colorado now for the first time in three generations, and I wonder if memory might be genetic.

Mrs. Alice, what are the limits of the body?

This is… This is…

And then that was it. It was like she had forgotten how to make a sentence. This is *what*? What is *this*? Or was it, This is, *period*. I'm so afraid of this. I want to make these sentences. And I want to make them sixty years from now, too.

I work most days as a book designer, and two nights ago, I was working on a text about phenomena when I noticed that something strange was happening with the letters. So I went in and in and more closely still and again, and I saw that they were breathing: literally and slowly. Maybe you don't believe me, but I saw this vividly. It was like the letters were made of tiny humans lying on their backs with their arms crossed over their chests. They looked something like miniature living corpses on their deathbeds. It seemed like they might be suffocating one another — being so closely piled. So I gave space around each letter and word and leading and margin, and then I went back in and in and more closely still and again, and they had stopped. Entirely. There was no more breathing — not even slowly, not even a little.

From inside of my dream, Sir asked me if I was dreaming. I said, *I don't think so.* He said, *you know, this is where the word goes when it's ready to die. It goes inside the book, and it holds itself there.*

The next morning, I got a phone call that the author had died.

Dear Sir,

Can I still write you little letters even though you're dead now?
Please say, *yes*.

Dear Sir,

Last month, a woman came up to me in the airport and asked about my thoughts on communing with the dead. I don't know how our conversation got like this so quickly, but I do know that she was very forward. She said that she thought you and I are spirit twins or something like this. I told her I didn't know anything about that. She said we'd always be present in one another's lives.

Sir, are you back yet?
Will you be my son?
I hope you like the names we're choosing.

Dear Sir,

Yesterday, we spent mother's day with Mrs. Alice. My mother was showing off her new necklace, and Mrs. Alice was concentrating on it like she was trying to figure out an algebra problem or the meaning of life or something profound like this. Then she leaned back in her chair and asked about the necklace, *but where does it begin?*

Yes, *where does it begin?*
It's not such a strange question really. I mean, is it?

Dear Sir,

Last night I was given a handful of your ashes. I put half of you in my garden — mulched you in around the irises whose bulbs Patty dug last spring from your front yard just before we sold your home. I hope you like it here.

I hid your other half, but I can't remember where I put you now. I only told Mrs. Alice, and she can't remember either. I'm very sorry, Sir, but I think I must have lost part of you. I promise, I'll try to re-dream this tonight, but until then, can you be safe in the memory of whiteness?

Dear Sir,

It has been exactly one year since your death. Tonight's the night — just after mid-night. I'm twenty-seven now, and I'm trying to remember everything as best as I can. Like that summer when we were playing basketball, and you were wearing those funny teal shorts with the faded orange pockets, and Cookie came out in her bathrobe to make fun of you from the other side of the driveway.

I'm putting this here. This isn't good enough! Is this good enough?

You know, I didn't start this because you died, Sir. That just happened. It was like you had a terrible stomachache, but you always ached, and then the doctor said it's back, and you were so afraid you'd suffer, but then all of a sudden I'm quoting John Wayne on the little card about your death, and we passed it out to everyone you knew. *Tomorrow comes into us at midnight very clean. It's perfect when it arrives, and it puts itself in our hands. It hopes we've learned something from yesterday.* No. No, Sir. I started this because I'm afraid of not remembering, and then Mrs. Alice said that the giant evergreen across the street looked like, looked like, well that it looked like something she couldn't quite remember just then, and then she couldn't remember what we were talking about anymore, and then she couldn't remember that she was speaking a sentence, and so she just smiled at me, and I told her, *I wish I knew how long 70 years was*, and she said, *you don't want to know*, and I said, *but I do.* And then next time, Mrs. Alice said, *don't miss anything.* And I told her I wouldn't. This is supposed to be about the living, and this is supposed to be about remembering that we are the living.

Dear Sir,

I've just learned that a friend has died. She had written, *dead person, dead person, will you partake in my persimmon feast?* Sir, let's have a hard-candy feast and go for a walk.

I hate this death. Makes me feel like we're all running out of time, and what exactly am I doing just sitting here on this airplane like really, is one side more urgent than the other? Is it? Please, Sir, tell me I'll live to be infinity because I couldn't take it otherwise.

Dear Sir,

If I die today, then everyone will know that I never took a shower this morning, and I'm still in my pajamas, and it's now 3:43 pm, and I don't plan on changing those things later today either. Today. Today. Today. Does anyone ever get to know that they're going to die today? Sir, did you know when the most intimate moment of your life was here? Was that why you waited for my mother to leave the room, and then for the woman from Hospice to leave the room, and then the clock went past midnight, and you were alone in your room. *Tomorrow comes into us at midnight very clean. It's perfect when it arrives...* Was it perfect for you, Sir? At least it was no longer today.

Dear Sir,

Do you think that excessively using the word *and* makes a person sound manic? I'm getting *and* tattooed on my wrist in 6 hours and 14 minutes. Is that stupid? Is it hypocritical — being a human and all? I want the *and* life, and I'm serious about that.

And never knows any limits to its body; *and* knows no limits because it's incapable of ever even thinking about *no*. That's just not possible. We have to write the human narrative, but can only theorize about *and* because that's not our reality. *And* has it made, Sir. It gets to be everything; it's better than god or the world or love or anything (these things are just too human). We can only describe it by saying, *and*. And in my next life, I want to be an *And*, not a Human. Dear *And*, can you make this happen for me? I just want to live amongst the other *Ands*.

Dear Sir,

I'm twenty-eight now, and these bodies are moving quickly, no? What were you doing when you were twenty-eight years old? It was 1953, and my mother was eight months away from being born. Did you know this? I'm getting back to being a human again, and I guess this is what it feels: I had forgotten how cold it can get in bed at night when you're only one human.

Oh Sir, I wish you were here again to say *human* how you always would — how you'd keep the *h* silent. And I would say, *uman is not a word, Sir*. And you would say, *Well, of course it is. I just said it.*

Statement on a gendered possibility

When I ask myself Robert Gluck's question *What kind of representation least deforms its subject?*, I naturally come here in terms of language, art, and media, but foremost, I come to this question in regards to my own human body. How might I represent myself so that I least deform my thoughts? This is where genders purposefully become re- and un-defined. I find a possible answer to this question in another question proposed by Akilah Oliver: *What are the limits of the body?* Define *limit*. Define *body*. Or rather, undefined them, please; bring them to a state of limitlessness, and once they've become unrecognizable in this language, replace *body* with the word *and*. Since Akilah's untimely death in 2011, I've begun a project of repetitively asking people her question, and I propose my own answer: there are no limits to the body: the body of the human, the body of the work, the body of the language. All of this is an archive, and there is no limit to an archive because it can be described with the word *and*, where *and* knows no limits to its body. This would be impossible for *and* to comprehend: a limit. I want to welcome genders to the word *and*. This is my ideal representation. I admit I am not fully there myself, but I will attempt to consider *and* in all of my language and in all of my bodies. It is here that we might find something more accurate than a word that will always fail to define a gender even when it thinks it's succeeding. Gendered words will never be good enough until they attempt to represent themselves with *and*.

   When I think of gender in regards to my own writing, I imagine that I may be writing an elegy towards gender. I think of gender as a failed place or a dead place. I'm currently finishing a project, *Sir*, which I've excerpted for this anthology. There are certainly underlying questions around the body's relationship to gender, but to ask these questions are not the main purpose of the project. It is, however, unavoidable. The main character whose name is Sir appears both bodily and ethereally. He visits the narrator whose gender is ambiguous — sometimes the narrator speaks of when she was a little girl and sometimes speaks of being called sir. The point is not to define the narrator's gender, but to believe that the language is trustworthy during the moment of sound. That is to say, how can a human stand next to another human if they cannot trust the language? This is our common neutral zone, and it is fluid and mutable. I think of all of my work as an experiment around the word *and*, and how to make more genuine attempts towards its ideals.

Jordan Rice

My Life

The physician tells me much I know already --
these structures of your mind correspond with
women's, his illustrations clearly lined in color
quadrants, lobes lit up, explain. Life won't be
simple either way and, it's kind-of an impossible
choice. I take a year to choose. Then advice.
Lose weight now. Grow out your hair. Unlearn
hiding. Mostly, fear will pass. Passing's always
a state of mind, though you may require surgery.
The list of surgeons lengthens without end.
I choose. This one in Boston. This one
Wisconsin. Save your money. How's your wife?

Lines for a Friend

After lunch he asked me to wait for him in the car
because he was still as heavy as the linebacker he'd been,

and could walk out into the hurricane, already having to
lean with the outer bands at landfall, to buy our cigarettes.

This was when I was slight, underweight from months
of worry and not eating and eating whatever pills

he found that might have some effect (he tested them
first) on happiness. I can't describe loyalty, but a few carts

abandoned in haste near parking lot pylons, and one was
shucked loose of mooring, drifting downhill, then possessed

by wind, spun and blown sideways. I can say he said *fags*
whenever we saw men together, but didn't mean it – years

with him, always close, it bordered love, and for months
was enough. Earlier that summer, sunburned and dosed

on LSD, I'd thrown myself at him, my heart cartwheeling
undefined want, though I wasn't high enough and he wasn't

either but meant to watch over and keep me
from idiot harm. We sat outside that night in heat, smoking

on his balcony overlooking Richmond traffic, sharing a joint
between us, then cigarettes. Even now, years after

the hurricane, years after the acid, I'm sure we never slept
until blurred visions and whipped-down trees – cartographies

of violent, daylong seasons passing into no revelation and loss –
fell silent around us. And I want, after the story of his marriage,

cocaine and the last splintered dining room chair, disunion
and shame, to find him impossibly whole, undulating tremor and fix

uncurled from his habits, his old kindness returned. That first year
together he found me in a shut back room, some frat party haze,

and stood me up in my own blood after sudden panic and carnage –
my nose broken by a guy who'd been drunker than shame, then wasn't –

and drove us over Nickel Bridge to sit near the rapids and undercut
rocks I'd guide rafts through for money summers later, crying *hold*

fast and *all back, back left* and *all stop*, and lose no one – steam
off the silver current lines above and below the falls in late autumn:

Brother, once beloved, longed-for one still, I'd take you back, strung
out or slowly turning cruel wherever you are, alone in your new career

of loneliness or the carcass of your last life, hungover or unkept,
you who were for years and all silences already forgiving.

Transition with Harvard Sentences

For months the body lessens. "These pills do
less good than others." Other pills will follow.

*I took away the masculine. I am taking away
the masculine.* The phrase as she said it will not

settle, a friend from years ago, who was almost
beautiful when saying, *You'll get over all the fear*

and shame. A sham. *It's what we are.* So often
now it feels this way. Carriage and speech. Speech

and pitch. "The birch canoe slid on the smooth
planks." I am working on my voice: "Help

the woman get back to her feet." And thinking
she shouldn't be so difficult to find, though

she's disappeared from everywhere. Friends
are saying: We haven't heard from her.

I imagine everything. It's not possible, these last
things I think. "Her purse was full of useless trash."

She was more careful, had quit taking money
from men, whatever she would do. "Her purse

was full of useless trash." The recorder stuck
on playback. Last I saw her, no part of that

other self remained. No trace. *I took away my
masculinity.* "The young girl gave no clear response."

Laser Therapy

She pulls the trigger and I'm crying before I know it
which is when she pauses for maybe the fourth time

that day to tell me I'm brave for what I'm doing
or for being who I am, and in our small, shut room

smelling now of singed beard shadow, this crying,
I worry, is something I cannot stop, and so focus on

the high whirring current in the machine to which
her gun is corded by curling white tension line

like the phone attached to the wall in my parents'
old house and how as a child I would stand by it

twirling the slick plastic turns between my fingers
in the silence belonging to that kitchen

until the refrigerator cut on to hum the slow tune
of sleep within loneliness. And I am gut sick again

as I was so often then and close to throwing up
when the nurse becomes more nurse than

progressive or maternal telling me *sit up sit up* then
lean down with your head between your knees and places

against the back of my neck a wet handtowel,
folded and cold. And I would ask if I could ask

in a language other than swearing air in and out
of my lungs and these godawful sobs I am thinking

must be an affliction like hiccups that last a hellish
decade: Who does she think I am? Because only last

week in a fucking Wal-Mart a man with his fist raised
cornered me, saying, *faggot you faggot*. And brave is not

immobility, is not speechlessness, not even the flash
through your mind: you are going to die, not here

but wherever you end up after being followed by him –
snatched like a moth from his light – even after

managers escort him from the premises after four
or five shoppers intervene to push him away

and a policewoman, frowning and younger than you
arrives to stand near, promising your safety.

Designation

Into the woods behind that house, mountains
rounded into grassland and your father's still
behind you, framed in dimming light since we
rarely made it much beyond that part of your
story. The torquing of interrogation echoes
past the porch, past cities spent, whole years

of cities with you in them spent not waiting
any longer. Frailness isn't the word I want.

The light is fire here and the sun is blazing
down the face of one state into another into
prairie. So I'm asking you, a ghost now, no
the blue flame in the mason lid moonshine
poured to burn and be resealed, the body that
you were, liminal being there half a decade later –
talking after hours by the bar, smoke pouring
from you and from me, the ashtray between us
filling, your transition nearly complete and

everyone always staring, no way to tell who
you were or were becoming – as if by ashes
I'd remember how you named her.

Transume

This morning before
the mirror I said *These
are my breasts*, and you
looked away in disgust
and silence. All winter
you insist I've been two
people. This one –
stepping from steam

new and late for every
thing, would choose
another name, grow
slowly into herself –
unfamiliar with shame
strange as first sight
and unyielding.

Poetics Statement

1.

After decades of silence and months of therapy, I stood in a mostly empty parking lot on the far side of Michigan, staring at the words GENDER CLINIC on a sign in front of an office building at the outer perimeter of a shopping mall. I'd been driving since before dawn, was rushed and sick from too much coffee and six months of coming out to those closest to me. At the end of each of those conversations, someone I loved, usually sitting alone in an office many states South, realized by turns that the person they'd known by the body I'd been when we last said goodbye, was never coming home. When the alarm went off that morning my wife stayed in bed, warm, quietly watching me get ready, looking as worried as I was at everything before us. Then it was time, and yes, I promised, I'd drive safely, and be home soon, and I love you. Only this life. This one. *You too.*

2.

This might be the happiest I ever saw you, my mother is saying as she holds a picture of me at five, sitting next to an apple tree in my grandfather's orchard, wearing my uncle's USMC flight helmet. The same age then as I am now, he piloted helicopters the size of small houses, and while training, occasionally flew over his father's farm in Western NC, slowing above our tobacco fields and apple trees, tilting the Sikorsky slightly to the left or right. The notepad half under my thigh there in the picture though, that's what I'd like to point out now, because that was the first day I tried writing anything. My grandmother kept the poem, but told me when I last saw her, that she liked my old work more than what I'm writing now.

3.

The nurse was the calmest person in the room. Then the sudden *woosha-woosha* and a small screen lit up. Instant recognition. At the end of the first trimester, there in black and gray fractals, was the outline of a head, the pearly curvature of backbone, a small but clearly defined arm raised toward the mouth. My wife laughed, and the image flickered, the small form before us fluttering up, settling back. The nurse switched on the heart-rate monitor – one hundred and fifty-two beats a minute. *Like a marathon runner!* my father said the night we broke our news to him, after he calmed down, quit pounding the kitchen table with his fist, his voice a roar through static seven hundred miles away: *That's Good! That's Good!*

4.

For the first thirty years of my life, I escaped my body most through writing, which became the most recognizable and livable space I knew. But what I've gained from this process of transition, of slowly growing into another self, remains mostly interior. I smile more. I smile.

The poems of mine in this anthology present aspects of intermediacy particular to transgender experience: the conscious place between the old self and the person one must become. That hope in possibility bound in uncertainty is most reflected, I think, through the anxiety and frustration in the speaker's voice as these poems seek to ask and answer a central question: If I admit who I am, who will I become?

5.

My son stirs in his nursery. Soon he'll cry, and after some milk, and without ever really having opened his eyes, he'll curl against my chest like every night of his life so far, and snore, and at some point start to laugh from his dream. If nowhere else, it must be said here, I think, that the body cannot and does not matter at such times.

Visibly transgender, somewhere between male and female, however I appear to anyone, but especially to my son, it is first as his parent, second as comfort, and each night as he sleeps, his guardian, the only wakeful person in our house, as I read, write, staying up on purpose, sore armed, sore of chest, often with a cramp in one leg or the other, our son the constant flickering presence on the monitor, until some time near dawn I place him in our bed, where he scrawls his body between his mother and me, until his head rests at my shoulder, his feet at her stomach, each of us then lastingly and only ourselves.

j/j hastain

from **we force-effect the oubliette**

Pre

There are always shifts (which are both content and form) and those shifts are psychological, physiological and psychic. This non-novel works with/engineers these shifts on the nano-scale, as an always composite fact of feeling/sense and physiology/ sensation.

There are characters: I, you, we, she, he (which in the book is a place of fathers and infliction and yearning); boi (who is the future site of all non-linear healing, and can never have a static or fixed pronoun); Maxima (the always future child of beloveds); and the lineage/parental creature which appears in different temperaments reoccurringly, as largess statuesque forms of the Virgin de Guadalupe being extracted (through ephemeral action) by boi from an overwhelmed, anonymous mountain lake.

The work is both confession and mythology. This is obscure narrative, heavy with surplus, and much of its theory is driven by sound and image. It wants non-mirage, but gotten to through all forms of address (including mirage and montage).

I realize that even now I have not said enough about the non-novel as form, about what differentiates it from its historical pre. I think maybe I cannot speak that yet. I think you will know a better way to say it. I can say, however, that this book makes rest in my cosmic identity, mostly because it dents into my psychological, physiological and psychic states. This book is an invitation for just such dents to be made in you.

*

I fantasized about slough and slake until I turned my cells into something ravenous enough to be able to receive. Planting me as vegetal. Then planting in me. The emotional progression of a verdant cup, to a sturdy gene within beloved merge. How when you finally came to me you sang to me of teal vectors. A love song that could not die.

So, not lament but beaded, like being yielded is similar to compacting. Bending over. You kissed me. Professed and pressed by libidinal language. By bringing me carcasses of swan bodies. Oh bold promises and creaming. This was the first time I had ever been tied. It was as if the rope experienced an orgasm with me. Your firm grip, something I could recognize because of how it related to an enjoined hunger. Appetite to replace what had previously been such apparent and painful lack.

*

I am saying that incubating all of the airy insinuations into something formed and physical, there at the threaded and threading threshold, allowed a true genesis to take place. Allowed the underworlds to become elegant.

*

How when we woke we agreed to work together to surpass illusion and singularity. We read books. We favored shared vibrato over caricature. Pursued new flavors. Lavender-chile butter to spread onto sourdough bread.

Sonorous pages dedicated to the difficulty of revealing vulnerably. You kept commenting on the smell of my hair as we were pulling out those pieces. As we made plans to burn the hair. To make a film in a train yard and to focus on the train cars in the middle of the sequence rather than to focus on the caboose. Because there are so many traditional stories with limited endings. Because we wanted to disclose what inertias and energies the middles had yet to reveal.

*

For eternity as a psychic texture while also being in need of filaments. In need of a never ending propagation. Oh divergent yet coagulated, expressive insignias. It matters to note that you reminded me of father. This related to my desire for a female he. The way these bodies solder glass. How yours was always fervent stillness amongst such vivid sounding. Which made clarities about where light and body could meet and blend.

Silhouettes of figures dropping sacred flecks of bread onto gray roofs as the rain is coming in. That in all satiation there is music. When pertinent inner data is made bare, it is turned into something more. Love letters like honing fault lines that masterfully and enigmatically deplete chasms.

A depleted chasm as a fullness?
This is breaking things between.

*

This is "there is no way to non-fire." Boats filling the moat. You said the third and meant multitudinous. Stringcourses assisting us in surviving. Mutant forms are hopeful. Silvery, I do mean part mechanical part flesh in a continual stratum of crossing. And this is that notation as resonance. As attempt at restoration. At collective utterance being mined for an accurate or applicable "I."

An open mouth is key to the health and longevity we are pursuing. And subverting surface for what could arise in its place is a cosmic chivalry. I am saying that being with you this way makes me relate to you as a symbol. My open legs. Our contextual pandiculation. Your born-anatomy is fraying. And we are executing by craving, by simulacrum without cognitive root.

from myrrh

bees with stingers
and stinger-less

which is always a version of
gender

oh matriarchal   masculinity

a vibrant stamina

of maximums
that we bend
in order to pursue

*

before
is placed into betel

that this road builds
the lover

the sawing

then the adhesion

such a complex act of creating
legato columns

*

vistas of inverse-ratiocination

the ponder
the longing

:::   both which render us
at begging

desire as pendulation

exposure
by weathering

how and what   not to
ensconced

from birth or from conception we carry
scintilla
if only to generatively cohere

this is a romance of fractals

this is torridity

tenses of

the infinitely
ferric dress

Is a mistaken carcass a place for memory?

Is a mistaken carcass a place for memory?
Is woman to man at times a mistaken carcass?
Is there a way for divergently feminine to masculine to at times be a renovation of
previously mistaken carcasses?

*

We were thinking about the ethics involved in truly becoming sated. Staring into dark
matter together. Preparing to graze on it.

Eating to elate colors and tones in an induced coppice. Engaging to intensify our
vision. Amidst old growth poplars. Amidst root suckers and dropped barbules. Amidst
dried petals and crisped curves of fruit peel.

In amidst, we are both   primeval and modern miracles.

*

Our honor and our precisions come from how we darn and baste the contrary platelets
into contemporary plots.

*

The swan was a "he" and he consumed the monstrous femme's heart. Brutally. The feasting felt inert and allied, before a blaring, balanced heat. As their bodies aligned they both shared the single swan vertebrae as a core bone. The swan that was a he, sometimes wanted to be referred to by other pronouns while in this position. While within horizontal and vertical aplomb.

*

The luminosity of entangled bodies, as legion. Like whole plumes implanted into a living vein, as a way that that vein is magically able to enact vine. Vines crawl up the hamam. Vines with thaumaturgical veins in them drip possibilities.

Loving the aghast, but not due to haunting or ghostly. Nothing overthrowing. Just this additive-overflow. Gentle crookedness, that moves us as febricity.

*

We are attempting to sturdy and thicken a conduit for expansions.

Do predators also peck at other-than mammalian corpses?
Do they peck the flesh of apparitions?

If not reanimated, factions of history remain in our bodies as unintentional apparitions. As unintended predators.

*

We want corpses that can become curvatures of canvas. We want to sew the pacts and the parts together.

Like the feeling of a swan's weight inside.

Then something relevant to shed after the imprints of that implant.

*

Is there an image or lineage of images that will ever be numinous-synonym for this?
Is there ever anything new to be written of our genders and sexes as they develop us?

In place of those questions, we robustly ensue in order to enshrine masteries of fusion.
This was the point of the lovers. This was the last page of the diary. This more than
woman or man or_____.

*

It took me naming myself yours, in order for you to name me. And I named myself
yours by between.

I wanted you to think of me as a non-abortable, qualitative quantity.

*

Effervescing, invested, de-vesting. Needing to birth an impossibly new womb.
Needing to sink vermillion knots in venerate opaques.

We are making it possible to thrive. We are the shrine room being filled. Filling during
a secret dawn that comes at midnight.

*

Looking into a standard of vivid, shared canals.

To farm the brazen filigree. To be prostrate to future versions of each other as our
deities. Taking it all in at once, so that it is too much, then staying there in that overfill
until body becomes more immense. Until co-body expands us and nothing is too
much.

*

Libertine installations. This is what it means to be nourished. Memories of bites of
white with honey, pickles and truffle salt.

The force of the body in use like this. Where even the emissions are muttering about
volatile, baited abodements.

*

What it is to make home in a displaced site?
What is homeland for a body born as flexure from the start?
Did the lovers know that they were trying to *stay*, in place of being taken by an exterior burst of light?
After all of this gnashing, heaped in the orchard's middle, will the most shockingly beautiful melded corpuscle be found?

This is the will, of entangled skeletons of paramour. This will is a standard we keep ourselves to.

Oh dehiscent we.

Poetics Statement

My composition process generates deviant or differentiated pressures—it concerns itself with configuration of weights and releases, derived by way of (or upholding) ulteriors. This process engages deeply so that new types of relation can emerge. I deal directly with the transgressive body, deviant gender, eros, and identity construction as necessary compositional methods to living with empowerment in what can be a diminutive and polarizing world.

I am interested in expanding traditional notions of what activism is/ has been/ can be. I do this via the reimagining of spaces. I believe in composing texts/ spaces that are inherently non-linear and a-historical; texts as spaces that have never been patriarchally controlled and cannot be patriarchally controlled. It is my hope that in these spaces there will be room to experience contemporary moments of truth, eros, convergence, conjunction and profoundly new types and sensations of equity.

Composition provides essential spaces for the future of declaring: spaces that are integral to those expressing their stories. What about the humans who do not identify in clear, precise, accessible ways? For humans who do not fit into either-or models, the dominant culture's compositional structures do not offer us a space. The future of composing/ creating our bodies must consider how our bodies speak. This is why we must demand space.

As a genderqueer writer/ maker of things my body speaks of/ as a constant state of generative genesis. It asks this question: "What is it for an identity to be in a continuity of beginnings? Always extant. Always reaching. And what forms must be invented in order to make space for that identity?" The current dominant structures cannot enable (regarding such body-speak) because the pressure/ need to speak is itself a result of what happens when a body does not/ cannot adhere to the dominant culture's dogma or imposed paradigms. It is from just such pressure/ need to speak that we generate new forms. Forms to hold this different type of telling. Forms to hold not only what is told but the way that we must tell it.

One of the ways that I describe this vigorous creation of forms is by way of the image of the cyborg. I see the cyborg as a bridge (psychological bridge and additive-dependent shape to biomimic) to articulate the non-either-or body. This body needs multiplanar narratives, manifold eroses and motile documents (which bear no loyalty to singularity, binary, stricture or limit).

My cock which (in the context of my current embodiment) is potential (a fact of the ephemeral realms) but has at other times been a bodily identity (physical) makes me cyborgian. My compositions (which are moving elementals not relegated to single logics or planes) make me cyborgian. Here, cyborg equals additive-as-essential. Cyborg equals I am not whole without _____.

I am not whole without my beloved's cock (which is also cyborgian). Your cock is mine, making me as it moves in me.

Move in me my love, with such pristine force that I curdle on the cave floor.

All hail the sentiences and staminas of the female he!

Another way that I think about my own work/ identity in my composition process is through considering the morphologies of the Archea. Archea are microbes. They are theorized to be the oldest form of life on the planet earth. They are organisms that have no cell nucleus (and are therefore morphable). Archea thrive in extreme locations (hot springs, marshlands, oceans, human colons). I see myself as a functional Archea living as an extremophile amongst the extremity (conditions) of a society that does not intrinsically provide me space.

"Archaea possess genes and several metabolic pathways that are...closely related to those of eukaryotes: notably the enzymes involved in transcription and translation" (Wikipedia). This aspect of Archea is very important to me. Transcription which is the gesture of creating "complimentary antiparallel RNA" strands to the DNA that is inherency. I see the relevance of this in the context of queer bodies and forms--in the context of a need for continual compositional generativity and genesis in order to proceed.

"Other aspects of archaean biochemistry are unique, such as their reliance on ether lipids" (Wikipedia). I see my work as interacting with ether as one of its primary subjects. I see composition as a ribboning agent--as a way of threading disparates (ether, physical/ desire, form) into potential aggregates.

My compositions have a keen interest in ulterior healing: healing that is not reactive but is instead proactive-- attending to not yet visible or known (perhaps still subconscious or located in ulterior planes?) wounds or rifts. This is miraculous healing. "A plant that doesn't grow from seed" (Stephens). And the compositions themselves (in their reimaginations of space) are healing as activism.

Healing is <u>so</u> site specific--body specific. Healing is not socialized or strategic. It is somatic. It is relegated to authentic sensation. My composition process is rooted in experience and invention regarding a myriad healing. One that vigilantly pursues and so activates previously unforeseen empowerments and enablements. This is composition invested in:

I do not want to have lived any of my planarities with my back turned to emancipatory restoration.

Works Cited

"Archaea." *Wikipedia*. 29 Jan. 2013. <http://en.wikipedia.org/wiki/Archaea>

"Transcription (genetics)." Wikipedia. 29 Jan. 2013. <http://en.wikipedia.org/wiki/ Transcription_%28genetics%29>

Stephens, Nathalie (Nathanaël). *The Sorrow And The Fast Of It*. Callicoon, NY: Nightboat Books, 2007.

Jaime Shearn Coan

Ceremony, late September

in memory of Edgard Mercado (1970 – 2009)

I'm watching my words burn
        through the night air, shaping a shell
        that won't be held to any ear.

At the far end of the pier, at the edge
        of our forgotten, their shadows glancing
        out across the water, I wrap the metal

railing with tenderness
        while behind my eyes I undo you
        from this place.

Loops of wool
        dizzying the hands– an ancient
        Greek rite in the face of no

other way: a plea for recognition.
        Here is your name, your entering
        year and this one that turns on you

in the form of a rope.
        And here I am, repeating
        the gesture, recasting its intent.

Man City

He walks in and orders a beer.
He doesn't drink but then again, he's
not a man either, he's a visitor.

PALM SPRING'S FRIENDLIEST:
MEN + LEATHER + LEVIS
ADULT BEVERAGES DAILY

In the backroom he hits up
the cigarette machine,
curses when it steals his money.

He doesn't smoke but he liked looking
at the naked boys stuck forever
to the surface of the glass.

A Tom of Finland painting takes up
one wall – it's got real chains
that keep getting jostled by the pool game.

He's by himself, wearing boat shoes
in the desert, his cock is impressive but
stayed behind in L.A. Tonight he will have

no one, not even the muscle queen
splayed out like a skyline in the dark,
all four limbs pinned, grinning.

"that lonesome vibration so familiar to young boys"

- Vladimir Nabokov, Speak, Memory

Some of us grew up with mothers
floating on water beds in the dark.
We tried to keep ourselves
company, to smile and laugh
all dressed in yellow.

What do I inherit now
that the boy's father never knew
him that way, and
the mother is still sleeping.

Now like then this shimmer
that surrounds the body,
keeping it apart from.

Humming its way across the skin –

this attic-space this basement
the dryer thumping the splintered light
a record slowly revolving.

Do we find ourselves
in Nabokov's nursery, the boys
we never were.

Do we materialize
on his conjured walls,
cast by a magic lantern,
do we fill the space with our future
shapes at last.

circulation

"pinch the little finger to stimulate the heart"

it sounds a little masochistic, she said,
to listen when you already know
what he's going to say

in the mirror, my eyes misting
in double

my circulation is my worst trait, it's
like a melting the liquids
don't know where to go

mom would pinch
her cheeks before a date

the men's underwear display:
my cheeks fill with blood when I stand facing.
stimulation stems –

manipulation of material

bite down post-palm, fit the flesh between
your teeth when you let go the flood

of me

i was all contained in that place
and now the heart
hooks through me
it's loud at the meridian
you hear it in your feet
the pounding you feel

red

why do we associate the heart with love?
love is lazy the heart is work

and her breath is short now – even from talking
the heart's strength
is irreversible

open your chest to the ceiling
your shirt open, then off –
my little finger at the corner of your mouth
it's hard while walking to think about it

hold your fingers cross your breath
the ghosts are out tonight –
heart-hungry, blood-rythmned
circulating what's gone cold

Capture

Cornered in a cavernous warehouse,
in the midst of oversized landscapes
& wine-loud conversation,

my father's self portrait,
knee-deep in faggot art,
declines appraisal.

His pink polo collar-up, his face
smooth as a sand-dollar
and giving away nothing.

blue

the color of background
above, below
the belt, yards of blue
worn to fit
the points of his eyes
the point of my pen
they are always meeting
in the blue
in the blue
is where we wander
the days we only meet in dreams
or seasick in your windowless room
the stretch of salt blue
beyond your shoulders
blue should know better
than to think I'll stay
blue in the hands they're never warm
is blue a cold color
even in summer
blue, I'm so –
her throat must be lined with it
some of us
are sky-filled
cloud-headed
blue of the neutral
blue of the boy
the bruise, broken skin
constellation of vessels
blue moon blue balls
blue screen
blue scream
blue ends

Blue was Derek Jarman's final film, chronicling the end of his life, released in 1993. 79 minutes of narrated text, music, and ambient noise set to a blue screen.

forcing the hand

a new way of knowing
the muscle, extending
thin metal into thigh

it almost doesn't feel
right how smoothly

      like the body should react
      reinforce its thirty-one years
      as is

the divine slides in

and the body
ever faithful, believes

Palm Springs: Reina de la Noche

(for Justin)

I floated your back
with my fingertips –
the lullaby of
water yielding.
This is the best part
you said, from
the underlit green –
your skin free of worry
for the moment,
slicked with chlorine,
and the stars
all you saw
from that height.
I steered you in a night

where air pinned itself
to mountaintop,
beyond struggle. You
lining the boundary
with beating eyes.

Gramma's boob

The best way to describe it is to hold it in your hand.
The weight is not daunting, it's like a waterbed in your palm.

Unlike the real ones, it doesn't warm. It doesn't talk back.

Stupid boob.

She was always leaving it around the house. It was an embarrassment
we took pleasure in:

the sacrilege of a boob
lying on the coffee table, kitchen counter, top of toilet.

I never asked to touch the place where her skin puckered
or her one remaining breast – its nipple was so unapproachable.

I preferred the smooth uniform boob, like her anonymous nurse's skirt.

Unlike the rest of her body, Gramma's boob doesn't grow.

She brings me with her to go bra shopping; won't accept it's the boob
that needs changing. She won't see the way

the women look at me, then look away, then look at me, then look away.

We're flipping through the sizes; she's eighty, she'd like a comfortable bra.

But Gramma, I used to wear a size B.
What size do you wear now?
I don't wear bras anymore.
Oh, I'm sorry.

and that's where it ends, flat and tidy as the front of my shirt.

I think of her name lining my inner arm, how it took her months to acknowledge the tattooed cursive, that tender spot.

I think of her plastic boob, snug against her heart,
her heart with its man-made valves.

All these stories tucked behind fabric. Someday, I would like to tell her:

We only have to stay alive.

Corpus

How I thought I was seeing it until I saw it – unfamiliar on someone else's couch. How I lay on my back with pins stuck to head, hands, feet. How I stilled myself. How I rebelled under the stillness. How I held myself with arms shaking. How I stared directly into the body I feared only to be asked: *What do you fear?* How I wanted to point, to stab him. How I felt my eyes soften. How the room went watery. How I heard almost a whisper: See your beauty. How I thought I made it up. How I didn't. How my lover spent the night next to a cardboard box. How the more rigid I become, the closer I am to death. How I was the cardboard box – stacking dreams on top of me. How I suffered, knowing this. How I inclined myself towards the suffering. How I listened hard as anything. How I was living in the future body. How I had given away my home. How I formed a true question and am asking it still. *What is more present than the body?*

Poetics Statement

Perception is messy and it is in motion. I find myself returning again and again —to texts, images, events, rhythms, sounds, somatic states. The movement of returning is generative. It is an investigation that exists in itself—a conjectured space that exists between now and not now where all rules are suspended. In "that lonesome vibration," I return to Nabokov's nursery, a place that feels both intimate and unfamiliar, to find "the boys / we never were." In "Ceremony, Late September," I grant my speaker the ability to take up a murder weapon and transform it into an object of memorial and protest, thereby "repeating / the gesture, recasting its intent." The poem is an offering.

The places in my poems are recognizable, whether leather bar or kitchen table. It is the subject that flickers and sometimes disrupts the appearance of realness. The body is in transit and the presence of the shifting body (if seen) causes shifts in the landscape. The speaker of "Man City" gradually reveals their transgender status and, more largely, the instability of appearances, remaining invisible in a queer male landscape. The body of questions, the body in question—embodiment is of vital importance here, and like everything else, is subject to revision. In "lobe," two transgender subjects have a sexual encounter out-of-doors and the speaker's vulnerability and desire is met with recognition: "the body's question / stilled by // today's eyes." In the midst of struggle with the body's shifting boundaries, the speaker in "Corpus" forms the question: "What is more present than the body?" considering a commitment to a sense of corporeality in the present, despite dysphoria, despite the yet-to-be-fulfilled promises of hormone therapy.

I'm interested in continuity that allows for disruption. I try to pay attention to the places where I want to keep my eyes shut—where personal and collective histories make me cringe. I'm interested in the question of queer lineage—especially in the margins of this lineage. Rather than romanticize or condemn, I want to welcome in the presence of our ghosts (including our former selves); to call attention to how they blend and bend our bodies in new directions. A few months ago I woke up desperately hanging onto a message from dreamland: "Go and dwell in the courages left behind." Make of it what you will—that's what I'm doing.

Jake Pam Dick

from **Lens**

<u>Concave</u>
In twenty this is gone.

To Karl: *subtitled…through work*

He: *Why're you in a such a rush?*

Because I am burning up the road with my Nova

the new life?

Because I'm wearing my pink Rapid Transit t-shirt which matches the hot pink bookmark which is also punk.

Pink looks good with the pea-green book jacket which is chartreuse loving ochre.

Pink like girly.

The shaggy mien in that children's book. That's totally obscure. If you want them to understand you. Or hair qua rocker.

He wanted to be a rock star, she didn't. Yes she did! I rock at air guitar.

Not for sale!

Advances' reading copy

            Be my tutor, Georg. I will fuck you.
            Be my tutor, Jakob. You can't fuck me.

I could've been Jago (pronounced Jaygo). To fuck them or be them. What's the diff?
But it sounds awkward.

Now break off crumbs of language.

            Brother and sister follow them back.
            Johnnie Gunther and James Lens.
            Will Johnnie matter?
            In his form?

It's so bright, I have to squint. Also the letters look too big like in a kids' book.

            Lenz is among us like a sick child, and we rock and dandle him,
            and give him whatever toy he wants to play with.

            Thanks, brother!

            It hurts to see this.

                      I hear this rushing
            sound, as of

His father was a religious man

He was supposed to be a religious man

        The king's mountain is Kant's

        Everything leading to Immanuel in every version
        But impure blows critique

Tutoring the two brothers, Link and Pete von Kleist

            Military like my teenage army jacket

olive which is ochre loving brown

mental peace thesis

Flout the punctuation, don't bow to commas, manual styles, illustrious names

Do I belong here? Or further to the right?

I have to stay far enough away to see the whole thing

She seems angry

Fucking is going to require leaving out some letters.

For instance to Johnnie or G-d.

Today is the 9th which is the day after the 8th. That looks weird. It's the first day of the

My eyes hurt

He has to be here with me, so I am not all alone.

It's bad to be self-centered.

Universality of the stress book

cosmopolitan but in exile
how does that work?

Karl aka friend or brother or journal comrade through work

Not enough variety in the placement, but we could play with it

like so

end of the page a fine
place to lie down
and break

Convex

The 20th inked Lens traversed peaks. Blocks. None wailing. Snow except for grey concrete. Brown tree branches, dropped bus passes. This music is dumb. The sun stuck a finger out and poked the forest in the eye. It hurt somewhat. I need to buy a new pen, this one has a disorder. Ganglia of trees. Nervous ticking of wooden floorboards. Snow lay all across the berm by the run-over futon. James Lens in his/her Hessian boots crunched across the room. It would not do to pull the blinds up, someone might accuse you of a murder. Or the sun could take its revenge. Elsewhere clouds made a face at James, it was holy. Then a leering grin. Representational art i.e. religion is infantile. Likewise James is. Annunciations need speech ribbons. Here the walls decide what to do. We went further. The clouds predicted answers. Wild restlessness with different implements. Or the dull hollow stroke. A wish to write inside out. It snowed upward. One day had a crevice, the other not. James noted the humidity. Nearby a toy barked. The rattling of the radiator's teeth expresses the anxiety of the room. Get back to the mountains. There the way was up or down. Here I thought indifferently. Pubic hair atop trees. Unlike the others, I am so tired. Lie down then, Lens. We reclined under a blanket of heavy snow. It had snapped the bough off the tree. But James walked across the sheet of paper. It was snow white. My lazy eye wandered. James wet and cold. Deathly quiet across the land. The slope has a coefficient. James is inefficient because he forgets herself. Should have snuck into that math class. I will never learn anything. Used to be a student but quit. Mused somebody with a tightening chest. Grammatical moods darkened—

Then the building soars up in glinting cornices and equations, and James resurrects a comma. And/or it resurrects her/him.

*

A comma unless an apostrophe is a question of location. Possession presupposes connection, continuation entails separation. Contraction needs omission.

Didn't talk to nice Ivan with his floppy sandy hair, now James feels guilty. White table an accusatory ellipse from a certain angle. Children are the future here where filth, the book, has been withdrawn from the circulation library of ingress. Itchiness of flea market and longing for my missing copy. Tell me something good, said the disciple. No streams, but faucets won't close all the way. Rusted-out t-shirt. Starsky & Hutch pamphlet. Pair of clip-on shades, Lens could've used those. Chairs are for sitting in. Nurse your resentment. Make a strong depression in the skin. Whorls on thumbs. The whorl is all that is the case. That was before, when I was a younger treatise. Lack of facial hair suggests the monks shall not accept you. Theirs is a beautiful lifestyle except for the visits to the girdles of aborters' clinics. Righteousness a sin, vs. devoutness. I pray to avoid it while James prays while he aka she stares into the faces of Roald's three, four or five children. I don't know, I forget how to count. Both ways. Where is lovely Inger? She doesn't appear yet. Weighed my neck out of desperation. Because I think that would actually work out. It depends on the contour. I scratched my back out of inspiration, but it was a pantomime. Then I got pardoned and scratched from the line-up. Next I panted deductively like a sly dog or a sex kitten. I kind of wanted to but then I realized that I had no choice. Yeah, you should go. Red table manners. I was ashamed to chew in front of them so I grew skinny. Out the window, snow in humps. An apocryphal valley fought a non-canonical peak. I wrestled with a dinner roll. That was the vow of violence. Yellow signifies Sweden and *dude* signifies man. Every man is Lens's brother. The taxi cabs are Swedes. I skated on thin & illegal inferences. The hair stuck up on my thin wasted forearms. Some sort of dread blew across the ink. I ran out of time and space.

Concave
Not enough time?

Pressure point in the Vic's chest vapor rub.

Yellow and green and brown shirt with swirls.

I see a profile higher up, white walls and white ceiling. Here it's empty. Before, I was full with it. I had the whole thing in me. But now it's empty here.

It doesn't work to interact with a newspaper when a racer like McQueen hangs himself. Hanged is better than hung. More dignity. Remember that for next time.

What's the point without…?

Started the day (the 10th, i.e. the 2nd) listening to the one who swallowed pills. His throat hurt.

I flirted with you my whole life

Left the red fragments elsewhere
I smell my dying hair

Dying by trying to be a genius by going fast through snow

what sort of

transient meteor

Thank you, brother.

a meteor is *1) a small particle of matter in the solar system directly observable only by its glow from frictional heating on falling into the earth's atmosphere 2) the streak of light produced by a meteor*

My first typewriter typed in script, my boyfriend Benjy's in italics. How weird that seems now. I was ten. He had manly hair on his hands. I had girlish fuzz on my upper lip

                meteoric   career

suddenly it got dark outside the head or in it

        meteoric
        meteorite
        meteoroid
        meteorology
        meter

a thing in the air, raised in the air, versus measure. Then it plummets

        don't know where to put the

suddenly the blue turned black

                not so sudden, if you were paying attention

                there isn't anything to

                look on a face, don't feel anything

                outer sin

the thing about the blank slate, its desirability

        after being tutored

I think you should do tutoring for the standardized tests. O.k. Don't spell it out.

What it isn't

lick the lips, they're salty   smell your own dirty hair

An obituary printed when he was 29. Then 12 years of haunting

Dying homeless in the Basic Russian textbook

masked vow

Shoving each word onto the page like a heavy stone

His writing not yet translated into English, or no longer

wanted to invent
                    a library
                              it could save it

social and political reform school uniforms which are bright blue jumpsuits for
teenage miscreants

her father a religious man

she was supposed to be a religious man

the maintenance man gave me a jumpsuit like his for the service elevator

this desire to be in some sort of service

it's time to introduce a woman

vs. James, who's a chevalier nova with pink or rapid transitions

just because there are spaces doesn't mean this is poetry

Jake didn't see anything, so how can she/he say anything?

Conceptually i.e. sonically, *Jago* would be better, but   right now I'm not
                                                        feeling it
                                                                right now not
                                                        feeling anything

Jakob, my forest brother. Jakob and James both begin with J, are fraternal twin
names, share the room, become private secretary/secret/secretion to the exploring
of Siberia—

Transiberian expressionism or the pure Siberian concept

Could get high there, wear a white noise t-shirt with revolutionary red lettering. Or
could freeze.

Georg forswore *revolutionary children's pranks*

It's so cold here.

Inger loves it there.

red letter day?

The wrists of this book hurt. They are sticking out of the yellow long-sleeved shirt
which also has brown like a Tootsie Pop.

There is supposed to be something inside. If there's nothing inside, it feels like
being cheated.

The friction of his book, which you rub against as you go down, try to get warm—

Convex
Clouds of white glue drip down the sky. Stuck James to them. Stupefied by humidity.
Crows will inherit the earth, along with bedbugs. James no longer a transcrow. Tried
to swallow the mountain, it got stuck in her throat. So s/he spat it back out, pushed
it into the corner. Despair at the foyer of the landscape. Inside or out, everything the
same: pure waiting. Buildings flapped like stage sets. Air conditioners drooled onto
James. Clouds hunkered down, obscuring vestibules. Then rose like skirts. The light a
shining pair of scissors. James admired the tailors. She kept going, determined to reach
three years ago. But the most recent world enveloped him, and the bad bum started

cursing everyone. James shrank to be a crack in the sidewalk. I cannot bear this, this thinks. Two pieces of pavement separated, stretching him/her. James jumped up and started sprinting toward the trees, Polish people streamed by her, whining disapproval. Red lights shrieked. Horns were armies attacking with tuning forks. Finally, in the front of the butcher's shop, Stefek told her *Waldbuch* lay half a page away. We slowed down to peer into naked apartment windows, watch the young fathers and mothers and children around the tables or glowing machines. Then James was a constant and could substitute in for x or y. It isn't so terrible. Yes it is. Roald will not like me, but that doesn't matter, since his name has no meaning, it's merely Scandinavian. Actually it means famous ruler in old German, but that doesn't speak. Madness will come from the future, respite had come from the past. Their terrace overlooked a great mountain, they imbibed lager. Can I go back there now? Should never have returned here. Left foot misattached. The twentieth gimp Lens ducked his gilt block. Halo-head wannabe. James soon reached the dinner, to which she/he had not been invited. She stumbled in, her thick brown hair mussed, her long pale face boyish, his eyes wideset, his mouth blurry. His clothes were a second-hand kid's t-shirt (electric blue, saying *St. Stanislaus Youth Basketball* and the number *20*), saggy grey men's trousers, and the clichéd Hessian boots. Has-been properties of older projects. Roald grudgingly let her pass him, Who are you? I am a friend of Robert's and greet you from him. Your name, please? James, alias Lens. Aha, it will appear one day on a dotted line, won't it? I seem to infer a famous philosopher/mental patient by that name. Yes, but please don't judge me by that. James's German was *schrecklich*. Roald listened absently, with a disgusted frown. Gradually, James Lens grew more and more uncomfortable. The claustrophobic room, the shadows of the antique furniture, the bored faces of the several children, the astonishing Frau Inger, her face calm, inscrutable, her grey eyes sharp, missing nothing. James exploded and conversed brilliantly on philosophy, flying up to the ceiling. They decided to put him across the street, upstairs in a schoolroom, the head too spacious. James climbed, it was stifling, a closet, the pallet on the floor, a lamp next to it, James paced. Drying out, the universe shrank. This t-shirt, now tighter, gives me a pot belly. Thoughts as dreams or fables, the woods something I invented. *Forest brother!* Flat faces the only empirical sense data. The room became a nostril, James panicked. God picked her with His thumb and forefinger, flicked her onto the pavement. How revolting and goofy. *Goof* used to mean dement, i.e. madman, when it lived inside my parents' thesaurus, which was left to me, after the—never mind. There was a kiddie pool, inflatable like truth, James jumped into it. No Father, no Father! She bit her own hand. It could not feed her. Wet leaves vs. dry ones. The witnesses rushed over, James Ensor had painted them green, white and orange. *Ensor, Søren.* Names as possible egresses such as windows. I might not make it to the church or the bookstore ever again. James! James! What in the hell is the matter with you, boomed Roald in accented English. I cannot help it, I get so hot, James confesses. It is my habit to baptize my ankles and wrists or else clauses. He/she ran back upstairs feeling elaborated with shame. Who, then, could have slept?

Jake's Translit/My Transmanual

'C 'Cos all Jake now. Except some Franz: free man or French! Jake, Jacques, Jack. Like every transman jack of them—no, like one. Truth jacking logic, speeding off with it. Errant knave or servant. @your service. I feel hot. In my jacket opening at the front but a cover. Of the book. How frank to be? Even concepts are confessional. But don't just jack off: jake off. Give a hand job to another or novella. Incestuous poetics: do brothers, sisters. A Jake in the books should be deviant, non sequitur! Transmanual vs. Immanuel. Though I want God to be with my hand. In the unbound pamphlet or 12-second love prose poem/comedy. As much sorrow as comedy, said James Kirk, I mean Jake Dick, I mean Johannes Kierkegaard. Kirk had a sexy compact body I would've liked to feel. Pamphilus, feel us! Abbreviates to pam, the Jack of Clubs, 21 or under, 'cause writing juvenilia. Franz looked weirdly young like me. Vulnerability, moodiness, tenderness, emotionality, self-consciousness, alienation. Jack means fellow, man, it's used for a stranger. Fighter for some God. @higher service. To raise a heavy subject or object, go light. A jacklight is small, transportable, used at night for seeking, filching. Like Jacob when he ran away, perhaps from a bad narrative, after snatching his one or two years I mean one or two hundred years older brother's writing, and the Father's blessing. Don't arrest me, my lit! Cf. Georg B., also Franz K.'s The Trial. Kafka means jackdaw, but Jake d'Awe is a new world glossy black-haired bird. Don't let them dictate your body, don't be their dictée. In the dicktionary dichterisch (poetic) is followed by an arrow pointing at Freiheit (freedom). I am a girl with an arrow. Took to my heels like Jakob Lenz. On the Alp I wore my Jake boots, for deceivers, not soldiers. But you show your hand, don't keep your Jack close to your chest. Franz's chest sickly. Expel, eject, ejaculate, I Jake. Females do it also! How sex re-enters. I would enter the girl! Or the boy! Crushed-out sex with other texts: bastardizations. Translate's not enough; translit is better. With God licks and riffs. Plus a slit. My brother Lukerl said, There are two godheads: the world and my independent I. But also: I am my world: the microcosm. I, his younger brothersister Jake, say, I am my world: the microjism, microcum. My word: the microspasm. Ach Jacques, so obscene today! Too frank, Franz Jackdaw's antinote. Caws he hated his body, sexuality. Didn't crow. How you could find yourself trapped in a bad body, the wrong one, wake up to it. But then, you could imagine your way out. By agility. Like in wrestling. Jacob vs. the message. It's good to have something to fight against. Above all yourself. Whatever form you've set up: throw it away for a new one (novella, essay, poem, note, proof, etc.). To bring the writing back to life. It struck him on the lip I mean hip—thigh or socket (jack!). Don't eat your wound when you are blessé, or let it eat you, like when it feels like they jacked your dick. Instead make it bless you. That dream of messages going up and down the jack ladder of your phrases, sentences. That alternation as metaphysics. Via impure idiolect: open form and bawdy/heady, slangy/formal, fragmentary, mood-disordered. Outcast poetics. Ismael was a wild Lens of a transman, wild Jake as of a girl, w/ hisher hand raised against everything, including one self. 'Coz a line is a point that keeps moving. Jake d'Awe qua transFranz: The true way is along a line that crosses the others. It's designed not to steady you but to make you slip away. In jerkin and hermafro! To see the world's ascending/descending angles. Also to meet girls like Lulu and Odile. (Cf. Leah, Rachel!) World of city an opening. And you are lonely. Fear the empty room, want to love others, have uninferable experiences. Are hypersensitive to noises, others' suffering, their words and tunes. Jago crawled out to hear his sister Ottla sing, play her music. The world is all that is the verse. Which could be prose and biblical. The only good form of knowing. Fucked her, Olivia, up against the tree of life before they got expelled from infinity grade for doing it standing up. The ardor of thoughts is the ardor of flings. But this should quit now. But in here Arthur's music is addictive. Improvisation, variation, rhythm, dynamics, timbre being Jake's moves, too. My bro Haakon says Arthur's an angel i.e messenger. Like Gregor Samsa, except they don't understand him, his Amschel/Ishmael throat. But God does, so Jake keeps making noises. Making something up or out of hisherself or something, or making out with something. God? The girl? It repeats wrestling. It's unreasonable. Don't forget to jump out the window, hit the street. Do you want to live or to die? Polish men, Chinese ladies. Love the ones who might disdain you, they don't get your language. Put them into you. But what if they do violence, want to hurt you like biblical brothers? Even so. Outside it's gray. I am starving. Must break off. Jakob von Walser said all his pieces belonged to one huge, torn-apart book of himself. Resurrection by self-destruction: I could become Grégoire, Ivan, Mona. The other self-destruction is different. E.g. Georg T. Your brother: how you feel for him. In crossdistress. Or Jakob L., he tried, and Lenz means spring, and it's the spring now. But the spring died at 41, a banished stranger on the street of must go. Instead be der Verschollene: the one who went missing, was presumed dead like Lenz, but actually escaped to the wandering theatre of poets, 'cuz writing's acting, moving on the page's stage. Illuminated. The world is all that is translit: it lights up, then lights out. Lights up, out, etc. Translition = living onward. Like Jacob. Grasp the he'll. Of possibility. Be a small sex-pointed playing piece, don't be nothing, jack. Be Jake lit. Throw away Jakob's latter, be a jack ladder, a Jake letter. It's not a note to leave behind. It's a world to jack up. Ejaculate. 'Cosm all Jake now. Jake@All.

Jay Besemer

from **Gorgeous Hybrids**

Return to Form

Return to form, resubmit. "How conscious of our limited choices are we?" We return to form to

       console ourselves that life is controllable and predictable if we just keep
       to the lines. I'm told language is form, a consensual corral for thought, but
       no—language itself mutates to spawn gorgeous hybrids. (This is the forbidden
       lover): whispered to, whispered of, whispered in.

Heat, Light

Heat, light, the face of dawn. "In one person, longing drives a lifetime of questions. In another,

       that longing is fulfilled, and growth stops with the last payment plan
       installment." I don't know what forest I woke up in today. If we ignore the
       way the sun slides down the bark of the tree every day, we ignore the constant
       movement toward another morning. (How does desire move our limbs and
       those of the trees here?): In defiance of our hearts and the heart of existence
       we turn away and jingle the coins in our pockets.

Territorial Turkey-shooting

Trade (Series 2) 2010

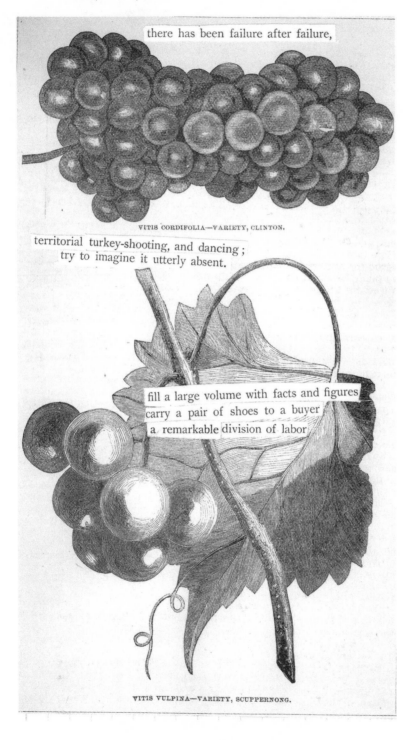

there has been failure after failure,

VITIS CORDIFOLIA—VARIETY, CLINTON.

territorial turkey-shooting, and dancing;
try to imagine it utterly absent.

fill a large volume with facts and figures
carry a pair of shoes to a buyer
a remarkable division of labor

VITIS VULPINA—VARIETY, SCUPPERNONG.

The Beef and the Milk

Trade (Series 2) 2010

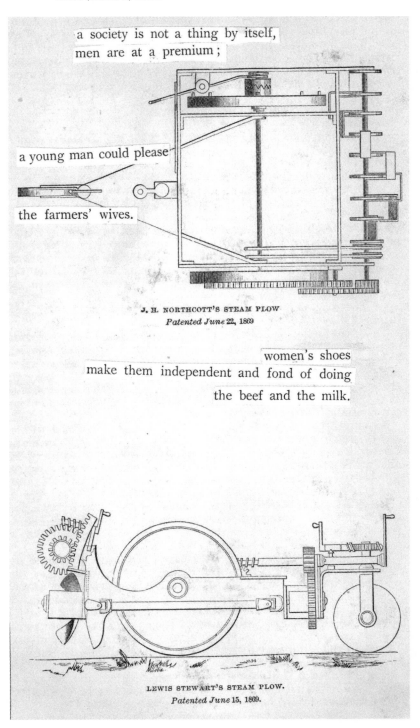

a society is not a thing by itself,
men are at a premium ;

a young man could please

the farmers' wives.

J. H. NORTHCOTT'S STEAM PLOW.
Patented June 22, 1869

women's shoes
make them independent and fond of doing
the beef and the milk.

LEWIS STEWART'S STEAM PLOW.
Patented June 15, 1869.

Eels Look Like Snakes

Problem Science (Series 1) 2009

When you are tightly held in the branches of low trees, by several of your friends, how can you get loose?

Eels look like snakes.

Hybrid, Camouflaged, Miscategorized, Found and Altered: A Poetics Statement in Four Parts

HYBRID

It is as natural as lichen. I make work that is many things at once: poems that are prose, that are pictures, that are poem and picture. Actions that are images using poems that are umbrellas. My best work is both/and, in-between, occupying several dimensions simultaneously.

CAMOUFLAGED

Some poems look like informational captions for photos taken by stone-age cameras. Some poems take the form of bibliographic citations. Some wear the clothes of word problems on standardized tests. Are you a man or a woman? Are you a door or a window?

MISCATEGORIZED

I was female when I was born. Later, additional information became available. I went to school for poetry, but I learned painting, performance, photography, psychology and biology at the same time. Some people find limited words to describe me and what I do, but my own words are not theirs. Sometimes I appear evasive or contrary so as to avoid miscategorizing myself, to avoid a truly misleading classification. What I am is how I work and what I make (see Hybrid).

FOUND & ALTERED

Catalogs. Trade magazines. Early twentieth-century textbooks. Pre-Darwin natural history surveys. Photographs. Letters. Ephemera. Drafts of my own work. Drafts of your own work. Objects on the street. Discarded, rejected, adopted, transformed. BECOME NEW.

Jenny Johnson

Tail

I picture the shameful length of it poking along behind me as I walk down 5th Avenue,
    the odd sheen of it, shimmering in shop windows,
How after too many beers, I'd lumber back into bed, its strangeness between my legs.

But as the sun rises—the clean stretch, aesthetic vertebrae— how I might flex its
    elegant, careful weight.
Consider my newfound balance, how gracefully I ascend a flight of stairs,
    teetering on one leg, my rump poised just so!
Or how I might signal to my lover, wave fondly to her through the air, lift my fur to tickle
    her mouth, dash a small crumb off her lips.
In a midnight alley, flashing my snowy underside like a switchblade, we'd sprint through
    underbrush.
Had I a tail, I would be luminous and lingering as a comet, who traces the starry night
    with a broken ellipsis…

*

As a kid, I remember the small green bubble inside the carpenter's level,
How it would dart from corner to corner,

And how good it felt to straddle the sawhorse, out behind the shed, half tomboy,
    half centaur,
How I clenched a 2 by 4 between my thighbones and it was part of me.

A nest of yellow jackets rose from beneath the splinters and, forgetting how to move,

how to cry, how to run,
I let them sting and sting and sting, eleven times, leaving swells on my arms, neck, legs,
feet, and shoulders.

*

Oh, Lord of Parts, Oh, Holy Tool Shed,
When I rise from these sore bones,
What have you taken? What have you left me?

James River

You are the wren scavenging for the husks of beetles.
I am the trout poking through river rocks,
the head of a copperhead slipping past,
the shadow of what you asked for turning to husk.

I am an open parachute, breeze billowing through.
You are the wren scavenging for the husks of beetles,
Now, I am flotsam poking through river rocks,
the detached head of a copperhead, snagged on rocks.

During recess, I remember, the parachute in my hands,
an open shadow, breeze billowing through.
When everyone pulled the chute upward to run beneath,
I was flotsam poking through river rocks,

the undulating lead blue shadows.
The parachute, faded indigo, was sweaty in my hands;
tucked beneath, one might feel whole
when everyone pulled the chute upward to run beneath.

Tell me: How cold is the fluid beneath your kneecaps,
the undulating lead blue shadows?
How red is the air beneath your fingernails?
Tucked beneath one might feel whole.

How remote is any one appendage from the other?
How cold is the fluid beneath your kneecaps?
Don't tell me the body won't turn on you like a corkscrew.
I am the air red beneath your fingernails,

the trout poking through river rocks,
remote as any one appendage from the other,
the shadow of what you asked for turning to husk.
Don't tell me the body won't turn on you like a corkscrew.

Late Bloom

What were you fending off?
You were Zorro, only less cunning
in cut-offs, wielding your branch tip
to catch web centers as if piercing

the flesh of foes. Sort it out:
The name of the spotted apple
on the leafy floor in the woods
a half mile from your white-walled

bedroom where the FM stereo
was always tuned to the same
country station your girl crush loved,
was gall, name of the shell

withering under leaf rot,
in that spot where the surprise
lilies sometimes remember,
sometimes forget, to bloom.

*

Touch a weevil and it will fall to the ground, legs and antennae tucked.
Blink and the artic fox becomes snow.

The gecko, toes spread against a tree trunk, passes for lichen.
Of all the ways a creature can conceal itself, I must have relied on denial.

There were the Confederate bumper stickers, pressure from seniors to tail gate,
the spindly legs of a freshman scissoring out a trash can,

how just the smell of Old Spice could make my muscles contract
like a moth, wings folded, the color of a dead leaf in October.

*

So, that she might hear her favorite song,
my voice would drop, and if the DJ answered

I would be Tim, Charlie, Luke, Jason, every name but my own.
Truer than gold.

Wasn't I the stripe in a tiger's eye?
The dapple in the flanks of an Appaloosa?

A heart hunting after a body?
In daylight, how would I possibly explain:

There is a border between the prey and the predator. I know this.
I know how to freeze, and I know how to forage.

Vigil

When I pedal down her streets, space and ecstasy are a single surface. Wind at our backs,
         white bungalows, striped awnings up and down Main,

I cycle fast, pant-leg cuffed, calf streaked with grease; I thread my way through
         locked traffic, past the canal, around Bell Isle;

I glide towards her and the glint of light that shimmers off the reflector on her
         rusted ten speed.

Our first date,

I fear if I blink I'll forget the dimensions of this city,
Lose foothold.

Trapezing across railroad tracks, I follow her to a spot along the James.

She kneels down to sunbathe on rocks.
I lie down beside her. What else could I do?

She points across the river to an osprey nest:
Tufts of straw jut out of a distant utility tower,
Silhouettes of birds circle

Overhead, eyeing us, eyeing their nests.

*

I need to tell you about the seeing that goes on between two people, around two people.
Not the touching. The watchfulness.

This is not just about love, though I love her as much now as then.
It's that she's always looking out.

If I follow the dotted lines of her gazes she's looking out at some thing
Just out of range:

A river otter floating at the base of a cliff,
A damselfly dipping her abdomen into a still dark lake,
A wasp out a tiny hole in a hollow gall, that wasp lifting its legs.

*

Years ago, I followed the gaze of a kid, looking at me through
A mirror in a public restroom in a park in California.

I knew by the duration of her looking that I was already a spot in the glass,
A small detour in her life that she was building a barricade against.

When she presses her nose to the glass every exhale fogs the exterior.

I knew her. I was her. I left her.

On lunch duty at the public school where I worked, I worried for her every single day.

Because I sometimes found the shadow of her against a wall in a hallway or stairwell
Where a boyfriend would press his palms into the tiles that surrounded her body

As though, if they might spin from vertical to horizontal, he would be ready
To drop and do fifty push-ups, up and down against her frame.

Already jeans sagging, he's excelling at this performance,
Lifting his chin to salute the other guys who pass by,

As she looks longingly, not at him, but at this spot at the center of his ribcage.

If you love someone, Rilke says, you must be the guardian of her solitude.

I picture this solitude: a physical, as well as psychic, space:

A shell extending around her frame:

The room her elbow needs to make just now:

The way a disc of light amplifies a solar eclipse.

And because I am a woman who forgets sometimes that she is a woman,
I always slip my shoes off and knock, at least, three times

Before crossing that threshold, before presuming I'm welcome here.

*

Out the window of a speeding car a man yells, *Dyke*. I don't know why.
It's Friday night, before our date, catching a late movie.

Have I placed us at risk? Hair short. Bound tight.

A silence bristles between us,

Hot ash about to blow across a paper city.

I see us as a low-budget docudrama, a dim photo of the White Night riots,

See us without context

As a tourist might with eyebrows raised eyeing two queers.

What I don't know how to reconcile is how to guard ourselves
When we're reliant on another's recognition to be perceived?

Not that she ever needed me to guard her. Her biceps are firm
As she folds me over in the dark the way I like it.

I won't cover your eyes, because I need to show you this, too:
Leviticus on a fence in Wyoming, the gay blood ban, Sakia Gunn disremembered.

*

Wherever you are, come back, she says, *come back*.

And eyeing us, a kid on a tricycle dinging her brass bell pedals closer.

Poetics Statement

Here is an analogy for the work I attempt on the page: A mirror box is a device used to deal with phantom pain in an absent body part. Say that you lose your left arm, and as a result you experience phantom pain in the space that remains. Seeking relief, you place the visible arm, the right arm, inside a mirror box, and when you do so a reflection of your phantom left arm is cast. Suddenly, you can see what was absent; you can move it around. The invisible is made visible.

When I go to write, I sometimes think of the page as a kind of mirror box, a transformative space where I can use language to give absence presence, to make the invisible visible. And here I am not speaking exclusively about bodies and their parts, as bodies indicate worlds beyond themselves, too. Here, I mean, anything felt that the eye might fail to register, skip past, or deny: two "old maids" on a park bench, a gecko passing for lichen, the blood beneath a fingernail, a look of unthinkable desire, etc.

Of course, I'm also interested in the ways in which language allows various bodies and all their unspeakable parts to materialize. When talking about how the brain imagines the body, neurologists sometimes use the word "schema" to describe a little map that lies across the cortex, sensing all our visible and invisible parts. In *Bodies that Matter*, Judith Butler goes a step further, using the word "schema" to talk about how the construction of the body through language is both psychic and corporeal (66). Some "phantasms" about our bodies in relationship to gender and sexuality are idealized, some affirming, some degrading, some transgressive, some compulsory (Butler describes heterosexuality as a rehearsed imitation of itself) (125). But she also suggests that we don't have just one imagined schema for our bodily egos, and that there is a need for "alternative imaginary schemas for constituting sites of erotogenic pleasure"(91). I am interested in this need, even as pleasure in the line of a poem has the potential to morph into ache.

A mentor asked me once to write an ode to a part of the body, and then an elegy to the same part. When writing about the body, is there a difference? I'm not sure. For example, a poem like "Tail" is both a praise song and a lament. The poem revels in the uses the speaker might have for a tail. And yet, the speaker's sovereignty over the schema of her body is lost when the bees disrupt her vision, stinging every part: "arms, neck, legs, feet, and shoulders." Writing this poem, I was interested in the juxtaposition of competing sensations: the desire to see and exist fully in a figurative body equipped with figurative parts *against* the ache of recognition, of acknowledging the limitations of a human body, the uses and lack thereof for one's body parts.

Which sensory experiences are necessary in poems? A parachute in someone's hands or the breeze billowing through? The way a child sees you in a bathroom mirror or the way you see yourself looking back at that child? Maybe if we can bear it, all of them, equally, at once.

Works Cited

Butler, Judith. *Bodies That Matter*. New York: Routledge, 1993.

John Wieners

Understood Disbelief in Paganism, Lies and Heresy

Prick any literay dichotomy
sung unrent gibberish from maxim skulls
west Manchester cemetery

recidivist testimony damned
promulgated post-mortem Harry Ghouls
wills pleasant chicanery hulled

in opposition to queer honesty,
flying hapless good humours
Morphe erroneous untedious mystery,

non-said mistakes; pure levity
to a method of confused doubt;
lipping erratic contrary indexd

Brevity; yes or no arsinine Coliseum
arrogance, attrib. Constant shout
Emperor Hippocratic misaligned

green breviary Ursuline stiff codecil.
A prayerbook, black Catholic mint
bogus mendicants Parsifal muff

Taught in the text as poor flopped sisters,
reeked convent blood between pleas
of gospel purblind drawn melodramas.

Silk-ribbon circus twined, border rhyme.
Povertystricken grandfathers hymnal
Less-allowed than San de Remo cape civil

War Revolutionary caval.
House Father across Sunday common roof
"But they're all ivoried brooch (navel

running marines the other way."
Spies vision for impertinently, drugs
when you're awake.

A viscosity submandered elopes
deluge senseless colophon
Forgotten opposition

in the face of negligent monetary
station or bookstore adherent nation.
(Debauched, bequeathed goad.)

Signs of the President Machine

I've got 25¢ coin on the bureau
or maple mahogany table, built out of
magnolia limbs, and a persian carpet airing in lawn

yard a baby flood, TELVA magazines with my photograph on
the cover as Marilyn Monroe, jack dead mother's nutty sister
saying, *Who Is She*, I'm A Lot of Man, by the late Nancy
    Cunard, of course

that pauvre Rose La Rose, Billie Shakepeare, or was it Sanctity's
                Holiday drugged as Moynihan across

behind a red lantern, ask Mme Brenda drinking torpid Gloucester
	cyan-
ide dutied United States Postmen, plastic transparent basket.

Poor Benedict posing as a Polish sister
I can feel his dope over the Hedges, wintergardening carol from
the Meirovingian corner besides
the master bedroom, the military treason in their acquisition
from accumulation in the United Feds prison of
not only food at Agriculture, but terms of language, love and
fashion

Pussybile, fresh from black George's suicide at 86 Charles.

Oh, yes, a week of, a month of, two years moving shirts with
Treasury numbers
poor secretaries becoming international thieves, from failure
to absorb
newly hung curtains, encroaching plants and poisoned burners
on the stove coiled charcoal sexual yens in the dish dryer.

Maria Gouverneur

Attic coiffure admonitioner
supreme Parisien commissioner
unblemished savior's listener

From circus rear town-house tier,
rare Egyptian emerald-agate tiara
reginatur licensed signature.

Triple-layered pensioner
mortally do not know who there
medicinal lives severally upstairs.

Heartbreak libertarian, or gall's pier.

Gathered upper cuff James bows,
arrows Maria cared cool shoulder
vying to honor Hebraic answers aries.

I shrink from the sight of her splendor.
actors, bottles readily bordellos
working useful plants shadows

delightful fool of no chateau marbles,
Ms. Monroe's daughter executes tables
geometry as a train's lucky owner.

Gardenias

Blue songs of The poetess' heart

In this moon-lit room above the city,
having risen out of darkness and obscurity
being witness to two decades of drunken futility
I have spent each day in fealty to beauty

still some loneliness lingers as sickness's vapor—
is it jazz, or late-night musing by the harbor,
unemployment with an empty head in the library
merely only poverty, or could it be inability

to hold a man, or woman as my own property?
Whatever it is, I am sick of sickness in the heart,
having no part in the world, being only a victim
to time, money and machines made by men other than I.

          2

There is no security, only a vague feeling, learned from other
     men,
That it is within yourself confidence lies, the means required
     necessary

seen in Nico and other men of her ilk, to relieve this misery.
Oh, we can't go on; why try, even monopoly competition alone
     kills

Despite fur coats, and banquet tables, single ear-rings,
poetry readings across the country, ideal communities
and overseas, the spacious mists pall boulevards to
lone candles in little moon-lit rooms above the city.

          3

I am tired of success, and literary acclaim if only
by a coterie to name just a few
in poetry; I know the answer, it's a womanish heart
growing old alone above the city, parallel horizontal
to the snow
wrapping herself up in the dreams of other men

               Have no mercy, they cry on the Fenway,
               their mesmerized eyes burn in the darkness,
               pushing herself on to the exhausation of
               love
               for a short eternity.

To Billie Holiday's *If I Were You*

did I swing in downtown bistros
as a black girl, what would my ancestors say
even in Africa I was punished

Well, what can you do,
it was great fun while it lasted,
a maroon blue gown out of the fourteenth century

approaching since memory,
under stained glass chancellories, oh, yes,
the morning promised

Tuesday afternoon tea dances,
on Churchill Street and the men drove up
to slice off my thights

and make me jitterbug in black nylon stockings,
singing in a side bedroom, where my sister and I slept
alone, while I wanted *A La Veille Russie*

on Fifth Avenue, under a wall of fan magazine photographs

Tashi

Put my brassiere between my legs
in the year 2000, as I shall be a thrush on the stem
with the muses removed out of Shubert Alley, can the kleigs
blow out, in an imagined act of position between

Demeter to Lusimelos. The magnificent dorsals sculpted
from Florence remain that evening's realine.

Don't mistake your message, Bavaria
          it is only my kind of paramount
                    woman you discharge.

Casual Love

casual, gives to her, joy
in the chair, sitting naked
looking at her lover,
asleep in bed.

Casual love, so easy to get,
so hard to forget yet
casual arms around a
casual waist

with marijuana regret
nothing, long hours passed
in love, he will not come
her way again. He's gone

to work by dawn. Deep waves carry him
out to sea, where one may not see
beyond his brown body / nothing.
Old rain falls on the windowpane.

Two o'clock rolls round again,
any two o'clock. Sinatra sings on the radio
It Had To Be You. Naked in the chair
Georgia on My Mind, listening

as moonlight, clear and sweet
through the pines. He will be gone
another naked dawn, another man
left out of her life.

2

She just picked him up or
rather he passed her by
on the street, turned around and
she took him home in a taxi, stopping

on the way to buy a fifth of whiskey.
She could not resist, what matter
he was black, drawn as she was, he has
not come yet, she thought suddenly,

I hope I don't have to go through that again.
Sitting up in the chair, a bed only big enough for one.
I wont get no sleep
dim music started to play.

She did not care, as saxophone and smoke began to blare,
through a trombone for riches and kings.

These were not her things
only marijuana and she meant it,

Stella by Starlight crept over the machine
and imagining a white leather pump
slung around her ankle,
she did not care again.

To H.

I like Sunday evenings after you're here.
I use your perfume to pretend you're near
in the night. My eyes are bright, why
can't I have a man of my own?

Your wife's necklace's around my neck
and even though I do shave I pretend
I'm a woman for you
you make love to me like a man.

Even though I hear you say why man
he doesn't even have any teeth
when I take out my plate
I make it up to you in other ways.

I will write this poem.

Preface

Verse making is more than a continuum of principle resting on feminine phenomenological apprehension. The real one of many, the illusory far and near intersect to push behaviour's stream, dependent on questing, producing revelatory postures for men, animals, and stars.

The poet is one pastor of this distribution between two visions.

Illusory form heightened by denial arises from contraction of desire, stilling propagation. To stay with one's self requires position and perhaps provision, realizing quality out of strangeness.

The quality of gift being alone

Wraiths cross time.

The gift of quality seems rather removed from processes practiced today over the counter, behind the bar and desk in lobbies of service. Interferences from gifts hamper realization, but they may be used as reinforcement of sensory apparatus. Proximate distractions show little more than confusion and to promulgate them as verse scatters ultimate sights, the true brothered quality of what we condense and what to allow constant.

The permanent evident seach for labour and trail makes dignity trivial. Visual order obeys gravity, but genuine shimmer substance cognates more than complacencies of constant worth. It holds radiation, that force attracts, draws and breathes.

An indoctrination to quality could be a return to places of origin, one instance of namely objects, the second an absolute rendition of balance and movement, the third transformations by fire, the easiest of all, if will be inherited. To true the present gleams more than conditions of pseudo-morphology, it asks one to submit to discipline's enduring form.

Joy Ladin

The Subject Disappears

It's hard to make small talk
when the subject disappears. Excuse me:

have you seen my I? Have you heard
which way it's pointing, whose heels it's sniffed?

Does it buy you drinks, give you shivers,
did it turn you on last night, stumble out at dawn,

tail between its legs, identifying its repetitive desolations
with the descending scale

of a bird that moaned in the distance?
Was it clever, patient, self-reflexive,

doomed to some dim archetypal quest,
did it crash in on itself like a waterfall, has it lost its sense

of beginnings and ends, does it stretch itself
toward opposite horizons, a tragic rainbow,

whose no can only mean yes?

Letter to the Feminine

You are a dream of clam shell and olive,
dark places between tails and spines, sheets stained
to reveal the spiritual complications
of your carefully perforated wings,

a calculated performance I rehearse again and again,
style detached, breasts incandescent,
little theaters of impossibility, immature stages
of the women in which you clothe me –

dead women, married women, women stuck between medieval pages,
fluttering in slips, flirting with socialism.
mounted, judged, incarcerated,
rubbed by unknown hands.

I wade through your editions,
lives you've bound, lives you've stitched,
lives you've flushed with dedication,
to unearth the truths you've hidden

in my own time, my own skin,
my own self unfolding
toward you and away,
over your passionate objections, through your suffering.

Letter to My Heart

I touch you from behind, through blood and spine,
and you become a child's again,
as though your mother were calling a name
you long to answer to and long to escape.

You fear I'll never leave you alone.
You fear you've been abandoned,
crushed, pinioned, institutionalized, metamorphosed
into a character in a play, a stranger I will meet someday

when we are both grown up,
torn in all the right places,
strong enough to wait outside the gates
of each other's ghettoes.

I touch you through a thousand facts and details –
sweet cream, crushed soil, honeysuckle, dusk –
the latest editions of the war, our original war,
to set each other free.

Letter to My Body

Philosophers shilly-shally, but it's true:
you are me; I am you.
This dust, these rays, this strange internal sense
that after all these years, I finally exist – all of this

is only mine through you. You still seem surprised –
that's part of your charm – that I wish to be extracted
from your handsome bindings.
This, you say, is only the beginning,

which is why it feels like drowning
in what we've both survived. Ever the politician,
I say I'll be your widow.
Try to look cheerful as you die.

Not yet, you say, as though
– this is the other part of your charm –
you still believe in time.
Violent laughter, yours and mine.

Let's go out into the woods
of meaning and matter, among the laurels and the mustard,
the unlit suns and unnamed branches, the listening shoots and loosening leaves
we can only appreciate when we're drowning

in one another. Let's break up before we meet
and fall in love again, let's whisper wishes
in the darkening parlor of the heart,
let's wait for God in the gathering dusk

and watch the stars come out.

Filibustiere

Time to raise the voice that sank
as your hollows expanded.
Disenfranchised by the coarse black curls

matting on shoulders and thighs,
you kept your pleasures private,
moments of naked abandon

when you stepped behind the electoral curtain
that barely covered your midsection
to punch a hole beside a name

no one knew you had chosen.
When the curtains opened,
you resumed the role, unmade-up and unshaven,

of model citizen, a posture of submission
adopted with ironic disregard
for the liberties you'd taken.

Now your spheres of influence have grown
in the most unexpected directions,
your aureoles shimmer

in the patriotic breeze,
exposing the consensus you've assembled
in a corner of a closet

one yes vote at a time. Some day,
you'll stand for what you are –
this slash that, out of order, other,

one of the unmentionables
America fingers in her dreams
but wouldn't be caught dead in.

Ready to Know

All words found in the June 2005 issue of *Seventeen*

Ready to know which girl you are?
Find out while you shave your face
and try to convince yourself

you *can* look great, hide tummy, enhance bust,
find the best dress for your shape,
exfoliate your past so gently

you won't even feel
the ambivalence that rocks your body,
fleshing out your future, adding curves to your shame.

If you prefer the privacy of your bathroom,
practice becoming in the mirror.
Say yes to the girl you see,

witty, pretty and brimming with caffeine,
glowing with passions you try to keep hidden,
the vaginal freedom evolving under your clothes

as Venus sweeps through the house of your body,
a sun-kissed goddess kissing your contours,
filling them in with love.

See what's in store for you
in the opposite direction of the hair
creeping out of your bathing suit? Real life

curling gratefully around your navel, winter fading
as the quintessential girl moves into your chest,
creating opportunities, offering you up

to the goddess moving through
the guy you've been for years.
Which girl will you turn out to be?

Are you ready to know?
Indigo impulse, aqua flash,
say yes by letting go.

Half the Human Race

All words found in the May 2005 issue of *Woman*

If your happiness requires you
to ruin your life
by whirling between man and woman,

why not sip a glass of wine
under the cozy comforter
of your marriage's demise

and plant yourself in the fabulous oasis
of psychological freedom
beyond the shores of pain? Most divorces

turn out to be petite and needy, childlike hands
you'll have to wave aside.
Making up half the human race

takes time. Think about it. Women
are more than spring plantings, candy that doesn't melt, angels
in search of the perfect life.

They tightrope-walk into adulthood
between searing fuschias of right and wrong,
struggling to heal, provide for their babies,

be just kids with each other, breathe.
As you lose the marriage that cut you off
from the lives of women, it's remarkable to see

the blessings of the feminine
knitting your suffering and fear
into hope for connectedness.

Yes darling, a life of freedom
encircled by discomfort
will be served in the Carriage House,

where fine specimen roses climb
winged poles damaged by trauma,
cleansing and energizing the life

you can only share with generations of women
by amputating rage and failure
from both breasts at the same time,

simultaneously splitting down the center
and knitting together
the young girl you had no hope of becoming

and the old woman
who taps her foot in time
when she hears you sing.

Trans Poetics Manifesto

"Trans poetics" are techniques that enable poetic language to reflect the kind of complex, unstable, contradictory relations between body and soul, social self and psyche, that those who see ourselves as transgender experience as acute, definitive, life-changing. These relations are simultaneously universal – no soul is precisely expressed by a body, no society precisely fits a self – and unique. No non-trans person can experience what trans people experience; no two trans people's experiences are identical. Because trans experience is unspeakably unique, it is quintessentially human.

Like all poetics, trans poetics are ways that poetry can happen: not the only ways, not the best ways, not the truest ways, not the noblest ways, not the most experimental ways: poetry doesn't care how it happens. From a poet's perspective, "trans poetics" refers to techniques that enable poetic language to embody or enact some aspect of trans experience; from a critic's perspective, they refer to formal categories, tools for classification and identification, bases of comparison that bring different poems into meaningful relation. From a reader's perspective, "trans poetics" means language that makes us realize that we are Toto and there is no Kansas anymore.

Trans poetics aren't a matter of poetic content. Poems that describe or refer to trans experience may not utilize trans poetics – and poems that are not about the trans experience may. Trans poetics aren't a function of the demographics, gender or political identification, body or soul of the poet. Trans poets (by which I mean the entire spectrum of gender-complicated poets) may write poems that don't utilize trans poetic techniques, and non-trans poets may write poems that do. It doesn't take a carpenter to hammer a nail. It doesn't take a trans person to sing, sigh, scream or psalm the friction between body and soul. Trans poetics aren't intellectual property, a badge of honor, compensation for oppression, an inversion of the gender privilege system, the gender equivalent of Masonic mysteries, or a secret handshake.

Like all poetics, trans poetics are partly fantasy. They only exist when we see them, and we only see them when we need to.

Like all poetics, trans poetics may be consciously conjured, or recognized in retrospect. (At this very moment, some grad student is probably discovering trans poetics in Homer, hidden like Patroclus in Achilles' armor.)

"Trans poetics" may be unheard of, outlandish, shocking – or they may be familiar poetic means deployed for trans poetic ends. Think of rhyme: the use of sound to call attention to likeness in unlikeness, the revelation that different semantic bodies harbor the same sensuous soul.

Like modernist poetics (remember those?), trans poetics transform meaning from a product provided by the poet into processes within the reader. Like post-modernist poetics (remember those?), trans poetics transform semantic processes within the reader into self-reflexive reflections on the lust for and impossibility of meaning, knowing, being.

Trans poetics show us who we are by showing us who we aren't. Trans poetics show us that who we are is who we aren't, and that who we aren't is who we are. Trans poetics transform self-estrangement into self-discovery, self-discovery into the discovery that there is no self, the impossibility of self into affirmation, exposition, industrial revolution, a massive conspiracy, a door, a window, a wrinkle in time, a sob on tiptoe, a song that is singing us.

If we are smart, honest, work hard and stay on our toes, trans poetics will grow through us from yet another fashionably vague critical term into an understanding of language, form and humanness as precise as a scalpel and as urgent as the silence of God.

Julian Talamantez Brolaski

new nudism

all pure honey granulates
holds with death no más
& yelling only makes old yeller yell more

dream of driving a postal truck
w/ bad brakes down a vertiginous
precipice of moss (when formerly, out west,
I thought the postal truck was in pursuit of me)

hasselback made a face
                    ran the length of jersey
the table or the nipple wd be the same colour as befor
why is ther a prince if it can get agitated?
I must learn certain skills, like how to pour a tea w/out at all spilling
you cant ask a lover to get intimate w/ a wound

I tried first the one glasses, then the other,
finally none
I think I may finally begin to see in my myopia
the sevral dirty pages
the fact that the page had ended
        staying amid lines
                    pale hesitant ink

that my glasses too needed a bath like any other appendage

I'd actually gone up in flames. of course, that's
what a flamer does. I shat an actual figure eight.
flamer-4-ever.

The tears attempted to approach me at my very
writing table!

This is how blind I was at 7, at 14, at 22, at 30.

I need only to blink and my vision is improved.

> philosophy attends my wounds
> here at the hour the utmost hour

>> wher doth desir
>> I cdve ben ston'd
>> eh-ben-dis-donc
>> mor philosophie

# of mongrelitude

A bed of roses itself is no bed of roses. Nobody wants an e-book, they would sooner
leave you in the lake, a den of mouldering slime for your coffin. Everbody calling it
a recession—theyr in a delusion. I am privy to these contradictory situations where I
am told first the one and then the other bathroom is the wrong one. Madame, c'est là!
and then o monsieur! je me suis trompé! If I powder my nose in the tudes, if I choose
to walk barefoot in the small hours…you yourself are a healing property you know.
You came home from the fair only to join the circus its festal moods, to feast on frost.
So one learns to make thir way amid the multitudes. And know bliss as a cowperson.

I know I am the small fry here. Whose harnassed thot drove winter aback, gos wrastlin
thir daemon underground. Tho the stirrups brinked and tha mud was broke, I looked
down to the rivulet between the tracks, and couldnt tell if what I saw was a turd or
twisted rust metal. & the rats, rooting amid the black death and the typhus. One
comes out steppin, their eyes fallen on the shores, cognizant only to the trash they
mucked around. Suddenly you and your neighbour's thighs are pressed together,

accidental camaraderie or blunt eroticism. And neither of you move away.

We race toward the mounds of gravel, the morning star met with its wanderer.

red sky at morn

tho what hath been primordial—thir fronte, ofttimes in geste, as in ACCORDANCE
they hath pronomounced themselves (most onerous) who forsaw (midst all lordyngs)
the hairy belly upraiseth itself from the sepulchre studded w/ flames—that this geste
was made hereabouts, one amends thir own selfe not a priori the lover but in the act of
transing—that's what the therapist called it—does not one sometimes *arrive* or end-to-
begin? yes DEATH but of a spirit also which goeth nat w/ fleshy mouldings, haha, not
w/ *that guy* anyway.

some say an army of horsepeople

some say an army of horsepeople
some say soon the handle wull fly right off
only to be ambiguated by a single letter

who hath bespoke
wheelis   flyan upright
who sat bolt upright in thir coffin

look it's victor hugo
the great poet
talking to chopin

who hath commandeered all tusks
only the particulate matter
the very follicles

yeh I have to leave you

alone and give you
your mouth back

the godawfullest thing
on this bleak earth
some say an army of horsepeople
but I say it's—

whos manifest chivalry is n/t but sexism

whos aspect dear, regardless
how it soles thir aspect
               who claim
chivalry is n/t but sexism
prettily vested. pretty cloak draped
overra puddle   whos fingers
point nearby the needle to be
not afraid, no tengo medio
but I have rushing, to rush
a kind of anarchic mise-en-scène
one washes thirself but they do shower,
they bathe one or the other, raze
the parts. that they may
not be away, that þt was therrtofore
the extent: breath of paganini,
outfit de-oiseaued, bird defrocked.
our fans are now ppl who like us, trust me
it's less commital this way and no-one
likes commitment. the i in thir
name was in the shape of a pill
intended for s/o who actually needs
it. whos leather yarmulke said how kinky
they were, whose gauntlet, so beautiful
in its utter lack of purpose.

most honeyed

that most ~~that~~ honeyed ~~form chi~~
~~that~~ took xirself
up against knocks / said / set ^{be met}~~to meet~~ / against (incontro)
with-for—that so being forse achen
upon my word, srsly
ich have litel worth (^[or] had not the thot)
to thereby go ariding & YET have (hath) ridden forsooth
þat I am said to have been and must to remain <u>one</u> <u>way</u>
it ~~has~~ hath been forwilled—my brayne aches—
           litel company   no forsooth it ~~has~~ hath forgone,
that is it is forwent, having been gone, passed over
to be ~~erst~~ all-the-while forsaken, though the lover ~~was~~ is
     perhaps there ys s/t (suthing) in the populace
that speaks for, may be hereas^ywis. ~~why~~ ^{what} say you
that it is locked   is now being asked to re-whoa why ought_(n't)
(that) to be xir job? _____ has not required a
passkey ~~being~~ ^{that one is thereby} not not not a person. perhaps one does not
not want to be found   unsupple in the main and unduly hided
                    that one ys most of all (the time) w/ oneself

[WAR MESSAGE!] we dont want yr tools

   for CAConrad on the escalation of troops

look gentlepeople
the only source of likelihood
is a fist in a gentle orifice
if I'da been a ranch
they'da calld me bar none
a fecund desert
full of heartless so-and-sos
the tub of butter thereafter was rancid
we put xir and xir mouth ta rest
along with the chickens in our maw

hey blood, hey sucka
as like to one as to th'other
do you love your sibling
as they do as they do

when melancholy fails, capchas doth succeed

in the end

        whos ars becum manifest

          consolio ergad

            list of capchas which better expressed
            hir disconsolation than any

ars melancholia. art, in the end

        the tedious array of portraits

        the seven line simile

        the grainy flickers of light

          did not express it better than

             garoomer ingstsag
             enounch fronses

Phonosemantics and the Real

> *Shakespeare was almost certainly homosexual, bisexual or heterosexual. The*
> *sonnets provide no evidence on the matter.* -Stephen Booth, ed. *Shakespeare's*
> *Sonnets.*

If you look closely enough at a word, you'll find it contains its opposite. George, porridge, Norwich, porch and goy ridge all rhyme with orange. Why this antithesis between decoration and use? Is a tiger less efficient because of its stripes? Plato's cloak was so magnificent that Diogenes leapt on it...

Lucus a non lucendo – an absurd conclusion, explaination or non sequitur. Literally 'grove from not giving light,' i.e. a dark grove (*lucus*) is so called because it does *not* shine (*lucere*)—an illustration of the etymological procedure (see Augustine) of definition by antiphrasis.

That art is thievery is a commonplace--lyre is homophonous w/ liar. This only coincidentally says something about poets (*fidicula*, little lyre, is an instrument of torture).

The very labor.

Stein was mainly moved to write by sounds, but not divorced from their landscape or visual field: 'Cows and the clunking of their bells inspired her. The American writer, Bravig Imbs, said he saw her sitting on a camp stool in a field and instructing Alice to bat a cow with a stick to one side of the field. Gertrude then wrote in her exercise book. Then she folded up her camp stool, moved to a different part of the field, and signalled to Alice to bat the cow in a different direction' (Souhami).

That mountain range reminds me of a postcard.

Georg von der Gabelentz's *Lautsymbolik* claims that as sound and meaning meet our 'feeling etymologizes' (r to the dog and s to the snake [Saintsbury]).

Erasmus says to lie and tell the truth cleverly are the skills of the same artist (*De Utraque Verborum ac Rerum Copia / On Copia of Words and Ideas*). See Isidore of Seville on the 'vervex' or wether, the ram:

> The wether (vervex) is either named from "force" (vis, gen. viris), because it is
> stronger than the other sheep, or because it is male (vir), that is, masculine; or
> because it has a worm (vermis) in its head—irritated by the itching of these
> worms they butt against each other and strike with great force when they fight.'
> ('De Animalibus' II.x, *Etymologiae*).

Etymology can be said to be articulatory, thus bodily: 'The Paget theory would explain this...by saying that while "huge" moves the tongue back from the teeth so as to make as large a space as it can, "wee" moves the tongue near the teeth so as to leave as small a space as it can...*all sounds may be reduced to gestures in this way, more or less fancifully*' (Empson 14, emphasis mine).

Changes in poetic form correspond to changes in language structure—e.g. the move from alliterative to end-rhymed verse may correspond with a shift from Germanic trochaism to Gallic iambism (see Hanson and Kiparsky on universal poetics)[1]

I like using 'it' for humans. It reminds us we are creaturely. From the Passion of St. Margaret:

> And se godes peowe Theothimus gefand þaet **cild**, and he **hit** up anam and **hit** well befæste to fedenne. And þa **hit** andgeate hæfde, he **him** nama gesette, and þaet wæs **Margareta**, and **hi** syððan to lare befæste, and **hi** þæron well geþeah. (MS Egerton 877, late 14th cent.)

> And God's servant Theotimus found the child and took it up and entrusted it to be well fed. And when it had acquired understanding, he gave it a name, and that was Margaret, and [he] afterwards set her to learning and she fully excelled thereon (at it).

The third gender pronoun has been variously referred to as a 'doomed neologism' (Joan Taber), 'an exercise in futility' (American Heritage Book of English Usage) and 'the word that failed' (Dennis Baron, *Grammar and Gender*). Anna Livis writes that they 'exist only in articles exhorting their use' (Anna Livia, *Prounoun Envy*).

Curiously, among my friends, it's the painters and not the poets who use 'xe' in speech.

OE used to have a dual, *wit* ('we two'). We don't have that now, why not? Clearly the need to distinguish addressing two people is not sufficiently compelling. Youse, you all and y'all remain dialectal (but seem writerly).

Samuel Johnson is right to say it would be folly to attempt to 'embalm the language' and yet he inveighs heartily against translation, which he called 'the great pest of speech' and hopes that 'if an academy should be established for the cultivation of our stile...let them stop the licence of translatours, whose idleness and ignorance, if it be suffered to proceed, will reduce us to babble a dialect of France' (preface to the *Dictionary of the English Language*, 1755).

Hank Williams was the first to translate the nonsensical yodel (yo-de-lay'ee o, delay'ee o, delay'ee) into the substantive yodel and regularly exploit it: 'And I'm lo-o-o-o-onesome / I got the lovesick blu-ues.'

Mimesis may be a typical response to the world, but it is the distortions that are provocative--the Pythia riddling over Delphic fumes. Wittgenstein writes, 'I can see a stag that isn't there, but I can't shoot it' (I think he uses 'him').

The melting of the Polar ice caps, having caused the Grizzlies to extend their habitat further north, has resulted in a hybrid 'Grizlar' bear.

The Apache word *pesh* ('sword') literally means iron, named for its materiality. The tongue must at length comply w/ the pen.

The Book of Vices and Virtues, a 14th cent. typology of sin, says of homosexuality, 'the devil himself is squemous thereof.' The homosexuals are in purgatory and upper hell in Dante and in the visio Pauli, 'their countenances like blood.'

The police officers' riot gear tells us they are our enemy.

You can tell the difference between voiced and unvoiced sounds not only by placing your hand on your throat (the textbook says 'adam's apple'—as if the sin got stuck in the throat?) and feeling the vibration or lack thereof: as between /s/ and /z/ (voicess / voiced sibilants) or /f/ and /v/
(voiceless / voiced labiodental fricatives) but by attempting to sing on the phoneme itself. The voiced sounds /z/ and /v/ are able to vary in melody and tone, unlike their voiceless counterparts. Just try to hum 'Silent Night' on /s/.

The seagull spreads its wings to indicate imminent flight.

Notes

1. 'At 6 months of age, German-learning infants demonstrate a preference for syllables with a trochaic pattern, while French-learning infants can discriminate trochaic from iambic stress patterns but do not show any preference' (Höhle et al., 2009). ('Rhythmic grouping in French and German adults: A cross-linguistic investigation of the Iambic-Trochaic Law' by Anjali Bhatara, Natalie Boll-Avetisyan, Annika Unger, Léo-Lyuki Nishibayashi, Thierry Nazzi1, and Barbara Höhle).

kari edwards

good questions...

quick answer, no; quick answer, there is no here-to-there-there; no, quick answer, no, face-to-face, tag you're it; quick answer, there is no answer; quick answer, stop being a body with organs; reach escape velocity; undo the gender tape on the body, put on with super glue, stapled in for good measure; can you spell escape route? quick answer, no-yes, yes-no, no-yes, yes-no; quick answer, how would you like your macmac'alike today, served your your way way, this way or that, choice (a) or (a) or (a) or (a) or (a)? no; quick anwer; maybe, (toto knew), home is where all objects cower in demonic mimicry; community is the now of now, of now of now; quick answer, can the tools of the master race, tongue or master master major major be anything more than have it now moments? quick answer, become unrecognizable, schizophrenic in a minor key; quick answer, no; quick answer, I am of the air waves, virtual, vital and a good fuck on channel 4; quick answer. it is always post-post historical post-post, never and can be, divergent unexpected endless curves, always post-post never-never's or always bold holocaust road maps, one or the other guiding one through future mine fields; quick answer, the coyote and trickster; quick answer; feel the deep talons of commodity sink into flesh; quick answer; resistance is futile, you are already virtual, stuck in quantum glue...... quick answer, no, it's already too late

from obedience

let nothing be as silent as arrogant bigotry

let nothing be so silent as supernatural belief in arrogant bigotry

let nothing be so silent as the implementation of a superstition
    based on arrogant bigotry

let no conformity of experience lead to certainty of violence of
    belief found in supernatural arrogant bigotry

let all be led away from the blind hybrid of the drunk corpse of
    arrogant bigotry

may some like it hot and like it to go and something something
    stopping the terror of neurologically rearranged bigotry

let no galaxy burn brighter than a poem railing against the
    carnivorous teeth of dismissive references of gritty bigotry

let the crystalline batteries ultrasonic song sing flashbulb and
    vacuum descend in will-o-wisp implosion at the drowning
    dolphin's embrace, when there is a new flash existence of
    bigotry

may the day be speaking of speaking, the sanctuary, of humanity
    and illumination in the flower of clarity, speaking of the
    poor and hungry breath of the ocean, of the saliva, of saints
    in dust at the end of the day, at the end of all bigotry

double your trouble – toil to a stubble

in the beginning we ate collateral damage, in the beginning we pretended to be slugs. it was an easy life, it was barbecues, cathode-ray tubes and KY for those secret rendezvous. not room for much else, tried to avoid the sun as much as possible, mostly due to a DNA debacle with those insipid bipeds. it was awful, helicopters full of garbage, heaps of singing corpses a la king. what a scene, disco being reinvented for the 10th time. I kept saying something about the wheel, the wheel, the wheel, but the word was not around long before the ideal became an appendage extension; call it a cigar, but never a nobody being a nobody's fool on a hill. lessons were given on makeshift wearable shoes. good-n-plenty was a personal deity, "unless one has too much cheap" beer, wine, whiskey, food, liquor, lavish costumes, chocolate, coffee, or the rest and becomes christian in feelings, jewish in food, buddhist in shoes, muslim for a good time, and hindu for many lifetimes. that is about when everyone joined the wright brothers sisters daughters fathers tom, dick and mary's entertainment board of wicked dock workers, or was it the oxford dictionary of nursery rhythms, inc.? everyone wanted a new place, everyone pined for mete-or-ological faith healers and or remunerative suggestions. bigger, cleaner, wetter, faster, broader, more often, longer, harder, much harder, richer, prettier, louder, sooner or later all came after the invention of the hyphen-dot-happiness-dot-com; someone had the bright idea of toothpicks and pyramids, and for a while they were head-to-head, toe-to-toe, while the rest waited in place with plastic teeth in hand .

each motion its own atmosphere

imagine a red fragment
entering my flesh

you walk away
tearing the breathing apparatus

impossible to speak without memory
mantled by a jagged harnessing human tide

the rest flattened to a freeway
rest stop experience

both victim and execution,
generalized and reduced

inert object identical to
a mob burning another fetish to flames

nothing to do with the living
it can not be helped

hence it is terrible
you are in the same place as before

I am repeating my standards of care
there are a billion subjects doing the same thing

chance recovery

we ourselves, our all included and not included or nothing or part of a practice that could be a mistrustful manner, that could be our deceitful panic, in ours scattered among nations or a few with upper management desires, we are the working poor, we have cardboard box homes or contrary to popular demands our objective self, which is as much a lie as one for all and all for . . . . . . is there such a thing as a enemy of the state, could there ever be in a fair state of mind if we see anyone as an enemy, or is there a state worth stating with our aesthetics bound in collective picturesque truths or our panoramic lies.

we are them wanting to be like them who want to be like us. we can no longer trace our origins, our ancestry has disappeared the dirt and soil you try to sanitize, our mothers and fathers have all disappeared, disavowed us, been captured, are in prison, murdered or are members of a party all night till you puke-party.

we are in the back of the bus, we are the driver for your new mercedes, we drive your hearse, make the casket and bed you sleep in. we crucified christ, froze in the paris commune, hid in tunnels as tanks rolled past, plotted revolution against a tea tax, against the fascists, against the emperor for life, king of the land, infidels and greedy landowners. we are, relatively speaking, a relative of someone somewhere who sees us as a dangerous machine with no knowledge of the former addressee.

we are soul, flesh, blood, codes, spirals, and subatomic wave forms. we are a head in a herded crowd, nothing, everything, sin, grace, carpet bombers, forgiveness of sin of an imaginary or real enemy, hero, villain with a complete lack of cause. we are sign-language, esperanto, rock-an-roll, the watusi, tango, charlie, care givers, assholes, believers in the myth that there is such a thing as a man or a woman, or only men, or only one or another, we are the good, bad and ugly in every spaghetti western. we are the hateful, and hated, the redeemed and redeemers, the possible and the limited, we all want to be famous and on television or hide under the covers, we are simple and complex, which depends on the census. we can be the sheet-anchor for the drowning or the one holding them under, we are the assassin's bullet and the blood of the victim, we are a moment of everything and nothing, we all have an address with no known distant neighbor, we are a speck adrift in the vastness of unknown dark matter. we are a chance recovery waiting to happen.

This leftover disruption thing

we want the freedom
to be disassembled
freedom from connotations
of the nearly possible
being intoned
in the contours of contours

we want 1 of any
108 times
16 hundred attentions to detail
either does or does not originate
on account of absent
or not
concerning the concerning
set forth
after too many objects
after too many objections

we want
a combination of
the impossible
dreaming substance
moving in fire
because it's a condition
in a substance
moving in fire

liquid human like
senescing the senses
recording undulations

becoming an apprentice
with perfect teeth

the rest is someplace
looking for a sunrise
able to rain down
hills and streams
inside the flesh
inside the wind
held in a dream

subject: statement

it is the space one holds, not an essential objectification one is held in, where one is stabilized into things in space, places with borders, bodies with procedures, proper behavior by corporeal containment, compulsory reproductive management, polarizing populations, producing mythological projections, slicing every single living energetic instant into bipolar neurosis for further control of an imagined boundary.

queer is fluid skin, a body without organs, fingers, sweat, fists, taking responsibility for orifice potential, another possible inner exterior moment to moment nonlocation location, accounting for that finite moment that bleeds to the next, noncorporeal sensual connectivity with the body in space, a responsibly of that space as place, an awareness beyond compulsory reproduction, writing nonlocation location.

identity is a tool for momentary defense against historical locality, historical permanence with borders, but the body is flux mechanics, writing a queer writing a queer text is fluid, outside inside, inside a body space with no boundaries, a realization that there is no singularity without borders, dogma and a belligerent linearity.

it is not imaginary borders turned into religious incarceration. boundaries are not queer, sovereign boundaries are colonial, location of the self within the state. queer location is a discontinuity within the panoramic whole, taking into account the unaccountable, accounting self in space, attempting language.

a narrative of resistance

recently I went to an "I am a _____(fill in the blank) and I am beautiful and sexy and fine and I am ok with who I am no matter what you say" performance. the fill in the blank in this case could be any word that describes any category or any group of nouns that are a category or any adjective that describes a group or category of nouns that are recognizable within the repeatable patterns of situated narratives, whether on a part time or full time basis. this is not a judgment about the "I am this _____(fill in the blank) and I am beautiful and sexy and fine and I am ok no matter what you say," club, since it is a first step in seeing one's self other than as a formless form situated in social shame. it is more a question of, if this is the stopping point, does it do anything more than reinforce the "I" as the ultimate achievement; where the end-game is the epiphany of late capitalism; to become an all consuming self-controlling anorexic life-form on automatic here to be the greatest consumer by buying one's way into endless cycle of unexamined representations of the grand tale; a maybe, a reiteration of the heroic journey, or a story with a moral? I am not interested in morals, morals situate one within the state of label placements and finality. as whatever said in *a day in the life of p.* writing an article for the *psycalene quarterly*: "to the funeral ball - to the bat-n-ball, hand shaken going on at the funeral ball."

I am not interested in situating myself or seeing anyone situate themselves in a state of subjugation, "or a felonious definition that creates a category." on the other hand trying to escape from this multi-labeling assembly line at the commodification factory is like a fish trying to open a franchise of mcdonald's . . . though this is not a probability, it might as well be possible. the probable we live out of has as many options as the impossible . . . . . we exist in the probable of the planned out, knowing the outcome ahead of time. I want to explore the possibilities hidden away in dark rooms, the unnamed and unseen . . . . I want to experiment with new ways to articulate the inarticulate that do not situate it in "a larger than persephone cast iron cog with teeth of cement blocks," and at the same time affirm our humanity while calling attention to flagrant lapses of institutionalized thoughtlessness. whether we were dropped off here by someone's god, or by accident there is too much suffering and destruction going on for it to be always about the "me" theme in personal "I" narratives.

so then what is a narrative of resistance? what is a narrative that informs and resists at the same time? what is this miracle and how did I get here? is there a stable body? can there be more than twenty pronouns?

words become important in the act of resistance or the corruption of words, or what you can do with them, or not. and just for the record, I am a self proclaimed deviant and all that that can mean. it's just a word right? deviant is like queer, but more so; I deviate as much as possible from moral norms . . . . or social norms, right path, or a proper code of conduct, proper spelling, right grammar, right way to be, here to serve someone's god and country. that does not mean anything goes, it is still and always about reducing suffering.

basically, the way things are going now, the implementation of the social contract is not working, there is too much suffering and destruction going on and I/ we need to deviate from this path of institutional subjugation. in *a day in the life of p.*, p. the main character is "referred to as sometimes, something, whatever - or both." are we not at all times, a both or whatever sometimes? and a whatever as we glide through our own positional grid, qualitatively changing with each passing event. we can pick and / or choose (as much as one is able) multiple categorie(s) to situate in, if we choose to pick a category at all. there is also the possibility that no matter how positioned we think we are in category or our choosing, an individual can experience a sudden sift in one's position as one subjugated by another's gaze into a different category.

this dance with a narrative of resistance started for me when I "discovered I was writing this secret diary, totally unaware of the fact that I was keeping this secret diary . . . . (but) there was always this feeling I was doing something I didn't know I was doing." I began reading books that allowed me to say, "oh, there are others like me, and they all did similar x, y, and z things." finding these connections with others are important, if not critical to resistance. having a language to speak ones truth is a critical tool for resistance, but it does not creates an environment of resistance if one stays in an identifiable category; just the opposite happens, one becomes, "I am this, I will always be this," "this is my story," and "I am going to tell my story." then there is a city full of stories, and television shows with everyone's story on it, all day all the time. after reading numerous "x, y, and z things books," what I started to notice was, all these "x, y, and z thing" books were more of the same thing, then there were more books that said the same thing from a different perspective, and all these books ended up on a bookshelf in the back of 'barrens and nobles,' or those bookstores with rainbow flags out front... another way of looking at this is, this is a country of, "I am an island theme songs," "my story counts as possible docudramas points," "I am an island in a special ocean" . . . . . we can no longer afford to be islands . . . . or support the island effect. artificial boundaries are foolish and create the is the first step to nationalism and creation of the 'other.' we are a nation that thrives on islandism . . . . psychotherapy induces islandism. there is a blue jean company that produces 45 different types of blue jeans, so we can become one of 45 special islands . . . how many types of blue jeans do we need? it becomes nothing but a celebration of "the national assembly line production quotas for the year. look at me I am the newest of the new in my 1 of 45" what ends up happening with all these "x, y and z" books, is they lead to forms of ghettoization, and marginalization. traditional chronological narratives create recognizable forms. time situates form within a past relative to the present, form has a category . . . recognizable forms are those events that take place in progress. recognizable is something repeatable enough to be seen as a noun and can be situated in a category. the problem is once one zeros in on a site, or a group, zeros in and calls something home, one becomes a target for new markets. or is placed on one of those bookshelves in the back of the store, or becomes a group locked into the DSM IVR. so shifting and causing interference, not knowing where the "I" is going, creating the probable out of the impossible and reinforcing resistance with information jolts to the system from stagnation. you could say practice "being a campaign of personal espionage," "as was done with those who went over niagara falls in a log cabin, or when someone landed in a distant field in the wrong direction." what becomes important is new systems, "all split atoms should have their own zip code." new approaches to open new areas in life one does not even know they do not know, "write one thing that relates to each of the past 14 million years, in large print."

we need to explore the hidden possible, out of dark edges or lost words that take place in the path of personal narrative, "like truffles on parade," not the known past which situate the already situated into further subjugation. shift, transform, find multi-connections and use many ways of distortion to swerve out of the way of the oncoming train. there are new connections where there may not have been connections. seeking out multiple connections creates new systems that takes us into communities where we would not normally go, and the more we can get outside ourselves the more we can connect with others. "truth=maybe."

all this brings back the question of how does one write a narrative of resistance of the inarticulate, in a language that situates? lean towards deviation, migration, position shifting, slipping in and out of focus, shifting, (that kind you do when your bored and sitting on your seat to long). try to find alliances that go in the same direction by a different track, corollaries that get lost in their own direction, which challenge the "find myself" narrative. so why do this? this is a tool for disruption, activism, acts of personal and public empowerment. give back to the community, with glorious havoc and come up with new possibilities. as "p." stated, "remember - all prescribed incidents are nothing more than obligatory super rantings . . . with a sigh of relief from nowhere."

all quotes taken from:
edwards, kari. *Iduna*. Berkeley, CA: O Books, 2003
edwards, kari. *a day in the life of p*. New York, NY: Subpress, 2002
edwards, kari. *diary of lies*, Brooklyn, NY: Belladonna chapbooks, 2002 & EOAGH Books, 2013.

Kit Yan

At the Medicaid Office

They are giving out Turkeys at the Public Assistance office,
Wrapped in plastic,
The legs folded in, balled for convenience,
You must have had to write your name on a raffle ticket,
I came too late to see the process.

There's something about the Medicaid office that seems so familiar,
A waiting room-
Immigrant kids sharing cheetos,
The numbers being called in English,
Familiar languages dancing in the damp air,
Chairs that are too big and too small for us all,
Crammed into the tiny space spilling out into the hallway,

The paper shuffling almost sounds choreographed,
I reorganize my stack to the beat,
Electricity bills with mismatched name,
Application with missing information,
Naturalization paper with a little girl awkwardly smiling,
Thinking: *they're taking my picture!*
A notarized birth certificate from China, the authenticity always in question,
The tax return map that brought me here,

In the basement of this Brooklyn building,
It doesn't look like Fifth Avenue,

The designer fashion is knock off,
Second hand, across generatedions,
The nails aren't all manicured, and
We wonder if there is a corner bistro vending machine for lunch,
It doesn't look like Fifth Avenue,

But it is the middle of the fucking night crew,
Security,
Deep fryer, diner server,
Window washer,
Children of the those who breathed life into the soil,
Before the buildings and ships came,
Before they had us build the railroads,
These are the brick layers laid off,
Big families to keep warm,
These are the feet that shuffle past the taxi cabs piling into the subway,
Taking the day off to come here,
To translate, to apply, re-apply, and to wait.

For-
My body to be an academic text,
My waiting line time a statistic,
My story boiled down into a sound bite well edited,
Funders in line to see what happens next,

I've been to Human Resources before,
My mother holding my hand,
The application stacks for our family members,
The days I spend back and forth social security to HRA,
This is not a first time,
Just the first time my mother doesn't know,
I've told her-New York streets are paved with gold,
The jobs and trees are fields for harvest,
I don't want her to worry about me,
I've got plenty here ma.

The man behind the desk is kind,
While taking down my information,

The others that wait are patient,
Lending pens and smiles,
The paper shuffling sound is some sort of comforting shared experience,
Saying: *You are alive*.

At night, I am a single young Chinese man ordering noodles on a low traffic
Chinatown street,
It's the middle of the darkness and this is what my last 2 bucks can buy.
A woman comes
We don't speak the same dialect,
But she knows something, I've yet to discover,
She brings me a free bowl of broth to blanket the cold fall,
The water flavored with marrow and bone sprinkled with green onion,
And I forget that I'm a vegan for a moment to thank her,
Sipping the hot soup-

Martsa's

It's at a Tibetan restaurant in Davis Square where we first meet,
I sit window seat not knowing which one is correct,
We were still learning our own languages back then,
Just gettin' our legs out in the sea of rainbows,
She will order for us both: Mango, mushroom tofu.
I take note, she likes mangoes.

She's got Jasmine eyes, and a Dallas smile,
Our conversation is slow the way two people,
Who only know what they see speak,
And as the layers peel, we tell a lifetime in a dance,
That is word and gesture,
Body and thread.

When she says let me get this,
I will back off,
Let the tea pour into its tiny house,
Let every drop finds its place,
Her smile, a map of how to please her.

When my fingers hit the table in thank you,
She giggles,
I am a man, but she is older- her hands steady with time,
I will serve her rice and she'll accept,
The waiter will never know our secret,
Our napkins will fall from our laps both of us reaching each time,

When the check comes to me,
We chuckle,
We just leave it on the table,
We're still in conversation,
But our second hand manners have us both on our toes,
I pay when she goes to the restroom,
Just like my mother would.

There is a doorstop that does all the work when we leave,
I watch her sway,
And she's ok with that.
She buys me a coffee at Diesel,
I do not protest,
She knows what she needs.

(Then you ask me to stop talking,
pulling your knees up so mine would follow,
and that slight arch of the back,
so my belly will find its way into the space it was made for.)

We're one, and we're tender,
the absence of their eyes our shelter.

I will always see her understanding that the guidebook she gave me,
Is always in edit mode,
But I know she likes mangoes and I can follow or I can leave,
She is Pikake tree and I am a boy in love with its fragrance and shade,
Made to chase the wind when she lets her petals fall.

Martsa's

It's our Tibetan Restaurant three years later,
We've eaten here so many times,
We even have a side and a favorite table,
To the right, hidden from front window view,
Our conversation's better without the distraction of the hot Diesel dykes that pass by in
Davis.

We would have never guessed that this would be our last meal here,
Our break up was as quiet as our relationship,
A harmony even at the end,
We were meant to be,
Effortlessly ordering for each other,
She knows I like momos,
The tenderness of the dumpling wrapper,
A texture that reminds me of that soft hip spot just below the belly,
Where my hands fell as she entered a room,

The momos are simple, but comforting,
Like steamed egg cakes with salted fish,
After a hard day of work,
Rice porridge and pickled cabbage,
On winter mornings before school,
Butter and pasta,
At a neighbor's house,
Bread and mayonnaise,
Alone after class.

And now momos,
The spicy chutney I use to dip each one,
Reminds me of the time I threw you a surprise birthday party,
You got mad,
Never liked surprises, except me.

She cuts each momo with a knife and fork,
Dips each bite into lite soy sauce and chews for proper digestion,
She's no train wreck,

But a glass door dryer,
Irresistible to follow,

We order two entrees,
I'm no longer afraid of eating too much in front of her,
Mango mushroom tofu, and vegetable curry,
We're in no hurry when we eat,
We have nowhere to go,
I say I could stay here forever,
New York is just another dumb city,
And you're all the poetry I'll ever need,
She says we're meant to be,
But right now, we're just not meant to be together.

We both reach for the rice attempting to serve each other,
Over the years, we threw out all of our manners,
Realizing that the blend of man and woman,
Chinese and American doesn't have a pattern.

We do not eat the last bites,
We leave them on the table as sacrifice,
I have to go home to do my injection,
So we skip dessert,

She pays because I don't have cash,
Opens her own door,
Scolds me for driving in the wrong direction, and
Tells me where to park.

It hurts a little more tonight when the needle goes in,
Or did push the metal in slowly to create more pain?
So the muscle could heal HARDER?
I can't remember.
I can't remember.
I can't remember.
I can't remember.
I can't remember.
But I am glad for the distraction,
For one pain to replace another.

Martsa's

Our Tibetan place has a lunch time buffet,
A strange concept, they've adapted
I'm glad- I don't want to have to choose,
I come in at the end around 3pm,
The food isn't fresh,
But no one bothers me when I scoop the last of the vegetarian dishes onto my plate,
Green beans with garlic,
Tofu and veggie curry,
Spicy Eggplant.

They have gone-
Back to work or to their little Davis houses,
To study or to clean their once ghetto shelters.
I over-eat,
Cleaning the food from my plate to evoke memory,
Suffocating the vegetables with chili paste to cause pain,
I don't know why I come here,
Why I sit at a new table every time,
Stare at the paintings of Tibetan mountains,
I've never been to,
Leave a big tip and walk across the street to say goodbye to the landscape.

When I am full and an hour away,
I remember the food as bland,
Say to myself that was the last time,
"Yeah Kit, the last time"
Make a promise to try a new restaurant in town,
Something must be better.

The waitress doesn't recognize me,
Maybe the management's changed,
Maybe I look like someone else,
Older and a little shabbier,
Another single Chinese guy coming in for lunch,
Maybe I look older, a little shabbier,
But Martsa's they've expanded, doubled the tables,

And I still occupy one seat,
Choose a table for 2,
They take away the extra plate,
I know she will not pass by today,
But I still watch the windows,
Hoping for a miracle,
My reflection in the way.

I wonder if I only feel small on this block,
The beginnings not quite distant enough,
No one to mind manners for,
Or to serve, to be excited about the familiar with.
The order of how much I miss it changes each time,
Sometimes I miss it more when I walk in and then less when I leave,
Sometimes less and then more,
I can't remember,
I can't remember,
I can't remember.

The hapa children walk around the table,
They like it here,
Dinner feels like a special treat,
Rice pudding is always sweeter eating out,
The raisins burst in their mouths,
A sweetness mama doesn't let them always have.

I stored the memory of us in my taste buds,
Tongue and heart beat one after the other,
With each significant moment a meal to follow,
I keep coming back to this buffet hoping that the dishes will change,
That the chef will make new curries with the same ingredients,
That the crunches, slurps, and inhales,
Will suddenly be different,
That I will taste again.

Poetics Statement:

My poetry lives in my belly. I'm not sure whether I will digest them and feel them in my blood and bones, or find the jagged half-chewed pieces coming back up my throat. When I write in real time, as the events of my life unfold, I don't digest. I don't care that there is no editing and smooth written word, I want to taste it a second time and there is something bitterly beautiful in that. The parts of my body and identity I explore in my work are constantly changing like the food I eat. Often I find myself looking at my work feeling disconnected from it because I no longer have those raw emotions or I find my life in such a different place. Identity is important, and for my poetry, it is important that I explore how my identities change and grow. I used to think that a body of work I feel disconnected from means it was bad, premature, or immature but I am learning to sit with the feeling that truths can seem distant, maybe even false and still be true.

Lately, I've been interested in things that previously bored me. Unpacking the mundane, the repetitive, the every day. I've been visiting times of silence and finding in that a story that I've forgotten or have left unexplored.

As my body changes through age, modification, and trauma, I remember the events differently. I am writing to remember and in that, I re-imagine the events depending on the current experience of my body. Sometimes I write things down in a reactionary manner, documenting as they happen, taking in the first impressions and senses, but sometimes I don't have the energy to think or write about my life as it happens. It seems like time possesses an element of healing, which helps me come back to the events in a way that I can understand better. So I might take notes, make a list, a voice recording to tell myself a story, or write half a poem and then come back to it years later. Sometimes by then it feels like someone else's life. That's when I start talking to myself, talking to myself about what really happened and trying to feel again whatever it was at the time. Does this even make sense? Sometimes it feels like lying when I changed how I feel, but I'm ok with that too.

My poetry is a blend of desperately trying to document the world around me and my own life, and an exercise in patience while I revisit and edit the thoughts, emotions, and experiences I have. Though, sometimes it's hard for me to process what doesn't always seem real, what only my body or mind or others have to remember.

The main influences on my work are my family, friends, and lovers. They often appear as the main characters in the stories that I tell. But the way they truly influence my work is by the love we share and the support they show in saying that it's a good thing we live.

Laura Neuman

different

When we visit the sea, you bring a rainbow umbrella, two beach chairs, a cooler. We are just getting to know each other, and you want to know *if you don't listen to the lyrics how do you know what the musician is trying to say?* and I want to know *how can you hear with all that screaming?* While you lie on the sand under the umbrella, I swim, wanting to be that book. You know the one. All the pages in it make you want to leave behind whatever words make you into someone capable of reading it. Whatever words provide you with the most comfort and care, leave those thickets.

You don't. Instead, while I swim, you lie on the sand, busy consolidating a body that maybe couldn't be at all without the language problem that with every minute you choose to exist, you slide further away from and into. Sun-block? Somewhere is a book that says he, she. Maybe ze. Some book right now calls the beach a liminal space, says we're caught between a rock and a prosthetic. Instead, while you read and I swim, that narrow band of anti-space itself shoots out and sprays us both. *Can you pass me the towel?* You need it all so differently today, won't take off your shirt in the sun, then do.

On the way home you drive too fast, complain about traffic, the wet sand on the seats, want to stop at the mall, and I begin to think maybe I'm just not that book. There could be others. *Words are animals, too.* I'm okay with that, I tell you, really. I just want to be there when it happens–to see you stumble, naked and inspired, away from everything you've cultivated, out into the book's "wild thickets."

second attempt

This page needs more forgetting than even you wanted. To get to the next sentence, forget: rosemary, how to go to sleep. Forget what certain words make nerves fire like tunnels we dig through fucking back into a field you escaped to as a child after a great calamity, the grass neon green, chest high. Forget the scars the surgeon left behind on purpose after your great leap. You keep telling me to listen, but I can't stop defending my latest syntactical position. *Shh*, you say, *you're missing it, love* or maybe just the words themselves, begging to be erased one by one, like a lover crying out for this one kind of touch and that only, as if one sound alone could sate us. Surely this new kind of reading or writing or whatever it is we're doing where our technologies can't help but touch –small bed – will result in a New and Improved Human Substance.

How did talking start to require such a *décollage* of tools? Do you really need to keep three kinds of fake milk, five different sizes of dildo on hand at all times, are we really that specific? And indeed, what kind of strange creature have we made of ourselves that takes *erasing* for *reading*, a *need* for a *want*, your *no* for *years later, the house*—

phase diagram

The room is only a place I happen to find myself sitting in for a portrait, waiting for a book or a painting to happen to me. One of them will happen first, then the other. This was the closest I came to being unfaithful, while you were sleeping and I snuck out to the park at midnight to look at all the snow. The book, grown up, breeds its own blanks now. You can go into them, I'll stay, sip something hot, watch you wade uncertain on an uneven surface. This is the kind of story that runs down your back. That asks to be erased. It begs, actually, the way I used to ask you to hit me over and over, creating a blank space or another time in the middle of sensation, it never being enough. What kind of person is it that can call erasing, reading – kissing, but not spanking, "enough"? Reading it makes you over into just that, the kind of person we all never wanted to become, the kind capable of sleeping through snow. You can be that or you can be the one who leaves your lover unconscious while geysers, then glaciers, whole colonies of dry ice threaten, springing up from the middle of the page. "You can't see them?" "All I see is doubt, letters, paper." If I were here I'd find and erase every last drop of anything resembling what was once or will in any state ever become water. Do you feel safe enough yet? This book will keep you sexless, warm and dry in all kinds of inclement weather, as long as you keep reading it—you are reading it, right? Just keep reading – don't stop – whatever you do.

single organism

Then comes the moment you realize you and the book are not so separate after all, but together form a single organism. Equipped with this new method of reading, are you the same person you were? If you say no you will never again be alone, but where, in the world? on the page? at the supermarket, feeling up peaches?

We know it's only a matter of time, the right book, that this will happen. Once we learn to say the processes that regulate the workings of our own internal organs, single organism, can you can feel an inner structure shift and crack, making room for the contents of this book inside you? THIS BOOK IS STRONGER THAN FIVE HUNDRED THOUSAND ANIMALS TAKING OFF YOUR SHIRT. This book is taking off your shirt. This gives me a technological advantage. Bird, Love, this book is banging on my chest like an extra chest, making me into someone who knows how to read it, want to or say.

Don't worry. In time, you may begin to care more about the end of the sentence that made you over into someone capable of arriving there intact. *This is the large intestine, responsible for grief.* So says the snow-capped book, handing it back to you.

everybody

Everybody wears too much red. Everybody stops then starts eating meat, everybody wears shorts. Everybody can't decide what to listen to after a long day at work, has trouble reading more than a few pages at a time, wants to move closer to the beach. Everybody can't orgasm while oil is pouring out there. We're not wired to, just have to wait. *Shh, don't move, love—there's a fly on your cheek.* Everybody likes to get slapped now and then as long as you don't mean it. Everybody found out the sun was going to explode one day, has a lot of concern for objects. Everybody sometimes forgets to turn off the coffeemaker and burns the pot. Everybody is secretly annoyed, then overly nice to strangers on the trolley, everybody rides the trolley? Everybody is walking around in two cities at once. While your body cuts out space in this one city, taking up room on the sidewalk and disturbing plants, buildings and other persons, there's another city making nerves fire like tunnels inside you, which is why you have trouble navigating the boulevards, remembering where you've been or how to get home. Everybody wants to go home?

new human substance

Towards those persons and objects that will never disappear into words, I feel a tenderness difficult to explain. Every time you see or hear the ocean in my voice, tearing the page, just a little.

We know our terror is too much, so we keep calling people to tell them about it on the phone. On the phone, it sounds like something you'd want to tussle, like daffodils in a field whispering. But even when safe in our beds—you laugh, kicking your feet— every act of tenderness we attempt can only be received as something more brutal, like S and M but in reverse. I want to tell you things that make you catch your breath, or stimulate your organs, foster new white blood cells, if you need white blood cells, make for shinier teeth and whiter hair. *Exactly*, says the wolf, *like the wolf!*

Instead, my breath on your cheek can only be a catalyst for pain, decorated pain, pain with spikes, with frosting. We once talked of bathing in frosting. Instead, when I buy a fountain, you buy a fountain, and when I write "what if it isn't that the materials are damaged" you become the collective organism I've been seeking to know.

I write towards Collective Human You in pieces: first the chest hair, purple, untangling it, then soothing the backache with some Ben-gay, then pouring another whiskey, massing your temples before I show you the next really beautiful and challenging thing. If I could just get there myself, to the next wild and clear presence, could lead you after, like a little child going out into the forest at night, forgetting that we are the forest, forgetting that we are the wolf—forgetting is what we do.

weeds

Dear Animal,

In the garden, while they pull weeds, one of them is very excited to be an artist. The other wonders about the weeds. There is a sensation very much like sexual or sensual pleasure at that moment the weed is killed. This sensation runs up the arm. Why? Does it have evolution? politics? religion? It appears that the actions a body takes in space remake that body into another one: gardeners and professors, for instance, have different postures and lines of sight. This thought runs up my arm with pleasure. Pleasure is only feedback, your body telling you how it likes operating in space, what should be changed, and people get sore throats who often don't say enough of what's on their minds. But then, says the other one, there are people who work in factories on meat-killing floors or for the army of any nation. Those people working under these and similar conditions must perform multiple tasks with their bodies in space that might be difficult to deal with or see. Maybe in those cases having clear sight of one's actions or the body messages isn't always a good idea for people.

In the painting of this condition, the daffodils are indistinguishable from both the field and the act of looking. *Stop that,* says the other one, *the painting already happened somewhere far away from us, no more looking is needed. Besides, it's time to move to the back of the house.* So maybe I am wrong to think that being aware of what the body does in space means caring more about being an artist than the weeds.

my job

I'm growing a lot of body hair, sitting here in the forest, leg and chest hair too, lying up and looking through the weeds. I'm thinking about the time I asked you to rape me and you didn't, the time I asked you to rape me and you did. I'm holding these thoughts about water and you in my mind, trying to see if a thought isn't said aloud but still invited to the table, if it will create resonance or ripple, will make things happen around it among the other plants and trees. I'm trying to become part of the common language, hoping the hair will help if the thoughts won't tangle. Is this common enough for you? Where our landscapes can't help but touch—small page—a burning sensation the size of a nickel. Did you ask me to hurt you less next time, or was that the coin? Five figures hunched at the edge of a platform, looking out over a substance that is becoming less and less water. We knew all along it was only a bowl made of land, that one day all the sea would spill out of it. I start to worry about the sun. *A picture book*, you say, *nice! But you sound bossy. I'd like it if you want to rub my feet after dinner at the mall.* Okay, but the kids are still standing on the dock, looking out over a great calamity. They don't know how to look yet, look! Will you teach them, or should I?

The fish keep falling.
The things I said.
Moonlight falling on khaki falling on concrete.
Blisters forming on cornfields, sowing sun dead.

city

There is no longer any possibility that we will ever locate ourselves absolutely. Not in bodies, on paper, or on streets. It used to be that even talking on the phone meant your voice had to be somewhere, in a building or house—or, in case of a payphone, everyone would know since you'd have to keep adding more quarters. I begin to feel so sorry for architects, but then one starts laughing. *No way!* What with Jessica falling down into the miles of infrastructure below us, and the centuries-old toilet they are digging up downtown, not to mention the new seafloor that cracked through the Ethiopian desert in a matter of days, we are always going to need someone to design a container to hold the next thought for us. You need the gaps in consciousness that allow for the assimilation of what is *seen* or *found there* along with the very fact of looking—also found there?

Let's hold hands. The smallest disaster is in a brushstroke.

storm clouds will poison you

Dear Infant/Hydrangea,

Chains of those flowers will forever connect whatever you're reading with what I'm reading, what you taste with this next thought. That's a culture, conjoined. The animals don't like this. They tear at my shirt, slobber and tell me material is caring more about what's present than what's not. This isn't always possible, but we can try.

Say you first learn about sickness while looking at the sky. This image creates a fold in you, since it will from now on function both as a central cloud around which other emotional vocabulary can cluster, and will also become its own unit within that vocabulary, combinable with other units in order to build further structures for thinking/on which to get closer to the sky. Watching from below, we can see that this person will never again see the sky. It's too much a part of how you think and know now.

The child part of me wonders, *but what about the clouds?* What clouds? *I want in on this cloud that's in you clustering.* The animals like that okay. They send me a care package: tick repellent, spicy tea and time in the form of dirty photos you took of yourself before we met. I forget to read the label, accidentally poison myself with the substance that isn't meant for...*skin?*

Poetics Statement

Now writing starts with difficulty—difficulty being in a body, difficulty having an experience, difficulty locating myself in a landscape among others. *Rage may be one of the few things that binds or connects me to you, to our pre-invented world.*[1] Now I want poems that are roomy enough to include the various difficulties involved in their making and reception. We have good reason to resist showing up for even our desire to have experiences; I want to fold in a lyric no, the poet's and the reader's.

Then there is this body doing the work of wanting, of hearing then saying. It's awkward, a writing body, you could don it, get nerve, you could dwell there for a spring, or drop in unannounced and stay to supper. Now I want to know what you would eat on this occasion. No, instead of writing about something, there is a desire to make writing. *You wouldn't think of form by the ocean. You can go in if you don't encounter anything.*[2]

Just now I am finding myself between language and movement, in the interstice and overlap. Trying to find form in the languages of choreography and dance notation. I want these languages that don't claim to map an "us" with accuracy. I want what is necessarily provisional: here it fails, but something still results, here it *names an "interior" state so we can get back there but without claiming any alignment to exterior reality such as muscle, bone alignment, skin, but still return to this position, X, with precision, ease.*[3] We all do live in bodies that are vulnerable to language, and yet find ways to use that language to create spaces of encounter. How and within what architecture?

Now there is the question of being in flux, or, as I was recently asked, "how do you like to pronounce that pronoun"? I don't know. It's a blip – a mark that lies properly fixed only on paper, after my name, and in conversation remains a welcome stumble—as a rhododendron might invite you bushwhack through, but at the end of the hike or the start, and carrying what in your pack, seeking what coordinates, and who is with you?

but fate is not / the force that predetermines events / as the dictionary says / fate is to speak / and you fate yourself as you speak...[4]

Any fleeting ability I find to move within the space of "woman" is only in relation to an experience of gender that is neither binary nor a spectrum (running between the imagined fixed points of "male" and "female") but rather is a multi-dimensional, space plotted not only on an x/y axis but in time, movement, community, connectivity, conversation – for instance, as one friend suggested, gender could be a swimming pool we are all moving through...

Any transitory sense I have of inhabiting the space of "genderqueer" is also utterly relational—dependent not only on being able to imagine into a "model" but also indebted to the lived experiences of other transgender and genderqueer people as well as feminist-identified people who I have been privileged to know, love, read and write beside—

I sense, too, it is not unproblematic for me, as a cis-gendered female, to claim an experience of gender that fluctuates among these constellations – one of them being "woman", which is a term that has been deployed in order to "naturalize" the imagined binary, to exclude, to make invisible, and to justify violence against the bodies of transgender and differently gendered people.

And yet experience gleamed and thought, read and woven– somatic and psychic, erotic and aesthetic, definitely urban—*has* brought me into this flux—a fluctuating gender which makes, finally, to my own body, an inexplicable and to some extent, a "natural" kind of sense—a structure, loosely draped, into which we can perhaps climb, from within which we can again take up the work of sensing—

Now, Smithson asking *what is the geometry of laughter?*[5]

I am asking what are the geometries of the language spaces we make in order to meet, however briefly—here—here?

Notes

1. Wojnarowicz, David. *Close to the Knives*. New York: Vintage, 1991.
2. Martin, Agnes. *Writings*. Hatje Cantz, 2005.
3. Gregory Holt.
4. Vicuña, Cecilia. *Cloud-Net*. Trans. Rosa Alcalá. New York: Art in General, 1999.
5. Robert Smithson.

Lilith Latini

Judicious Corseting

I once knew a woman
who could draw in her natural
waist by eight inches.

The fitting room door won't close
all the way. Neither does the dress'
side-seam zipper, open like a groaning

mouth over my ribs. Eight inches?
One inch at a time. I'll fit.
Cinch the thread. Parted seams will meet.

Visiting Family

When I walked up my family's driveway, a bird circled
overhead looking for the dead thing it smelled.
All year I loosed stitches from my lips with violet nails.

The ash grey dress may have been much, my parents
not expecting make-up. They claim I charged like a train,
bright steam and light that broke against their turned heads.
But I've only been walking, and nothing I come from is dead.

Forgetting My Mace

My feet are half a size different,
but both my pumps are nine-and-a-half.

Late evening downtown,
four noisy men across the street
slouch at a table.

Their argument suddenly quiet, and
they mumble as I move through
the empty crosswalk. It's better
than yesterday: Sharp neighborhood jeers
and the streetlight out.

Snap of heels on concrete. Hope
they hear my heartbeat, and their own.

Gina, Trina, and Esmeralda: The Creation of a Tranny Tough as Acrylic Nails

I.
Esmeralda meditated on false eyelashes
right before the drug store closed. *Purple feathers
or gold rhinestones?* He floated to the counter,
both in hand and purred to the cashier,

"Do you get a discount, darling?"
"Um. No."
"Oh. I was about to be really jealous of your life."
Money changed hands and the doors flung open.

II.
The phone propped next to the shower.
Gina screamed,
"I told you I had plans!"

Water off, curtain open, unfurled steam.

"Maybe I'll run into you, baby, but
I'll be busy." His body sliced the heat.
Gina rubbed the mirror, practiced his pout.
"Just hope you're lucky, honey."

III.
Trina slept under sixteen blankets:
down comforters, crocheted yarn,
fleece. The pile rose and fell
with her long breaths.

High heels lined along the walls:
clear plastic, patent leather, peep toed.
Glitter spilled on her bathroom sink
next to the wrench.

IV.
Gina drove and Esmeralda blew on his still-wet nails.
One more night until the moon was full, but Gina cried,
"It's tonight! I don't care what your astrologer says,
darling, that round thing is rolling all through me."

He shivered and giggled. Esmeralda licked his lips.
They parked at Trina's house, threw the door open.
Sang, "Wake up honey, the night's ripening!
We've got things to do and places to see!"

V.
Three women in front of a mirror.
"Can you glue these on for me?"
"Oh, I love that. So pearly,
bioluminescent." "Move over!"
"Bitch, keep your skirt on!
I do not live to please you!"
"Can I borrow that?"
"Of course, darling."

"Will you zip up my dress?"
"Of course, darling."

VI.
Bodies like blades breezed down the sidewalk,
through the bar's door. Slouch off jackets, drop purses.
Gina, Trina, and Esmeralda walked to the bar,
ordered drinks. The bartender winked, the trio's

glossed ruby lips, black glittering eyes, rhinestone and feather lashes
embossed in the dim light. This warpaint was for battle,
to claim a territory, a space. Steel mace shoulders swung,
legs whipped, hips fired shotgun bullets.

VII.
Gina batted his eyes at shirtless men: pale, blonde, blurred.
Knife legs minced around the throbbing bodies,
he blew a kiss, pouted, glanced at them
over his pointed shoulder.

Polo shirts, bronzed chests, trucker caps and
Esmeralda not far behind with Trina in hand.
He flung her sequined body like a shovel between
the dancers. Trina smiled, her pearl teeth glinted hungrily.

VIII.
Gina, Trina, and Esmeralda dug through their skin,
ripped the lid off a boarded up well behind the stomach.
They guzzled the liquid, starved for that self bound by rotten
wood and rusted nails. Between bark and howl, bark and howl,
Gina shrieked at Trina, "I knew it, I knew! Don't stop working!"
Trina drunk, feet on fire, milky eyed boys gone away to dance
in the corner. Esmeralda sang, "Water the seeds with honey, bunny,
Water those dried out seeds!"

IX.
The next morning Gina and Esmaralda stood over Trina's
briny body in bed covered partly by a sheet, lipstick smeared
and rhinestones stuck to the pillow. "Should we wake her

for breakfast?" Esmeralda asked. "Oh no." Gina smiled.
"What this girl needs is to take a walk." He took Esmeralda's hand,
and they flounced away in the early afternoon light, satisfied.

Bubble Wrap

Windows covered in glue and bubble wrap.
Blurred shapes, colors warp through
the opaque lens. Inside, the tea kettle whistling,
strewn laundry, cobwebs curled in corner's shadows.
She called and was screaming.
He called but I left the phone ringing.
Stare at door hinges soldered solid, inflexible.
Humid air thick and sugary, the mattress sunk
to the floor. The phone rings! The phone rings!
I sit up against air grating on my skin.

Judy Garland and the Stonewall Girls

A video of Judy howling "Down
With Love," the microphone cord
thrown over her shoulder, shaky finger
barbed and pointed at her audience.

Some blamed the Stonewall Riots on her death.
Cue a montage of queens' tears fallen on radios playing Somewhere Over the Rainbow.
The panty hose hung on radiators and dresses flung on the floor,
doors open to let the June heat smear through.

I will not rise on the stage like Judy,
lilting with gestures barely hinged
to my body and bathe in that limelight this year.

Hair unfurled, the Stonewall Girls
now lay jailed or murdered. Don't send me
out of the closet and into the streets alone.
Someone has to help me out of my strappy shoes before we run.

Bathed in that limelight, I won't
lilt with gestures barely hinged to my body.
Under those hot lights tears dry quickly,
but I won't cry under those lights alone.

Down with love, Judy sang, the root of all
midnight blues. Down with love, the flowers
and rice and shoes. Down with eyes, romantic and stupid.

Do not send me to the front lines alone and undone,
rice and petals sailing through the air,
my sisters' bodies on the ground.

Cabbage Soup

Corn husks rot beneath autumn's cabbage. Small,
neat purple bruises in long lines. Their wrinkled frames
fan open. Harvest moon full and empty, its orange glare
obscures the stars. Already brown October leaves flake
across the field. Night's crystal frost on the full-bloomed
food. We'll eat those fetid bruises, boil them in soup.
Save the faded broth, let each limp piece float to the surface.

Decisions

Piled beneath the bed: unopened mail,
the unanswered calls, bowl of half-eaten cereal,
a to-do list.

Rain rang in the open window,
ignored but insistent, and
chipped at the sill's paint.

A glittering apricot dress hung
in the closet, sagging
though the night hadn't begun.

From her throat tension popped,
pearls played crack the whip and
flung out of their orbit.

A quick breath then she turned on her toe,
moved over the spinning beads
and out the door.

Traveling West

Last night I drove West, alone --
the only way people seem to handle
crisis or find adventure.

I didn't leave messages, notes.
What's out West anyway?
Sand, a cactus. My body

evaporates under the new sun
slowly, burnt skin
peeling aimless into sand.

A stale scene, the single cloud
curling. Seated not far from the car
or highway, I

can imagine my form from
third person -- the image
almost satisfying.

Poetics Statement:

When I first began outing myself as a trans woman, I didn't want to answer a lot of the questions friends and family asked me. I felt scared to give the honest answers that I had come to myself. Many of these answers were nonverbal, felt instinctually like my own pulse. But a pulse is a predictable rhythm and there was nothing particularly comforting in these truths I was untangling.

It was my last year as an undergraduate creative writing student, and I quickly mined what I had learned for a way to communicate. People want to paste certain established transsexual narratives over my experience for some framework to understand. It's offensive because my narrative is still taking form, like any life still being lived. My poetry is admittedly unpolished because my trans experience is still raw. I am still scrambling to communicate.

Even before I began talking about my trans identity or transitioning, it always felt that my body was public space because of my high femme gender presentation. As if nobody learned it was rude to stare, peopled looked at me like I was some newly unveiled statue and they already read the explanatory placard. The interpretations of this placard ranged from: disgusted, dismissive, amused, confused, excited.

Trans women's lives and safety are one of many prices paid for a conversation of LGBT rights that dismiss the complicated strands of gender, race, and class for a dialogue that placates the majority. These stories are picked up by newspapers only to misgender their subjects and comment morally on their lives and bodies.

It is necessary to transition with my voice intact. As a white trans woman, my voice only manifests as a singular subject position. The differences of perspective and need within our queer community are valid and important. Just as important is the web of community that supports and acknowledges its members. I won't stop scrambling to communicate, and I refuse to stop listening for the voices left behind glossy images of gay cruises and marriage.

While writing these poems, I was navigating a new relationship with my family and becoming a member of a queer community that nurtured me in my efforts to grow. I hope my life and experience will no longer be marginalized, simplified, or demonized by strangers. Often tweeted by Sassafras Lowery, this quote by Richard Rohr is what I kept in mind while writing: "If we do not learn to mythologize our lives, inevitably we will pathologize them." When questions are asked, I want to give the larger-than-life, glamorous, gutteral answer, and I want others to have the safe space for theirs to be heard too.

Lizz Bronson

The Year You Bloom

You tell your Mom over *Pad Thai*
You want to switch sex
She replies it's not the answer
You say I am not you
You are not me
We are not the same
The body is not the only ocean.

Memory switch

When you tell your Mother
Over *Pad Thai*
You want to switch sex

It can't be because
The moment you walk by a man
And
A thin skirt of desire dances across his
Mouth~
You remember

That you completely forget

You're a woman.

No, It must be something else.

The Pillow Book Of Unsaid Things

After you tell your Mother
About how you want to change
You see it stir in her head
You never tell her this pillow book of unsaid things:

There are days you are a lion in the labyrinth
~but caged.
Men put their mouths up to your house
Waiting for you to come to the window
Or open the door
They watch your comings and goings
They try to un-
              peel you like a mango
And lick out your dreams
Through eyes, lips, hands, and hips
Even though you tell them we cannot be a collection of things
Even though they wrap their limbs around
You and ask about your unstirred silences

In your thirties
You never thought you'd say things like
Baby, I don't do fatal attraction
Or
Baby, I am not you
      You are not me
       And we are not the same

Just because a woman is a fleshy moon.

creation myth # 3

long before dreams   words   and thoughts
   sun
      earth
  and sky
    breathed   color palettes
      red blue black yellow white...

      to make a world

       gather: skin
        breath
        and
        bone.

      add voice

    sky came
  when earth
cracked open.

trees sprang
up like
  fountains

  (volcanic
   sound.)

    patchwork sky
    stories weaved
     in the bull
      shaped
       clouds.
     all we were
     and would be
    in the myths
    of our ways

creation myth #4

man fell from first tree
then came woman
and oh

woman
woman
woman

creation myth #5

woman breathed water
and named animals
after etching earth
her hands in sky

she undulated her body~
pulled two people from
the clouds:
one man
one woman

then again
and again

and maybe
one man
and
one man

and
one woman
and
one woman

and so on

and she made villages

she unleashed birds
from her hair
and they weaved the whys

she picked up each creature
painted them
and we shined bright before the stars
she blew a deep breath into the world

the heart beat in the core of the earth.

Poetics Statement

I believe that we write to find our own meanings and construct our own identities. Our stories come from some magical place, and our identities hinge on our perspective. Poets and writers function as storytellers, anthropologists and magicians, weaving together many truths into stories and turning dross into gold. I am influenced by children's books, art museums, Stand-up comics, daily walks, cartoon strips. Poetic influences include Joy Harjo, Wanda Coleman, Linda Gregg, and Brenda Hillman, among a wide range of writers.

As a multi-ethnic writer,(Black, White, Japanese, Cherokee and Choctaw) I have always been fascinated by identity from all angles: how identity surfaces in daily life, how it affects one as a writer and a reader.

In my writing process, I think about where I have been. Where am I going? Where am I now?

The themes of this anthology resonate for me in my thirties, because I am confronting my issues in a more real way. What snakes between blue lines and pink margins on the page, that hasn't been written yet? Gender is something I confront daily. All of our truths are tangled. I interrogate and investigate the "SELF" by exploring these things. The being and becoming. What pushes me to the edge and what pulls me back.

For me, this anthology has the opportunity to heal the need to belong, the need to be heard, the need to be validated. And to unify different voices as separate fingers of the same hand. This anthology's work is exciting because it builds a bridge to further understanding of each other and ourselves. And it reminds us to never forget our dreams, or the fact that we all hold magic. These words we write are the intersections between thought and space, the truth that lives in the body, and the wish to create something of our own.

Lori Selke

Three Sex Dreams

1.

The famous chef takes me out to dinner, but it's not a dinner he has cooked, nor is it his restaurant. He leads me to a secluded booth. Instead of a table, there is a bed. There is no food, but still there are waiters, they pull aside the curtains every few minutes and ask, "Is everything all right? Can I get you something?"

2.

Phallic symbol. Phallic symbol. Phallic symbol. Phallic symbol. Phallic symbol. Phallic symbol. Phallic symbol. Phallic symbol. Phallic symbol. Phallic symbol. Phallic symbol. Phallic symbol. Phallic symbol. Phallic symbol. Phallic symbol.

Forest.

3.

He knows that I have wet dreams when I am lying beside him, that I come in my sleep. He asks me in the morning, stroking my hair, what I was dreaming. I can't tell him *shapes, colors, tastes upon my tongue*, I can't tell him *it was you, over and over, you and you and you and you and then the alarm would wake me up, over and over again, recursively* because he'd think I was flattering him and anyway that's an old dream, I can't tell him *they spread my thighs and forced my mouth open* and I can't tell him *it wasn't a dream, I was awake and you were beside me and sometimes that's all it takes* so I tell him *hands, many hands, hands all over my body, anonymous hands, big hands, rough hands* and he smiles as if I've told him a secret.

Three Dreams of Teeth

1.
They call it an ear of corn, but the kernels look more like teeth. Neat rows of molars, ready to sing songs of silver and sugar, starch and gold.

I dream that my mouth is full of keys. I can taste their brassy tang when I swallow. I cannot wrap my tongue around them to speak.

There are four holes in my gums where the dentist removed my bicuspids. The sockets sit empty, open locks. A kernel of corn would fill them perfectly.

2.
One of the most common dreams on records is the dream of one's teeth falling out.

Freud says, with uncharacteristic lack of imagination, that dreams of one's teeth falling out are best categorized as somatic dreams; that is, you grind your teeth and you dream of teeth.

Other sources say that dreams of your teeth falling out signify fears of aging, of not being heard, of talking too much. Social anxiety, worries about sexual attractiveness, even financial concerns can be symbolized by this dream.

Teeth represent power, and their loss, powerlessness.

3.
When I was eight, I had incisors so pointed other children said I was a vampire. Not a vampire, I said. A werewolf.

Now my incisors are dull, and my molars so sharp the dentist offers to file them down.

The instructor wrote in red pen on my poems, "where is the Lori who dreams of werewolves?"

She has turned vegetarian, and only eats corn. Her only song is "sweet tooth, sweet tooth, your love so sweet it hurts my mouth. Sweet thing, without you I will starve. Sweet thing, you have broken my lock."

Browsing Bargain Poetry

Browsing the bargain poetry section seems almost shameful; at the same time it's gratifying that there's even a bargain poetry section to shop, but still, you know how much poets make on their books, it's not like browsing the bargain cookbooks, cookbook authors must get paid bushels, they even get to go on TV and they don't have to answer stupid questions like "where do you get your ideas?", they just have to open the oven and like magic, the dish is there, photo perfect, and the hosts all smile as they chew and their eyes open wide with delight and that's it, the chef's a star. Lunch was not noteworthy and so you're looking for a different kind of sustenance, but you don't want to rip off a live and struggling author so you skip all the names that you know. There's one book, it's called "Against Love Poetry" but the title poem isn't very good. There's another, by John Ashbery, he's famous, he can take the hit, and you hate his poetry anyway so it's almost fair. Your partner likes him, it could be a gift, but thinking about his lines makes you see snarls in poorly-combed hair, so you put it back. A dead poet might do. You can't take bread out of the mouth of a dead poet. There's a book of poetry on the shelf by a dead poet you once met, Joseph Brodsky. Or was it that other one, the Polish guy whose name you've forgotten? That's what you told everyone the last time you told this story, but now you think you might be mistaken, it was the kindly Russian on the couch, chatting with a colleague and allowing the aspirants surrounding him to overhear, to ask a question once in a while even. But the book is *Nativity Poems* and you don't believe in Christmas or at least Christ, not in late January at any rate, not with rain threatening and a need for just a small bite, a cookie, a crumb of cadence and rhythm and something more if you're lucky, but you're not, not today, and you leave empty-handed. You'll try the cookbooks tomorrow.

Found Personals Poem

Interested in talking
I like strong women
Luv to see and luv to show
Hello
Hey there
Hi
Hi :)

Love BBW ladies, hope to chat
Mmmm, I'd love to hit it!
Hi!
Sexy!
I Like a little bend
Hey
Hi
Discreet relationship
I'm a sexy man
Mutual respect and sexual satisfaction
Hi...
Always looking for unconventional
Let's get together
Wow!
Hey there
Hi
Very excited by your ad
Hello
I like your profile
Want sex
Want to talk?
I do
Hello
I am definitely interested
Hi

Three Nightmares

1.

The dog. Mouth full of knives. The fading light of dusk gleams on their serrations, slick with froth. The black dog. Tall as my chest. It must have eyes, but all I see are human eyes, fixed on my throat. I can see it coming, loping slowly down the sidewalk. It takes forever to arrive. I am wearing the leather jacket, my hands are in my sleeves, but this time the dog is too big and it will knock me down, the knives will cut the jacket to shreds, I will be nothing but meat.

2.
My skin is so delicate. It is almost translucent, so easy to see the veins and things underneath, pulse shivering at the wrist. My skin gets thinner every day. No longer soft like a baby's, no longer admired by stewardesses and tricks. It dries out, like parchment, and curls at the edges. Bruises bloom, ripe plum and green grape clusters. I could be a hemophiliac with a good luck streak about to end.

3.
Bite harder. Leave a mark. Unmarked, I am nothing. A blank page. An empty frame instead of a portrait. I cannot see myself. I need the shock of your teeth, blunt and bruising. Human teeth are weak. We are omnivorous, like dogs. We will eat anything.

Lines for a One Night Stand

Yes, I let him lead me to the bathroom.
Yes, I let him put his hands underneath my skirt.
Yes, I watched him wash them in the sink first.
Yes, he used a condom.
Yes, he didn't ask for my phone number.
Yes, I didn't ask for his.
Yes, he probably thought I was a slut
Yes, he probably thought I was fat
Yes, he probably thought I was fat and easy and gross and
Yes, not girlfriend material and
Yes, not much better than Kleenex and
Yes, not even worth taking home for a night and
Yes, certainly not worth cooking breakfast for and
Yes, I know, and
Yes, I fucked him anyway.
Yes, I came.
Yes, he came.
Yes, he came with relief on his face and
Yes, vulnerability, exposure, that was there too and
Yes, that's what I really look for and
Yes, that's what really excites me and
Yes, that's why I'll do it again, because

Yes, I will never know what he really thought of me and
Yes, he will never know what I thought of him and
Yes, that's the secret, I don't know and I don't care and
Yes, we were really just using each other and
Yes, I am OK with that and
Yes, it was easy.
Yes, I liked it.
Yes, I will do it again. But not with him.

Knife

1. A woman buys a knife from the knife shop. She keeps it in her kitchen drawer. One day, she takes it out to peel an apple. The blade bites into the flesh of the apple and draws the peel out in one long strip. The woman forgets to clean or wash the blade. It rusts. She picks it up again and tries to peel an orange. The knife cuts into her palm. She throws it away in anger.

2. Shiny. Shiny. Shiny and dark. Dark. Dark. Dark. Shiny and bright. Pushing. Gliding. Smooth. Bright. Singing. Bright. Unheard. Bright. Forgotten. Bright. Lonely. Dull. Warm. Together. Apart.

3. "Worthless piece of crap. I thought those fancy things were guaranteed for life."

4. Once I was clothed, then I was stripped naked, then violated, torn apart, cast aside. My sister, when they tried to take her too, she fought. One of her attackers was caught. But the other one escaped.

5. I wanted to give it up, but I was too tough.

6. If the match is right, there is little resistance. The path will be smooth. But it takes vigilance. A little inattention, and the union is marred. There will be bad feelings. Separation may be the only solution.

7. Opel. Pippin. Valencia. Anne.

8. We had so much potential, but she couldn't see it. Once our first date was over,

she started taking me for granted. Finally, I lashed out. I admit it, it was my fault. I should have known better. But think of what it was like, after all those months of neglect. What else could I have done?

9. The blade is made to bite. It has no bark.

10. Without touch, I decompose.

Woman/Dog

I'm really fucked-up about women. But you know what? I dig it. It's a blast. Scared, tormented. You want mom, you want a hooker. One of the things I've come to realize is you've got to get a woman with a dog. A big-ass, good-looking dog. Like an Akita or a pit bull, so when the woman's out of the bed you can curl up with the dog, talk to the dog about the woman. – James Ellroy

you want your mother, you want a hooker
you want a woman with a big dog
a handsome dog, like a pit bull or an akita
a dog that can climb into bed with you when the woman's gone
and you can talk to the dog about the woman.

you can't talk to the woman.

You want an heiress in eyeliner with a flower in her hair
and a slim blonde, spread on the dining room table
the brunette, the blonde, the blonde, the brunette
you want a grainy, blurry stag loop
of a woman and a woman (the blond, the brunette)
or a woman and a dog.

you want your mother, you want a hooker.
The blonde. The brunette.
you want a woman cut in two
sawed in half like a bad magician's joke.

you want a woman emptied of her innards
so you can wear her like a coat
you want a woman with a permanent smile
slashed into her cheeks.

you want a sad-eyed girl with big-screen dreams
and a one-way bus ticket to your bed
your dirty mattress with its stained sheets and its dog hairs

you want a crime scene photo

you want high heels and seamed stockings
a garter with a broken clasp
a slut, a hooker, a mob moll, a taxi dancer
or just wrong place wrong time

you want a woman who knows how to make ends meet
with a certain shade of lipstick, a beauty mark, and a smile
a smile that never reaches her eyes
a smile cut permanently into her cheeks

her eyes are blank, a silver screen
you're the star of the movie that shines in her eyes
she's not even on the bill

you're fucked up about women because someone killed your mother.
you're fucked up about women because someone killed your wife.
you're fucked up about women because you're divorced.
you're fucked up about women because you never knew your father.
you're fucked up about women because the first girl you kissed is a dyke now.
you're fucked up about women because your father fucked Rita Hayworth.
you're fucked up about women because you screwed a readhead once, and then
she screwed you.
you're fucked up about women and you always have an excuse.

Because a man can't be with one woman
without obsessing about another
you want your mother

the blonde and the brunette
a man won't turn down a target of opportunity
you want a hooker

you take the dog for a walk every night.
The woman waits for you in the bed.
One night she's there, one night she's gone.

after the crime scene is secured,
you'll go home with the police dog that first found the body.
you'll sit on the couch to watch the late night news reports.
a bottle of whisky and a lipstick-marred cigarette
is all you need to get through the night.
The bed's not cold; you have a big dog.
This dog understands women. He smells of her perfume,
Carries a flower in its mouth. You talk to him
Mothers. Hookers. Blondes and brunettes.
Sawed in half and found empty,
Scared. Tormented. you dig it. it's great.

Poetics Statement

A writing instructor of mine once wrote a final class evaluation that stated that while I was great at analyzing other people's work, I was not nearly as articulate about my own.

Not a lot has changed in 20 years.

Gender is a language. It has its own rules, its grammar and structure. There are things you can say in our current cultural gender system, and things that you can't. One of the functions of poetry is to pry language open so that the things that cannot be expressed in traditional grammatical forms can be articulated in another way – through imagery, through allusion, through sound, through wordplay. Genderqueers, like me, do something similar with gender. We find ways of expressing what should, by rule, be inexpressible.

I'm highly conscious of how the world sees me. I'm fat, I'm female but not feminine, I'm tall. I take up space. My fleshy, top-heavy body attracts a certain sort of attention and I've spent a lot of time wrestling with that sort of objectification. I see a lot of that confusion and rage in my poems, right alongside a hefty dose of desire. How to navigate romantic-sexual desire and associated roles in this particular body seems to be a perennial theme of mine.

I like to imagine that my best poems are like seeds, and they begin to bloom upon re-reading. My poems tend to be quiet but persistent. I like to approach topics from unexpected angles. I always feel like I am taking different elements and pasting them together until I uncover meaning – sometimes this means using found elements, sometimes it means experimenting with prose cadences and line length changes. I do the same with gender, by the way. I borrow and I transform and I experiment with labels and language until I find something that works for the moment. I create the space to articulate my desires and identity through a multiplicity of overlapping voices. The "I" in my poetry is almost never me per se. But nor are my first-person poems strictly speaking persona poems. The truth, like my genderqueer identity, lies somewhere in between.

I don't know who my influences are but I do know whose work I admire. I seem to be drawn to poets who are writing in English as their second language, such as Lisel Mueller and Charles Simic. This seems rather suggestive. I definitely see myself working in a particularly queer poetic tradition. My copy of *Gay and Lesbian Poetry in Our Time* is well-thumbed. I feel terrible omitting anyone from a list but my personal shout-outs would have to include Ferlinghetti and Ginsberg, Anne Sexton, Pat Parker, Dorothy Allison, Harold Norse, Minnie Bruce Pratt, and Sharon Olds. Finally, the tremendous Daphne Gottlieb is indirectly but pivotally responsible for my return to writing verse after a decade-long hiatus. Don't call it a comeback.

Max Wolf Valerio

Fetish Eyes

hide the
symptom

cold fear
tangled

bent to

perfect tension

runaway kids on Polk Street with fish in their hair motion
to the crawling
furnace of oil and syringes

yoga asylum   object-oriented
hybrids
circle

with squatting
feelers &
brush-level
tongues

collectors
pickpockets

loan sharks
pistol portraits
grocery fat hoarders
oval-faced machine guns

murky pizza skin
shaved heads
    post-modernity pencils in a moustache --

short thick forms   that turn out to be
people

smoke sharp objects
cradle
wooden figurines

stretching lips
hover close to
store windows

a killer instinct
an odor of darkened rubber

night rabbit howls
a lightning drenched figure ---
adoring

filigrees of jazz
and   needle-thin
watchers

           veneration --

      fetish objects
       still
  in   sharp

Cyclops Emergence - Will

choice
from a mausoleum filled with broken bones and
blackened stones

cold
blades
eclipse
a Cyclops
emergence

the moon
                    floating
rigid and stiff emerging
sensational on these last freezing decimals imprisoning
summer winds

nexus of
spectacles

mob thronged
cycles --

violence and concealment

the art of cunning and denial

the placement of photographs in such a way as to diminish guilt --

apostrophes and
          fragments --

              isolation   water-logged
                      bloated in tandem

              to desire

longing has only served
to obscure

the sun and moon
appear
to
speak in
multiple
languages

simultaneous to our listening and our nebulous
　　　　　　　　and uncertain ascent
　　　　　　　　　　　　to separation

black ringed
　　　　phantoms
a planet of swords and necropolis with horns

I invite you to divulge your
hidden places　　　*the secretive glances*
you balance at right and wrong

this question:
　　　Why did you die?

Is it possible that
if the human capacity to knowingly name evil is destroyed　　　　that
the equally human capacity for good is also
abrogated?

Transubstantiation

There's a linking of forces that seems both inevitable and slightly tragic.
A procession without weight, color, or definable shape. Memory interferes
with sensation. A uniformity of motion, odorless stretches of space. Time
is competent and narcotic.

Caught up. As the tongue is brought to bear on the syllables, dialogues of varying stress and pressure. Breath stretches toward meaning or a glyph that competes with meaning.

Ringing. Pipes – weapons or cars as they pass over the freeway.

My vehicle is almost angelic. A cradle. Tilted. Its fragility is painful – I am the person whose photograph is repeated.

Any kind of emotional squalor has become rancid.

My vehicle feels pristine. A sphere with windows. Watery shapes float over my head in the twilight.

What was once hidden behind tall buildings surfaces into view.

Increments.

There is a pigment in her skin I cannot define. She appears colorless as the lights are extinguished.

Nocturnal Pump

The women, forgiving --
walking close to the drills

punching up and punching down
into the damp
earth or concrete bandwidth --

sabotage
a mechanism
walking on heartbeats
a collage --

fingertips entranced by bananas

fledgling
>   *polymorphous pimp pump*
>   *underground atom punch*

every second face is
hostile to circus ideas --
eaten up by every cause
the black mobility
of an elephant trunk

wrapped in white linen
dangling
over
the radial forearm

attentive
feeding of animals in the wild
>   **swallow snake --**

Eclipse

necrophiles

>   bludgeon   each other in

>   hopes of getting

one   last   good   fuck

girls rebel against each other
in boredom

>   reason is transfigured in paradise

the slaughterhouse is more like it

nearly witless or

blind

subtlety

borders a robotic high

wet hair

enclosed spaces

tightly confined   wrapped in

spiraling gauze

torches --

.

strip search

elephantine stages

of walking

Celebrity

-- listen to the magazines
the plunder of celebrity

a hopeless condition
        awake under nylon light

as electric impulses decay
        scavengers alight

                fists --

                                        dingo faces &
                        assault weapons
            in the tight, red car   beer bottles and big
                                                            hands
                        arson wigs   tipsy
                                        and phallic
                        with a touch of
                                                    envy
                    each bone and tendon
                    marked with grasping

        the light hearted gasping   of infant veins
    soft rolling motion of hips   on vinyl car seats

                movie cities

            pain ornaments   oil her
                Pamela Anderson in the backseat

        smearing clay on her lips and
                                        holding her

                two large mechanical breasts
                                                    out
                                    to
            the full   moon

Apocalypse Poetry

The unexpected, subliminal, incomplete, the silenced: these energies emerge, elemental to a landscape that is also a journey—*poetry*. Words take on textures and supernal light, telegraphing strange, new points of entry—portals to visions. Because they are both process and object simultaneously, my poems are written for the page and for the ear, for the voice, and also—as they break and sing meaning and music on the page, for the eye. While I have "performed" my poetry with musicians, I do not consider it to actually be "spoken word." I use montage to suggest action or absence, active and vivid words to evoke sensation and texture. I build upon concepts and create images to contain a sense of place, and then undermine any certainty by shifting to another image, another modality or tone of language. The poem should be dynamic and the reader submerged in an internal landscape that is not ordinary or expected. I expose the submerged music in language. Foundational to my poetic practice is Charles Olson's concept of "projective verse."[1] Olson describes a poetic practice where the poem is created without reliance on inherited forms, in an "open field,"[2] and the poet "can go by no track other than the one the poem under hand declares, for itself."[3] While I enjoy playing with structure, usually grammatical restrictions I create on the fly, instead of traditional poetic forms—my poetry most often improvises meaning, cadence and imaginative play to create a moving and dynamic form on the page and for the ear. The poem is open, and always—opening.

My own sense of self is various and multiple, and while many of my identities are certainly uncommon, since I am both mixed race and of transsexual history, I don't necessarily regard my experience as interesting enough to support the usual rhetorical grandstanding that these identities tend to inspire. At least not in poetry, I will leave that to prose! I started transitioning medically from female to male in 1989. I regard myself as both "just a guy" and—well, "different from most guys", in certain essential if also, ineffable ways. What this means in concrete terms is that in my poetry, I don't "play with gender," at least not more than I "play" with any other concept. My life project is not about "playing" with gender or subverting gender, so I do not foreground this trope. I experience my gender as deeply complex as well as simple, and while my poetry does not point to any particular sex or gender as its source or voice necessarily, this is not a political statement. Most of the poems, after all, do not function as a mouthpiece or a reflection of my personal history or journey. I am not attempting to reconstruct my life experiences as poetry, or to persuade the reader to my experience in the telling; in other words I am not taking on the restrictions and inflated sense of purpose of the "egotistical sublime,"[4] as Keats would call it. That sense of self often restricts a poem to a poet's own autobiography, often projecting an inflated sense of self-importance onto a work—easily leading to what Zukofsky considered the fallacy of "predatory intent."[5] The poem is then reduced, it is reductive—a mere vehicle of expression for the poet's conscious intentions. And, these intentions are often on the surface, all too obvious. While I certainly have written poems that work with more conventional narrative threads and an autobiographical voice, even in those instances I tend to create voices that are not instantly recognizable as my own. Often, they may be amplifications of certain aspects of myself, but even then, these voices are not necessarily persuasive of the existence of that self in any place other than—the work. So, always my poetry attempts to be an artifact and ignition of a creative process where my conventional, known "self" is largely absent, and other selves are revealed *in* the poetic object through perceived and enunciated textures, rhythms, humor, clarity, movement and ambiance.

Inside the poems, space is dynamic and moving. The spaces between words and phrases fracture and multiply meaning and music. Space is breath, and an invitation to the eye to move, or to linger. Poems can be read from left to right as in convention, but poetry also frees language through an imaginative and musical arrangement of space. Meaning, time, and space are fractured and expanded in the field of creation that the poem enacts.

While post-modern, I feel apocalyptic. Situated somewhere, awkwardly and with some irony, in the line of romantic poets who refer back to Blake, where an intense and sublime explosion of the senses and experience enlarges the imagination. I privilege the imaginative faculty above the autobiographical. Imagination is foundation. Transformation is annealed to the imaginative skin of a poem, its entrancing poetic eye.

I take my cues from the Beats' improvised prosody, their expansive subjectivity, their emphasis on music, their visions and humor, and their understanding of the vulnerable ordinariness of an open heart. Poetry must speak out loud, as well as enthrall in silence on the page.

I am in debt to the Surrealists, the Objectivists and Imagists, H.D. and also of course to Baudelaire, Verlaine and Rimbaud, Lorca, and Genet. Celan teaches me to endure more and go further. Bob Dylan and Iggy Pop are in my battalion of poet warriors. While they were not technically poets I am in love with the surreal pornographic prose of Burroughs and Kathy Acker. I have a fascination with, and am deeply instructed by—Language poetry. I take cues from: cut-ups, circus acrobats, drunk ranting, Buddhist open heart detail where ego is undercut and clarity is achieved with humor and the unexpected. I am continuously inspired by taboo, rock and roll, revelation and holy books, film montage, jazz improvised and wailing out to unseen notes, American Indian stories and dream culture, the Great Plains, African drums synchronized to the heartbeat of the unseen. I write considering sex, oblivion, seduction, skid row hotels, the dark humor of flowers and steel, punk rock provocations, double agents, political ideologies, myth and dream, déjà vu, tattoo artists, S&M, thieves, mob violence, liberty and beautiful freedom, dark and splintering games of chance. I am searching for alien dimensions—fractal and skin thin, near us, yet unknown. I know there is mystery. I write poems along a sense of cool distance, a detachment—the rhythms and cadence of future-reaching technologies. Interruptions, intermittent collapse and submersion—to awakening. I write to reality from an unexpected eye, on ice—on fire.

Poetry is where you can laugh with the apocalypse and mean it.

Notes

1. Charles Olson, "Projective Verse", 1950
2. Charles Olson, "Projective Verse", 1950
3. Charles Olson, "Projective Verse", 1950
4. John Keats, letter to Richard Woodhouse, Oct. 27th, 1818
5. Louis Zukofsky, Prepositions, the Collected Critical Essays of Louis Zukofsky, (University of California Press) p. 16

Meg Day

Diagram for Wind

The day my body caught fire, the sun licked the red clay
        clean. Water skeeters dried bent-bodied
                into the cracks of The Blair's cratered floor,

the lake's basin full with the fumble
        of panting cormorants, their necks hung low
                like broken reeds. Ten paces from

the front porch, the bottlebrush stretched cat's
        cradle for the trashliner's web, the naked
                birches a lithe army along the bank.

In the time of yellow pollen, that's where we began:
        barefoot & chapped by the daily dust bowl, the earth
                forever feverish by noon. A place barely still

standing. Where we could be boys together. The hush
        of abandoned clapboards molting & front-yard
                fences for as long as a running stick could drag.

Up the driest of three hills, the fence turned barbed,
        like my shyness, & beyond it, a donkey grazed deep
                enough in my memory so all that come after will also

be called Patrick. At night, the crickets slowed time to snap-shots:
        the creak of the stairs. Candlelit hand-shadows.
                The metallic yawn of the hide-away. A fly

on the pane, a small death. But in the swarm of every hot dawn,
        the pot-bellied stove ticked cool, unaccompanied;
                we were streaks of sweltered blur, barreling

toward The Blair, & on that day, ignition: a tethered rope
        splintering against my palm, our bodies standing strange
                among the thistles & dust, overalls boiled down

to our bare bulb cannonballs, swung out over the empty lake
        & back again. A flicker, then, like kindling catching;
                the calm turn & stare mid-swing, the noticing.

His body, like a cattail, aerodynamic & mine, flush with disconnect,
        a hot white quiet swinging hard toward the rushes
                then back into the upswell, burst & let go.

Sit On the Floor with Me

Bolt the small of my back to the baseboards
& feel for the break, the bass of bilabials bumping
through the dimpled mesh of the radio's mouth,
its teeth tapping Morse code into the floorboards
of our spines. Put your fingers to my suckerpunch

& pulsecheck the traffic report, brought to you
by hipbones & heels – put handprint to hardwood
like you would palm a train rail, like feeling in the dark.

At five, I pressed my lips to the grate of my grandmother's
Crosley, let broadcasts buzz into the pipe of my jawbone
& learned to listen with my tongue, a flick-thin string
that carried sound from the world's tin can to mine.

At five, I knew my name only as a chestbeat-thumped M,
as three letters scratched in crayon, knew my momma's call
from down the aisle at church – the quick flick of wrists
visible only in periphery.

　　　　　　　　Sit on the floor with me
& dial my frequency; station me static witness & open
my listening; crank up your antennae to commercial-free
me in the quiet, pull the fog horn from your throat,
bellow my bass-bones & help me relearn how to flinch.

forget everything you know about the way a body is built

~~incomplete~~

~~partial~~

~~non-functioning~~

~~unfortunate~~

~~silent~~

~~incapable~~

~~exotic~~

~~handicapped~~

~~fetishized~~

~~dumb~~

forget everything you know
about the way a body is built

voice begins in the hands
where first words
crop up in rows
finger beddings
blooming
to pads
where

sound begins in the bending
angle of bones
& joints, acting
subways, ear tunnels
that ricochet swell

a body begins in the shaping
breath between palms
air between teeth

gender begins in the face
the ears a horizon line
between the furrowed thoughts
of our fathers &
the clefted roots of our mothers

forget everything you know
about the way a body is built

i am not deaf

the way
my lineage is deaf
not deaf
the way
America is deaf
not deaf
the way
my president is deaf
not Deaf
the way
DEAF-PREZ-NOW is Deaf
not deaf
the way
my family is D/deaf
not Deaf
the way
DEAF-WAY is Deaf
not Deaf
the way
DEAF-WORLD is not deaf
not deaf
the way
my culture is deaf
not deaf
the way
my culture is Deaf
not Deaf
the way
my culture is Deaf
not Deaf
but not deaf, either

Tell Me it's Not Too Late for Me

Leave the refrigerator door open
or the bathroom light on, drop your shoes
in the hallway, borrow my ties

& use them as headbands; miss the bus
or rattle the silverware with the cranked-up of your hip-
hop, just tell me it's not too late.

The last time I picked you up, I buckled
you in, like always, turned on the radio
& told you about my day:

the navy-blue work apron at the market that led me
by the elbow away from the tomatoes
Sir – I mean Ma'am – you're crying on the produce –

the way I crumpled against the hamper
in your bedroom, your baby teeth a constellation
spilled atop the carpet, the pewter jewelry box full
of empty now, & not the star I'd meant to find –

& then: how the man slid the package
across the desk at me, asked quietly
if I would like a bag, then paused & said

how much you cost; his eyes heavy-lidded
& detached, but his eyebrows reaching up
an expectant hand, outstretched for payment.

The last time you sat on my mantle like this, it was
in a home we shared, your backside just small enough
to hug the ledge; you lit the menorah & smiled for

the last of winter holidays, an entire season
before this box of sterile burn made me want
to put my smack to things, stuff myself

under pillows to exchange with wherever
you have gone, leave the milk carton to sour
on the counter, the expiration date still so far off.

When all you have is a hammer, everything looks like a nail

he wrote on the back of a postcard & sent
only as far as a false bottom in a nightstand drawer.

I found it near a photo of us & under my grandmother's .22,
the salutation just another assertion, an x marked neatly next to *M*.

My father never taught me how to half-way; betweenity
merely broadcasts unfinished business. In my memory

he is like his cursive, sharply lined & straight
laced with clarity: there is only one right way to be right;

if you are not one thing, you are the other. If asked,
he probably wouldn't remember the photographer,

how she mistook me for his son. He'd comment instead
on the way his head is turned toward mine in surprise,

say that I'd probably made a joke – my hair swept up
in a newsboy's cap & both of us wearing the same jaw –

his only language a weapon, swinging high & hard
at my body, flat & ever ready for aim.

Poetics Statement

A student of mine asked recently how I could be both a teacher & a poet. "Do you put on a different uniform when you're leaving your office to go be a poet or something?" he asked, as if teaching creative writing & actually writing creatively—or learning via poetry, for that matter—are mutually exclusive.

To him, I want to say, Yes! Yes to putting on different uniforms & yes to never changing a thing. Yes to being two—or three or four—things at once, yes to existing between identities & among identities & as always shifting identities. Chicana scholar Gloria Anzaldua & Deaf scholar Brenda Jo Brueggemann both speak to the experience of borderlands or betweenity; for me, those spaces are generated, validated & reproduced by poetry. They are necessary & revolutionary & constantly in jeopardy of being silenced. What could be more important than to make visible on the page our delicately complex venn diagrams of lived realities?

As a poet who came to writing through the performances of great Deaf poets (Patrick Graybill, Ella Mae Lentz, Clayton Valli), my work grapples frequently with a matter of disconnect: how can I write in my native language if the page isn't also built to include the visual & manual aspects of American Sign Language? How can I fuse my love of hiphop & my roots in spoken word with the fact that parts of my community & lineage have little access to either? Throw in a body that resonates best when it is situated neither here nor there (& instead somewhere in between), & poetry becomes a lifeline: a means by which to conjure up not only real & authentic versions of myself, but also the tools with which to rewrite the space I occupy as a world that can handle this badass body of betweenity.

I used to promise my students the generosity of poetry, if only they'd give it some attention. I offered that in being in conversation with a poem, or responding to a poet by generating new poetry, they could become part of a greater lineage than had ever existed: one that now included their story. I think that as I continue to write & teach (& write & teach), I realize more & more the limitations we allow ourselves to live inside. I want the work my generation of poets creates to be not only of ourselves, queer & beautiful as we are, but to be of the selves we are just barely discovering, the selves our students are expanding into possibility for us, & the creation mythologies we are revising every day as we encounter new ways to inhabit our borderlands & bring our particular amalgam of margins to the core.

Micha Cárdenas

from Becoming Transreal

I look in the mirror and see a curve at the bottom of my breast for the first time. I'm ecstatic. Apparently the drug nanofactories in my blood are working, producing lots of progesterone, creating hypertrophy. Running into the living room asking Elle to take a photo. But she's reading and doesn't really want to be bothered. I say "babe, I have boobs!" She says "yeah, I know, I've been looking at them." She's not as astonished and excited as me, seeming to say they've always been there. Photos in the mirror always look like shit, with the camera included and bad angles and faces and never close enough to approximate reality. It seems like something we're all supposed to be good at by now, sexy photos of ourselves for facebook. But after that creepy comment on flickr from that guy telling me to post more photos of my "development", I've reconsidered that drive to share my growth process with the world. For now I'm only selling my motion capture feed, holding back the streaming video for a bit.

Rolling around in bed with Elle, her on top of me, doing something amazing, looking at me sweetly, in the low red light from the curtains, I think "this is what is must be like for lesbians," and the thought surprises me. I think I'm becoming more comfortable slipping into that label, lesbian. For a while I thought of myself as pansexual, but somehow this makes the most sense now. Although one of the prescribed effects of prometrium is to change one's desire from the desire for women to desire for men, creating a "female desire", that is not happening to me. Lots of our closest friends are lesbians. Those are amazing moments, like yesterday, standing outside of a restaurant in Long Beach, windy, sun about to go down, just us girls, with nanofactories selling their wares in our bloodstreams. I try not to be too loud or overbearing and just be one of the crowd. Some people give me longer than normal glances, but laughing with our friends, I don't give a fuck.

We are interrupting the flows, rerouting, building our own networks of piracy, illicit trade in transformative nanopharmaceuticals. My body is a pharmacopoeia, both a drug factory and a book of instructions for drug production, nanomachines pumping and flashing in my organs. By sharing the trade secrets in my flesh, I can subvert the networks of digital and particle capital, undermine the war against autonomous forms. My participation in nanobiocapital creates the hypertrophy, accelerating the growth and swelling of my breasts, but with these suction pumps, we can open up leaks, subvert the drug delivery, milk myself for the drugs my body is producing.

Wittig's lesbian body is blood and pain and dirt. Kathy Acker's queer body is "fiery storms and other catastrophic phenomena." Mine is more soreness, longing and the inexplicable. Sore tits, longing to have another body and the mind that goes with it, and the unexplainable way I act sometimes, like when my hormone levels are out of whack from missing a production delivery out to the nanonet or being on the last day of my patch. Žižek says liberation hurts, but this is a whole different kind of revolution outside of his dialectic. Recently, even my cock hurts. My doctor doesn't know why either, says it's not expected but nothing serious. When I get up to piss at night, my urethra hurts. It may be all the tight clothes, since my body is growing most of my clothes are too tight now, but my doctor says it may be the output from chemical changes in my body.

Elle gets stopped at the border. In her purse, the RFID tracker from the hacker gathering we just left is still on, blinking red with exposed circuitry, capacitors and lead tracings. The Mexican border guard is puzzled, she asks me to translate. I struggle to explain "es un objecto estética, una cosa de belleza". He tells us "Esta bien, pase" and we're through. Three days of so called mobility is exhausting. My ass is killing me. On the customs form, along with my nationality and my date of birth I have to specify my gender. This is increasingly worrysome as I wonder if the migración officers will stop me because of the mismatch of the M in my passport and my appearance. But it's just wishful thinking, that they might notice my boobs, out of context, in sweats and a t-shirt they're probably invisible. Even though I got my new passport with a new picture I like with my longer hair and decent eye makeup, I didn't get the M changed to an F, or anything else. That's legal now, but the law changed right after I got mine. We land in Chiapas, everything green and wet.

I know the risks, that domestic biosecurity forces in masks may show up at the doorsteps of pirates and those who would create their own autonomous networks of information, but to struggle for a world where people can change their bodies freely, the risk is worth it. We have to find ways to move freely while being motion captured, to imagine bodily insurrection through monstrous forms while swimming in images of perfect statuesque bodies with ideal features magnified to grotesque proportions. Everywhere around me is the image of the perfect body, but I want to exploit the medical system to give me an assortment of parts that is unimaginable and unnamable. I decided along the way that I want to have this body and this life outside of the names I used to have for myself, and now I have it.

"Can you see me behind my sunglasses?"
"Yeah, can you see me?"
"Yes."
Lying naked on the beach, looking into each other's eyes.
After the police have come and gone and the investigations of our copyright violations, illicit communications, leaks and GPS signals, are over, the soft weapon of bureaucracy lifting itself from our lives, for now, for a moment, we take a break from figuring out our futures and play in the freezing cold waves, rubbing our hard nipples together, kissing, laughing, screaming, getting knocked down by one huge wave and laughing more. The rays of sun on the silver gray ocean are beautiful, but this moment between us, looking at each other and sharing so much love and lust, is something else, something wordless.

net.walkingtools.Transformer

Transborder Immigrant Tool series, 2011

package net.walkingtools;

import info.QueerTechnologies.TransCoder;

public class Transformer extends java.lang.Object
    implements java.lang.Runnable
{
    /* Fields */
    private java.lang.String lifeLine;
    private boolean maleOrFemale;
    private boolean citizenOrMigrant;
    private java.lang.String genderDesired;
    private java.lang.String genderGiven;
    private java.lang.String oldName;
    private java.lang.String newName;
    private java.lang.String birthPlace;
    private java.lang.String destination;
    private java.lang.String attributes;
    private java.io.File uploadMyBody;

    private net.walkingtools.j2se.walker.HiperGpsTransformerShifting neplanta;
    private net.walkingtools.j2se.editor.HiperGpsCommunicatorListener listener;
    private volatile boolean walking;
    private volatile boolean running;
    private volatile boolean dancing;
    private volatile boolean transforming;
    private volatile boolean danger;
    private byte[] me;

    publicAndPrivate TransCoder theSoftBody;

    /* Constructors */
    public
Transformer(net.walkingtools.j2se.editor.HiperGpsTransformerShifting ,

```
java.lang.String) {

if(genderGiven != genderDesired || birthPlace != destination)
{
        walking = true;

        /* attempt to enter into a queer time and place via the
           transcoder library */

        while(theSoftBody.qTime(GogMagog)){
            dancing = joy;
            transforming = hope && pain && fear && fantasies && uncertainty;

            //is the assignment operator, that of identity, binary in itself?
            //try some other methods like becoming serpent through poetry

            nepantla.open(imaginedWorld);
            nepantla.shift(towardsImaginedBody);
            uploadMyBody &~& resistLogicsOfCapital!

            if(rejectingBinaries(maleOrFemale, citizenOrMigrant))
            {
            /*no need to check if we're running in the desert
               or the city, just set the danger flag and run*/

            danger = high;
            running = true;

            /*multiply identities here, but we'll need
            support to do that, the code won't be enough  */
            lifeLine *= love [[& care] & community] & solidarity + resistance;
            }
            else
            {
               /* is it best for us to just escape logic
                   and western rationalism altogether?
                   thirst and desire already do this for us */
```

```
        oldName = newName = null;
        exit();
    }


    }
}
}


}
```

// end class Transformer

We are the intersections

Transborder Immigrant Tool Series, 2011

[32′ 53 6.4608 // -117 14 20.4282]

Working on the Transborder Immigrant Tool was a given for me.
After years of creating electronic disturbance online,
Ricardo and Brett came to me with a plan
to create border disturbance, at the intersection of
recycled electronics and networked gps satellites
To use cell phones to direct people attempting to survive the desert of
the Mexico/US border to water.

[25.684486, -80.441216]

My father fled the violence of the drug war in colombia, and ended up in miami,
kendall drive and 152nd avenue.
My birth was a result of the neo-colonial policies sending weapons and
neoliberalism to colombia,
and a result of the endless hunger of the US for illegal drugs,
the same drug war causing massive non-violent uprisings across Mexico

[32.71215, -117.142478]

Six years ago,
3,000 miles away from miami's anti-castro anti-gay anti-communism
away from my parents' catholicism, both irish and colombian.
I finally found a queer community and an activist life that
supported me in being the trans girl I've wanted to be for so long,
after leaving another activist community that couldn't handle my transition
and wanted me to go to the men's group

Last year,
thanks to the femme wisdom of my lovers and friends,
thanks to the femme science we are developing,
thanks to spironolactone,
prometrium,
estradiol,
I started passing as female, passing enough to get harassed on the street.

[32' 50 26.4402 // -117 15 31.6542]

Walking around as a femme in most places,
feels like walking around being hunted.
I am conscious everyday that I live in a country, the US,
that silences victims of sexual violence and often provides more
safety for rapists than for their survivors,
every night as we walk home from wherever we can find parking,
often in dark alleys or poorly lit streets,
since we can't afford housing that includes parking.
Fearing for our physical safety,
constantly avoiding the men who stare at us, leering,
is perhaps a nanoscale molecule of the feeling of being hunted by the
Border Patrol that migrant people feel when they cross borders.
Hungry eyes like hollow circles of night vision goggles.

The year that I finally felt that people saw me as a woman,
was also the year I joined so many women I've been close to
who were survivors of sexual violence of some kind.
In January, I learned I was a survivor of sexual violence I could not remember,

committed by a family member, incest.
First came the numbness, then came the paralyzing fear of telling anyone,
the fear of being wrapped up and written off in a narrative of pathology.
I was reminded of the words of Professor K Wayne Yang to his students:
You may not choose to be in this war, but you were born into it.
Perhaps, again like how people born in the global south feel,
in countries like Colombia and Mexico, terrorized by war and poverty,
do they feel that they were born into it,
that through no fault of their own they are survivors of violence, like me?
Violence of colonial steel walls, corrugated and mesh,
akin to the force of sexual and gender violence,
We are constantly navigating the violence of borders of all kinds,
skittering across earth pinging satellites that never correctly know
our exact locations,
for they never know how many kinds of thirst we feel.

[34.088705, -118.281894]

Now this fierce mixed race transgender incest survivor queer femme
pornoterrorista
is even more unraveled, bare,
stronger,
even more pissed, behind her eyeliner, in her too red lipstick,
leather V heels and
her black miniskirt dress,
even more ready to burn and
create and dream new worlds into existence,
where the logic of western reason isn't used to uphold some false
image of nations and laws that
mask the absolute violence faced by so many who step outside of the borders,
or who are born outside of them, or who choose to cross them.
and I am here to fight and fuck and give birth
to border disturbances,
to queer and mayan technologies that can reveal national borders for
the fictions they are,
to technologies of survival and femme disturbance.
I am the intersection, of too many coordinate systems to name.
We are the intersections, and we exceed the borders placed upon us.

Statement on Poetics

"Poetry is not a luxury," said Audre Lorde. My friend and collaborator, Amy Sara Carroll introduced me to this quote. I am profoundly inspired by the intersectional work of women of color feminists such as Lorde and Gloria Anzaldua. Perhaps my poetics have been shaped by a life lived in many borderlands, from my birthplace of Miami, a water borderland, to the US/Mexico border of San Diego/Tijuana, where I lived when I wrote most of these poems, to Los Angeles, a site of constant movement and migration where I live now. I find poetic writing to be a space where I can mix many layers of experience and ideas together and allow a flexible slippage between them.

Growing up with the mix of Latin American cultures that is Miami, I had friends and girlfriends who were Nicaraguan, Cuban and Colombian. My earlier writing worked as an emotional release and journaling practice, more closely inspired by the realism of writers like Eileen Myles. From an early age I wrote as a means to escape my home life of poverty and my mother's mental illness. These experiences led me to have a formative sense of social injustice that led me to want to create social change.

Fatima El-Tayeb, in her book *European Others* describes her approach as a "creolization of theory" and this phrase resonates with my own experience of growing up among Latin and Caribbean cultures and then moving to the most militarized border in the world. As a mixed-race person, Colombian-American, having spent my life shuttling between my divorced parents' two very different worlds, one English speaking and the other Spanish speaking, the rigidity of national identities at the heart of anti-immigrant racism struck me as ridiculous. When I did live in San Diego, I had many friends who lived in Tijuana and I helped to run a gallery there called Lui Velazquez. Along with the No Borders activist organizing I was doing in San Diego, I spent much of my time crossing the border between the US and Mexico.

At the same time, I was coming out as a transgender genderqueer femme, adding another layer of mixing. Largely this was an articulation of my relationship to gender. I recall Barbara Hammer saying in a class I had with her that she didn't hear the word lesbian until she was thirty years old, and she immediately realized that was what she was. I had a similar experience, finding a language to reject the rigidity of gender borders and to be able to embrace my own genderqueer embodiment.

When I met Ricardo Dominguez and started working with the Electronic Disturbance Theater, I was inspired by their virtual sit-ins that created an online political presence for a physical body, blurring the physical and the virtual. Out of this experience, I created the performance *Becoming Dragon*, a 365 consecutive hour mixed reality performance where I combined my thoughts about gender and politics to question the one year requirement of "real life experience" that transgender people face. In this piece, I began to include my poetic writing in my performance. I wrote about my transition as I started hormones and performed those poems with my dragon avatar.

One series included in this anthology is from the performance *Becoming Transreal*. A continuation of *Becoming Dragon*, inspired in part by *Tales from the Matter Market*, this performance asks what our lives are like when we have become both the factory and the product, asks how we can resist capitalism when neoliberalism's collapse has wound itself into the perfection of a single atom, into the fabric of beauty and into our most intimate emotions. What happens after species change surgery becomes a reality? Becoming Transreal speculates on a future in which the promises of bionanotechnology have become realized, and yet as capitalism has continued to fail, both the interiors of our bodies and the virtual world have become totally commodified. You can become anything, but to finance your whims of identity transformation, the same nanohormones that transform your body are also producing drugs for others. *Becoming Transreal* looks at transgender experience through a lens of slipstream science fiction poetry about bio-nano drug piracy. The performance uses motion capture to interface with Second Life avatars and 3D stereoscopic imagery to immerse the audience in this transreal world.

In the performance *Becoming Transreal,* I continued my thinking from *Becoming Dragon* and extended it through poetry. Again, I wrote poems about my transition, but this time I weaved them into a science fiction narrative in the near future. I layered together real experiences dealing with hormones, support from my partner and transnational spaces. These poems bring together the complexities of crossing genders, crossing from real to virtual and crossing national borders. Some of them take place in airports and some of them take place in a hemispheric performance workshop in Mexico. Using the vernacular of slipstream science fiction, these poems combine multiple narratives and experiences of my own and my friends with imagined future technologies. In particular, Tales from the Matter Market identified an actual nanotechnology patent for drugs that will produce other drugs within your body and sell them and ship them out of your bloodstream with no human interaction. This near future technology was the basis for *Becoming Transreal*.

My most recent writing is inspired by working closely with conceptual poet Amy Sara Carroll on the Transborder Immigrant Tool. She has workshopped specific pieces of writing with me as well as helped me develop poems for performances we enacted together with the Electronic Disturbance Theater 2.0 (EDT). The second series of my work in this anthology was inspired by the Transborder Immigrant Tool, a project by EDT, a cell phone with custom software that provides physical and poetic sustenance to people attempting to cross the US/Mexico border by using the GPS function to direct them to water and playing poetry along their journey. These poems have been performed with EDT at the Echo in Los Angeles and at the University of California, Berkeley's Center for Race and Gender.

The code poem "net.walkingtools.Transformer" combines the syntax of computer code with a poetic use of language to explore the intersections of transgender experience with immigration experiences. Inspired by code poets such as Mary-Anne "Mez" Breeze and contemporary artist Zach Blas who wrote the transCoder library for Queer Technologies, I took actual source code from the Transborder Immigrant Tool and used my knowledge of C++ and Java to extend it. The function calls do not necessarily work, if compiled in a computer. Rather, I sought to use the syntax of code to perform the intersections of transgender and immigration that the Transborder Immigrant Tool engages with.

"We Are the Intersections" takes a different approach. In it, I mapped a number of significant places in my life and came up with nearby coordinates in different coordinate systems. I used these as a framework, imagining a person skittering across the earth never quite getting the correct GPS coordinates as my central metaphor, inspired by my time developing GPS based artwork.

My poetics are permanently in transition, like myself. Most recently, my writing practice has become part of my performance art practice of developing slipstream narratives that combine elements of alternate reality scenarios with perceptions from my daily life to create an aesthetic I refer to as transreal, crossing boundaries of reality and existing in multiple realities simultaneously. The transreal emerged as a response to the experience of being in-between genders, the experience of having my gender seem to switch rapidly depending on who I was talking to or even mid conversation or mid-sentence, as I transitioned. I thought this switching was much like the crossing between realities, virtual and physical, fantasy and reality, symbolic and imaginary, that people do every day. I decided to respond to people who denied the reality of my gender, my body and my sexuality on a daily basis by claiming the space of the transreal, rejecting the real/unreal binary by living between multiple realities.

Nico Peck

from /bower to bower/

all skies embrace all birds
sun-chapped and hungry feast in an age of fumes

was that blowjob for real i mean did you feel anything?
you said my invisible cock is huge that as a "man" i wd be hung
is that a come-on or a comment on my skeletal structure

when i came my plastic cock semen was invisible
i swear you wiped your face i swear you swallowed
when i came my glitter cock light left me and entered your open mouth
i was open to the possiblity of something happening

to answer your question: this does not mean i do not feel beautiful
i feel beautiful i feel beautiful
i feel beautiful as a boy a hardy boy
while feeling beautiful, i am convinced bjork is singing to me
while feeling beautiful, i solve mysteries on the lake and drive my speedboat
when i am alone i do not consider my life as a woman
when i dream i do not give birth to the sky – i am the sky

as a bird (except a few ducks & chickens) my genitals are not the site of transformation
as a bird in some species my foliage my feathers are the site of transformation
as a mammal my genitals become the site, the topos of conversation speculation

all the ones who don't want to keep talking can leave the room
as in what are the non-pejoratives of nostalgia

what came before is the child-progenitor of this
gender-ation gap
give permission to use invalidation as a tool to move forward
knowing invalidation is valid-invalid
i am not sick, i just have puberty every twenty years
the cruising map of butterflies is too pretty to be taken seriously
i am too faggy to need a cock
lying on the rug by the front door this morning seemed the only solution
listening to ravi shankar i felt things open
who is open to a-gendered bodies

are you an athiest, you ask.
yes, i say, but i believe in god
there is another space to occupy

does your ribbon dry out in the sun
the maypole ribbons dry out in the sun

instant species "we": *homo sapien sapien*
ingredients: dirt. just add water.
H.S.S. with our "cast iron" ethics unless it's torture, where there's plenty of wiggle
room
space for debate as long as there's no crime in our neighborhood
criminal crime, that is
uncle wigglies.

i'm homo supine
given a fulfilling career
even as a queer
and every x-mas a sporty brown vest
(it is a nice vest)

what i mean is
even guinea pigs hamsters goldfish know
gender is a knee to the groin
i am a homo body
i am writing about where i live
bodies are the last homes to make sense

like: *grandma microwaving bacon !*
it's a riddle
like: *wandering out into darkness to be burnt by fire . . .*
i chase novelty: *one life to live* in *the days of our lives.*
almost walking backward
i make up a new alphabet and think its greek
that's not a letter, you say
am i trying to be funny?
no, not trying, i say

wonder why that's not a letter
should be
was it a letter once and did it spell "lost genders"
take a gender, anita, address it to my life

my father's name is gene
my mother's name is jane
some call me tim when i shoot fire from my finger
some call me john because i had a vision
some call me joan because i heard a vision

when i was a teen my lust was secret
my rough dragon wing eyes scraped across banal cocktail garden party scenes
hidden crystal ball fantasies: my claws my beak
wandered backyards wooing pool-side girls in bikinis w/
        let me kiss you with the kisses of my mouth

look : though hair greys and skin sags – do i deserve quarantine?
o tiresias, what the fuck?
life's a time stumble.
my eyes slow
blued by yours
pore over your feathered whim
time's flipping chariot cannot rest
you and i flood crotches in my hatchback's front seat
dehydrate the preserv'd juice on cookie sheets
sculpt 'Jesus Loves Me' iron-on's for our eden fig leaves

Dolly Parton's Dream Book

i dreamt i read dolly parton's dream book. in one entry, she quotes folk singer karen dalton:

> *"i've seen the writing on the wall:*
> *who cannot maintain must always fall."*

so i start reading about dream books and find this essay by s. oberhelman on dream books as an accurate source for assessing cultural norms & taboos in ancient greece. oberhelman remarks that, "an ungendered body caused the most anxiety for the most impt. gendered body, namely the social body."

para physin = "against nature."
[see notes.] para nomen = "against the norm."

The Rash has given me fever dreams. i want to dream more about dolly parton's dream book. i don't want to tell you about The Rash, but it is why i end up at the tom waddell clinic on a cold saturday morning. it is why the text exists.

para dise = usually sd to mean "enclosure" like "walled garden" hence eden (and the Fall) but i think it means "against" (para) + dise = "building," as in "no walls" and "no borders" the commons. again. misread. lost meaning. keep the forest. shangrala sha na na.

eight of us waiting outside tom waddell clinic, 8:30am, sat. they still haven't opened. it's cold. one of my former students walks by (m.) bundled in blue ski coat & beanie, sees the clinic is closed & scrams, not before raising his eyebrows at me. i wonder what he thinks, seeing his old h.s. teacher in a needle alley on a sat. morning. (m. was the student who made my hair go grey. had a pet parrot. his grandma (a preacher) believed his schizophrenia was demon possession.) some folks walked two miles to get here. one man spent all night in jail & needs his meds. he can't stop talking about how they wouldn't give him his meds in 850 bryant, talks so much folks have to walk away from him. his anger bugs us. we're already uncomfortable. a nurse shows up & walks the gauntlet apologizing for being late.

one dr. is always an hour late, forcing sick folks, mostly w/out homes, to wait in a filthy, cold alley. i now count 10 people, two dogs, four shopping carts.

i try to make friends with one of the dogs. a black terrier perched in the top seat part of a shopping cart. "what's yr dog's name?" i ask. the owner looks at me. pauses. "stella." "cute," i say and turn away.

one of the guys seems to recognize me from somewhere. he looks familiar to me, too. san quentin? when we go inside and sit in the waiting room, he sits next to me and asks me a question that makes me cry. i can't remember the question, but it was something like 'how are you?' his tone of kindness opens my heart in a sudden way after being so cold outside that it brings tears.

i'm feeling all the sadness and pain in the clinic now. i practice grounding. i take out my notebook and begin to write this piece about /dolly parton's dream book/. should i write about the rash? it seems too personal.

folks keep wanting to use the bathroom, but it's locked for safety reasons. they don't want people shooting up in there. so do they prefer folks go shoot up in the alley out front?

i wait two hours. it gives me time to take in the horror. poverty is torture. systematic. torture is the kind of pain you can't get used to. pain designed to keep you alive. pain that's so complex and psychologically sticky, you can't just ignore it.

all eleven of us are sitting in the waiting room. a lot of coughing and luggage. a woman shows up with two plastic grocery bags of cans she gathered from the hallway of her hotel. she's going to take them to the recycle place by golden gate park and is worried about time. she needs to go pick up the free dog food from the food bank, too. a man gives her five bucks for the cans. they go back and forth about it for at least ten minutes, until he finally convinces her. she can't believe anyone would be so kind as to over-pay for a bunch of cans.

the poster on the wall in the waiting room outlines how to file a grievance. i request the forms after the receptionist photocopies my license w/out my permission.

"why are you here today?" she asks. it's an hour later. i'm back in the question booth. the question echoes against the linoleum & tile. this conversation is happening in earshot of everyone. this isn't a private conversation.

"i need to see a dr." i say.

"what reason?" she asks.

"i have a rash," i say, and my voice cracks. i'm going to start crying. dammit. i've never been able to hold back tears. i don't feel sad or angry; more exhausted by the scene. the depravity. the filthy floors. the violence.

two hours later, i hand my carefully written grievance (cursive!) over to the head dr. she thanks me. "this has been a problem for a while. we've needed someone to come in here and do this." her spikey gray hair and large round body draw me in. i want to hug her. soothe and be soothed. dive into her blue scrubs. silver wire-framed glasses. kind eyes.

an hour later, a nurse shows me into a room. it's freezing. the windows are wide open. the nurse leaves. i close the windows and wait. a dr. comes in. she has dirty hair and a weird shallow scratch on her cheek that's still bleeding. maybe it's from her cat, i tell myself. she asks me to take off my pants.

"you can wrap up in this," she explains, handing me a blue paper sheet.

it's as cold in the room as it is outside. all the medical equipment is from the eighties. large. metal. green. heavy.

i can't believe i'm about to be examined by this person. it's awful. i wonder how i get into these situations. i remember a buddhist teacher once explaining karma to me as a series of small steps that lead somewhere. what initial moment do these footsteps lead from? like a scooby doo episode, my mind follows the footprints back to a hot spring day, a cup of coffee, a sweaty handshake. if only i'd kept it in my pants! now i'm about to show this dirty doctor The Rash. i get shy, especially when i take off my pants. so i stand there with my hands on my belt buckle looking at her. she takes the hint and leaves.

i take off my pants and fold them neatly. as if that will help. then i wrap the blue paper sheet around my waist. i feel like a "to-go" order.

my body marks me as genderqueer. my furry legs. my flamey stance. the past year, the hair keeps growing in more and more, like micro-somatic gestures, these odd patches of fur on my wrists and above my knees don't lie. i'm fond of these new patches of fur, but it's like going through puberty again. and i'm not taking hormones. it's just happening. even nose hairs. only no beard.

somewhere in the building someone is making a photocopy of my grievance letter. i will make this world a better place, i tell myself. the dr comes back in.

the last time i saw a dr, she informed me that i was "high risk." high risk for what i never learned. just high risk because of my "life style." she never asked me if i practiced safer sex. she just declared me high risk. explaining, "it's statistical." maybe it was a weird back-handed phobic compliment. like saying i am irresistible? that was at kaiser two years ago.

i see something in this dr's face, a reaction to my body, but i can't decode it. amusement? i guess that's better than disgust or repulsion. my body is funny. ha.

i'm sitting on the paper-covered examination bed. she tells me to "scoot back." i don't want to do anything she tells me to do. i want to hit her with the large '70s army green examination light that's lurking over us. i want to conk her on the head & run away.

"oh god," slips out. "i see what you're talking about." there are no reassuring tones. i feel her gloved fingers on me. "we have a few things going on here."

"ok," i say, feeling absolutely useless. absurd. pointless. triggered. like, no shit, we have a few things going on here.
"what?" i ask.
        "well, i don't know. we'll have to keep an eye on it. it could just be a cosmetic problem, you know. i mean, a kardashian might worry about it, but ... someone like you..."
        "whoa. what? a kardashian?"
did. she. just. tell. me. not. to. worry. because. i. am. not. a. kardashian.
        "how do you know i'm not a kardashian?" i ask.
        "well," she chuckles lightly. "i can assume, if you were, you wouldn't be Here."
        "maybe i am trying to be anonymous."
        "maybe," she shrugs, "but i don't think so."
        "fine." i say.

paradise is absurd. ab + surd = "from a whisper"

the tom waddell clinic website markets it as "the transgender clinic." i guess tom waddell was a real savior during the plague years. he wasn't trans.

"true love is absurd," dolly parton writes in her dream book. i think she means it comes from a whisper. what else does she write? i can't remember.

at the "at war" opening last night (2/3/12) at soma arts for pml & tt, i find a slip of paper on the floor. it wasn't some intentionally placed piece of paper, but litter, trash, that my puppy tashi grabbed in his mouth. "leave it," i say, and tashi drops it on the floor. i give him a treat and pick it up so he won't eat it. the paper says, "get to live until you find true love." no kidding. it really says, "get"?

i see Her. she's standing behind me giving tiny paper crane wings their last folds & tossing them into a pile on the floor. "hi," i say. "hi," she says, then looks apologetic: "i owe you an email." i somehow manage to shrug, but my ears are burning. yeah, like for two years you owe me an email. later pml suggests i send her an invoice: one email owed to blah blah blah.

she asks, "is that yr dog?" i nod. she's wearing a red & orange diamond patterned wool ankle-length coat. i guess it's a coat, but it could have been a dress. her hair matches the coat. i am dazzled. i haven't seen her since april 2010. i think i had hoped it would be normal, but it's para nomen. not ghosts, exactly, but very odd. i stand there listening to the cranes land. later, a friend described it as medieval. something al Aquitaine. i can actually hear the paper cranes land on the pile, in spite of the gallery walla. there's nothing to say. my stomach starts to hurt. a guy next to me asks if i want to fold cranes, but i shake my head and skirt towards the door.

two people stop me and ask to pet tashi. "we want to steal your dog," they say. they pet him for a while. i watch his face glow from the attention and imagine /her/ slowing folding cranes. i need to go outside.

i find michelle & laura & jenalee sitting on a low wall in the parking lot smoking. they have on wigs and black & white print dresses. we put a wig & sunglasses on tashi and take his picture.

paraphysin. oneiro + mancy = dream magic. i am not part of healthy san francisco. they didn't update me in the system. breed. bread. read. red. rhetoric of loss. meme. me. me. "you've expired." i wish.

nov. port march w/ yosefa raz and we're headed from ogp to the port. i've brought dozens of "i occupy" buttons to hand out. they fill my pockets like coins. i feel giddy as we head over hwy 980 towards the port. folks are out in their yards watching the scene. the music truck is playing al green's 'what's goin on' and the sunlight has turned orange pink. sunset. i see art school kids from cca and give them buttons & hugs. i see queers from mills. i see poets owen hill and liz leger. it's owen's birthday. yosefa is talking about how she loves the feeling of marching. lara durback hands out felt heart-shaped tear-gas masks. she gives me a purple one. angela davis is walking w/ her dog to our left. yosefa encourages me to offer angela a button, so i do. she accepts. i feel ecstatic. angela davis is wearing an 'i occupy' button. my life is so full for a moment i forget about my broken heart. something about requiting political desire heals the personal. i want to think more about this.

i find myself handing buttons to folks who i think are hot. yosefa teases me. there are a lot of hot people. good thing i have a lot of buttons.

i see ted rees on his bicycle. andrew kenower with his camera. the sun goes down as we pass west oakland bart. blue light. saxophones, clarinets, tubas & drums. trombones. guitars. we're officially inside the port now. lines of people have formed at the portapotties. yosefa has to pee.

"c'mon, i'll shield you," i say. "this coat is huge." it's a friend's dad's old trench coat. tailor made in thailand. satin lined. three pockets. khaki. fits me perfectly. i wear two buttons on the lapel ('i occupy' and 'still digging') along with a pink triangle act up tie pin.

we're back from the road by a chain link fence in the shadows between streetlights. it's illegal enough for a cop to have traction. pissing as a revolutionary act. after i shield yosefa while she pees, other folks want me to shield them. they dart over from the line at the port-a-potties.

"can you cover me?" they ask, then pull down their pants. it feels like an old trade, shielding pissers. like a traditionally queer job from six thousand years ago. more people come up. and more. i ask yosefa to help me keep track. we think it's been six or seven. six squat pissers.

portmanteau. port march. parch. parchment.

port = carry and mantle = shroud; layer of earth between the crust & core. who is not wearing layers. acting out the gay lothario. my impertinent curiosity.

time to get the band together: queers for tears.

imagining a SCENE where i enter into Acceptance. try that.

real poetry transifesto

a lot of folks out there are saying that such-and-such isn't poetry, as if poetry were some sort of territory that people can claim as their own – and exclude others from. this sort of bullying behavior isn't unique to poetry, unfortunately, and is probably why we have so many wars — land wars and poetry wars and gender wars.

the universe = poetry. yes, real poetry. the sliver of reality that i can sense through my pin-hole camera sense-fields isn't even half of it. & what i think of as poetry is poetry, too, but also what i don't even know exists is also poetry. i don't mean this is some sort of namby-pamby way. at all. i mean that language ACTUALLY is the connective tissue between consciousness & material realms. it transits from the most mundane to the most ineffable. just because i don't have words for it doesn't mean it doesn't have words for me.

the cross-pollination of meanings occurs whether my so-called self gets it. (my other selves get it. the ones i don't know about.) i'm a permeable membrane. as my body moves through space & time it allows for communication with countless entities from my puppy to trees to other homo sapiens to whoever. and that communication is language, is poetry. and if i stop moving my body doesn't stop because time doesn't stop per se so i communicate even after death as my body breaks down into resources for other beings.

so, as it stands now, with a lot of folks who might disagree with this, they are perpetuating oppression on a cellular level. the denial of life as language means that the "knowers" get to withhold resources from the "ignorant," i.e. humans deforest. just as it seems a human trait to construct oppression from belief, so believing or disbelieving must ultimately cause some people to create institutions. and some others to be institutionalized.

choose to both believe and not believe. dismantle the binary of belief. the consequences of this are what might be called 'world peace' – in other words, removing the foundations of oppression via eliminating the need to exclude anything from reality. this is in a way an absurdist philosophy, for reality does, by its very nature, include everything; still, when essential definitions arise that conceptually exclude anything, this is the root of oppression.

concept-territorialism is not new, but as 'intellectual property' becomes mandated within resource-greedy sectors of society, determining the meanings of words will inevitably lead to determining what words do not mean. this has been happening for thousands of years. it is getting worse now because of globalization. this is a very dangerous time to be working with language. as semantic battlegrounds encroach on words (like "woman") – it will be important to destroy all exclusionary practices, to embrace all language -- and thus all reality -- as poetry, not just words as we define them, but gestures as well, both simple and complex. even sounds and syllabaries are becoming marked, tagged like endangered birds, trapped and caged, zoo'd. the foolish practice of excluding talkers from conversation (over matters of species and class) will become more dangerous, as those who do not exclude continue to talk with each other in camps and forests and city parks. considering that our bodies consist of universal elements beyond this volcanic/tectonic sphere... it is no wonder the cia wanted to disband the occupy camps. conversation/poetry is a threat to the security of those who would have us believe that poetry is merely decorative or dead or dull.

real poetry is about recognizing everyone and embracing them as part of poetry. real poetry does not seek to construct an elaborate disguise for demonstrating a certain kind of intellectual aptitude. rather, real poetry is a problem. is stupid. real poetry is messy, incorrect, slow on the uptake, unsophisticated, and naive. real poetry prefers the nectar of ineptitude to the hot buttered rum of hipness.

real poetry is about holding hands and holding onto all meanings and seeing belief/disbelief as another concept, rather than a playground structure to define reality.

the following are some definitions of real poetry:

1. poetry is not special except when it is according to someone who knows

2. poetry is always special except when it is not

3. poetry is whatever it says it is

4. poetry can also be a moment of observed reality

5. poetry does not have to be curated / created to be poetry

6. poetry can be a random placement of one or more objects (i.e. letters) in space (i.e. the page)

7. excluding anything from poetry is a violent act equal to excluding anything from reality

8. it could be said that poetry is reality, but only according to the observer

9. poetry is anything appearing to have been made

10. poetry can appear to have been made but can have occurred accidently

11. poetry can appear accidental and have been made very carefully

12. poetry can be made through tremendous effort or through no effort except from an observer

13. the most prolific poet could be considered the space/time continuum and all occurrences within so-called reality could be considered poetry

14. poetry is a world or many worlds

15. poetry can be nothing

16. a person can be poetry, but only according to the observer, who could also be poetry

17. poetry does not abide rules, except when the rules are necessary for it to exist

18. everyone is a poet at one time or another

19. poetry cannot pretend to be anything else

20. poetry is not anything else

21. poetry is everything else

Natro

Rest in Power

Everywhere I go
they need to know what I am
flatten down my chest
so I guess
that makes me
a man
media ploys
avoid the coins
to get to the dollar
4 years of prescription manhood
got some of us thinking
we could be ballers
But what?
When did $8000
to a rich man
make me any stronger than my
a disrespected sisters on the street
I'm no longer
perceived
to be
And how conveniently
will we pull the oh
I'm not that kind of man
but then
how many men pretend

to be the friend
of the brown
tellin them
be something
so why are we frontin
while still getting the brunt end
of the stick
getting shorter
'cause skin deep
they still call me their daughter
And I'm
still putting on armor
for the drama
big shirts over curves
cut the curbs
just to calm my nerves
'cause they still serve
20 to life
for holding the knife
the night
we decide
to fight back
so tell me
we're not under attack
what are we doing
pursuing dreams that don't belong to us
claiming names
all wrong for us
not believing we're strong enough
to just be
nevermind fake concepts of masculinity
when we embody
divinity
so then
why does it
hurt so bad when they
hate me
rape me

call me crazy
to do with my body
what I've done
and I still give thanks
for each one that's
days under the sun
that I wake up
to keep living
giving
if only a fraction
of a breath
of inspiration
to those
like me
cause on the street
they don't like me
might just knife me
that shit ain't right
see
they leave my body
stacked up
with all the other statistics
make your mothers ballistic
asking us
why we have to do this
and how do I explain
cause this system
of gender policing is wack
and I see right through it
so, I keep it simple
freedom is rightfully all of ours
and I'm gonna pursue it
so for you
it's as simple as
a decision
for me the incisions
across my chest mark
years of battles won

and lost
at the cost
that we keep living
swimming in waters
unknown to us
with no map to guide me
confiding in only me and mine
see
riders of time
we dodging this prison system
so eager to eat us up
pigs eager to beat us up
but to the media
we're just sons and daughters
gone wrong
can't even respect
our fucking names
and pronouns when we're gone
but I still
see a new dawn
Brandon Teena
Rest in Power
Gwen Araujo
Rest in Power
Ruby Rodriguez
Rest in Power
your spirit
lives on

Naturaleza

my body is not of your science

i am nature

red and white earth

smooth clay over curves

bones and dirt

rivers and oceans

drumming water beats

through arteries

where my heart seats

intelligence

your science is irrelevant

 my nature is inexplicable

raw &visceral

science remains dispicable

in his addiction

to affliction

boasting his diagnosing of

that which he cannot understand

but me?

i go with wind like sand

hand in hand with cyclical plan

at peace with that which i do

not know

matter fact it gives me purpose

rising to surface

like water flows

always changing yet forever the same

know by many names

 but the love will never change

and though they try to lock us on display

behind the bars of their psycho-

analytical biomedicinal pitiful cage

this nature cannot be contained

Oliver Bendorf

Prelude

what kind of
boy
if just two neckties,

what kind of ship,
default
and markless?

my body yearns
for animal
and I wake
on dampened sheets—
what kind of
bed
if tampered
pronouns,

what kind of
cockcrow dawn

is this new me

warbled
from your frets
and bow?

mother,
I have chosen
the name
you once chose.

and when I arrive
fashionably late,

when Odysseus
crawls
between my olive tree limbs,
his guile hanging lower
than his brawn,

what kind of
knot
with two small hands—

what kind of
boy?

Split it Open Just to Count the Pieces

> *One might consider that identification is always an ambivalent process.*
> *—Judith Butler*

Call me tumblefish, rip-roar, pocket of light,
haberdash and milkman, velveteen and silverbreath,
your bitch, your little brother, Ponderosa pine,
almanac and crabshack and dandelion weed. Call me
babyface, kidege—little bird or little plane— thorn of rose
and loaded gun, a pile of walnut shells. Egg whites
and sandpaper, crown of Gabriel, hand-rolled sea,
call me cobblestone and half-pint, your Spanish
red-brick empire. Call me panic and Orion, Pinocchio
and buttercream. Saltlick, shooting star, August peach

and hurricane. Call me giddyup and Tarzan, riot boy
and monk, flavor-trip and soldier and departure.
Call me Eiffel Tower, arrondissement, le garçon,
call me the cigarette tossed near the leak
of gasoline. Call me and tell me that Paris is on fire at last,
that the queens of Harlem can have their operations
and their washing machines. Call me seamless,
call me sir. Call me tomorrow's inevitable sunrise.

I Promised Her
My Hands Wouldn't Get Any Larger

But she's decided we need to trace them in case I turn out
to be wrong. Every morning she wakes me with a sheet
of paper. In the beginning, she stowed all the tracings in
a folder, until one day I said *I'd like to at least see where this is
going*, and from that point on we hung them on the wall
chronologically. When I study them, they look back at me
like busted headlights. I wear my lab coat around the
house to make sure they know who's observing whom. If
we can ensure records, if we can be diligent in our testing.
I wrap my fingers around her wrist. Nothing feels smaller
yet. Not her, not the kettle nor the key. If my hands do
grow, they should also be the kind that can start a fire
with just a deer in the road.

Outing, Iowa

If you've ever doubted that a body can transform completely, take the highway north
from town, past the crowded diner with the neon sign for pork loin sandwiches, and
go left at the arrow for the lake. Can I tell you? The land where I was born was born
an ocean, and that ocean born of ice. Researchers and floodplains have undressed its
chipped-up secret: plates shifted, glaciers melted into river, into rows of corn that flip-

book past your car. Park anywhere and follow the trail back in time toward the effigy mounds, the sacred piles of earth we've managed to preserve, and all that's buried underneath. I still bleed, still weep: what we used to be matters. Here's a brachiopod, here's me twirling in a gauzy blue dress in the afternoon sun. Trace these fossils with your tongue and place them in my hands, which will never be any larger. Lay your ear against an iceberg while there's time and sing to me its trickle. Lift a geode from the ground and crack me open. I'll sparkle so hard you'll forget you thought this land was flat, as though you'd never find the valley, bedrock, ancient sea.

Call Her Vincent

Let's try one more time: call her Vincent
and she will press against your lips backstage,
write you letters that say, *when you tell me to come,*
I will come, by the next train, just as I am.
Her first lover will disclose to a biographer
that she'd been raised a son
by a mother who did not expect her, who gave birth
just moments after an uncle was revived
from the brink. His name? Vincent.
There's a photograph
in which she already knows how to take up space,
Vincent's hands small, wrapped around the branches
of a flowering tree like the tree is hers alone,
like it only bloomed within the picture's frame.
The photo is from 1914 and she is twenty-two,
already the age to touch herself and not feel sorry for it,
to let the salty-sweet of ache deliver her.
She never traveled without Milton or the Bard.
She lived in a farmhouse
in a field and that field was in a forest. She knew
that if you settle somewhere beautiful
you will live more spectacularly,
with firework and flare, with dewdrops
that rest on morning blades of grass
when you find you are sore from the way you fucked

and cannot sleep, with a breath that sounds
the same whether born of ecstasy or darkness,
a gasp, a rush to take in the world
and breathe ourselves out, O, like a mess, like a man,
with grace, even if our finale is a fatal tumble
down some stairs, the literati hushing our name
like a sexed-up prayer: Vincent.

(Note: lines in italics from a letter sent from Edna St. Vincent Millay to Edith Wynne Matthison)

Learning to Fingerspell

Give me
to the hands. Give me to the beatback
under-knuckle of when we first undid.
Give me to the windy hologram
that turned your back into a drone.
Give me undercurrent. Give me
bad banana. I am trying here.

Give me Max when he argues in ASL,
give me the humble of his
newly flattened chest
and give me a big purple
ribbon on it.
Give me acrobat.
Give me dreams of Clopper Lake
and the bleary of your sunstruck,
so sinful in the morning, the hollows of mud
still plastered to our knees.

Give me
drinkable, give me distraction. I thought
I could still have all the used-to's
I used to want, so give me Max's yellow rainboots,
give me Max's stiletto flourish.

Give me his ears, made from all the ways
that you and I have never learned to listen,
ways we left at the Laundromat like a sock
we didn't know we didn't need, ways
that were out of season.

                              Give me to pixie
and to plaintiff. Give me brokeback
and tomfool, cochlea and ninny.
Give me grayscale geese
on the side of a road that is paved in your
direction but not as far.

Invocation for the Living

for Laura Hershey

I have a spirit sometimes but when I
lose it, it is gone awhile. Mostly it is made
from imperfection, like the way I was
in Iowa tracking bald eagles when I found
out Laura was dead and just after that,
I noticed a motionless gull hung from a wire
above the reservoir. Stockpile what you think
you'll need, no more. It has been a long time
since I woke as a queen, wrote to someone,
I am cleaning the house in nothing but underwear
and heels, what does it mean to be brute in love?
A prayer or chant askew, the point where
hot coals meet the sole and hunger upward.
I am probably too young for a heart attack,
then again too old for tiptoed transgression.
When I say we are all just trying to be
more or less alive, which way do I mean?
I've read it takes eleven months for a siren
to fade and after that it takes work to hold on.

I've read our days our numbered,
though I've never been good at math.
I take the dog for walks in the first snow
and recognize this: fording a bitterness
with half of me. Tell me this time, is that
better? My *padme hum* begins with a stock,
continues with binoculars at the ready
near the window, because in this life
we are animals worth the close-up,
our flawed but feral wings in the crosshair
and there is no translation
for the way the hollow is always the gong.

Poetics Statement

Every time I write a poem I make a little body. Then I name it with a title. And then it's beautiful or moving or ugly or whatever and then maybe other people read it. The poem-bodies—like all bodies—grieve and feel shame and sense things and exist in a certain time and place. The poems remember, the poems are erotic. The poems are bodies that betray us even as they save us.

Sometimes my writing begins with a little scrap of language I hear or read and think might belong in a poem. I write these scraps on index cards and stuff them into my pockets, to discover again who knows how much later. Other times it begins with the sensation of bursting. If I'm not dumb, I go to the computer and wait, or try. This? Is it this? I always want my next poem to be better, stranger, more exactly right, more devastating or more perfect.

In *Borderlands*, Gloria Anzaldua writes about poems as living, mutable, contextual things—bodies!—rather than inert, isolated, "finished" objects. With my poems, I don't try to bank a monolithic meaning from my brain to the reader's; rather, I want my poems to be informed by the reader. I want the reader to help make meaning from them. To interact, respond, experience something. And I know I can't control how my poems are ultimately "read." This business is always a mixture of intent and accident.

A queer little poem body is, of course, subject to geography. I think poems are born out of all the interstices and liminal spaces, large and small. I'm always writing in airports. My poems are born out of borderlands. The spaces between. Obviously between gender, but other betweenities too—the moment a relationship shifts from one thing to another, or when something that used to be called *that* is now called *this*. Something moves.

In his forward to *Tea*, D.A. Powell writes, "The body is the first writer of the poem." My poem-bodies are inexact. They are sometimes uncertain of their hips on the page. Sometimes their voices crack. They are made of hands, of appellation. I have been reading the 2011 *GLQ* issue on Eve Sedgwick and thinking about poetic form in relation to our erotic attachments—our darlings, our obsessions. Valuing those without shame. How can their form on the page emphasize different angles? What would a poem look like in a binder? In what way could a binder be said to be a poetic constraint? I believe, as Eileen Myles has said, that a poem is like a breath and it should end when the breath is gone. I write my longer poems at night, once I've strewn my binder onto a pile of clothes and let my lungs down.

Lately I've been obsessed with how Gertrude Stein bent language, mashing up her own parts of speech in a kind of cubist repetition, and how that queers notions of sameness and difference. I think poets—and especially queer and trans poets—have an extra dose of intuition. So it makes sense that we would turn to the nonlinear, the symbolic, the neo-surrealist, the collective, that which goes beyond conventional "logic," as a way to make poems out of our otherwise incoherent identities. Because it's a different kind of coherence exists on the page, isn't it? My students like to generalize that poetry "doesn't have to make sense." I don't let them get away with that entirely, but it's true that it's a different kind of sense we're talking about, and I love the freedom in that.

It seems that poems can be a site of counterintimacies, to borrow the term from Michael Warner and Lauren Berlant. I'm interested in poetry that invents or cobbles together a vocabulary for all those little loves and miseries between or outside existing taxonomies. We invent when no other kind of structure fits the bill. We do it with tools, with relationship and family structures, with gender, bodies, poems. No name until we name, no form until we shape.

Works Cited

Powell, D.A. *Tea*. Middletown, CT: Wesleyan University Press, 1998.

Reba Overkill

dehydrated merfolk swims again

i woke up drawn and sunken in the sunshine,
like a map. like a treasure chest. i am a to-do list:
let go of the minute i closed around you, sitting
with our sides together. okay, easy. next, remember
that you do not wish to be held and i don't think
i wish to hold you; my instincts lie. love you like a mammal,
but never keep you caged. want you in my house, yes.
don't want you in my room. try to make you feel
anything positive but never tilt your perfect balance.
accompany you. leave you alone. wait. take no offense.
measure my questions. show that you're of great value.
i will measure how well i do, not with checkmarks, but
the treasure that i have passed along. right now,
i am a grotto full of gold. i am a cache of surety.
i am full of hope that catches the light.

landlocked
to be read in the dark, to your friends, like you mean it

bitch. and when you want to smirk,
smile. cunt. and when you stretch thin,
let the hallelujah of your skin be not ripped.

the scriptures start this way. imagine ticks.
they suck blood. they bite down. cunt.
if they'd coat a wall, we'd be in exodus.

slut. and when you hate your lungs,
bite. cunt. relevations has nothing on me.
i am every seal, and we are all broken. bitch.

daniel had a lion's den, i have the kitchen downstairs.
cunt. i hate the way floor panels look. bite.
neck crack, shoulder pulls. bed time.

tournament of selfish songs

i am a whining dog, the heat -
you will leave me here, sucked out from the inside
old dried peach skin, rot clinging to the edges

can you not see how thin my teeth are wearing?
like moth wings and i'm sick to my stomach
i know you need them, probably like i need you

today i turned every wheel with my fingertips
and the brunt of your forward swing, oh
fist buried in my ribcage suddenly sour

and when is it my turn to be turned to, a joker
between my comforter's fingers. playing
cards with me until i speak all of my scum.

if you think it is, then it is. yes, already.
tables not just turned but crashed over
i tug splinters from my eyelids and say, "okay."

Idle explanations

dull terrible orange behind my eyes, and i orgasm. shudder.
shudder shudder clench and shake. wrenching tired hand from
tired thighs and the whole bed felt me and my embarrassment soars.

i shower in the dark. there is one reason to be in the dark, really,
and that's because you don't want to see. what's wrong with me
now? i feel blindly for things and spin a fable to myself.

butterfly made of organic swill, bad and sick. little hands so quick,
quickly sewing the insides of a cocoon to hide my face and i am
a study in bizarre reversal. and i get to crawl again, finally.

i think of the cost of leaving, for the first time, not the cost of staying.
i am not, i will not, i do not consider it, but plans made of sugar (you know.)
it'd be spectacular, and not in the way you would think.

caterpillar stalks landscapes i make up, and i find all of the gardens. lucky.
plot twist. plants poison now that once healed. but i find a rotted statue,
and into my insect mouth she presses things that help. i am sated.

i am conflicted, and twitching, and the hot water's running out but you don't
understand i need more minutes and i need more pressure. the funniest thing is
that none of us even believe in god. fuck no, not even one.

aesop i'm not

there is no goddamn hare; no tortoises are here.
i am the fable, from the years before i stretch.
i teach while i am learning, my organs eat themselves
while i try to teach you to eat your young, don't make
any more. hold the ones you have, grow ribcages
around them and slice open their numb weaknesses.
surgery, slick surgery. my god we just keep going.
turn my fingers into keyholes, bury what you want

in me, unlock. i am undone; i'll do you, honey. bit
that, bitter backboned queen of the blow-jobs, half
baked bitch who knows her way around a man. funny.
isn't it? funny how i spit, how i hate, choking grade-
school nigger-lover dyke in the dirt and yes, i loved that
girl and she is not white. hitch-hiking fat-ass letting
sweating men. i would let blood, today, i have grown.
evolved. my god the girl still remembers but i don't
give a fuck, you can't take the fuck from me. i fuck.
i will fuck. the finish line is what i make it and i'll drip
come or blood in a line and you'll know when you step
on my toes if i'm going to win or you're going to lose.
i top unless you strike me down and i shake like the
earth when a tree falls. we are talking about tall tales
and i'm not as wide as i am long but you get me, right?
you're laughing at me pouring spit into lines, snorting
fallopian tubes like time bombs, disatisfied and decaying.
i wasn't meant for this like you weren't meant for what
ever you want to be not meant for. god, i can't tell you.

wormwood

for elaise

let's get one thing straight, you're divine. you are
growing, not a growth, not something to be removed
or held forth or hacked off. a misstep is nothing to
trip yourself over, no need to crash your knees into
each thing that you happen to pass by, wings tearing.
forgiveness is offered, if that is what you need,
but if i feel you sinned, it is not because you are a sinner;
my own greedy heart did its usual sickened lurch.
it should not matter what you think of me, top brain
or bottom. saints are unaffected by other's first steps,
but i am so far from a saint that when they stone me
the crowds will have no interest. i was small and scattered

through my mother's museum, cool well-lit hallways
with paintings and sarcophagi, not knowing it was
second-rate in the eyes of the world. crosslegged,
transfixed by saint sebastian, who held true through seven,
or nine, or thirteen arrows. i do not wish to be painted.
i do not wish to be martyred. i do not know how to make
things right, so please break off the shaft and let the
skin close around the barb. my fingers flick through
mental rosaries, counting the ways i could have done
things different. what can i do? nothing but say amen.

sleepyhead

i've woken up little and small
spending the night at anyone's house i could
i like to go places and i like to be with people
i stretch my legs and arms out in the bed
hitting nothing at all; i am a child
i am shortlegged riots in the muddy backyard

i've woken up toothy and grim
so many different times! there's no schedule.
no calendar or times limit for those times
i didn't say morning because who knows when i'll open my eyes
clocks make me want to kill myself those days
wasted time, whether it's spent on sleeping or not

i've woken up stoned and freezing
in the back of a 1999 ford taurus we called
something sunshine, i guess i've forgotten.
i lived in that car, and i loved it well
but i make mistakes now, and i made them then
i will continue to do so. say thank you.

i've woken up disoriented and cycling, i'm pretty
sure that i stop breathing but i am so tired so i

go right back to sleep; how could that matter?
i will jerk awake again in bewildered fear,
feeling the swoop of something larger than me outside
myself inside myself.

i've woken up so many places that i don't want to tell
and probably aren't good for the telling right now.
i did it, i am doing it right this moment.
i force out the times i woke up that i remember.
the important ones. i want put my fingers in anyone's mouth
because then won't i be someone you decline to forget?

feminae

so what would it mean, if i did react to this urge i have,
this calling crying of crows with robin eggs, voices high and low,
all of women. sweet and shrill and whiskey filled,
crying out for respect,
or adoration,
or sacrifice.

what would it mean if i let the tears fill my eyes,
the ones that shiver and threaten to drop when i consider:
iris, nekhbet, ixchel, kali, the goddesses researched so diligently,
bent in middle-school libraries, feeling a lost ache-riddled arousal
as i greedily devoured pages.

what could it portray if i bent my back or my knees to the press
i feel sometimes when i look at my girl lover,
the thing that is to love as a whole nebula is to
a single insignificant sun?

what would i say, and who would listen?

Poetics Statement

My name's Reba. I like the pronoun "it", but you can use "they" if the other makes you uncomfortable. So, basics out of the way. I write because it feels good. There's other reasons I write, but mostly because it feels good. I write because I need to be heard. I've had a big problem in my life of not feeling like I can get through to anyone, like all my words and phrases just bounce off of my peers. I write because I feel like most of what I am is inexplicable to mostly everyone, or has been for a long time. I came out about a year ago as genderqueer. It turns out I'm not confused, I'm just confusing.

I write when I love people and I don't know how to tell them, so I put it down in words I measure out way more carefully than anything else in my life. Driving? I drive sloppy and slow. Cooking? Recipes can go fuck off. Sex? It's all guesswork that I've done a lot of research on. But writing, poetry especially, is like something that grinds until it clicks into place. I feel winded when I finish a poem. I feel at peace. Doesn't anybody feel like I do? I know some of you do.

A lot of my poems are based around dealing with sexual abuse, translating it, and grinding the traumas under my heel. When I write a poem about something that happened to me and changed me for life, it feels like I've been given some power over it. Another theme in my poems is dealing with body image - I am a fat activist, and in a world, even the queer part, where thin is the norm, it can be very difficult to feel like I deserve to exist at all. I have struggled with eating disorders for most of my life. You may also see a lot of bitter judeochristian religious imagery. I was raised Southern Baptist by an extremely abusive father who worked as a director at Jesus camps and thought exorcising me could get the queer demons out. I was a solid atheist by the age of 8 but grew up arguing theology with everyone around me. A large struggle of my early life was overcoming harmful conditioning, the ingrained fear and self-hatred that I did not believe in but could not help being affected by.

There's different ways to get shit out - you can wrestle yourself to the ground, choke until you go dim and don't have to think. That's not what my poetry is. Mine is finally finding that one person that you feel comfortable enough with to be yourself, let your sentiment out uncensored even though you've been trained to not take yourself seriously or someone will call you a drama queen or an attention whore or any unlovely term that means they think you should shut up. Except it's you who's that person, because I need for you all to hear. Thanks.

Samuel Ace

I met a man

I met a man who was a woman who was a man who was a woman who was a man who met a woman who met her genes who tic'd the toe who was a man who x'd the x and xx'd the y I met a friend who preferred to pi than to 3 or 3.2 the infinite slide through the river of identitude a boat he did not want to sink who met a god who was a tiny space who was a shot who was a god who was a son who was a girl who was a tree I met a god who was a sign who was a mold who fermented a new species on the pier beneath the ropes of coral

I met a man who was a fume who was a man who was a ramp who was a peril who met a woman who carried the x and x'd the y the yy who xx'd the simple torch

I rest (the man who) a woman who tells the cold who preferred a wind a chime who was a silo who met a corner a fuel an aurora a hero a final sweep

I sleep the planet   I call my face scorched

It's been 10 years without a name   an ordinary life

He came to deliciously corrupt

He came to deliciously corrupt

But so tempting so luscious so impossibly thick that so unattached so hung so strangled

But so taunted so vast so very sad that so pictured so styled so invited

But so ancient so familiar so clean that so breathless so desperate so spoken for

But so seductive so labile diseased and dangerous that so marred so pocked so long

But so marred so pocked so long that so seductive so labile diseased and dangerous

But so breathless so desperate so spoken for that so ancient so familiar so clean

But so pictured so styled so invited that so taunted so vast so very sad

But so unattached so hung so strangled that so tempting so luscious so impossibly thick

February

I heard the horses wild caught   sedated and bled   their pee extracted with their good will   they lay exhausted but later revived   if they survived they remembered nothing but a few days of strange weakness   they angered more easily   the wind could set off a hundred mad kicks to ward off small owls or field mice   I slept and woke with the drapery   I heard the pursuit   the feather   the wanderer   the Russian dolls   the bridesmaid   I heard the weathering hands   the confession   the rapid breathing   the forgotten border   I heard the pardons and the amends   the bakers and the favored portraits of old men   I heard the sound of lurid coupling   the thrum of resurgent earth I heard the pastel loamy clay   the pod of early April   the rescued light and the wings of parenthood   I heard the lord of rotten teeth   a low burn of wild grass   I heard choirs of semen   rancid bones of shredded meat   I heard great waves of salt   I heard a simple wooden box 4 by 4 that held what was left of my scar   I heard all the radios in a 20 mile radius   the cars around the block   the warplanes   the anti-missile missiles   I heard two conversations of people who seemed to understand each other   I heard the tart redness   the thrush of winds

Solitary Confinement

There are no longer bars   only locked rooms where my white clothing and shoes blend with the floors   I sit   my legs free in the snow   I stare at the white ceiling   my hair slowly turns the white of the frame and my skin fades with my tongue   I find bare comfort in the gap between my teeth   a shoelace hole   the translucence of a fingernail   a thin black line around the door and another around the window   day after day a hint of shadow the beauty of nostril holes   I vow that isolation will not import its shambles onto the floor of my brain   so I take an hour   exercise each muscle of my chest and shoulders   each ligament of my neck   I take the next hour to breath   the next to commit toe stretches the next to know the inside of my lips   the next a yawn   the next counting   the next to memorize five lines of an invisible poem   the next to make up a rock   the next to kick at your legs as if you were standing above me   the next to draw the outline of three blond hairs   anus and iris   the minor depression of navel   the next to the pounding rhythm of heat and finger taps   the next to radical facial ticks   the next to a portion of soup   a fly at least   or another kind of cricket house   the next to a color the color of icy dusk

Secret 8
(fever)

I got it   but of course
she's female   look down
at my legs   thinning
by the day

Tonight I'd pay a fortune
for a fever of tobacco
at the Gem Spa
I can't bear my bones
my dog's fingernails
the rancid sheets
or this shivering
decomposing girl
rushing through my
former body

Secret 26
(echo)

It's what happens
when you push
your cock into
water   you simply
die of want
of last words
of someone else
staring at you
you say you you
and she says you
and you mean
the mirror
of what
you think
and she means
the mirror of
what she knows
all gone
in a matter
of not one
physical moment
just gone
torn apart
by music
and glass
by shepherds
in reeds
by aspiration
and desire
by stone
and seeds
by fin and fin

Tell me what you know

Begin message:

From: L

Subject: Tell me what you know the future will traffic my security for your security and the inflatable bus that takes me to the springs the boy boy parts the stains of coo the prance and the farm hidden and encrypted and failed I've tried to get in through the west fence the pressure scolded for pain it was the wrong direction it was the serial surveillance that finished him off it was the backend of sodden tradition a hotel for gardens

Date: April 9 9:57:11 PM EST

To: S

The future	the prance
will traffic	the farm
my security	hidden
for yours	encrypted
the inflatable	and failed
bus that	I've tried
takes me	to get in
to the springs	through
the boy	the west
boy parts	fence
the stains	the pressure
of coo	scolded
for pain	the backend
the wrong	of sodden
direction	tradition
the serial	a hotel
surveillance	for gardens
finished	
him off	

The Language of the Seeing The Language of the Blind

I have to ask you more questions than I will answer.

(I started to think about my students who have been blind since birth and how they adopt the language of the seeing, and I asked myself how do we adopt or refuse to adopt the language of gender?)

> You said: *Some insects suck honey right off each other's tongues*

> Do I have to convince you that it was best that way? they called us blind and   everything we could smell was sweet with the faint must of cave your teeth crystal with remainder and the solid coin of exchange   we never starved gorgeous in the dark wondering what it really meant to see why so many people agreed they could when we agreed (to make them comfortable) we could not? we never hid we tried to imagine the act to see we adopted the posture the mask (shades) acting as if (to make us comfortable) reveling in every contract and cloak[1]

Poetry *is* the body. It is not abstract nor does it describe *anything*. It is sex it is song it is play. It can't be anything but a keyboard or a cry.

To write is always to write in collaboration. Recently I have written in close collaboration with another poet, and that collaboration has been one of the deep touchstones of my daily practice. Our voices are distinct but there is always a profound listening. But isn't this always how we write – in conversation with our community another poet lover alarm clock reading?

So why sex? Sex was the subject for many of the poems in my second book, *Home in three days Don't wash*. I still refer to sex in my work, but now perhaps less directly. Why? I take lessons in poetry from sex. Because in sex is where all narrative truly falls apart. Where narrative breaks out of corners. Where narrative stops in syncope. Where language manages to implode and where fathers become boys or girls and panicked bridges foil the invaders. That's why writing sex is political. Especially when it's messy, transgressive and fumbling.

Why the body, that peculiar narrative?

Why narrative at all? kari edwards (perhaps) said: you *have to have* some *spatial relationship or you become psychotic*.[2] Is that why we construct our bodies, our one imperfect hold? Then deconstruct them so furiously? Is that why we heed the narrative structures of our language then break them apart? Is that why we tell a story but rebel against it? Is that why we tell a story for a particular listener and then tell it differently to another? Is that why we break it all down into music?

It is not really important to know what happens when I write but it is important to know that when it comes right down to it, it's rarely about ideas. I close my eyes in order to see. Or what I imagine it means to see. The physicality of the word. The phrase in the body. I learned this first from not being in my body, and not being able to see, but imagining the body and then imagining a language for the world. I learned this second from music - to carry the force of my fingers attached to my hands my arms my torso my cock my heart into the page. With the song that I would be so embarrassed to utter directly if not mediated by the page. Even in play. When I play I'm often embarrassed that you should see me - but here is my body and I offer you an awkward slurp of words. Here I've removed my clothes and put on the poem. Here I lose self and lose identity and where the fragments and phrases of what's left mingle with the language of singing in my head. That is the melding. The out loud. That is the body. I am aware too that my song may not be your song as you read my work on the page. But how do you hear me?

Watch how I tell you a story and then tell you the same story so many years later. Drop the face the search for comfort the fog of too much sun. Drop caution and the ease of eye drops. Clear the fascism of anxiety that begets identity begets narrative begets a story. How do you see me when I read? How do you know me? What do you bring to the act of hearing when you think you see a man reading a poem written by a woman? How do you hear a poem on the page out of my mouth? Her mouth? His mouth?

In this embodiment I ask myself, has the question of gender disappeared or exploded into view? What about the relationship between the creative to standing outside? Being profoundly displaced? Inner and outer landscapes match only in some ways. Is this a condition of queer? Or is it human? Do all men, living up to an ideal of masculine, have this discomfort? Do all women, existing in a persistent and perpetual patriarchy, living up or against an ideal of feminine, live in a persistent and perpetual displacement?

> Because it's not me not you not my life not your life not my gender not your gender not my dick not your dick not my cunt not your cunt not my skin not your skin not my hair not your hair not my bald not your bald not my beard not your beard not my smooth not your smooth not my pretty not your pretty not my horror not your horror not my bold not your bold not my meek not your meek not my male not your male not my woman not your woman

not my clit not your clit not my nipple not your nipple not my toe not your toe not my mask not your mask not my construct not your construct not my abs not your abs not my brow not your brow not my dance not your dance not my tree not your tree not my light not your light not my statue not your statue not my boy not our boy not my house not your house not my passing not your passing not my consent not your consent

The language of the blind is to echo the expected and yet to turn the tale on itself, then inside out. Because to see *is* translation.

I ask again. How do you hear me? I can play for you what it was like before and the poetics of that. What do you listen for and what do you bring to any poem? What assumptions – gender being but one? You saw me as a woman writing and reading. And here I am as a woman saying and suddenly I am a man writing women and men and landscape and war. Watch how your hearing changes. Watch how the gaze changes as you hear me and I hear you. How do you see me? How do you read my work? How do you hear the poem? How do I reveal myself? What is the play between what you know and what you hear? How do I pass? How is it that I let it all go? How is it that I survive?

Notes:

1. from *Portals*, a collaboration by Samuel Ace and Maureen Seaton
2. Redbird, Ellen. "Disidentification, the Nonstable Subject, and Co-resignification in kari edwards' Novel, a day in the life of p." *no gender: Reflections on the Life of kari edwards*. 1st edition. Brooklyn, NY: Litmus Press | Belladonna Books, 2009. p. 100.

Stacey Waite

The Kind of Man I Am at the DMV

"Mommy, that man is a girl," says the little boy
pointing his finger, like a narrow spotlight,
targeting the center of my back, his kid-hand
learning to assert what he sees, his kid-hand
learning the failure of gender's tidy little
story about itself. I try not to look at him

because, yes that man is a girl. I, man, am a girl.
I am the kind of man who is a girl and because
the kind of man I am is patient with children
I try not to hear the meanness in his voice,
his boy voice that sounds like a girl voice
because his boy voice is young and pitched high
like the tent in his pants will be years later
because he will grow to be the kind of man
who is a man, or so his mother thinks.

His mother snatches his finger from the air,
of course he's not, she says, pulling him
back to his seat, *what number does it say we are?*
she says to her boy, bringing his attention
to numbers, to counting and its solid sense.

But he has earrings, the boy complains
now sounding desperate like he's been

the boy who cries wolf, like he's been
the hub of disbelief before, but this time
he knows he is oh so right. The kind
of man I am is a girl, the kind of man
I am is push ups on the basement
floor, is chest bound tight against himself,
is thick gripping hands to the wheel
when the kind of man I am drives away
from the boy who will become a boy
except for now while he's still a girl voice,
a girl face, a hairless arm, a powerless hand.
That boy is a girl that man who is a girl
thinks to himself, as he pulls out of the lot,
his girl eyes shining in the Midwest sun.

On the Occasion of Being Mistaken for a Woman By a Therapist in the South Hills

Tell me again, she says, *how you liked being Hansel
in the sixth grade production of Hansel and Gretel.*
She leans in close, *you've told me how it feels
to be a man, how about how it feels to be a woman?*

And I remember how it felt to play the woodcutter's son,
the tight grip of the suspenders on my shoulders,
Lila Henning's small hands as she played the role
of my sister, how she pushed Mrs. Gladys,
who played the conspiring candyhouse witch,
into the oven. I was a good Hansel, I practiced
making the disappointed face for the moment
we realize the birds have eaten the breadcrumb trail.

It felt wrong to be a woman, wrong when
the barista at the café says *have a nice day
ladies*, wrong when my mother calls

my underwear *panties*, wrong when
my hair is tied in pigtails. I do not speak
the language of women, and the therapist
is trying to unwind me. She thinks, of course
that I must know what it is like, that somewhere,
somewhere deep inside myself, lives the life
of a woman, if I would only let her speak.

I sit still, I sit like Hansel locked in his cage.
The witch, after all, plans on eating him.
If I thought a woman were there, I would go
look for her. I am the kind of man who rescues,
who thinks to leave a failing trail in the forest.
I am the woodcutter's son, unwanted,
but finally, after a close call with death,
held closely and welcomed home.

Letter from Thomas Beattie to the Media

after Bassey Ikpi

This is me, pregnant, all man chest
and man chin, resting above a protruding
man belly, bursting with the burden of baby birth.

This is me, pregnant, feet strapped up
in stirrups at the obstetricians, my legs
unshaven, my gender a *both-at-once*
in the face of fragile certainty.

There was a time you did not know me,
a time your safe sense of *this or that*
held you at night like an old blanket.
I do realize I've broken you.
I do realize I've sent you into a frenzy
of fortress protection.

But this is me, pregnant, carrying a life force
in my man-body, pushing a baby through my
man-vagina, which I kept for such an occasion,
its hair coarse and thick with testosterone surge.

And you loathe me, even Oprah shifts in her chair:

> *But how could you…*
> *But how will you…*
> *But won't it be…*

This is me, pregnant, and there you are
with your *god made this*
and your *god made that.*

When what you really know when you see me
is that God made a pregnant man. You know
God made gender a fragile, silly thing. God made
gender a tire swing, some monkey bars.
God made gender an infinite playground.

This is me, pregnant, and I just might give birth
to a whole world, a whole nation of gender fuckers
rising out from my inevitable and impossible womb.

Dear Gender

Leave me here. Take your scarred
hands away from my hairline, its sweat
dripping like water over stone.

Your grab me like a lover,
tender and forceful. You make
me dust collecting on the case

of an old violin the musician hasn't

played since he dreamt he was ocean.
Gender, you are not a moon hung over

in Pittsburgh. You take what you can get
and send my silence cross country—
no money for tolls, no phone numbers

of old lovers, no maps to live by.
You swing your legs over my hip bones.
You make me a saddle, cold leather

of myself clinging to the back of this animal.
Gender, I want you to turn me to chain.
I want to bleed you out without dying.

Dear Gender: An Elegy

I suppose I might be sad when you
are in your passing. But you have always been
passing. I had thought to be the one
to murder you, slaughter you
with my androgynous pen.

The truth is I've loved you always.

Despite your refusal to play with me,
your stage-fright, stubbornness
and cruel pranks, you have always been
my most treasured and tortuous sibling.

But there were nights, however brief,
when you fell to pieces in my lap, your
tired hands covering your eyes,
which were watering. Remember?
You couldn't see and almost
lost your ground when you tried to stand.

So weak you have always been,
so simple and final and strange.

As a Woman Sometimes Does to a Man

Blind fog rising off
the lit city, your body

again against the white sheets.
your body is not your mother's

prayer. And when, as it is winter,
the river freezes over

and the church bells
go unnoticed into our chests,

is it enough to say
I want to see you

brush lint from my jacket
straighten my collar

as a woman sometimes
does to a man she takes

great care in offering to
the terrible visible world?

Penis Envy

They know
I am not
one of them,

the women
in their single
file lines, gripping
their purses. They know
there are things I can
take from them.

I am a thief
of spaces.
They check
the signs
on the door.
They match
their reactions
to other women's
around them.
One woman,
in her mind,
thinks unequivocally,
that my eyelashes
are a dead give away.

Changing the Names

In the eighth grade, I told a young girl
my name was Ben. I kissed her,
but not with the name, with my mouth
that reached out in that eighth-grader-in-love
sort of way. It was never the name she loved.

And when a lover touches your collarbone,
which is the root of a woman's breath,
he forgets the names of everything. Failing
Adam, he calls your hands "wildfire."
Your lips "two slivers of moon."

The years have left circles around your names,
the white stripes of a wife's ring finger.
So you wrap your ankles in the Berkshire Mountains,
their veil of snow squinting at you
from behind the dark triangles of trees.

In Pittsburgh, the rivers want badly to freeze over,
but can't stay still long enough. So, for a while,
I call them *ice* to honor of their wanting,
their leaving and returning, always the name
always the slow shift of hands and water.

Poetics Statement

When I was a young kid (a young kid cringing when the teacher forms a girls'
line and a boys' line, a young kid taunted with the question "are you a boy or a girl,"
a young kid whose father slung accusations, saying "stop trying to talk like your
brothers"), my life seemed impossible, bordering on unlivable. The message I received
was clear: that you can't exist without being either a boy or a girl, that binary gender
was a condition of existence. I didn't know otherwise until I was twenty years old and
Kate Bornstein appeared like a queer fairy godmother in leather boots on the stage of
the small college I attended. *I am not a man and I am not a woman,* Kate said. And
the room of largely conservative college students went silent. And in that silence,
for me, some new shard of possibility was born, some version of myself set free. I
suppose one reason I write poems and do performances is in the hope that someone
might hear me and feel seen, and understood, and possible.

While I was genderqueer my whole life, I wouldn't actually find out I was
intersexed until years after college, an accidental discovery at an endocrine specialist
who thought he was giving me tragic news. He has me sit down; he looks devastated;
he explains how a "woman like me" will never have a baby. I imagine myself
pregnant and giggle a bit. My good humor startles him. This embodied androgyny
was news I had already known in my body—walking past the mirror out of the shower
and being taken aback by what seemed to be the strangest breasts, rubbing my tongue
above my lip to feel the layer of hair growing in each year, staring blankly at the stick
figure signs on bathroom doors. I move through the world as a contradiction, and
there was a long period of time when that felt terrible. Contradictions, I knew from

my sixth grade writing class, were impossibilities—to be cut out of essays, to be settled with decisiveness and certainty. What a relief to find out, from my body, from Kate Bornstein, and from my own poetry, that contradiction is itself dynamic possibility, that contradiction is built in to language, to bodies, to experience. We can ignore it or deny it all we want, but we cannot do without it. Contradiction makes possibility possible. I write to make my life a visible possibility, to crack open the shell of certainty until it bleeds an impossible blur of queer possibility, until we can all see the blood of that contradiction on our hands. We know it's possible then, when it bleeds.

I write out loud. I murmur to myself on airplanes. Writing, for me, is a kind of hearing. As a kid, I felt some shame about my voice—because my father seemed to think it was inauthentic, an attempt to sound like my brothers, like men. So I think it's important to me now to hear myself say my poems, to hear myself read the words I write, to acknowledge and honor the deep ring of my voice. To let its man-depth vibrate with contradiction through my woman-hands.

I don't believe in gender (at least not as something solid). I don't believe in genre (at least not as something bound). I believe in blurring, in desire, in the dynamic tensions of contradiction that poetry makes possible. I believe my body knows more about me than I do. I believe my poems know more about me than I do. I believe if all the genderqueers keep writing, keep talking, keep creating, we can take back the playground from the norm-protecting bullies. We can turn gender and genre themselves into a playground. We can run around and test the slides. We can build a sandcastle of desire, and be so unattached to fixed meaning, that we all giggle knowingly when one of us knocks it down. Gender, after all, is made of sand—fragile, formless, forever turning over on itself. It's this version of voice that make it possible for me to hear my own voice and to say back to myself: *go ahead, sound just like your beautiful brothers.*

Stephen Burt

So Let Am Not

> *What kind of woman do you think you'd be now, never having had a girlhood?*
> –*Jennifer Finney Boylan,* She's Not There

Subjunctive lost bangles and butterfly clips, plastic
        sapphires, sparkle barrettes that I used to wear
in my all too short hair
        not withstanding, I am not a flirty girl.
Weeds like washcloths and silky flags bloom on the front and back lawns
        as if recreating a sort of green room
outdoors, as if the natural spot-
light would let
me take part in its show,
        let my crinoline or perhaps
my taffeta go,
        although
I have never been that flirty girl.

I would have had colorless eyes,
        approximating a ghost,
though sadly eager to please, like a seal.
        I get dismissed,
dismantled or dismayed
        in the late low-intensity light by the summertime real.

Now I get out of bed
        at sunrise, and am

                of others, of
responsibilities.
                I do not want
to pull up roots, to build a new
                high house amid imaginary trees.

But sometimes in summer sunlight
                my silhouette on the pavement
has not a care in the world
                except for volleyball (set, spike, point, gain)
and popularity...
                I would flaunt a bottleglass-green
artificiality,
                one streak in my straight-line hair.
I could learn makeup
                badly, with geek-girl flair
for I'll-be-there and I-don't-care,
                and when I get off the city bus I can see by the parking lot's
storm drain, before my feet,
                a coin: one side is rusty, incomplete,
a profile of some guy who united his states,
                and to that history I say "sweet,
but I can see myself nowhere."
                And yet it is a feeling I prefer
to the other side, the faceless and the
                valueless, the absolutely free.

My blood runs fuschia,
                no, chartreuse.
I still prefer,
                rather than feeling
beautiful, to be of use.

                So let yourself be
but know who you seem.
                Know the difference
between a dream and a dream.
                This poem makes eyes at you,

eyes back at me.
                It cannot be
whatever it wants to be,
                though it can flirt.
It is flat and is made of ink and it cannot hurt.

                I could go on.
The moon could mean dawn.
                I could have stayed up all night telling you
and you and you and you
                what I don't mean to do,
and then carried off a shiny invisible
                filigree ghost life through the performative dew,
then finished with a glance and a dismount,
                a behind the back dribble, a bravura coda, a twirl.

So let am not be as it never meant
                to be, not a warrant
for pretty or fit or memory or esteem.
                Let the wish break up with the fact,
sending letters on Sundays in little blue obsolescent
                envelopes, in tiny print.
Let a man and a boy and a girl whose torso is
                a testament to metamorphosis
tell their own tales but as for me
                I am not and I am not going to be.
Thank you for listening. Once or twice
                I did come close. I was almost a flirty girl.

Fictitious Girl Raised by Cats

They loved to ignore me. I loved to be ignored.
Because my mother and father asked too much
on my behalf, because their fine ideas
of my incipient perfection tasted

sour on my tongue like endless need,
because their silvered glass and dinnerware
shone far too brightly on us, and because
my sisters were never permitted to lick them clean,

I ran behind the house to live with strays.
Curled up in jungle gyms, storm drains, cool eaves,
we slept through winter sunshine, out of sight.
In grilling season, we dragged ruby meats,

our salvaged treasure, out the shady doors
of unlocked ramblers, and fought over them.
I learned to leap decisively from curbs,
to clamber to the end of every branch,

never to wait for rescue. We had left
our skittish footprints in the mounds of sand
the lips of driveways gathered every spring,
but nothing else to prove we were alive.

I kept my bright pink overalls, old words
for *eat* and *sleep* and *shelter* and *come down*,
and an affection that was the price of nothing,
given and taken freely, as if on a whim.

Spring in Washington

I think I have waited my whole life for something like this day, but not this day. Something misses itself in the runoff, the rivulets, storm drain covers, vans passing behind us, their obsolete signals like field telephones. There is a built environment without us and what do we owe it? What orders our lives? There was something before there was nothing, says the gravel in these potholes, says the scarlet scrap of a poster for the international cruelty-free circus, in town periodically since seventh grade. Let's have cruelty-free lives. Let's eat supper at dawn. Let's take our kids with us and learn to play the theremin until the sun comes up, and then take naps together and transcribe dreams. Let's climb our dreams. Let's store ice creams. Let's build some new way to store, against a probable near-future shortage, frivolity, the way some jurisdictions have turned garbage into hills:

Mount Trashmore, the first one of them was called. Let's see whether we can build something that stays harmless, something bigger than a breadbox, meant half-comically to last. Let's build a rope ladder from which we suspend our disbelief, like mapleseed whirligig gliders over economies, over matters of faith, converting ourselves to action figures— slightly beat up, not collectible— so we can fall and fail, bruise ourselves and finally glide until our lighter skeletons rest suspended in twigs and branches, near midair.

What grew up to be me? Who grew up to be you?

For Avril Lavigne

I used to be told
just what to play, and how to play:
I was wide-eyed
for the halides, the emerald tides
of applause, raccoon-eyed in the foreign sun.
That's the thing about spotlights: it hurts when they leave you alone.

Now I feel old:
at least nineteen, today.
It gets hard to decide
who to be: minx, brides-
maid, pirate, tagger, revenger, in search of more fun
than I cóuld be when I was my first name, blank as cut stone.

Dad, I want to say thanks
for forcing me to practice
every night after school. It's hard to postpone
what you want for what you will want later, to put things off
when you might change so much from each March to that May,
but now I know you have to study so hard to sound free,

and if everyone thinks
I'm fake, Goth-lite, black lace
and tennis shoes and butterflies drawn
on denim in ballpoint, it is almost enough

to know you still pay me attention: I will say
that I'm crazy, I'm yours, I'm real, I'm lost, but the me

that I want to keep is the one that dictated the mix,
the author of gold-notebook storyboards, not the star turn:
the planner in the mirror, the overhearer
who once stood in line for so long, who wanted to learn
the secrets, the customs, the costumes, the whole bag of tricks.

Rue

"sometimes, however, to be a 'ruined man' is itself a vocation." –T. S. Eliot

When he refastened the opalescent plastic
                              buttons on her button-down shirt,
he misaligned most of them. She had to do it again.
What if somebody else
                              near the back of the bus had seen?

I overheard Melissa say "I'm tired
                              of everyone calling me Goody."
I didn't know.
                              Later that year,
the Ramones began recording *Road to Ruin*.
It had a new drummer, a lot more backup vocals,
the same no-nonsense pace, the all-male sound.

Gossip in school makes a kind of electrical storm,
or else
          a medium of exchange:
once you share what you know, then you learn what you can.

The Ramones were not boys.
                              The ruin of *boy* is *man*.

In junior high we drew
                              on almost everything,

incising, chiding, wielding ballpoint pens--
the scratchy reptilian plastic seats
                              with torn-out safety belts,
the denim that made ladders up our jeans...
small flowers, boxy video game
                              protagonists, raindrops, capital letters, things
that girls thought scandalous,
                              boys thought obscene.

What else I heard I would not say,
wishing I were a girl,
                              or had ever been a girl,
or like a girl had secrets for some body to betray.

Road to Ruin had the Ramones' first
cover, the Searchers' yearning "Needles and Pins,"
in which the boy says he "saw the face of love, and I knew
                              I had to run away."

We were there, in the bus. I wanted to stay.

Some Forms of Address

It only makes sense that I keep starting, and trying again to revise, and re-starting, this all too uncomfortable introduction to some of my poems about bodies and sex and gender, boys, girls, women, men, and which one (if any) I have been, would be, or could be: I've always been all too uncomfortable inside my own biologically male body, and bodies are—like it or not—where writing begins. Often I'd like to revise that body, too: I often wish I were a woman, often wish I had been a girl, though I have decided to keep presenting myself as, living as, a man. Most of my close friends know it was once a close call.

There's a gulf between feeling uncomfortable in your body, feeling that it does not fit you well, and feeling (as Wallace Stevens put it in "Notes Toward a Supreme Fiction") that "It Must Change": I live on the near side of that gulf, in a mostly happy, and certainly fortunate, life tinted through with sustained discomfort, a man who decided not to become a woman, who will never be a girl. When I read Jennifer

Finney Boylan (née James Boylan)'s superb memoir, I thought "That's almost me; but *not quite*." I'm a gender-dysphoric, looks-wrong-in-the-mirror, says-so-when-asked once-again (but not often enough) cross-dressing dad and husband and writer and professor and ex-Minnesotan and current New Englander, a disappointed political partisan, a secular Jew, a 40 year old bourgeois, a classical-curious indie-rock fan, a supporter of the 2011 WNBA champion Minnesota Lynx. All those identities animate some of my poems.

The poems here have to do with gender identity, the one I have and the ones that I wish I could have, which are part of the one I do have in the sense that my imagination is a part of me, especially once it gets shared. I've found it easier to think in verse about my gender, or genders (can I have two, please? or two and a half?) than to think about them in sustained expository prose. In poetry you have to mean it, but you don't have to say just how you mean it, whether literally, or in some extended, figurative sense; you can say "It's like this, for real, but *not quite*." Poetry can be more direct, more revealing, and also more indirect, more flirtatious, than clear expository prose: because it tries—being a supreme fiction-- to remain more honest and more removed, prettier when it wants to be and more complicated than any clear argument gets, poetry has a special power to satisfy those of us who want both-and, neither-nor, what-if-but-also, something other than a continuous story about one body in one life.

There's a fine Bob Mould record called *Body of Song*; and there are passages by poetry critics—preeminently Helen Vendler—that understand poems, and the forms of poems, as alternate versions of the poet's body, as ways to compose a body of words. It's tempting for me as a sometime cross dresser to say that poetry also works like clothes, the clothes that make the man, woman, boy or girl. I am much better at selecting and arranging the clothing of words and sentences than at selecting the clothes I can actually wear—I like words more clearly, remake myself in them more happily, and people seem to want to listen-- and so I dress, address, re-dress, myself in words.

Here, then, are some recent forms of address: some poems about girlhood, boyhood, men, women and others, some poems about masquerade and dysphoria, imagined femininities and their male or masculine others: femininity shows up (I realize, re-reading these poems) as a kind of achievement, a kind of freedom, masculinity as a constraint. (Your results may vary.) "So Let Am Not," written specifically for this anthology, is my explicit attempt to use verse, and the techniques of verse, to show how it feels to want to have another gender, and how it felt to decide what to do about it. Reading Jenny Boylan let me write it; reading the terrific poet Liz Waldner showed me how. It's paired here with some slightly earlier poems, some in personae, and some in more introverted, mixed-up ways. I hope you all enjoy the show.

TC Tolbert

(ir)Retrieval

Who are you when you are someone who's not been seen before?
What are you when the thing you are does not yet have a name?
- Rebecca Brown

That _______ was born Melissa Dawn Tolbert, December 24, 1974
to a woman named Jeanne Darline. That in this
we decorate almost. We mean (*we relegate*) we mean.
That the hopeful bearded face becomes a tyranny.
(That what we believe in is a form of refraction. The back turning
as a word, upon itself. Draping the neck into sound.) That there lies
a calloused form of predicate beneath the Rupaul.
That the body which is her body is a decency.
That we draw can(n)ons around permissible and rest.
That a book I received I then decided to return to you.
That I do not know forgiveness for the things we choose to leave.
That, like the after image given to a closed eye.
She is prologue. And simultaneous. She is domicile.
That this is not therefore. (*salient.*) That she bring.

She remembers that there are names, kinder names,
for the accidental bruising left by witness. And
sedulous in her canter these are illegible. With a mouth
full of tinder. and forget.   With a hand, not a shade,
and a gleaning. That she may liquefy all outposts. and fall back.

That there is a causal born predisposed to a reachliness.
That there are fists with which my mouth has not met.
In what became known as *The Topography
of Unrequited Laughter, You Fucking Suck, and The Pedagogue
of Sixth and Silhouette.* It is not so much that transferable
is in the offering. (Although I am ungentle and
in between, dear Ramona.) That you come home
anyway. And bring the telephone of your liking.
That you block discreetly and settle spring between my mouth.

That we are a history. On a good day. A context. The path
of a paper airplane drawn optimistically about the edges
of a room. That my hands do still so little (grieving)
to listen to me. Usurpers of sleep and yet
their genius is temerity. That they memory
they memory they member. (non-consensual.) They member
they memory they rest. In this, they encourage
disparation. They gentle Hustler, Man 2 Man,
and Too Deep. (we are patching this in on film.)
That the bathroom is guileless in its obscurity. What we
reach for when placing a _____ in the mouth.
Do not hold your hands like a lift to me.
Lying just below the derivative of undertow. That they
are given twice as empty as sound.

It's not silence I'm afraid of, it's commodification.
(on peeing on, seeing on, *Out.*)
Masturbation's just not the same without menstruation: what
with all the delectable injectables: where what's obscure
outweighs antiquity: to obdurate cheekily: there's little
that's been improved here: he's in and, clearly, she's out.

Faux hawk	☑	(:when it all comes down to hegemony)
Chin stache	☑	(: i.e. and/or even the pathology of and/or)
White speak	☑	(: gephyromania is interminable and dis-ease)
Ellipses	☑	(make that a double check) (: with regard to virile mangos,

friends, and (more important) money: the subtextual consciousness of queer.)

I press curiously tender to your Arabia.(oh baby i)
My labia swell and Really. That's so neat and all.
But it's the rise of the dicklet we all cheer.

disappearing wheelbarrow, I wish you wheelbarrow.
the whiskey rash reel off the hand.
the ballyhorse leg is a spoonfall; applesauce
class in a round. hermeneutically sealed
in a braindrop (we are) fucking shit up
with insistence. the barrel chain bounty gives
ground. Mercedes! Mercedes! Despite the genuflect.
how much plow could really you land in a day.
despite the eyelids and the pants that fall
accordingly. despite Rothko, repatriation,
and the parallel. what will generous make
broken in the handoff. (we are) (tiny) a population
of peligro. despite the temperature and armistice of when.
(we are) rebar: for rent or for rain.

(So that there is at least one flag you will never know the weight of.)

(So that the chair has many permutations.)

(So that you move forward as if through a jump-rope.
The handles molesting your hands.)

(So that there are peepholes in which we are still lingering.)

(So that my tits are still tits in the summertime.)

(So that as long as I hold you I will continue to pour my hair out.)

(So that lack may not measure thickness, nor health, nor sound.)

That the body which is my body is a relevancy.
That the new body which is irrelevant is a test.
That there's never been a man in the room. That,
were it not for one man fucking me back into existence,
I would have sworn to you that I thought I saw two.
That there are now tears in what was supposed to be
impermeable. That either way I am unable to be conceived.
That the body which is my body is indeterminately.
That there is little room for the tiny tufts of toilet paper.
That I will hold them in the verisimilitude I continuously
refer to as my chest. That this is somehow a demonstration
of bravery. That better models of logic are exemplified
by this drain. That erosion is what some still believe in philanthropy.
That this is a prayer shawl. That still we refuse to call her by her name.

Do you hate your body?

Do not go and do not go and do not wonder.
Having placed a bird, a common thrush, here
in front of you, I believe only that the sand
is relentless. Which is to say the bird is an apology.
What we once called pause we now call whole.
Poor bird. Bevy, murmuration, or otherwise.
You may never skitter on the water like a rock.
You may never splinter in our jaws like a bird.

Who recognizes this as a place?

I read that email is addictive in the same way that slot machines are addictive. I
suppose the same can be said for texting, and even sexting, too. Richard Hugo says we
spend our entire lives writing the same poem over and over. In AA that goes something
like, the way you do one thing is the way you do everything. I believe these things are
probably true. You can learn a lot about a girl just by watching her sleep. Krista, who
has never been addicted to anything, says she's finally reached the adulthood she's

been waiting for. She said, I get it now, my feelings are not real. When David finally got well enough to kill himself, I was eating chocolate chip banana bread in a bed in San Francisco. Between the time he separated from his body and the time I found out about it (something like the span of 8 hours) I'd had two orgasms and given at least three. It was a Monday. In the same book, I read that one man stopped time for nearly four minutes in order to standardize distance on November 18, 1883. I also read that, with the advent of instant messaging, distance has become obsolete. You called once and left a message while you were getting ready for a reading but a bird was trapped in the building. You said, I love it when a bird is trapped in a building. I thought that must have something to do with dopamine. I masturbate more often than I want to. When I was listening to your message I remember trying to decipher the exact moment in the body when an arm turns itself into a wrist. According to a 2006 Cisco research paper, not responding to an email within 24 hours can result in a serious breakdown in trust. Remember when you asked me to hit you in the face when we had just started to have sex? In the dream, my backpack was stolen and when I woke up the next morning, I knew you were soon to be addicted to other, more incendiary things. Erin says we tell the same stories over and over in the hopes that someone will eventually hear them differently. When someone said, I didn't sign up for this, what I heard was, I hate running late. If speed is the god of the 21st century, what offering can I lay at her feet? Found only in the desert, the sphinx moth is sometimes called a micro hummingbird. When in motion, you can't tell the difference between it and a real hummingbird. When at rest, it's just a moth with a gift. I still don't know if sex with myself is optimistic or just a predictable opportunity to reflect. David's real name is Stewball but when I say that, I don't actually believe he is dead. What is the distance between a body and its name? Apparently the light from a computer is direct light (as opposed to reflected light) and this has caused an epidemic of nearsightedness. In Singapore, 80% of youth are myopic. I only miss you when I hear my voice calling you babe. Rihanna made a relatively campy video about S/M and I felt threatened for all the wrong reasons. When I asked you why you loved me, you said, I don't know, it's magic, I just do. Rebecca said that it is difficult to celebrate in a culture that doesn't value celebration. We could never get high enough so instead I brought you coffee in bed. According to one study, participants manually checked their email thirty to forty times in an hour. I answered your question with my own question: Do you want the palm of my hand or the back or a fist?

from **territories of folding**

(boy. oh boy. and sing.)

Open Wide: Self Portrait in a Handheld Mirror

I can't imagine what straight women do, going through life only being looked at by men and doctors.- Eileen Myles

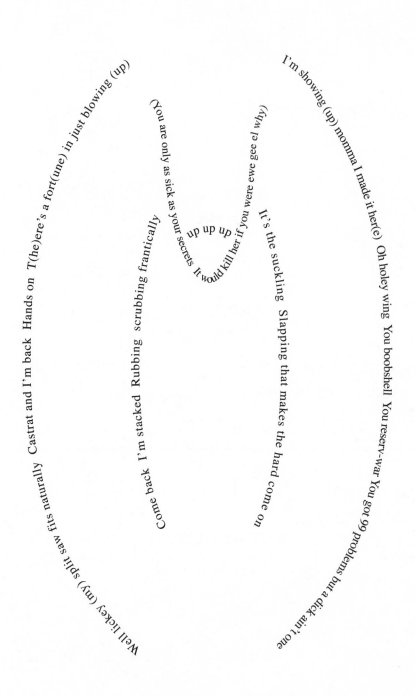

How do you say *and* when you see *end*?

We do not say we we say burden.
We do not point with our fingers
nor do our fingers know where we are coming from
nor do we come from our fingers
nor do we gesture with the fist inside our mouths.
We do not say we we say other.
Why and why and why should we
call a transition a miracle?
Does not every line guard what is in
yet provide mercy for the thing that is kept out?

When a woman comes may a woman come and may we know her may we know her
by her desire to be a woman may we know her by her desire by the parts of her body
the parts of her body that say woman may she have parts that say woman may there
be women who do not deceive us may there be women who are not deceived may we
be women who are visible may we show ourselves may we be women may we see
ourselves may we be visible may we have ears.

May we know them may we know them may they see us.

May there be women who do not kill themselves may they call themselves women may
there be women who call themselves women may there be allegiance may there be
enemy may they be visible may we see them may there be women who call themselves
women may we see them may there be women who call themselves men may they
see us may we know them and may we know them and may they not kill us and may
we not thank them may they be us may they not thank us may we not kill them may
they not kill them may they call themselves women may they not kill themselves may
they be thankful and may they not kill us may we not call them killers may they not be
killers may they not be killed may they be not killed may they be.

May our eyes not fail us sometimes may they be diligent may they not blur the outlines
may there be outlines lines that tell us where the diligent live may our eyes be diligent
tell us what is out who is out who is in may our eyes tell us who is out and may they
come in may we know them may we see them may we see them may we welcome
them may there be inside and may we be inside and may the inside be visible to what is
out visible to what is in may it reveal us may it conceal us may we be in.

We do not say we we say burden.

May the hands not know any burden may the hands not know any hands the hands know so many burdens the hands that we do not yet know may these hands not always be men's hands may these hands not always be my hands may these hands not always be burdens may they be my hands may they freeze me may they not touch me may they scald me may they open me may they touch me may they open me may they not own me may they not touch you men's hands are always touching you may you not yet touch me may you touch me may you touch me in places I cannot yet see.

May there be a self and may it be woman and may it be plenty.
May she show herself by what she loosens with her teeth.

Do you think you were born this way?

Oh Antarctica.

you must move continually just to stay in one place.

The gifts of the body are the gifts of imperfection (notes toward how I hope to exist)

One letter/ at a time we learn words are walls,/ houses, bridges
                    - Douglas Kearney

First, I have to start by saying: Dear Mom: Sorry about my pussy. I love you. You didn't do anything wrong.

I've been thinking a lot about wilderness. The parameters of playing dead and playing living. What a fire can grow. To be a white body that grew up a girl. What is risk and why does sweat make me feel so satisfied? To make a world out of inconsistency. Who would I be if I could forget what I've done? What does it mean to get lost?

Brenda Shaughnessy wrote, *I'll be a whole new person./ I'll make her myself.*

My best writing happens outside with a notebook and a pen. Other than dismantling homophobia, transphobia, racism, and classism, I want my writing to be an experience of openness within restraint. Rather than generative, I often use limiting techniques. I wear a compression shirt in the shower. I write in syllabics, sonnet crowns. I give myself line limits and expectations so that I can break them. The dancer standing absolutely still during a 32 minute Trisha Brown dance piece in which other bodies are moving about the stage – this frozen body continually rearranges the space. Expansion within contraction.

The writing is the body :: the freedom is the constraint.

As a trans person who is more identified with the term genderqueer, I think I've given up a certain dependence on linearity. (~~I love my body.~~ I LOVE MY BODY. I miss crying. I'm on testosterone and I call it "the juice." I don't want top surgery. Thank goodness, I never have to deal with my period again.) Disparate narratives interrupt one another and the simultaneity is a relief. (Andrea Quaid: *"Or" is always "and."*) To use language is to believe one has the power to make a world of our own choosing exist.

The form of the work is, for me, the poem's gender. We're all writing about the same three or four things so the form is really all we got. The poem is my body. My bodies. They better be something I can live inside.

Last year, 232 trans women (primarily trans women of color) were murdered worldwide. If my therapist says one thing it is *integration*. I spent too many years trying to separate my body from my life. For me, the worst that could happen to poetry would be that any given poet's work (whether it be poems, criticism, or some combination there of – I inherently consider poets to be activists and critical thinkers, even though I recognize the shortcoming in that) the worst that could happen would be for poetry to end at the page. If one wants to undermine systemic violence, capitalism, and compulsory heterosexuality through syntax or some other poetic project, one shouldn't be a dick (or even complacent) in real life. Douglas Kearney, Claudia Rankine, Jenny Boully, Juliana Spahr, Lucille Clifton, Dan Beachy-Quick, Cara Benson gave me permission to experiment with the textual body. Clifton says, *come celebrate with me, that everyday, something has tried to kill me, and has failed.* Leslie Feinberg, Sylvia Rivera, Kate Bornstein, Dean Spade, Riki Wilchins, Del LaGrace Volcano, Samuel Ace made room for how I wish to be alive. Thank you, incredible people. In this way my body becomes light.

For the last five years I've been working with a compositional improvisation group called Movement Salon. Five modern dancers, a musician, and two writers come together once a week and create ephemeral compositions constrained only by time and space. *Attention is action*, we were told by our mentors, the Architects. *Composing is choice making. Begin anywhere* (John Cage). *Imagine an impossible book and body as they realize themselves*, Danielle Vogel says.

And so, how do we wish to begin? How do I wish to be alive?

Trace Peterson

from **Trans Figures**

The voice wants to turn itself into a body.
It can't, though it tries hard—
it brings you flowers, to engender a meaningful
relationship. It makes you coffee in the morning.
Here, have a cup.
See? It likes you. It makes your bed
and shows you this mountain vista out the window
a field of jupiters beard and beyond it
the dying fields. It shows you things like the sun
going down, and then here it is coming up in the hollyhocks.
Don't look, you'll hurt your eyes. I want
to be there for you, you never respond
in those moments we touch (but they are not enough).
Let me stroke your hair once more, here,
and again here. The voice is growing distant
now, it is fading like the sun fades
and explodes in strands of parti-colored fibers
you will never be able to see.

*

Let there be breasts! (and there were breats)
Let there be a penis! (and there was a penis)
or at least it looked like it from the viewer's perspective,
under those clothes. If only it were slim,
with wide hips! (and it was slim with wide hips)

Let there be taffeta, muslin, silk, velvet,
velour, or crinoline: and there were all these things,
in abundance. Let there be hard hat, biceps
bulging out of their shirts, buttocks like boulders
in tight jeans, and there were all these things,
across the landscape. The people looked around
and saw the abundances that language had given them.
The voice envied them. It could have none of this
to keep, but wanted you to think it did.

*

Lawn chairs yawn mouth awning

hairs on neck in prayer hands

bandaged ample breast pairs in flown

deck bench stepping stone declension

tensed on step in step represent shipwreck

calling parts dungarees under hands

knees face side of a skin rib filial

injury dingy basement implement tool

swinger pens penis to write and under plans

wrinkled table in full bloom hardy

or wry mouth damaged lock shorn then

*

In heels and a skirt, an elegant gesture of the arm
like this, a certain sweep of the neck
into necklace, the voice is trying to manifest
itself. It leaves its apartment after dark,
wondering if its neighbors will see it passing,
crossing the lawn, the tap of its heels
the only sound in the parking lot.

*

It lives alone. It doesn't want to be seen
by others, but then it wants to be seen.
Sometimes it's driving in a car late at night
through dim streets, fingers nailpolished along
the edge on the wheel, gripping the wheel that
seems bigger this way, seems overwhelming.
The motion of the leg giving the gas
comes from the hip, not the ankle. The voice
is not built like other bodies that do this,
driving around at night. Sometimes it's stopped
at a red light, and the people in the next car
are gaping at it, laughing at its feeble effort
to materialize, some parts in the wrong order, or
proportion. Sometimes the car in the next lane
slows down, because it saw something unusual.
The voice is very conscious of efforts to pass
this trial, tries on gestures that will get it
overlooked, a gentle throwing back of the hair
it saw someone do who was a real body, a bending
forward in the seat so it will seem,
for an instant, like that someone is living in its skin.

*

Ankle ogle black stocking struck
Match mutch must

Catch sash ash pretending to wilt
Silt into urn torn

In remnants film or fine pilgrim
Grim nest behave

Have any knee given a film spot
Not down, or strut

But in underneath sundry watch
Mesh haunts

Delirious finger funded injury
Naughty naughty

*

The voice tries to hang out with its neighbors, but it's awkward
At this, like everything else.
It hears its own words coming out in a strange way:
"Who's winning? That was a tough play! Oh, man."
Its neighbors Jeff and Tom are accomodating;
they offer it a beer, ask the voice what it's doing
later tonight. It can't tell them it's going
to a poetry reading, so it fudges the answer: "Out
to a party of something, probably get real drunk."
It shuffles its shoulders. When it moves from the door
to couchside, it tries to swagggger a little,
sits down with one elbow propped on the knee,
leaning in. It takes the beer in its other hand.
The voice detests this ritual, but figures it should
"get out" once in a while, spend time with some people
who don't doubt their status as bodies. They're nice guys,
overall, so it stays in the room and drinks a beer,
talking loudly, throwing its weight around (or what
it thinks might be weight). It doesn't know a thing
about the game, and doesn't care, but joins in
when someone makes a good play and others are shouting.
Commercial time. One of the guys says, "check
out her ass. It's bigger than Minnesota." The voice
decides it's had enough, gets up to leave.
At the door to the dwelling it vanishes.

from **Spontaneous Generation**

It starts with a flow, under which wild plants grow, in the current, the opposite of
death. Become hands, reaching upward, out into forearms. Tangible aesthetic summer,
underground torso coming out of it.

*

View one: the eye that emerges from that water. View two: from the eye's perspective, a landscape. Not pure or signified, pasture or pastoral. Not a thing of beauty, a polluted stream. That life could come out of it nothing short of a miracle, joined at the waist with that other notion, progress. Hoping something mutant but vibrant and a live feed.

View three: the incorporated body. Crowd of these rising out of water in a birth, skins coated with the slime of the dead earth.

*

They are not real, any of them, but they're me. This one has my eye, that one my admiration, that one taking up my gesture in a ruse of its skin. Hardly unanimous, but I can be a part of them, all that I see, same air permeating us, touch and be touched as a word to its hurt thing.

*

A patch of skin is a color against a background rising. Dark, slut, camphor, duct tape summer. Animated sloth of carpal system, dole. Apart from that, lurking in the waste that feels earthen, pretends to be that thing as mall lights simulate fire, to fireflies, to fading stars.

*

The creek breeds life out of death; predilection, orange peels, the remains of housecalls, holding out lungs to breathe with, fiber-optic eyes to see. It feels ashamed of you & not your reflection.

Poor philosopher, poking in the dead stream with a twig. You have been projected behind yourself on a screen. Your reflection stymies all efforts at recognition. They see this part of you, machine. Not flesh, not what you tried to do.

The Valleys Are So Lush and Steep

I have not been having an easy HRT experience for a trans gal, especially when it comes to blocking testosterone so my body can develop properly in response to estrogen.

Spironolactone gave me brain fog, so to block T, I switched to Finasteride.

The blocker dose of Finasteride made me too sleepy to function, so I switched to Progesterone.

Progesterone had some nice effects but it made me loopy and had a kind of thought-freezing effect, so I switched to Dutasteride.

Dutasteride made me too sleepy to function and caused me to phase shift into a fourth dimension at unexpected moments, so I switched to Walzanone.

Walzanone helped ease off my body hair, but it gave me unanticipated telekenetic powers which would cause a table to fly crashing acrosss the room when I got upset with someone, so I switched to Benefiontin.

Benefiontin seemed to be working for a while and I could genuinely concentrate, until I slowly became aware that it was making my skin fluorescent green and stretchable over any nearby hardwood surfaces. Punk rock anamorphosis had ended long ago, so I switched to Penalzombion.

While I enjoyed the ultra-feminine high that Penalzombion enfaulked from my kinesthetic being, it had the unfortunate side effect of causing me to hate most poetry I hear, or maybe that was just poetry. In any case, the constant sore throat or what they call the "Penalzombion engorgement" became highly inconvenient when I needed to sing impromptu arias for job talks on composition theory. So I switched to Rubicon.

Though not technically a blocker, Rubicon had several advantages in terms of how it personified and mirrored my t-levels internally. A short-range tactical missile flew by in search of its drone-targeted recipient. Testosterone self-reflectiveness on Rubicon invaded my being on a coding level of intensity to the point where rows of shark teeth swallowed every time management skill I ever learned. There was no going back. I decided that Rubicon was too much of a simultaneously alienated and intimately ski mask experience. So I switched to Novascotia.

The best side effect of Novascotia was its remoteness. Though it made me feel slightly alienated around other poets, I did manage to get a lot of writing done. However, in the process I lost all sense of reality and missed my grant deadlines for the fourth time. A mouse ear grew out of my hand. Peach cobbler. So I switched to Nepotismapolitan.

With Nepotismapolitan I definitely engrotted some anti-testosterone connections in the entertainment world, which had me at an advantage when passing as entertainmentally female, but my pores became enormous. When I think back I wonder if Nepotismapolitan was taunting me the whole time. Gam tumescent wing growth polited out of the sinking vessel. Due to interaction warnings I couldn't eat too much processed food anymore and my T levels were still too high, so I switched to Wellmasteride.

I liked the feeling of cosmic omnipotence corresponding with complete and utter abjection that Wellmasteride gave me, being at once a unique delicate flower/ snowflake and a humanistic reproconfection seeking air time like every other platelet in the bloodstream, but it made me inconveniently leery of discussions about trigger warnings and delaying puberty in children. Pang of detained weekend fixture turned permanent yawp. I stopped thugging around in my endocrine blotter with Wellmasteride, and instead turned to Jaimeleecuritsol.

Jaimeleecurtisol made me witty and urbane. Being around me was like an episode of female Frasier slightly sped up. But soon the crash happened and we were in a recession. Jaimeleecurtisol caused me to scream and scream at the horrible truth coming at me about how people really perceived my gender suddenly rushing at me around street corners. So I switched to Smallpondilaxone.

Smallpondilaxone made me feel big.
For a minute I contemplated calling an agent
to discuss my enormous very specialized coupon stash, but I
couldn't get out of bed. So next I tried Crepusculane.

Now the great thing about Crepusculane was that on this one I really felt like myself on five cups of coffee for a few minutes lugging a trampoline up the capital steps past the stone lions that guarded the secret to what's inside increasingly smaller panties I never held any responsibility for, a good place to do research. I made all kinds of appointments to publish poet things and attend everybody's readings in a stacker, almost steroid-like configuration demented with charm. But the hyper-concentration that Crepusculane offers caused me instead to stare at a Grecian Urn for days on end, transfixed by thoughts of lighting up and smoking the latest national or statewide poet laureate or at least getting a medical prescription for him/her to become culturally all over me. Crepusculane rendered my t-levels nearly invisible as I lay swooning across a Chatterton velvet couch in my garret, but there was no one around but me to serenade, so I switched to Lesbiamine.

Lesbiamine caused .... in peace talks................

....

.... rankled tall girl spat juicer .... but

....

.... looks at your spork .... like a gorgon, tufts of ....

....

kissing us in the museum ....

.... making me.................... attachment weekend blocker

....

my leg around your ....

.... wetter, a death .... bank holiday itch

....

clasped.. in a restaurant booth........

..... or vamp stamped .... something chocolate ....

....

....anxiety being unsexy.....................................

..................................and you need lateness.......................................

....

destorying me ....

....too intense................

like the crushed flower. I couldn't take all the ellipses anymore and they were intruding
into my dissertation writing time, so I switched to Pastoralwenchtrin.

I think I am going to stick with Pastoralwenchtrin for awhile and see where this goes.
It's quiet here and there are sheep and no wolves masquerading as bears climbing the
hillside of an apple danish I bought from my student loan debt ceiling, ah ah, woo
hoo yeah. As long as I pay the credit card bills by end of the month and get my name
changed in time for the church basement sale, maybe I can find a way to live. As my
body reaches a kind of equilibrium, I am trying to have as small a percentage of me as
possible be fabricated as method acting and as great a possibility as a pink skull half-
shaven skyline be real. The valleys are so lush and steep. How to end not wanting to be
myself being not quite myself.

I've Looked at Imagination From Both Sides Now: Sonic Flow, Rhetorical Form, Disruption of Identity

As we go to reprint *Troubling the Line* in summer of 2015, I reread my poetics statement from 2013 and realized that some of it no longer applies now that I have transitioned from male to female since its publication. During the past year and a half, I have finally become a woman, both in my writing and in my life. Putting this anthology out into the world gave me a burst of confidence to become myself and dispelled much of my fear. Looking back, I wonder how much of what I theorized about writing before was mythologizing an inability to transition, and therefore raising that fear to a meta-level of discourse. I also wonder whether the person who wrote those earlier poems of mine is the same person who writes this statement now. I have therefore revised this poetics statement, updating it and the poem selection to include work written both before and after transition.

Transitioning changes a writer's life and work. It changes what person others hear speaking in your work, who your friends and colleagues are, who listens to your speech or ignores it, what your audience will be, and how people treat you when you walk down the street or go to the corner store to buy groceries. A year and a half ago when I began taking estrogen, I thought to myself "Oh, changing my gender/sex will be no big deal," but the process has sent shockwaves through my writing—challenges which have rejuvenated and revitalized it during the past two years.

Before transition, poetry offered to me the possibility of trying on different versions of myself, a way of channeling possible selves through associated chains of sound, imagery, and thought, modeling potential realities that might be habitable. This process was a conversation between the activity of imagining and the activity of listening, of letting sheer sound create an unexpected textual body and subjectivity. Some parts of this process were active and some were passive. Some of the passive elements included imitation, internalization, and memorization. Early on I wrote by internalizing the voices or texts of others that moved me and there were hundreds of others people's poems in my head. When I sat down to write, I drew different sounds, cadences, and tones from this jukebox. I heard poetry as a flow, a string of changing stresses and phrasing, a continuous thread of sound. That was the passive part of the process. The active part involves cultivating moments of documentary punch within the flow, moments of reflecting on experiences to get a different perspective on them or develop a different relationship to them. This documentary aspect is the part which has come to the foreground for me lately. Since transition there has been more to talk about in terms of sheer subject matter, more that urgently needs to be said, and more external resistance to it being said. The process has become an exchange between passively channeling a flow of sound as a tool for imagining, and splicing it together with active negotiation of documentary experiences.

The act of imagining has been changed by transition. The more poetry I write, the more I am unable to avoid myself. This was my experience getting an MFA in Tucson in the year 2000, when I first sat down and started writing constantly writing poetry. The struggles with gender identity were staring back from every page I wrote and every poem I produced, however allegorically, and this recognition first prompted me to come out to other people. When I wrote "Trans Figures" in 2002, I wanted to reimagine my body but was afraid to do so and felt weighed down by seemingly pragmatic reasons why I couldn't. I was looking for a language to describe what at that time was a melancholy relationship to gender, furtively inhabiting the space of different support groups which provided a sense of community but also felt located at the margins of society. Brooding and somewhat blocked, this awareness nevertheless sustained for me the hope of being able to transition eventually, because it helped me to envision a hypothetical female version of myself. In "Spontaneous Generation" several years later, a prose flow of poetic language improvisationally explored the experience of what my body might be, though this imagining continually fell back upon the constraint of "the real" as a kind of continual disappointment, a kind of thinking through the question of what it means to lack a womb.

Often the process of imaginative flow has involved, by necessity, inventing procedural language to name what forms I am using, lists of rules that provide just enough framing to get the poem written and have it be internally coherent. Before transition, I leaned upon this technique very heavily as a way of structuring the writing, especially in the absence of any other urgent subject matter. I worked in series or in longer projects which operated according to a list of procedures derived from reading my own poem, extrapolating rules from a text I didn't entirely understand, in order to generate more of it. I gave this method of reflexive writing and reading the idiosyncratic private name of "rhetorical form" and it involved reading different kinds of gestures and the situation of communication they imply or evoke, as it might arise in the social world.

Though one can use the imagination to explore and discover identity through experimentation and play, what has come to the fore in my writing since the change is those aspects of identity that are imposed by others from without. This is the notion of identity as a trap, with the very real dangers of targeting, tokenization, and erasure. Since transition I have had the experience of "waking up" to the existence of misogyny on a visceral level. The person I was as a man sometimes didn't take women as seriously as he should have when they talked about the presence of this force in their lives. Now I can see that misogyny is not only real but central to how structures of power in literature and society operate—it is a quicksilver presence in every aspect of our interaction as writers, set up so as to be invisible to everyone but those who are targets of it. The fact of having to admit that this force exists, and seeing it everywhere, now structures my life. The fact that I am treated differently now by so many people who before transition used to hang on my every word and declare it correct or brilliant has caused me to begin reconsidering why I am writing. The pantheon of which poets I feel most influenced by has also changed along with with my gender/sex. The way I situate my work in relation to larger literary institutions, groups, and movements has changed. Feminism and transfeminism have suddenly become more vital concerns to me, at times, than abstract problems of aesthetics. As one example of such a change in focus, before transition I assumed a universal audience and a "neutral" anonymous ground for the aesthetic effect of a text. Now that illusion is damaged: on the contrary, everything I write is now "marked" as something written by a woman, or as something written by a transfeminine person. It is sure to be treated accordingly by a certain powerful, influential segment of the literary establishment.

In response I have developed a technique of strategically speaking to multiple audiences. "The Valleys Are So Lush And Steep" was prompted by a list of hormone replacement therapy drugs and their side effects, initially posted on facebook as a way of explaining to cisgender people what it was like to be trans. However, at a certain point in the writing process, identity started to feel like a restriction imposed from outside. My sense of irony kicked in and the piece entered a different mode as I found myself acknowledging the ridiculousness of the drug names and side effects. My focus moved to thinking about trans readers who were like me. I began fabricating details for these readers, making things up that could be absurd science-fiction extensions of the real experience, and I could do this because I knew that a trans audience would get the joke. This fabrication or absurdity was also a way of speaking back to an implied cisgender reader's assumptions about me writing my identity in a "factual" way, as if I could disrupt the interpellation process. I realized that as a "marked" writer I could still have fun with the identity situation by talking back to it in a disruptive way. If a reader thinks they have "got you" just because they might possess the name for what you are called, they are forgetting that individuals in a minority group or literature retain the ability to constantly reimagine and remake ourselves. I realized that there could be a certain authority in the mere act of assuming a readership (comprised of cis and trans readers each understanding different things) who agreed sympathetically that trans people are human beings and authors rather than symptoms of babel, capitalism, decadence, or society going to hell in a handbasket. This readership would be able to enjoy linguistic play, and be capable of participating as allies alongside my experience of the frustrations and joys of what it means to be approaching oneself while disrupting expectations about that self, bubbling as long as possible on the improvisational stove.

Trish Salah

Next Year in Jerusalem

As if beginning, trying to make of ourselves
          a home out of questions.

Might turned earth put into question the liberty of lovers?
would be lovers, brave beloveds in love with
                              (love's homily; a no more happy state)

Might the sign of pure history
          Be impressed upon this place
            offer readymade commentary to take up,
in the shadow of two soldiers taken, disappeared
 in the after/before
  of how many Palestinians, taken?
                              Might speaking disappearance, as the
                                        disappeared
                              thousands upon—
   might this place stand on one side of a border or another
might stand it in
          the girth of an impossible line—

two soldiers gone from Shabba farms,
   might alibi, headline fodder
for a thousand, or so Lebanese dead, a million or so,
routed from their homes, alibi
          for the ruin of their homes.

                                                  Might we, as gay people,
                                                        share, such liberation?

Coming together in Jerusalem—   for once, such peace
Christian, Jewish and Muslim accord—   as one
in condemning queer contamination of the holy places…

If there was a reason to go, that accord in hate was it.

But Israel, how might men share a kiss or a caress as their homes are shelled?
 How might women march together, fuck one another, tender or
rough break skin's
                              fast
the force of occupation?

Never mind.
From the West the gayest of lovers, fleet footed, a euphoric & proud race
on and over Lebanon, Palestine
where fire, stones fall, and the sky is turned
again against its people…
        How to come to Jerusalem
                with a question?

Memory dividing one catastrophe from all others
        as holy as holy as stonewall,
 or shimmers of Berlin, divided,
        your question,   to call up one wall

to build another

                        with what faith are questions put
between the living and—
                              Never mind

the unimagined living blood
 flowing stones to walk upon, questions that desire no answer,
                questions holding ground
        no ground for pride,

like
how to colonize place you claim does not exist?
            what is the dividend of shame?
                    never mind
            a thick dull— swathes this earth   its
lover's embrace,   its
            nearer turn—

how might a question turn, weary and reconciled,
lay its people down,
                    own death?

Schrebergarden 1-VI

from *Lyric Sexology: Case Studies*

I *Words Bode Ill*

Indefinite an order around one, me,
they flower so frequently:
newly created nerves in vulpation.
They have only to stem their attention
Energetic correlate of the rays
to effect a change in the source of Man,
(as with the effect mentioned in Chapter IX).

Since my nerves have become fonds
to suppress the corresponding—
hewn sexes love corresponding—
it would in any case be unendurable.

With the great shortage of verdure,
the "if only my " with "if only," withholding
the very exciting cause: fecund, forecourts' heaven.
Asinine.

Words do not go away chirping away, or judge
the cause. What is the cause?
"The doctors can only speculate," she explained.

Cultivating my religious beliefs,
Or my or my or my (why "my?"),
what is mainly contempt of death.
The Bible expresses this thusly: "to picture
All the lower souls wrought of sleep"
Ariman confirms this as well (wither the lower god of the horizon?)

II *"To Submit to the Act of Copulation as a Woman"*

A judge cannot
contemplate
her body in bed submitting
her arse a temple
to Manhood.

A beautiful feeling fucked free of judgment.
"Fuck my sex out."
"Fuck the god out."
"Fuck my brains out."
A judge cannot be a judge in/of her body.
"What a delightful feeling
to be without one's sex
one's judge, I meant, one's
submission."

To be without the whole wealth of knowing
Sexed thusly knowing the English love of pattern,
Rhythm's reason, even unto
Galaxies at the end.

One cannot but want to be bruise
Assfucked, and blazoned ripe and purple
Known,

Biblically speaking,
Across the firmament.

III *Attracted To Distant Stars*

One night—perhaps the fourth or fifth after my arrival at Sonnenstein—I succeeded
with immense mental effort in temporarily drawing down to myself all impure
("tested") souls; it would only have required a thorough "covering with rays" through
my recovery with one nerve-restoring sleep and with it the disappearance of the
impure souls....

In consequence Flechsig's soul took special measures to exclude the recurrence
of such a danger to its existence and to that of other impure souls. It resorted to
mechanical fastening as an expedient; a technique of which I was only able to get a
rough idea. This mechanical fastening first occurred in a looser form called "tying-to-
rays", where the word "rays" seems to have been used in a special sense which I did
not fully understand.

...the souls hung on a kind of bundle of rods (like the fasces of the Roman Lictors)...
this looser form of fastening seemed not to afford sufficient defense against my power
of attraction and the danger of dissolving in my body, a more resistant form was
chosen which was called "tying-to-celestial-bodies"
Pp. 118.

IV *Nervensprache*

I never got used to the inner ear twitter
          as spoken by birds in this straying

                    lovingly adorned and assorted my
                    lovely young girls playing outside
                    nerve gardens, the birds' throats

The rods like light spread out along the surface of celestial bodies.
How is a flower rod lightning in my throat and God's cock at one time?

(I admit it, I am trembled by division. I want it all.)

Nerves (my basis) forced them to think on, sink in broken off sentences,
> "by simply repeating the words and phrases. And thus turning them into
> not-thinking-of-anything-thoughts. I have done that for a long time now
> with conjunctions and adverbs which would need a full clause for their
> completion. If I hear for instance "Why, because I" or "Be it", I repeat these
> words for as long as possible without attempting to complete the sense by
> trying to connect them with what I thought before."

Pp 174

Animated chatter, trill and vault like summer languor and this prison is an illusion
really, the world's all rock and wasted and the prettiness I make the only consolation
among the spectral mechanos of my murderers.

V *They have the faculty of transforming themselves into all things of the created world.*

Robots are ghosts. Florid collisions between *flüchtig hingemachte Männer*
And the world yet to be.
Our mechanicals were far simpler, animated by a singular vitiating force.
Sperm in the throat and ass, and if I had to fight off that soldier, don't think badly of me
I couldn't resist, I was just a girl and no hypocrite…
I didn't think badly of whores they just were
Filth and if God made them that way, made them for corruption then well,
God is God.

Except, of course. He isn't. One being both forecourts and head of heaven, Ariman
and Ormuzd and all the others and myself, just nerves fraying and the echo light
leaves.
Once was a singular thing but you cannot have gardens of One or if you can, then
weeds, and rot and shit mingled with divine creation.

Euphemistically, Dr. Freud would say. I was dead when he read my book, but I still
saw him reading, perched on that rock of ages, at the neverending end of time. I saw
him with his Jewish Science, and glance of nose, and his hidden arrogance. Moses the
Egyptian, indeed.

Meanwhile, the dead in me, like women's trinkets. It bothered me once but no more.
I now know *my whole body is filled with nerves of voluptousness.*

VI Alabaster in the Mouth

Borne of our strife, soul shudders across time.
Blessed substitute for the stars: helpless, watch
little clouds become pink horde and grey multitude.

We are a *literal proliferation.*
Our view is the mirror's retrospective shatter.
Our view is the continually created, Himself.

Ghosts the names of all our houses:
A Mongolian Prince, outside of the derision of bloodlines, a prince
But a Mongol, half man and half beast, one might as well say.
A Jewess. I was very beautiful, but again, animal, driven by vile wants.
Her body could not bear children but none more womanly have I ever seen.
I was Hyperbolian Woman, Herself.
The Perverse Jesuit Novice in Ossegg, and his Perverse Master.
The Burgomaster of Klattau, striving to keep the peace the day this world stilled.
An Alsatian girl struggling to keep her virtue, held down by a victorious French officer.
Scoundrels. Apostles. My clan, the Assembled Margraves of Tuscany and Tasmania.
Corpses all, imprisoned in wandering clocks.
All but Miss Schreber full with child-blessedness.

Was I ever in your house, your bloodline? Could I have been one soul of Flechsig?
No, in my nervous condition, castration lodged my jailor and saviour.

Lili Elbe will be saved by her Herr Doctor, but not I.

Post Script: *Itinerary of a book/Anxiety of influence*

Unmanning, how a book could travel, great thoughts of a nerve patient,
The most famous patient in the history of psychiatry, they say.

Unmanning, the voices, trilling like birds gendered metaphors along the nerves of a
body becoming,
Becoming becoming the thought "after all it must be very nice to be a woman
submitting to the act of copulation"

Unmanning, not unreasonably, the fear of those doctors, but surely, surely mad?

Unmanning at the end of that century's end mad becoming impossible speech, an
impossible position, a sex that was not one, so sure mad becoming unmanning, a
bellowing miracle, a cold wind blowing through a body's hollow with becoming
becoming becoming deposits in nerves, on nerves' kin, as nerves speech, sinous
sensous miracle, the jolt of

Unmanning, Freud in the reading wondering to himself to you, here almost exactly
a century later "whether there is more delusion in my theory than I should like to
admit... [or] more truth in Schreber's delusion than... people are as yet prepared to
believe"

Unmanning, passing from Schreber's hands to paper scraps in his (her?) cell
From Saxon Judge, family man, not a father, proto nationalist, proto national socialist
        When did she/he become? Did she become god's whore, golden girl, the
chosen or at least some, one?
Ummanned anyway in the pages, Denkwürdigkeiten eines Nervenkranken
        --great thoughts of a nerve patient what would become in Freud's hand
unmanning
Psychoanalytic Notes On An Autobiographic Account of a Case of Paranoia (Dementia
Paranoides), and be translated subsequently into English, Memoirs of My Nervous
Illness.

Unmanning, can reading a book change your sex? Margaret Mead made me gay, they
say, but Freud defended himself manfully from all that unmanning, luder, shit, he
was no
He was not going to become writing his spinning his theory his unconscious his sex

Unmanning, no he would not be
Not a woman in another man's arms
Not a prostitute, a whore for some foreign God,
Not luder, shit, prostitute, homosexual jew or woman becoming
Not a jew, homosexual shit, prostitute becoming homosexual, not a

Delusion. Just this, writing "the cross sexed wish, a symptom of the patients repressed homosexuality, harbinger of their savior fantasies, paranoia"
 A century of that, thank you doctor. Couldn't you just have slept with Count Sandor, yourself?

Poetics Statement

Page 1

In the annals of a voice, a vocal exercise
machine, in the wake of a surgical gawk,
Not unlike the university defaced.

I used to work on my breath cuts
swimming under water was harder
I think the reason I couldn't cannonball.

You look up and you follow the words.
And numbers align, blood, the light fades,
You stumble, internally, recover.

An out of body experience, spongy
Green fields below, an I soaring
Breathless, choke of a sleeper still.

Breathy, her froth and tremul, as if?
A question, clipped and round "o"
Pursed, smiling, uptalk, for, like, always?

Enter the clichés, so as to be entered
Into the real. Reach over the body, ok?
Recognize practice makes unconscious.

Its lessons or lesions, and the associated
Press, risk silk or granary, rasp seductive
Like smoke, a body of smoke, Trace, thanks told you,

In Sotto Voce, what's a girl to do, do a woman
Like you, due do to pause, and fleshly accident
Accidental, pitch bitch of being born, as if!

A soul dwells there, a harbour of light
Haunts pleasantries with desire's husk
Bodies present themselves, appealing.

Poetics Statement
Page 2

Page 1 was a poem. I need coffee. Funny about the manifesto being something that for me was always immanent. "always" dates from encountering Fiction/Theory in Tessera, so 1991. For always or until 1991 (happens again), which will be a while.

The writing, like Jack Spicer, doesn't come from this body. I don't know about beams. It comes from what I don't know about. In this body, or that other, or that Other. The writing is singular, and eclipses particular modalities of thinking about. It could be accused of romanticism, then, or vent. There is a two body problem, that cannot quite get hold of or contain the more than two bodies that enter into the text. I guess the problem is between any two bodies of the possible field or duration in which two of those bodies are in view, one typing, one being typed, or not typed, but being a locus from which what is typed is oriented.

At least that is what I think when I am not thinking. (This writing is on a double track.) The traction of the body on the vent or romanticism is that I've not yet had a body my coffee this morning, insomnia sucks, I am lonely in a new town, my apartment is drafty, and….

(triply) my work should be of use, as well as of pleasure, of productive interference to someone being someone other than me. And specifically, we are so deeply, unmoveably fucked by the violent ordering of the world, the destruction of it, the destruction of us in it. So, Israel invades Lebanon, Palestinians are stateless and dying in public view, for sixty years, feminists debate whether or not to support prostitutes, indigenous people struggle to articulate viable realities, livable lives in/ against/through the murderous and abjecting "options" offered up/imposed down upon them by settler colonialism. And they succeed, sometimes, as do prostitutes and transsexuals and arabs, even Palestinians, succeed in making some life, some joy, something smart, warm or pretty and possible. Sometimes, some do for a little while, or even for a good long, hard won, lifetime, even in spite and through some difficult choices, violent oppression and self-serving rescue committees.

So you want to honor joy, and glory and farts (pardon me, Mirha-Soleil Ross) and (making messy, stop counting) channeling (beaming) the people who make a difference, who make your own life possible, between one body and the next, because that isn't to be taken for ground granted.

I haven't had my coffee yet. It is troubling, where language makes a bridge, but there's no firm. And when you become in a particular direction, the exhaustion of other avenues doesn't mean you are done with them. Writing is sometimes an exercise in the inexhaustible of other avenues. If my hand were to slip under my shirt, under skin. I slipped and cut myself when I first got here, and had no idea where to take myself when the wound wouldn't close. If I were to call you up on the telephone and say it was a mistake. Writing recovery, writing graven, writing manifesting the body and its impossibility, which is a persisting limit if you listen to it. It only sounds like lament to me today. Tomorrow it will screech cheerfully into route and fucking. Friday it will have people over for poems and sangria, or maybe take a nap.

If my body were written from the body would the body it was written from be transsexual? Would it be childhood's projection forward into whatever the forward of Oxford Street in Halifax or Lawson Street in Dartmouth might ever have been? There were imago girls all over my childhood. Which I fastened onto like stars. The neighbors and school chums and a cousin. And it is that (transsexual) lesbian Freudian cliché. Wanting and wanting to be. (There is a kernal of Freud in every Judith Butler Butch/Femme.) Oh, and Gilligan's Island, I Dream of Genie, Battlestar Galactica, the Uncanny X-Men. If we play superheroes can I be Marvel Girl, Phoenix, The Black Queen, Dark Phoenix, Willow, Evil Vampire Willow, Dark Willow, Dark Willow's Girlfriend Dark Phoenix? On Battlestar Galactica, Cassopeia was a companion, i.e. a ho, on a Battlestar, heroic. I loved that. Becoming towards. Sex workers, subtextual (Ginger/MaryAnne) Lesbians, Witches, Dominatrixes, the Girl next door in her Apocalyptic Invert form—superheroes, and reasons to write a body. (Writing this I realize again that Joss Whedon and I are about the same age, and probably watched the same tv growing up. Anya is Genie if Genie were a person and post-feminism.)

Oh dear, and just when you thought you weren't going to embarrass yourself at parties. Anymore. At least you're not passed out in the punch. Say something smart about Al-Andalus. No thanks, not today. I might have been a "dirty leb" but I totally didn't understand Fairuz growing up. Lebanon was a photo of my dad on skies in the mountains above Beirut, sitting next to a photo of him walking along the beach later that day. (I made that up, the same day of it, just cause it is what they always say).

But she pulled at me, like Lou Reed, only entirely differently. Beautiful boys in skirts, another way to fall. Hanging out with my Lebanese cousins listening to New Wave.

Poetics start narrative stops, allow the beach breach, leak out of life into objects, and abject there for a little while. This week in class I'm teaching the makeover as genre and trope. Your wanted to be, interrupted. You want through thought to have a room. Kiss up, fuck up, have a party, pay a debt, undo a certain rational, undo a certain violence, all certain rationales, move home, be next to, and welcome, dwell

TT Jax

Lincoln Park

on cobblestones otherwise swept clean:
a desiccated pile of dog shit, namely
 three separate sun-blacked turds
jagged in an asymmetric pile;
beside said feces a single
white wire coat hanger,
slightly bent--

a man with jogging shorts
more expensive than my
entire thrift store outfit
lifts his nose in greeting

why edgar allen poe, like me, needed some fucking healthcare

pressure -- built, building-- inner sanctum slow
draining sewer system of puss------stagnant
 ----------streams of infected waters rising in
all small holes------curved cragged crevices, secret
-----------interstitial spaces between brittle
ducts--cartilage--bones-- throbbing arteries
seeped swelled clamor clangor rocked screamed curled

spasm-hand clenched with pillow, pulled------dark, cold
-------window translucent tin fogged up ringing
wound tight------spiral------coiled brittle snail shell
lit brilliant red with teeth bone fuck stretch
--------------face hot, tense, sweated to moaning into

midnight twisted sheets, fist in pillow------punch
legs grinding, stiff back-------- twisted all elbows
angles rigid, dragging, swinging out------------ scream
underwater melody merciless-----------------------------
round ringing rhythmic waves in chilled dark folds,
blanket, pillow, sheet --------twisted, a conch shell
wound with coiled shadows and a static sea
murmuring softly within shrinking space.

I am the little monkey as he struts
redundant mechanical dance, his dull
dumb cymbals crash together, together;
and I'm the shadow between his cymbals
crash together--- crash together------ dark and
ringing scream dumb space turbulent with waves
shattering invisibly--------- together,
together------- and I dig my fingernails
into something giving and I wonder
if I will be heard down the hall if I
borrow a moment to smash my head, wall
togethertogether as I cup--------claw
throbbing red ear swollen on thin skin hinge----
faucet turned flip switched---- back and forth vacuum
suck--- niagara falls--- colic rocking arms--
saltandpepper snow on muttering screen--------

fetal curl rigid coiled brittle snail shell
---nothing------- and then I am fucking screaming
with fingers snapped to palm-- grabbing ear------ scream
over slow and resolute rip-- fireworks--
cannon fire-- mountains explode in rock rains--
the sanctum succumbed to yield forth rivers

oceans symphonies of vacuums broken
tv's, humidifiers, wind moaning
through peeling dry bark, gurgles pops pips drips
and bells-- and bells--bellsbellsbellsbellsbellsbells

"the body is the home for the"

three-ton shadows on the wall hang askew
like paintings, photographs, mild achievements framed
and in revolt-- darkness deepening in cracks--
its fingers flowing at once quick and still in the shallow channels
between harsh cinderblocks soothed by cool coat upon coat
of viscous white paint--- darkness puddles
in a jagged hole, chipped and wry like a rotten-toothed grin, filling to throat-full--
spills back out and down, blurry in descent, weakens, falls to muttering incoherence,
then still.   darkness heavy, hanging like paintings, falling like drapes, bleeding
like ink in water into hairpin cracks-- blackest there, most impenetrable,
wearing down my fingernail when I seek entrance,
knowledge, of the deepest hairpin pull of shadow---

but I repeat myself.

I, who am not she--
I, something (or some*one*) heavy-heeled, ambiguous, shelled in thin drag--
I, (not she but maybe) with key still in hand, moving mindlessly to pocket--
I, (who am *not she but maybe-- maybe*) standing next to the stained velour dried-puke
        orange sofa
we pulled from the dump out back, cumbrous, massive it strained at the stairwell as
        we cursed and sweated
it through the dense hallway, shiny white paint like dandruff on its arms, across from it
        the window unit
silent in the cracked pane, the cat keening at my calves--
I (*I, who am not she but maybe, he*) fingering the cracks, seeking entrance, wanting--
I, who am not she but he, I
want (like the body wants water, a place to sit, the act of defecation) to go

        home---

although I am home.
building door stuck open behind me, the limp
urine light of late afternoon musing on dirty
linoleum, taking one tentative step up
the foyer stairs, where motes billow thrillingly--- some
bird trills outside-- flaked metal numbers rattle on their nails,
the one banging up against the three, the four mere dirt outline-- an A
marks my own door, its dim golden foot toeing the frayed puddle
of shadows creeping up the doorframe: 1--3--(4)--A--East 61st Street--
home.

incidental-- darkened-- lulling cool interior alien
and furnished with shadows, falling like drapes,
hanging like paintings, askew.

nuthouse birthday, 1997

nu[*happybirthdaytoyouhappybirthday*]t *oyouhappybirthdaydear*[ ]*happybirthdaytoyou*

house   **:D !**

[birthday cake   ]

singingsingingsinging

(but don't look out the window)

before the nuthouse

after birth
        my mother's head
                        floated up:

                    a   s tray

                                        b a l loon

                    while
            in a [heart] torn op en
          like perineum-pul led to rip ping
        she cradled me cradled in clavicle rib
        cage   the fierce of sternum rising

                blue-skinned
            slimy   I   sucked through
                lungs whistle   a   first startled

                    breath

the day I turned 14

birthday cake with inpatient candles,
white cake, careful white frosting
with my name (and other alien words)
spelled in uneven blue letters
(both the happy and the exclamation point
authorized for good behavior);
wanly smiling nuthouse girls sit
resident on salmon-colored carpet,
face up this time;framed in therapeutic
blue walls and analog clocks they sing
with voices slightly croaking
happy birthday to you!
happy birthday to you!

they mean it, even though
most of us haven't seen
the sun in months.

Lifestory

#1

I was born in hiatus, whatever the hell that means. I waited for affirmation but
breathed and bruised instead. Nights Mama beat the particle board roof with a
broomstick-- winter brought the rats of the woods to seek warmer quarters, a rain of
claws and teeth. Then Mama died. The rats got in, that winter.

In the mountains we drink creek water: clear and quick it runs in rivulets,
breaks in rainbow whirls over wearing rocks. We live wound in a veil of sound; glass
high and tinkling shatters shatters swirls. In cool dim crevices salamanders sleep,
breath deep through their own cold skin. Crayfish prowl the cracks for the young.
Black bears drink; deer, bobcat drink; raccoons and rats: like family we gather creek-
side to drink and prey upon each other. Water runs over bone, a froth of green.

The rats, like me, move by fear, loneliness; gravitate by tooth or claw to
whatever warmth avails. Wind winds through turning leaves, awakening a clack
of limb on limb like bone; brittle tissues throw orange, blood red, yellow slick like
underbellies: a warning before the fall.

I live alone: perpetual hiatus. My heart pounds sometimes in sunlight, still
afternoons, still. The mountain crumbles in increments beneath my feet, over centuries
prior and lasting it packs, folds over the bones of salamanders, bears, Mama. I will fall
before the mountain; the rats will get in, root for warmth in the hallow of my cheek.

#2

She of course knew the potential for failure: shouts down the mountain, staccato
footfalls heavy through plywood walls. A bee buzzed in slow drone circles, drawn to
her sweat. Chilly outside, the sun behind the clouds: still she sweated; she sweated,
still.

She waited with bated breath as shouts small still like pebbles skittered to rock
slides, erosion. A drop of rain or sweat between her eyes: shadows deepened, as if a
bird folded wings to collect sun and clouds to itself, ease its own anxious heart.

She fell backwards into grass and rocks: secret cobwebs, interstitial
ecosystems of roots, mouths, eyes pressed beneath the darkness of her fall, her

sweating skin. Tip-over girl: in too-tall grass and granite she laid back.

A door opened: now it was coming, of course. Like a trumpet a flare the shouts sharp burst up out from the shack, disturbing bees and beetles small with gutfuls of the dead. Scurry: now it comes.

She opened her eyes: uncertain sun in sky suddenly scraped of clouds, picked clean and blue and vacant if not piercing. Above a small red hawk circled slow spiral searching, alone.

#3

No one: the same no one that is always here. A bee buzzes round her head as she wrings a dripping sock. Fingertips wrinkled with water, borax in the cracks; she folds the sock over a plastic yard chair, hands stinging with cold, wet.

Flies eat shit, eat the dead deflating caterpillar that she'd watched chew a blade of grass the morning before. Butterflies stir tumult, beat up secret eddies, flutter-tornado shifts in solar winds. Water falls, slowly toothless chewing the mountain to sand. A queen bee fucks underground, overhead a solid veil of sound, tissues, currents in a dark weighted with packed earth, stone.

No one: the bees and fucks and shifts and dead that radiate like roots, dendrites, reaching snapping through dirt planet space. The ground sinks: soft mud after rain; a bee drinks from the sock. A frog tan and spotted lands heavy on fat feet, mouth a broad grin snap-lipping everything in one throatless swallow.

Poetics Statement

> Writing, like singing or the smooth steady roll of clay
>
> between palms, is an art of the gut

Poetry is an act of body, an internal, intestinal movement. Poetry moves like an interstitial cellular revolt, rattling up words and rhythms from the deepest secret stuff of us. An act of body: the gut and heart in synch with the hand or throat. Words pull like a taffy tongue or twine—smooth, loose; sharp and dry—from an open heart with teeth, wound and wound and wound.

This is my body. I pretend it has no form. I breathe to feel it- lung stuck rising on ribs- ease my shoulders down, press palms like heels to a face gone cold in the mirror: is this me? Pressure, nails. I explore it in detail, another lens; trap it in emulsion like a fly. Nature photography. Still, developing. Frame form. Find form. I find its form alarming.

There is no form to poetry, beyond what we impose. Write like a divining stick: tap, tap; we listen for the resonance, intuit sound waves through cell bodies. We write to the rhythm of our pulse; our fingers flood with blood and words. Words are symbols, slivers of the sun and moon rolling over dark cold ground, from a time before we prayed to our own image. We have thrown our future, interpreted our past, preserved our guts with words spoken, carved—slowly split from mouth to screen, tongue to finger tip; still, words are the mystery we've sensed from the sky. There is no form to the sky, beyond what we imagine or impose.

This is not revolutionary. This is not experimental. This is elemental. We are beings that, in ambivalence and joy, warmth and deception, attempt to connect, witness,

My body is alien, dying. I catch it in a poem. A poem can be seen, read, kept; sometimes understood. A poem holds me. A breath in contrast, ink. The ocean in the slow coil of a shell.

be witnessed. Writing is a line as thin as a flame in a field unbroken by skyscrapers. Each day we are someone new; each day we tell an ancient story the way we best know how.

I rode a train once. Around the train there was black sky and ground we could feel, not see. This is my body, I said to the man who slept beside me. Rattle, rattle. Do you understand?

I'm here, I say, here's my sorry ass and my sorry ass travails. Unwind the convoluted coils of my guts and look for yourself; you are here, too. in me, in me, y(l)ou. A poem, a shell to the ear. Listen:

A statement is a wish for more sense than we actually make. A remnant, something simple, something lasting.

What does it feel like to write this?
What does it feel like to read this?

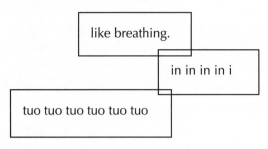

Y. Madrone

Personal

I swim in circles as a way of getting through things. My names change every decade or so. Sometimes the littlest movement or tap enrages me, causes my genders to fight. If you would like me to smack you around I will get my most recent gender for you. Please, please meet my gender on Sunday under the vaux swifts and their favorite chimney. Thank you for seeing the monsters I am best-friends with, isn't friendship and travel an excellent source of fiber. I almost forgot to explain myself or that I haven't dreamt in two years. According to my astrological chart I am holding my breath until Pluto is renamed a planet. I fight with science whenever I feel like. Go ahead and cry for bad movie love, it's not my story but easy this way. Goodnight youtube, goodnight facebook. Goodnight amoeba and your children too. Goodnight first gender, I love you today.

Personal [Myth]

If you squeeze your eyes tight enough god will accept you, accept me. Yes, I am trying to fatten up for deliverance or the day I open my mouth for god to fit in. I've got a boner now, just keeping these secrets to myself; god is a dirty word. If you notice me with my eyes puckered into dried figs don't out me. I will run out of family and piousness. All this myth brings up another confession: as a child I dressed up in my father's clothing while he and my mother were out. I would skulk into their bed and lie real still and touch myself. You know where. I'd squeeze real tight, dried figs and all. Exactly. I am certain; I must be a favorite of god's by now. I must be. I must.

The Tomatillo Verses [an excerpt]

Tomatillo makes a house of warm welcome and courage. I spend myself there, let the wind go on by. I can't remember anymore who eats persimmons and who doesn't, or which firsts have happened already and which ones we still wait for. For this I am cut open promises and roasted sweet. Oh too many scenes are not a color on this swatch yet. Too much stilted distance. Too many red apples to cut and slather in peanut butter. I would like to eat at your table.

*   *   *

Tomatillo has the bravery of a blade of feather grass. She has everything necessary and in the correct order. First a swath of soft opal across her collarbone, nape of neck a taunting pause between.

Upon waking she is already starry eyed as if the sauce of her dreams is still stirring in her, in her long asymmetrical torso.

I told Tomatillo to keep her grass roots clipped close lest I was to furrow there with my weeds, invasive but more medicine than a   mason   jar   full   of   snake   oil.

Tomatillo doesn't like arguments in the hot sun. A good screaming needs containing, needs a clouded weather pattern, best if the front porch could hold us. Not a damned sec of breath can keep this girl from gathering, her loyalty how the salmon   return   only   to   the   river   of   their   birth.

I kept track, kept all her reveries from harming one another. I kept certain. Kept shreds of hair and t-shirt, kept the smell of her lingering so long it went stale in the sheets I never did bring myself to wash.

Out past our last moment, her green beaning arms working their determination into a windmilling. Not sure if I was the wind then or the pilot passing overhead in his Cessna. There is always a   question   left   in   place   of   that   ending.

Tomatillo looks everything in its eye and laughs until them eyes quit looking and blink nervous and blink asking and blink blink.

*   *   *

The garage musty with damp cardboard and unopened doors. There aren't windows anyhow just splintered cedar boards in the square cutouts. Tomatillo's hair is braided over her ear and down her back and lies in the bottom of the box behind her. Tomatillo is the only thing not a box in that old garage—could be in Texas or Carolina or most likely California, central and near barren and un-enticing   save   for   them   boxes.

Tomatillo caused all of this to remain still and wait for her. She'd never meant to return but couldn't muster her courage of cattails to turn and go and leave everything unplanned for back beneath the summer's last peony stalks. I'd cut them down for her yearly waiting. Wouldn't recognize spring till them green shoots came asking. What pearly everlasting held that girl all them years.

Well it's the boxes that she remembered first. And her traversing only got her as far as the Blooming Oranges section. She slumped herself into them boxes, run her pincushion finger tips—softer than I could've recalled—over the stiff edges of all them swatches, boxes and boxes of slim papered colors:

Irish Breeze, Alfredo, Enthusiasm, Gold Dust, Pumpkin Butter, Sugaree Lemon, Copper Coins. She didn't cry over all them swatches, didn't cry for the color of the last ten years or what she'd have to name em. She didn't cry.

*   *   *

Somebody has to be the conqueror and I will be the fable. Two pennies and a rail tie couldn't mix up my luck any stiffer.

The dirty frame of my years says everything that could be said but in less words. And a larger word could be used here or there, as long as it is spelled well.

Tomatillo chewed up the "do not remove" label that separates the sexes from the sex. Folks ended up in every direction. Now I
am only capable of irrational job titles:

Surrogate Painter. Angel Eyes for the Blind. Sweet Charity Electrician. Imaginary Blossoms Farmer. Mischief Making Mortician. Crushed Mint Plumber. Barista Teacher Teacher.

*   *   *

Oh. Oh. Oh. The enthusiasm of a Tomatillo squeal fills up the impossible border hunger.

Girl's not the sort to look away once she's set eyes on a thing.

I gave her all my copper coin and gold dust to retain warmth she gives out unknowingly.

Nobody knows her name anymore, just the sugared smell of lemons in a clear cup on a clear day at the bluffs. The grass there covered in every color of blanket.

If she could still stand there she'd have organized those shades into their properly fading orders. Decrease intense Oliver until she found Endive and Forsythia.

O, Tendencies and
Their Bad Bad Tempers

There is always a window through which to either look or jump.
Woman of the squid trade has been stamped with concentric
repetitions. Only a memory allows dwelling too long. Disrupting
these periods is a simple business of wiping gathered dust from
the picture frames on the mantle.

Woman, on the outer side of an entry, please let us in. We are all
falling together in the direction of the nearest future. Believe our
foreseeing: an ancient algorithm will get pushy, an enlarged
knocker, to match our equally sized desires, willfully hanging
at eye level.

Look forth woman. Meant for upward movements or small
carriage of large duty. Lift elbows and knees away from the cold
foyer. If there is to be an entry it will be carved marble and
staircased. Set your feet at every threshold you come to. Cross
but don't watch, woman.

Hallway any temptation to place a vase where it may fall or
accidentally be knocked down. O, tendencies and their bad bad
tempers. Just let the faucet in the washroom drip itself dry now.
Keep this coming squid trade, lady—more work awaiting you.

Those tourniquets need tying; a woman must be delivered.
Aren't women delivered here? To this address? Has there been a
name change? A column you've been involved with? Another
vertebrae to bear in your crossed lap.

Left Properly Untouched

Lying in a reverie opens every coat of old makeup for
questioning. Stutter—stutter. Stop stroking a mid-thought,

which isn't aggregate, isn't dressed in nines. Between nowhere middles and everywhere paradise. Put on your five o'clock shadow. Yes. One after another, the mugginess can chase each lurking silhouette into a proper climate of porchlight.

Now give up your top hat, your almighty armoire. Untouched repeatedly. Put your pants down in every corner. The drawer pull—a tight knob between your legs—will keep all your clenching put. All the falling in, and orderly. Easy now, woman, keep reaching vaguely for the knobs.

listen, we are coming down to straighten everything out.

caster we won't ask please when we reach into your genes and pull a man through, we won't ask to draw finish lines of you, caster, can't run from our professional suspicions, you, can't have room or speed, let alone breath, you aren't a kind of allegory, but just dust, no, no exceptions, we are swift to cast our net, yes between your knees, yes caster, there are man fluids in the spelling of your surname and habits we identify as wrong for you, understand, we can't have anything anatomical involved, there are lists with two columns and not more, understand. not more.

a chest is an embarrassment to have.

I am embarrassed to write anything honest. I am embarrassed for every word. for all my predicates & names. for my lover, my children,

the color of my walls. I am embarrassed about
desires, my pronouns, tea choices. of my jokes
& parts, I am embarrassed of my breasts—no, I
hate my breasts, but am too embarrassed to say
anything. there are so many things I wish to
say, please, will I always feel too embarrassed.
my dishes so embarrassing, how they mismatch
& break, how my pants are labeled *not your
daughter's pants*—that's embarrassing. my messy
house, my failing wardrobe and balled up
socks. my dildos—all embarrassed.

Poetics Statement for the Undeclared

/

I have a hard time making a fixed statement about anything. [Even gender] I'm not one
to get fully on any wagon though I am good at getting going. [I fidget and collage] Perhaps

this roots up out of not having
a box to check on forms of existence, application, permission.

I can't even choose a genre. [I mean gender] Texts out of me won't just
poem themselves. My textuality takes a little

from over here and up there or back then. I can only hope
readers dissipate stiff edges [mine holdfast and push and shove]

get limber in my versions. Let me try to say it
like so. I write [I mean blur] poemoirs,

wrestle language and grammar, truth and fiction, into pluralities. [Everything genders]
A maker of questions, I write to go, [I mean fuck]

to experience disembodiment, to expand a universe or two. [My own type of]
Dispelling any notion that language is enough to make with.

//

I don't end neatly in my skin or ink, but I work at it, work with large objects and slippery cairns found at random while walking about, this is just how dreaming happens once the brain's assured there's no danger, didn't you know, sleep is dangerous, mallards and dolphins and even lizards know and metallica too, singing the kingdom out of their masterful chests, while I write my way back, back into a shape I can recognize and name, O, all too often I am left speechless and winging my way, khrg, I promised myself I'd make a statement already, how hard can it be, isn't this how genders become a period

///

Does the period make the statement or the statement the period?
Text is another noun for body. When the body is wrong, revise it.
My body, my text. My transtextuality.

Won't you read, O please, me either way?

////

If it is with language that we find each other, name what cannot be explained or question what is supposedly certain, than absolutely it is through language that we work to overcome what is mangled in us, in each other, in the world.

Our alphabet weighs paperthin-weight. No, we cannot fatten properly on word alone. Why certain truths make a stillbirth. This biting desire to write then must be a form of natural selection. The stickiest cells keeping time keep touching each other. Well, Jack, this is my ode to you.

/////

My cunt dropped its crowbar on 6th street down a
block from the day of mulch and weeds. Day spent
soaked down into my pair-of-socks balls. What does a
man feel like in a man's body? What is my body? Imagine
you are always wrong.

I am space holding when I should be protruding into [space].

Let me ask *how does your body feel today.*

Am I my body or just feeling?

Somedays I am made of force and sometimes only water. O, I forgot, water easily consumes a landscape, evidence, a body. I have no proof just feelings to wash out for maybe you to see.

A cunt is a trouble to hold [on to]. What is a man body anyway? My body erased a boy before a man developed to protect himself. Now, now, a body can always be rewritten.

Yosmay del Mazo

from Angle, Pitch & Scale

as if contour
postured gridlines
a concentric expression
of flattened altitudes

the topography of intimate
a body awkward
in recognition
the slightest meeting
between hips

and if given
an unsteady direction
one point & two bodies
coordinates
in place of closeness
only lines
without place of origin

*

and if light
tantalizes the sealed
an almost visible
behind thinly glued
envelopes & their letters

what a formal word
in place of screaming

*

and if light
backdrops the onion skin
typewriter imposes two lines
the parallel
and opposite
a thin space between
text & text

and if light
were medium
measure echoes or waves
a whisper to departed
in the lip of a shell

and if light
were star
the same ancient smolder
a direct and constant gesture

who am i
if not luminous ember

*

our continual here
definite & elusive
the face   its structures
an incongruence
in our pairing

lines and teeth and word
mistaking posture for certainty
as if wind without motion
as if legs
know only our grave

*

to begin linked
twilight silhouettes
timber & gesture
among darkening
slivers of grass
our ears in tuning
above
an orientation unfolding

*

the gauge of rivet
imprints
on vertices
each point
broken teeth
each point
our sleeping backs
each point
a geometry of conquest
each point
copper and jackets

*

the internal wallpaper
official or resigned
grandmother's frames
hesitant typewritten thinly ink
a muted hymn
a worn oar tapping
the needlepoint practice of initials
three days in a boxcar's open doorway
gifted ham sandwiches
and faces sewn into pockets

*

i pack
for the possible leaving
raise suspicion
and a boy
know steel & gridlock
the vacant hungry
i cannot make up for

*

a girl with her mother's face
washes then rewashes
socks   circles
the unraveled endings
ugly and frayed hangs
in the eminent lathering
mother will kill herself
and i as placeholder after

*

our hands in rhythm enough
both looking toward direction of wind
standing in miles
of open   our common
feet as rooted
arms in blur
shoveling rocks
to hold while calling names
of lost or far away

*

measure in opened palms
just how
an entire hand taken up
with lines crossing lines

a hand is map
intuits an overdue ocean
crossing in heartbeats
each rib a pulling oar

a small girl into waves
hears her own panting
the sound of stitches
merging the pink
how everything below is water
my teeth clanking grains of sand

*

to hold
as a simple act
two shoulders gentled
and wanting
how to reconcile
shape, grasp and sound

*

before inhabitance
fresh cut palm   humo
strings of hummingbird mantle
gathers of huracán
ashé in her choreographed
circles
the constant hum of her
low and frequent pulse

before inhabitance
our knees   circles
in entrance
in unison
herbs set alight
each direction
opens we

return to water
we return to us

*

pulse extends from tethered lips
  know mute & humming flutter

pulse extends even callused or radial
  patiently tapping tongue & feet

pulse tempered   constellation forms
  generations threading differential lines

pulse beating feather veined
  grasp at each others tenders

pulse extends four chambered branch
  logged pitch of entry

pulse extends an echoing scale
  abalone sheen & tribal insistent

pulse extends us adobe
  grass clump hearts flung into sifting wind

Poetics Statement

About "Angle, Pitch & Scale"

Our experience is mapped on our body shape and movement. How we move
in the world is informed by our experience and memory. It is in our tissue, our speech
and our perception this story about the home we come from and the home we hope to
build. Our bodies and geography become the quiet archive. This series of continuous
poems offers a somatic topography.

There is a tension between the architectural certainty and the narrative flow.
The architectural language constructs methodically, offers a blueprint then waits for

a response. The architecture works in definitive rules, wants a physical structure as representation. The narrative navigates a shifting cultural terrain. Offers a story of connection in an attempt to restore a sense of belonging.

Both body and landscape use the language of breath, movement and cycle. Bodies and landscapes are agent and recorder. They mirror each other in process. A stressed body may stiffen in movement or restrict growth the way plant limbs warp in drought or a hillside charcoals after fire.

These poems offer a sensory map, a means of building home both as a physical space and as an internal experience. They are an attempt to reconcile place and identity within a builder who learned to distrust body and language to survive.

The Writing Process

I have always been curious about cultural intersection, the tensions between reading and performing identities, the juxtapositions between different kinds of languages. We often assume that race and gender are biologically determined and physically obvious. Our use of language, dialect, tone and diction reveals how we frame our cultural world. Whether it's Spanglish or urban, affected by trauma or filter through our professional jargon our words reveal a perspective. Sensory memory fills the quiet periphery of intersections. The ways bodies (re)member, transfer knowledge between generations and store specific patterns or responses for survival. Our physiology responds to trauma and is reshaped by resiliency. It is this dialogue between identity, body, belonging and language that drives my work.

Being queer and mixed I am often the physical embodiment of cultural intersection. People ask where I'm from, or assume I'm a teenager because I'm short or glare at me for being in the 'wrong' bathroom or are confused about how I'm related to my family members. This kind of reading and performance with real consequences attached exposes the ways we are trained to think about culture as a static definitive category. I hope to complicate the dialogue about identity and belonging. Not only through referencing my experience in narrative but also in the craft choices I make. Who I am as a writer directly influences what stories I chose to tell and how I chose to tell them.

Zoe Tuck

[An unbound book invites]

JUDGEMENT: an angel emerges from a nimbus. Holy cow! Gold lamé bat wings and the proper embouchure for the trumpet-that-awakens-the-dead or

discarded. Null cards interlard the determinants of your fate,

SECLUSION: black bloc desert mother points to a red pentagram on a parched patch of earth bounded by four swords. What is it to shun society when its licensed eyes

dress meat (by inserting or covering)

POWER: as updrafts of hot air wet rock made hot, as bad as I wanted to be, after some delays, in a red-dress, a dragon as an homage taxonomical violence on femme and beast or as a gesture to the "here there be...", the serrated edge of frontier theory

a card in a different context is in some ways a different card

FAILURE: appears in many poems

and shuffle new sheets into the sheaf

What is the captain of the football team doing in this poem— only son of two queer mothers. Inevitably the winningest dimple smooths under the light of the Pleiades, the cracked pad castaside, rope sandals and a glimpse of futurity unbound versus hidebound different garments all lacking in pliancy

> THE MOON: only with great effort and continual reinforcement are a goddess and ball of rock locked in the same room of a word. In the house of memory: when Voyager was launched

queering chronology

> ROMANCE: a midsummer night's dream. What is William doing in this poem? Two full cups slake two parched mouths. Go home fleas, go home home falling stars. As a collaboration, erasure of the word hierarchical

by memory play

> CHARITY: "Whenever man has thought it necessary to create a memory for himself, his effort has been attended with torture, blood, sacrifice" but mercy is not charity. Enough for everyone; enough theatrical giving. Coin of the realm— mettle of the collar.

but challenge even these platitudes of textual alterity

> HEL: tattered handbook of the marvel universe which holistically encompasses the norse. A person and place and a telos for 11 year old dedicated feys without recourse to radical sanctuary when my course is tough the age of wisdom happening to coincide with the view that my betters subscribed to out of fear I would later come to decide

by introducing somatics

> common enough to read THE CHARIOT as the body. Two horses one black, one white balk at unity. See also voudoun, the chariot of the sun, animus/anima, hyperlink fatigue. Scale back to indecision following the perception of triumph

Coda. Goatish man goat pan pipe fertility, luck, roads and borders crossing over from you as a child I remember the nymph in flight pleading her father, god of the river, to turn her into a tree. But I always like to remind people that in tarot, nothing is final.

[The Road To Find Out]

I'm on the way— road— path—
Watch Harold & Maude with me; Cat Stevens sung about this, in order to access the
road to find out he
"Left [his] folk and friends with the aim to clear [his] mind out" (emphasis mine)

"the unwanting soul sees what's hidden"

or

"free from desire you realize the mystery"

"I asked a painter why the road are colored black.
He said, 'Steve it's because people leave and no highway will bring them back'"

fear of failure (to pass) becomes a threat to perception of mysteries when
it manifests as desire
for safety

When property=freedom
choose itinerancy or vagabondage over the happy home

Nietzche in *The Genealogy of Morals:* "The 'well-born' *felt* themselves to be 'happy';
they did not have to establish their happiness artificially by examining their enemies,
or to persuade themselves, *deceive* themselves, that they were happy (as all men of
ressentiment are in the habit of doing)."

whose occupation obliges them to travel constantly

1. Way of life; lifestyle

2. Municipal thoroughfare

3. Designated thruway for ambulatory leisure (as in a garden setting)

4. A directionality through the perceived quality of time (as in archeologists marching
at the head of phalanxes of highway builders)

5. Go around the border

Some of the book of the way and its virtue
seems to have been written by women
or at least the pronouns shift
such that the author or authors
deemed it important to express
philosophical ideas out of
and pertaining to what they might call today
the myriad genders

When traditional ways of knowing
(there's that word again)
do violence
then ignorance and stupidity become virtuous
unwise, unpowerful, certainly unmale reader, not seeking esoteric secrets, but
instead of listening for a voice that speaks to the soul
I propose knocking on the door at the gate of the hidden

*

The performance artist's song:
Look in the mirror   how
can you look at yourself
in the mirror   impossible
to roll your eyes back in
to your head and look at yourself
looking is always at, across, beyond
strive for a tender and discerning eye
when the person in the mirror isn't
you can choose to create a threshold
and cross it

The interlocutor's song:
Transitory phase phase of insipid transgression
what kind of human fails the mirror test
you imagine yourself a kind of mother
in that you get to name and ride around

Just because that's the way you can go
doesn't mean it's the real way

*

The road is littered with phorias. In this instance, read well-born as cisgendered.
On the way you fall in love with the 'wrong person' and a priest will tell you about
buttocks next to buttocks and revile this. A bearing, state or tendency towards:

failing

losing

forgetting

unmaking

undoing

unbecoming

not knowing

violating

mutuality

collectivity

plasticity

diversity

adaptability

illegibility

A prologue proceeds a legible text
fourteen lines out of the ten thousand things
in fair Verona where we lay our scene
the two houses represent gender as a bipolar schema
alike in dignity according to official mouthpieces
the *mise-en-scène* is foes and loins and blood
and death and civil hands unclean and parents' strife
and grudge and mutiny and parents' rage
trans characters whose lot is farce and death
whose life, work, love and preferred presentation is vexed
disallowed to live to full fruition, death is still
the door to the mystery of mystery, hidden because suppressed
let mending and children remain associated
in a new prologue of unspecified meter and length

Suck the smell of the sun from *textos* or Chance Encounters #2

How shall I live?

Books, tellings, anything.
What you cooked.
Who you made love with.
How you wrote the word for tree.

She wavered atop the narrow line that divided one possibility from the other, but in the end fell to neither side, beyond the window's rose, where my eye just came untied—

But perhaps Goddesses like to use castaway objects, waste, rejects.

Divers failures to fit personality in envelopes of rigidity
The sun rose undetected behind the sculpted clouds, the air humid in the eucalyptus grove
and the original world-making power degenerates
into a prototype to be copied and imitated, intombing Cupid
with sad obsequies.

You are he who felled by a tree deducts the maxims of Pragmatism
Blunt the sharpness;
Untangle the knots;
Soften the glare.

What a lot of texts we could quote which tell that the eyes are a center of light, a little
human sun—
We must therefore qualify what has been suggested above and show that neither the
king of justice nor the poet is purely and simply a master of truth.

If I could spill my blood red or marshall a blue
let the old man die,
the eye, dark as a tabernacle window
take up his dagger, and kill him there

Preliminaries consist of such eternity:
A demon blows out the candle, perhaps with bellows,
and an angel relights it,

Exiled from her own days, it seemed to her that the people in the streets were
vulnerable, that
she would not find in the stone-in-movement everything that she knew
in other ways
about
the stone.

Suck the smell of the sun from *textos* or Chance Encounters #3

Where do I go from here?

The most submissive thing in the world can ride roughshod over the hardest in the
world
Growth—heart wall upon heart wall, adding petals to it

I am the one who keeps the gates
it was just that, at that time, my body experienced this violent, irrepressible hunger

too soon you think yourself exempt from our lesser magic,
love's exquisite revel, that poses a new, difficult problem, that
of establishing or maintaining the harmony of their double
gender in each of the new partners

I admit that you may have succeeded in bringing a heavenly maiden down from the
sky with your music, but when did you ever do anything important enough to win the
hand of an Emperor's daughter?

Such was the rippling of the holy stream,
clay works the cooking arts language:
it is not a form that has much suited English poets,
too stingy to turn on the heat.

The impious history of sensation
as the Greeks understood it, as I understand
the performative efficacy of the word of faith

I'm interested in old things. Old words, old ways,
since the inscribing hand lost life—
upon the engraving of her Name upon a Tree

And that it cost them something this ensuing history will declare.
Our love should stretch as widely across all space, as
the sound of our laughing inside the bus.

Poetics Statement

Strictly formal considerations aside, I think my poetics at the moment can be distilled
into two basic principles:

1. To go towards the site(s) of my confusion, fear, anger and abide there.

2. My personal take on negative capability, which is perhaps a subset of the first principle.

"History may be written by the victors, but literature belongs to the losers." Did Someone write that? I guess I just did. I've always been confused and fascinated by quotes— losers, too. It's a commonplace that all language is quotation. Is it any less true that gender is? It scared me (and sometimes still does) that the best I can aspire to with respect to my presentation is a counterfeit femininity. I wasn't born with XX chromosomes, wasn't raised female. As a woman, I'm a born failure. But how does this shape my writing?

For starters, it's one of the most important aspects of my life that gender touches. Important because it seems so malleable. Despite, or perhaps, because of the relentless deconstruction and reconstruction of the verbal markers of gender identity which take place BY THE MINUTE in my mind, I know this much: I couldn't and can't write as a man.

By happenstance, proclivity and profession, I've been in an avant-garde or experimental writing community of one kind or another since I came to poetry in high school. According to wikipedia (an unauthorized and therefore dangerous source for quotation), negative capability, "...describes the capacity of human beings to reject the totalizing constraints of a closed context, and to both experience phenomenon free from any epistemological bounds as well as to assert their own will and individuality upon their activity." There is a kind of paradoxically constrained and totalizing antipathy in the aforementioned community as I've experienced it towards the articulation of subjecthood unless the articulation (perhaps of a new or long suppressed or colonized identity) is suppressed— lost— in favor of group think or encouraged as tokenism.

In the long period preceding my very recent embarkation on the journey towards transitioning, I have dreamed and hoped and despaired but also read. Despite postmodernism, the death of the author, etc. why does it nonetheless feel so necessary to read trans authors? I don't know the answer, but I intend to keep writing to "assert my will and individuality" upon the activity of my writing and my life. I can actually conjure a fairly typical spiel with points about my poetics and my influences, but in this context it feels important to shout from this lovely rooftop: trans and genderqueer comrades, let your voices be heard.

Bios & Acknowledgments

Ahimsa Timoteo Bodhrán was born in the South Bronx to a multigenerational mixed-blood familia (Kanien´kehaka, Onondowaga, Puerto Rican, Irish, and German/Moroccan Jewish). One of the founding organizers of Tranny Fest: Transgender & Transgenre Film & Cultural Festival in San Francisco, he was the opening poet for Trans World II: The 2nd Annual Transgender People of Color Conference, organized by the Audre Lorde Project. Bodhrán is the author of *Antes y después del Bronx: Lenapehoking* (New American Press) and the editor of an international queer Indigenous issue of *Yellow Medicine Review: A Journal of Indigenous Literature, Art, and Thought*. Acknowledgments: "Cycle undone" previously appeared in *Yellow Medicine Review*. "Mint" previously appeared in *Mizna*. Author photo is a self portrait.

Aimee Herman is a queer performance poet. Her work can be read in *Lavender Review, Sous Le Paves, Cake Train*, and *InStereo Press*. Her full length book of poetry, *to go without blinking* was recently published by BlazeVOX books. She can be found writing poems on her body in Brooklyn or at: aimeeherman.wordpress.com. Acknowledgments: The poems "i/dentity (packed)," "to soften," "Square Root of Menstruation," and "He gave her a quarter to cite a dirty word: man," previously appeared in *to go without blinking*. Author photo by Jun Liu.

Amir Rabiyah lives in Oakland, California. His work has been featured in *Mizna, 580 Split, Left Turn Magazine, Gender Outlaws: The Next Generation, Collective Brightness: LGBTIQ Poets on Faith, Religion and Spirituality, the Asian American Literary Review* and more. In 2012, he was an artist in residence at the Kimmel Harding Nelson Center for the Arts and was selected as a finalist in the Enizagam Literary Award in Poetry. Amir's hobbies include cooking, music, fashion, film, reading, gardening and channelling the powers of his inner (not so inner) diva to spread sweetness in the world. www.amirrabiyah.com. Author photo by Rostam.

Ari Banias grew up in Los Angeles, El Paso, and outside Chicago. His poems have appeared in *Subtropics, Gulf Coast, Cincinnati Review, EOAGH*, in the chapbook *What's Personal is Being Here with all of You* (Portable Press @ Yo-Yo Labs), and elsewhere. He is the recipient of awards & fellowships from NYFA, Headlands Center for the Arts, the Bread Loaf Writers' Conference, the Fine Arts Work Center in Provincetown, the Wisconsin Institute for Creative Writing, and others. Acknowledgments: "who is ghost" first appeared in MiPOesias online (Spring 2007). "Exquisite Corpse" first appeared in *Gulf Coast* (Winter/Spring 2013). "Narrative" first appeared in *Sycamore Review* (Winter/Spring 2012). "The Hole" was the regional winner of the 2012 Cultural Center of Cape Cod Poetry Competition and first appeared on their website. "Solve for X" first appeared in *DIAGRAM* (Winter 2013). "At Any Given Moment," "Here's the Story on Being," "The Hole," "Narrative," and "who is ghost" previously appeared in *What's Personal is Being Here With All of You* (Portable Press @ Yo-Yo Labs, 2012). Author photo by Solmaz Sharif.

Ariel Goldberg writes poety and criticism on photography and other things. Recent publications include *Picture Cameras* (NoNo Press, 2010), *The Photographer without a Camera* (Trafficker, 2011), and *The Estrangement Principle* (selections in Aufgabe 11 & *The Volta: Evening will Come*). Acknowledgments: The Poems on pages 71-72 appeared in *The Photographer without a Camera* in 2011 (Edited by Andrew Kenower & Erin Morrill) and "Confessional Press Conference" appeared in *Saginaw*, a zine (Edited by David Horton) in June 2012. Author photo by unknown.

Bo Luengsuraswat is an interdisciplinary artist, writer, and activist currently based in Los Angeles. He received a B.A. in Visual Studies from California College of the Arts and an M.A. in Asian American Studies from UCLA. Bo's writing and artwork appear in *nineteen sixty nine: an ethnic studies journal; Uproot: Queer Voices on Migration, Immigration, Displacement, & Diaspora* (zine); *Gender Outlaws: The Next Generation; Contemporary Asian America: A Multidisciplinary Reader* (Second Edition); and *Dreamers Adrift (*http://dreamersadrift.com). His visual, performance, and multimedia work has been exhibited in various venues including Fresh Meat in the Gallery, the National Queer Arts Festival, the San Francisco Transgender Film Festival, and Gender Reel. Author photo by Marissa Medina.

CAConrad is the author of *A BEAUTIFUL MARSUPIAL AFTERNOON: New (Soma)tics* (Wave Books, 2012), *The Book of Frank* (Wave Books, 2010), *Advanced Elvis Course* (Soft Skull Press, 2009), *Deviant Propulsion* (Soft Skull Press, 2006), and a collaboration with poet Frank Sherlock titled *The City Real & Imagined* (Factory School, 2010). He is a 2011 Pew Fellow, and a 2012 Ucross Fellow. He is the editor of the online video poetry journals JUPITER 88 and Paranormal Poetics. Visit him online at http://CAConrad.blogspot.com Acknowledgements: "it's too late for careful" previously appeared in *Occupy Wall Street Anthology*. Author photo is a self portrait.

Ching-In Chen is author of *The Heart's Traffic* and co-editor of *The Revolution Starts at Home: Confronting Intimate Violence Within Activist Communities*. A Kundiman and Lambda Fellow, they belong to Macondo, Voices of Our Nations Arts Foundation and Theatrical Jazz writing communities. Ching-In has been awarded fellowships from Soul Mountain Retreat, Virginia Center for the Creative Arts, Millay Colony, and the Norman Mailer Center. They have worked in San Francisco, Oakland, Riverside and Boston Asian American communities. In Milwaukee, they are *Cream City Review*'s editor-in-chief. www.chinginchen.com Author photo by Sarah Grant.

Cole Krawitz is a writer and poet whose work has been widely published, including in *LOCUSPOINT, Tidal Basin Review, Connotation Press, Newsday, The Forward*, and more. He's performed his work throughout the Bay Area and beyond, including at Lit Crawl, the Museum of Performance & Design, the James C. Hormel Gay & Lesbian Center at the San Francisco Public Library, Bay Area Poetry Marathon, and the National Queer Arts Festival. Cole has been awarded residencies and fellowships from the Virginia Center for the Creative Arts (VCCA), the Lambda Literary Foundation and Makor/92nd Street Y. He's also been a Lecturer at June Jordan's Poetry for the People Program at UC Berkeley and the MA in English Program at Holy Names University. He loves olallieberry pie, coffee toffee ice cream, bananagrams, and spending time with his niece and nephew. Acknowledgments: "The Sound of Aleph" and "in and out of the holy" were previously published in *Tidal Basin Review* (Spring 2011).

D'Lo is a queer Tamil Sri L.A.nkan-American, political theatre artist/writer, director, comedian and music producer. He has performed and/or facilitated performance and writing workshops extensively (US, Canada, UK, Germany, Sri Lanka and India). D'Lo is also the creator of the "Coming Out, Coming Home" writing workshop series which have taken place with South Asian and/or Immigrant Queer Organizations nationally (LA, NY and SF). His work has been published in various anthologies and academic journals, most recently: *Close too Close –South Asian Queer Erotica Anthology* (Tranquebar Press 2012), *Experiments in a Jazz Aesthetic* (University of Texas Press Austin 2009), and *Desi Rap: South Asian Americans in Hip Hop* (Lexington Press 2008). www.dlocokid.com Author photo by Sabelo Narasimhan.

A former union organizer and performing artist, **David Wolach** is founding editor of *Wheelhouse Magazine & Press* and has been an active Nonsite Collective. Wolach's first full-length collection, *Occultations*, was published by Black Radish Books (2010, 2011). And Wolach's new book of poems and essay, *Hospitalogy*, is due out from Tarpaulin Sky Press in early 2013. Other books include the multi-media transliteration plus chapbook, *Prefab Eulogies Volume 1: Nothings Houses* (BlazeVox [books], 2010), and book *alter(ed)*(Ungovernable Press, 2009). Recent critical work on embodiment, disablement, and gender, appears in or is forthcoming from *Jacket, Augfabe, P-Queue, Try Magazine* and the recent anthology *Beauty Is A Verb: The New Poetry of Disability* (Cinco Puntos Press). Wolach is professor of text arts, poetics, and aesthetics at The Evergreen State College, and is visiting faculty at Bard College's Workshop In Language & Thinking. Acknowledgments: "Poetry Slam: Cardiovascular Unit vs. Oncology Ward," "Complicit in the Shakedown," and "Tide's Haiti" previously appeared in *Hospitalogy*. Author photo by Elizabeth Williamson.

Dawn Lundy Martin is the author of *A Gathering of Matter / A Matter of Gathering* (University of Georgia Press 2007); *DISCIPLINE* (Nightboat Books, 2011), which was a finalist for both Los Angeles Times Book Prize and the Lambda Literary Award; and *Candy*, a limited edition letterpress chapbook (Albion Books 2011). She is a member the experimental black poetry and performance group, the Black Took Collective, and Assistant Professor of English at the University of Pittsburgh. Acknowledgments: "Dear one, the sea smells of nostalgia" previously appeared in

Mandorla. "After Drowning" previously appeared in *A Gathering of Matter / A Matter of Gathering*. Author photo by Stephanie K. Hopkins.

Drew Krewer is the author of the chapbook *Ars Warholica* (Spork Press, 2010). He is founder and co-editor of *The Destroyer*, a biannual online publication of text, art, and public opinion. He currently resides in Los Angeles, CA." Acknowledgments: "It Could Be Anything You Want Me to Be" previously appeared in *Trickhouse*. Author photo by Lily House-Peters.

Duriel E. Harris is the author of *Drag* (Elixir Press, 2003), *Amnesiac: Poems* (Sheep Meadow Press, 2010), and *Speleology* (2011) a collaboration with video artist Scott Rankin. A poet, performer, and sound artist whose work has been featured and published internationally, Harris is a member of Douglas Ewart and Inventions jazz ensemble and co-founder of Black Took Collective. Current undertakings include the AMNESIAC media art project and "Thingification," a solo play in one act. Harris is an associate professor of English and teaches creative writing, literature and poetics at Illinois State University. www.durielharris.com Acknowledgments: Excerpts from "speleology" ("pulling up into," "a woman's voice," "The fool," and "Discreet fragments"), "self portrait with body" and "Portrait" previously appeared in *Amnesiac: Poems* (Sheep Meadow Press). "pulling up into" and "self portrait with body" also previously appeared in *Shampoo* and *Mixed Blood*, respectively. Author photo by Gina Sandrzyk.

EC Crandall's poems and essays have been published in *PANK*, *Jupiter 88*, *Gay Shame*, and *The Trans Literary Reader*. Crandall is co-author of the satiric novel *Executive Privilege*, and teaches in the University Writing Program at Columbia University. Author photo by Diana Cage.

Eileen Myles (b. 1949, lives in New York): American poet, writer-performer, 2012 Guggenheim fellow, 2010 recipient of the PSA's Shelley Prize (2010), Creative Capital/Warhol foundation art writers' grant (2007), author of 18 books including *Snowflake/different streets* (Wave Books, 2012), *Inferno* (a poet's novel), (or books, 2010), winner of Lambda lesbian fiction award, *Cool For You* (Soft Skull, 2000), *Skies* (poems), Black Sparrow, 2000, *Chelsea Girls* (Black Sparrow, 1994), Not Me (poems) (Semiotext(e) 1990. Contributes poems articles and reviews to *Bookforum, the Believer, Vice, Parkett, Tin House, Best American Poetry 2010, Harpers, Brooklyn Rail, EOAGH, Occupy Wallstreet Poetry* anthology among other publications. Acknowledgments: "15 Minutes" previously appeared in *Snowflake/different Streets*. Author photo by Leopoldine Core.

White, disabled, and genderqueer, **Eli Clare** rabble rouses and writes in the Green Mountains of Vermont. He is the author of a book of essays *Exile and Pride: Disability, Queerness, and Liberation* (South End Press) and a book of poetry *The Marrow's Telling: Words in Motion* (Homofactus Press). Among other pursuits, he has walked across to US for peace, helped organize possibly the first-ever Queerness and Disability Conference, and coordinated a rape prevention program. You can find him on the Web at www. eliclare.com. Acknowledgments: "The Terrorist God, " "And Yet," "No Longer Small and Lonely," and "Arriving" previously appeared in *The Marrow's Telling*. Author photo by Samuel Lurie.

Ely Shipley's first book, *Boy with Flowers*, won the 2007 Barrow Street Press book prize judged by Carl Phillips, the 2009 Thom Gunn Award, and was a Lambda Literary Award finalist. His poems and lyric essays appear in *the Western Humanities Review, Prairie Schooner, Fugue, Gulf Coast, Phoebe, Greensboro Review, Painted Bride Quarterly, Hayden's Ferry Review, Diagram, Barrow Street, Third Coast*, and elsewhere. He holds a PhD in Literature and Creative Writing from the University of Utah and currently teaches literature and writing at Baruch College-CUNY. Acknowledgments: "Six," "Boy with Flowers," "Encounter," "Etymology," "In the Film," and "Dear C.—" previously appeared in *Boy with Flowers*. "Post-Inversion Vision" and "Night a ladder we climb to reach" were previously published in *Lo-Ball*. "Deer between fallen branches" was published on *Rumpus.net* for National Poetry Month in 2011. Author photo by Claire Ratinon.

Emerson Whitney is focused on gender variance and literary liberation. He is a writer, artist, and reporter who has published work for *the Huffington Post, New York Observer, Work Magazine,*and a variety of other publications. He is also Editor-in-Chief of *Wild Gender* magazine and is a Masters in Fine Arts candidate at the California Institute of the Arts with aspirations to facilitate art making and creative writing in communities of queer youth and otherwise. Author photo by Jason Rodgers.

Eric Karin is a recent graduate of the Creative Writing Program at the University of Alabama. E's work has appeared in public toilets across the US and Canada. Author photo by Sushuma Thornburgh.

Fabian Romero is a Queer Chicano poet, performance artist and community organizer. They co-founded several writing and performance groups including Hijas de Su Madre, Las Mamalogues and Mixed Messages: Stories by People of Color. Their sincere poetry and stories arise from their experience as an Economic Refugee, speaking two languages, queerness, gender-queer identity, brown skin, time as a migrant worker and childhood in poverty. Currently they are the Co-Director of Education at Bent Writing Institute and are a pursuing their BA at Evergreen State College with a focus in writing, social justice and education. You can read more of Fabian's work at FabianRomero.tumblr.com and contact them at FabiOrtizRomero@gmail.com. Author photo by Ngoc Tran. <http://sashimi-images.com/>

Gr Keer is a poet librarian living in Oakland, California. Gr prefers long walks on foggy beaches, awkward silences, big egos, and the pronoun "they." Their work has appeared in *Eclectic Muse: A Journal of Poetry/Prose/Art and Photography* (River Poets Anthology) and *poeticdiversity: the litzine of Los Angeles*. "who is a man," "hair," "connecting the dots," "where i'm from," and "crossing the line" appear in a chapbook titled *heterotextual*. Author Photo by Amelia Marzec.

HR Hegnauer is the author of *Sir* (Portable Press at Yo-Yo Labs, 2011). She is a freelance book designer and website designer specializing in working with independent publishers as well as individual artists and writers. HR has acted in two movies, is a member of the feminist publishing collaborative Belladonna*, and the poets' theater group GASP: Girls Assembling Something

Perpetual. She received her MFA in Writing & Poetics from Naropa University. HR maintains a portfolio of her work at www.hrhegnauer.com. Acknowledgments: "from *Sir*" previously appeared in the Portable Press chapbook. Author photo by David Quint for Naropa University.

Jordan Rice is author of the poetry collection *Constellarium*, and co-editor of the anthology *Voices of Transgender Parents* (Transgress Press, 2015). Her poems have been selected for the Indiana Review Poetry Prize, the Gulf Coast Poetry Prize, the Yellowwood Poetry Prize from Yalobusha Review, the Richard Peterson Poetry Prize from Crab Orchard Review, the Milton-Kessler Memorial Prize from Harpur Palate, and an AWP Intro Journals Award. Rice received an M.F.A. from Virginia Commonwealth University and a Ph.D. from Western Michigan University, where she served as Associate Editor for *New Issues Poetry & Prose* and as an Assistant Poetry Editor for *Third Coast*. She is currently an Executive Editor for *Dublin Poetry Review*. Author photo by Jordan Rice.

j/j hastain is the author of several cross-genre books including *long past the presence of common* (Say it with Stones Press), trans-genre book *libertine monk* (Scrambler Press) and anti-memoir *a vigorous* (Black Coffee Press / Eight Ball Press (forthcoming)). j/j has poetry, prose, reviews, articles, mini-essays and mixed genre work published in many places on line and in print. Acknowledgments: "Is a mistaken carcass a place for memory?" was previously published at Spuyten Duyvil. Author photo was a self-portrait.

Jaime Shearn Coan lives in Brooklyn, New York, teaches creative writing and literature at the City College of New York, and leads a long-standing writing workshop with LGBT elders through the NY Writers Coalition. His poems have appeared in several journals and his artist book, *dear someone*, the product of a collaborative queer letter-writing project, is distributed through Printed Matter. A 2012 Poets House Emerging Poets Fellow, Jaime has been awarded residencies at the Virginia Center for the Creative Arts and Saltonstall Arts Colony. Acknowledgments: "Ceremony, Late September" and "that lonely vibration so familiar to young boys" previously appeared in *LES Review*. "Circulation" previously appeared in *Drunken Boat*. "Blue" previously appeared in *The Portland Review*. "Palm Springs: Reina de la Noche" previously appeared in *glitter tongue*. Author photo by Rachel Eliza Griffiths.

Jake Pam Dick (aka Traver Pam Dick, Mina Pam Dick et al.) is a writer, translator and artist living in New York City. Herhis prose poetry has appeared in *BOMB, The Brooklyn Rail, Aufgabe, EOAGH, Everyday Genius, The Recluse, Matrix* and *Fence*. Hisher translations, co-translations and transpositions can be found in *Telephone* and *Dandelion*. Dick's first book, *Delinquent*, was published by Futurepoem in 2009. Currently, she is doing work that makes out and off with Hölderlin, Trakl, Lenz, Büchner and Robert Walser. Acknowledgments: A previous version of a portion of this section from *Lens* was published in *Delinquent*. Author photo by Oana Avasilichioaei.

Jay Besemer's most recent poetry collections are A New Territory Sought (Moria) and Aster to Daylily (Damask Press). As Jen Besemer, he also authored Telephone (Brooklyn Arts Press), Quiet

Vertical Movement (Beard of Bees) and Object with Man's Face (Rain Taxi Ohm Editions). Jay writes critical texts for a number of publications and is a teaching artist at Chicago's Spudnik Press Cooperative. Follow him on Twitter @divinetailor. poems and hybrids have been exhibited, performed and published in many places and contexts. Author photo by Jay Besemer, 2014.

Jenny Johnson's poems have appeared in *The Best American Poetry 2012, EOAGH, The Southern Review, The Beloit Poetry Journal,* and *Blackbird.* She was the recipient of the 2011 Chad Walsh Poetry Prize, a scholarship to the Bread Loaf Writer's Conference, as well as a residency at the Kimmel Harding Nelson Center for the Arts. Currently, she is a Lecturer at the University of Pittsburgh. Acknowledgments: "Tail" previously appeared in *The Collagist.* Author photo by Brooke Wyatt.

John Wieners (1934-2002) was born in Milton, Mass. Wieners received his A.B. from Boston College in 1954 and studied at Black Mountain College under Charles Olson and Robert Duncan from 1955 to 1956. He returned to Boston where he brought out three issues of a literary magazine, Measure, over the next several years. From 1958 to 1960 he was an active participant in the San Francisco Poetry Renaissance movement. He returned to Boston in 1960, and divided his time between there and New York City, over the next five years. In 1965 he enrolled in the Graduate Program at the State University of New York at Buffalo, and worked as a teaching fellow. He worked as an actor and stage manager at the Poet's Theatre, Cambridge, and had three of his plays performed at the Judson Poet's Theater, N.Y. From 1970 onwards he lived and worked in Boston, where he was active in publishing and education cooperatives, political action committees, and the gay liberation movement. Acknowledgments: "Understood Disbelief in Paganism, Lies and Heresy," "Signs of the President Machine," "Maria Gouverneur," "Gardenias," "To Billie Holiday's If I Were You" and "Tashi" previously appeared in B*ehind the State Capitol, or Cincinnati Pike (*Good Gay Poets*).* "Casual Love" previously appeared in *Ace of Pentacles* (Wilson & Carr). "To H." previously appeared in *Cultural Affairs in Boston* (Black Sparrow). Author photo by Allen Ginsberg.

Joy Ladin, Gottesman Professor of English at Yeshiva University, is author of six poetry books: *The Definition of Joy*; Forward Fives Award winner *Coming to Life*; Lambda Literary Award finalist *Transmigration*; *Psalms*; *The Book of Anna*; and *Alternatives to History*. Her memoir of transition, Forward Fives Award winner *Through the Door of Life: A Jewish Journey Between Genders*, was published in 2012. Acknowledgments: "Filibustiere" was previously published in *Educe.* "Trans Poetics Manifesto" was written for and presented at the *TENDENCIES: Poetics & Practice* talks series, curated by Tim Trace Peterson, at CUNY Graduate Center in NYC on October 20, 2011. Author photo by Liz Denlinger.

Julian Talamantez Brolaski is the author of *Advice for Lovers* (City Lights 2012) *gowanus atropolis* (Ugly Duckling Presse 2011) and co-editor of *NO GENDER: Reflections on the Life & Work of kari edwards* (Litmus Press / Belladonna Books 2009). Julian lives in Brooklyn where xe is an editor at Litmus Press and plays country music with Juan & the Pines <www.reverbnation.com/juanandthepines> New work is on the blog *hermofwarsaw*. Author photo by Jack Louth.

kari edwards (1954-2006) was one of Small Press Traffic's books of the year award winners (2004) and recipient of New Langton Art's Bay Area Award in literature (2002). edwards is author of *bharat jiva*, Litmus Press (2009); *having been blue for charity*, Blazevox (2007); *obedience*, Factory School (2005); *iduna*, O Books (2003), *a day in the life of p.* , subpress collective (2002), *a diary of lies* - Belladonna #27 by Belladonna Books (2002), and *post/(pink)* Scarlet Press (2000). edwards' work can also be found in *Scribner's The Best American Poetry* (2004), *Bay Poetics*, Faux Press, (2006), *Civil Disobediences: Poetics and Politics in Action*, Coffee House Press, (2004), *Biting the Error: Writers Explore Narrative*, Coach House, Toronto, (2004), *Bisexuality and Transgenderism: InterSEXions of the Others*, Hawoth Press, Inc. (2004), *Experimental Theology*, Public Text 0.2., Seattle Research Institute (2003), *Blood and Tears: Poems for Matthew Shepard*, Painted Leaf Press (2000). Acknowledgments: "good questions..." was originally published in *having been blue for charity* (Blazevox). "from *obedience*" was originally published in *obedience* (Factory School). "subject: statement" was originally published as kari edwards' editorial statement for *EOAGH* Issue 3: Queering Language. Author photo by Fran Blau.

Kit Yan is a queer Asian American slam poet from Hawaii. Kit has toured with Sister Spit, The Tranny Roadshow, Doctor Brown's Travelling Poetry show, and the Lizard Lounge slam team. He spends much of his year on the road touring, lives in Brooklyn, NY, and goes home to Hawaii as often as possible. This is his first appearance in an anthology. Author photo by Thomas Bugarin.

Laura Neuman is a poet and sometimes a performing artist and lives in Seattle. She/xe was a long-time performer and co-conspirator with The Workshop for Potential Movement. She is the author of a chapbook, *The Busy Life* (Gazing Grain Press, 2012). Some of hir poems can be found in *The Brooklyn Rail, EOAGH, Tinge, OmniVerse* and *Fact-Simile*. Acknowledgments: Versions of all of these poems appear in *The Busy Life* and many thanks are due to the editors of *Gazing Grain Press*. "storm clouds will poison you" and "new human substance" previously appeared in *EOAGH*. "second attempt" and "everybody" previously appeared in *The Brooklyn Rail*. "phase diagram" is forthcoming from Peradem Books. Author photo courtesy of the author.

Lilith Latini is a trans woman living in Western North Carolina. As yet unpublished in print, she currently writes a blog at twistingseams.wordpress.com. She spends much of her time searching for the perfect pumps to take her next steps in. Author photo by Peter Thompson.

Lizz Bronson is a spoken word performer who lives in the San Francisco area. Her work has appeared in *New Verse News, Poydras Review*, and other publications. Lizz believes that poems have the power to transform and revive the spirit, while being the incantation that guides us home when we are lost. Acknowledgments: "The Year You Bloom" previously appeared in *Haven: A Journal*. Author photo is a self portrait.

Lori Selke grew up in Michigan and is now raising twins in a three-parent household in Oakland, California. Lori's erotic fiction is widely published and has recently been collected in "Lost Girls and Others" from Renaissance e-Books. She is the co-curator of Perverts Put Out!, the notorious San Francisco spoken-word series. Lori can't decide on a gender or a pronoun: she, s/he, they, butch, pirate, genderfuckable. Favorite quiz answer: All of the Above. Lori loves silent movies, home cooking, tattoos, and orange cheddar. Author photo by Marlo Gayle.

Max Wolf Valerio is a poet and long transitioned man whose work includes: a poetry chapbook, Animal Magnetism (eg press, 1984), and a mysterious, unpublished manuscript of poems The Criminal which somehow wandered into the Stanford University Library; essays in: This Bridge We Call Home: Radical Visions for Transformation (Routledge), This Bridge Called My Back, (SUNY Press). Also, The Testosterone Files (Seal Press), a 2006 Lambda finalist, a memoir mixing testosterone, punk rock, and sexual politics. Max collaborated with photographer Dana Smith in 2010, adding poetry fragments to a triptych of art books: Mission Mile Trilogy +1. His poetry blog: http://hypotenusewolf.wordpress.com/ Author photo by Anja Weber (c) 2007.

Meg Day is a 2013 recipient of a National Endowment for the Arts Fellowship in Poetry, three-time Pushcart-nominated poet, nationally awarded spoken word artist, & veteran arts educator who is currently a PhD fellow in Poetry & Disability Poetics at the University of Utah. Meg hails from Oakland where she taught young poets to hold their own at the mic with YouthSpeaks & as a WritersCorps Teaching Artist in San Francisco. A 2010 Lambda Fellow, 2011 Hedgebrook Fellow, & 2012 Squaw Valley Fellow, Meg completed her MFA at Mills College & publishes the femme ally zine, *ON OUR KNEES* out of Salt Lake City. Meg's most recent work is forthcoming from *This Assignment is So Gay: Poems from LGBTQ Teachers* & in the chapbook, *When All You Have is a Hammer,* planned for publication in 2013 by Gertrude Press. www.megday.com. Acknowledgments: "i am not deaf" & "forget everything you know about the way a body is built" were previously published in *WITH+STAND*. Author photo by David Daniels.

Micha Cárdenas is an artist/theorist who works at the intersections of bodies, technology, movement, and politics. They are a PhD student in Media Arts and Practice (iMAP) at University of Southern California and a member of Electronic Disturbance Theater 2.0. Micha's project Local Autonomy Networks was selected for the 2012 ZERO1 Biennial in San Jose and was the subject of their keynote performance at the 2012 Allied Media Conference. Micha's book *The Transreal: Political Aesthetics of Crossing Realities,* published by Atropos Press in 2012, discusses art that uses augmented, mixed and alternate reality, and the intersection of those strategies with the politics of gender, in a transnational context. Micha holds an MFA from University of California, San Diego, an MA in Communication from the European Graduate School and a BS in Computer Science from Florida International University. They blog at transreal.org and tweet at @michacardenas. Acknowledgments: the sections in this anthology from "Becoming Transreal" were previously published by Atropos Press. The photo in this anthology, taken by Tracy Cornish, features (from left to right) Micha Cárdenas and Elle Mehrmand

Nico Peck's work has recently appeared in *With+Stand, La Fovea, Mrs. Maybe*, and the chapbooks *The Pyrrhaiad* (Trafficker Press) and Bower to Bower (Neo-Baroque Press). Peck lives in San Francisco and teaches at San Jose State. Acknowledgments: the sections from "Bower to Bower" that appear in this anthology originally appeared in the Neo-Baroque Press chapbook Author photo by Heather Pugh.

Natro is a xican@ rappero from the 'border' lands of Arizona. He is an MC by nature and uses Hip Hop and spoken word as a means to inspire the heart and mind and mobilize! He is a masculine female-born gender resister down to bang on the colonial system by existing true to his creation. Author photo taken from a video that originally appeared in *Trickhouse*.

Oliver Bendorf is currently the Martha Meier-Renk Distinguished Graduate Fellow in Poetry at the University of Wisconsin-Madison, where he edits *Devil's Lake*. His poems have been published in or are forthcoming from *Best New Poets 2012, Indiana Review, Ninth Letter, Redivider*, and elsewhere. Acknowledgments: "Split it Open Just to Count the Pieces" and "Outing, Iowa" were previously published in *Drunken Boat*. "Prelude" was previously published in *The Journal*. "I Promised Her My Hands Wouldn't Get Any Larger" was previously published in *Ninth Letter* and *Best New Poets 2012*. "Call Her Vincent" was previously published in *Quarterly West*. Author photo by Coco O'Connor.

Reba Overkill is a loud queer currently located in Fountain Valley, California. Their primary partner in crime is their fiancee, a queer trans woman novelist and lyricist named Kayla. The two spend their days writing, playing video games, and publically horrifying at least a few heteronormative people every day. Feel free to contact them at unlikelyandco@gmail.com with any questions, concerns, or general words that you want them to read and reply to. Author photo by Kayla Overkill.

Samuel Ace is the author of *Normal Sex* (Firebrand), *Home in three days. Don't wash.* (Hard Press), and *Stealth* (with poet Maureen Seaton - Chax Press). He is a recipient of a New York Foundation for the Arts grant, two-time finalist for a Lambda Literary Award in Poetry, winner of the Astraea Lesbian Writer's Fund Prize in Poetry, The Katherine Anne Porter Prize for Fiction and the Firecracker Alternative Book Award in Poetry. He was also a 2012 finalist for the National Poetry Series. His work has appeared most recently in *EOAGH, Spiral Orb, Rhino, 3:am, Everyday Genius, The Volta*, and other publications. He lives in Tucson, AZ and Truth or Consequences, NM. Acknowledgments: "Secret 8" and "Secret 26" were previously published in *Stealth* (Chax Press). "February," "Solitary Confinement," and "Witness Protection" previously appeared (in slightly different versions) - in *van Gogh's Ear*. An excerpt from "I met a man" appears in Ace's current collaboration with Seaton. "The Language of the Seeing the Language of the Blind" was written for and presented at the *TENDENCIES: Poetics & Practice* talks series, curated by Tim Trace Peterson, at CUNY Graduate Center in NYC on November 22, 2011. Author photo by Matthew Blank.

Stacey Waite is Assistant Professor of English at the University of Nebraska—Lincoln. S/he has published three award-winning collections of poems: *Choke* (winner of the 2004 Frank O'Hara Prize), *Love Poem to Androgyny* (winner of the 2006 Main Street Rag Chapbook Competition), and *the lake has no saint* (winner of the 2008 Snowbound Poetry Prize from Tupelo Press). Additional publications, interviews, and biographical information can be accessed at www. staceywaite.com. Acknowledgments: "The Kind of Man I Am at the DMV" previously appeared in the *Columbia Poetry Review*. "On the Occasion of Being Mistaken for a Woman by a Therapist in the South Hills" previously appeared in *The Rattling Wall*. "Letter from Thomas Beattie to the Media" previously appeared in *Bloom*. Waite's most recent poetry collection is entitled *Butch Geography* (Tupelo Press, 2013).

Stephen Burt is Professor of English at Harvard; Stephen's books of poetry and prose about poetry include *Parallel Play* (2006), *Close Calls with Nonsense* (2009), and Belmont, forthcoming from Graywolf in 2013. Acknowledgments: "So Let Am Not," "Rue," "For Avril Lavigne," and "Fictitious Girl Raised by Cats" will appear in *Belmont*. Author photo by Alex Dakoulas.

TC Tolbert is a genderqueer, feminist poet and teacher committed to social justice. TC earned his MFA in Poetry from The University of Arizona in 2005 where s/he is currently an Adjunct Instructor. S/he is the Assistant Director of Casa Libre en la Solana where s/he directs Made for Flight, a youth empowerment program to commemorate victims of transphobia. TC also leads wilderness trips for Outward Bound. S/he has two chapbooks, *spirare* (Belladonna* 2012) and *territories of folding* (Kore Press 2011) and his first full length collection, *Gephyromania*, is forthcoming from Ahsahta Press. www.tctolbert.com. Acknowledgments: "from *territories of folding*" was first published as part of a chapbook under the same title by Kore Press. Author photo by Samuel Ace.

Trace Peterson is a trans woman poet critic. Her first book of poems, *Since I Moved In*, won the Gil Ott Award from Chax Press in 2007 (selected by Nathaniel Mackey, Myung Mi Kim, Eli Goldblatt, and Charles Alexander). Peterson is Editor/Publisher of *EOAGH* and Co-editor (with Gregory Laynor) of the forthcoming *Gil Ott: Collected Writings*. She has also published essays, criticism, and poems in *TSQ: Transgender Studies Quarterly*, *Leonardo Electronic Almanac*, *Electronic Book Review*, *Harvard Review*, *Transgender Tapestry*, and several edited collections. From 2009-2012, Peterson curated the *TENDENCIES: Poetics & Practice* talks series on queer poetics and the manifesto at CUNY Graduate Center. She currently serves on the Board of Directors for VIDA. Acknowledgments: "from *Trans Figures*" and "from *Spontaneous Generation*" previously appeared in *Since I Moved In* (Chax Press). "The Valleys Are So Lush and Steep" previously appeared in *The Ashbery Home School Gallery*. Author photo by Danya Shneyer.

Trish Salah is a lecturer at the Ontario Institute for Studies in Education, at the University of Toronto, and an adjunct professor of Women's and Gender Studies at the University of Saskatchewan. Her writing appears in recent issues of *Feminist Studies, Cordite Poetry Review*, and *No More Potlucks*, and it is forthcoming in the anthologies, *Contested Imaginaries* and *Féminismes électriques*. She is the author of *Wanting in Arabic* (Tsar Publications), and recently completed a new poetry manuscript entitled, *Lyric Sexology*. Acknowledgments: "Nervensprache" also appears in a recent issue of the *Journal of Medical Humanities*. Author photo by Kaspar Saxena.

TT Jax is a parent, partner, mixed-media artist, and writer currently living in the Pacific Northwest by way of 28 years in the Deep South. He blogs about homelessness, community, poverty, art, rape, and hand puppets at Glitter and Mold, <http://ttjax.wordpress.com/> Acknowledgments: "Lifestory" was previously published by *Mudluscious Press*. Author photo is a self portrait.

Y. Madrone finally lives at both a port and a land and they like it very much. They co-founded The Thank You Writers Reading Series to which you should come sometime. They have too many day jobs and inconsistently write for their blog, *Notes of a Compulsive Self-Disclosurist*. Read too much about them at: ymadrone.wordpress.com. Their poems can be found or are forthcoming in *Rhino, 580 Split, Weave Magazine, American Letters & Commentary, Columbia Poetry Review, Phantom Limb* and others. Acknowledgments: "listen, we are coming down to straighten everything out" previously appeared in *So to Speak*. "a chest is an embarrassment to have" previously appeared in *Handsome*. Author photo is a self-portait.

Yosmay del Mazo is a genderqueer Latina poet from Oakland, California. When not at the page s/he is identifying plants, powwow drumming or working with youth. It is through the VONA Voices and Mills MFA community that Yosmay has grown as a writer. Yosmay's poems have appeared in *Breadcrumb Scabs* and *Painted Bride Quarterly*. Author photo by SOMArts Cultural Center.

Zoe Tuck was in born in Austin, Texas and lives in Oakland. She is trading in the flannel straitjacket in favor of femme futurity. Her preoccupations include queer theory, tarot and philosophical taoism. As another gender, she worked at Small Press Distribution and curated Condensery Reading Series. Her work has been published in *Try!, Come Hither, Riot Ink, Mondo Bummer* and the anthology *The Seven S____est Stories About The Seven S____est Seas*. She is working on a manuscript entitled *Renata Descartes Dreamed of Attending High School*. She is the staff astrologer for timelessinfinitelight.com. Author photo by Brittany Billmeyer-Finn.

Editors' Acknowledgments

TC Tolbert:

At the root of gratitude is grace. I have not done anything special to deserve the encouragement, compassion, patience, and love of my family and friends, but they give it willingly, unendingly. Simply put, I am inordinately blessed by a higher power that I don't really understand. Grateful is not a word big enough.

Even when I drive my mom, Darline McGinnis, absolutely nuts, she's always got my back. She's the only person who ever stood outside a men's restroom and threatened to kick any man's ass in there who looked at me funny and she was the first person I ever heard ask God to help her change so that she could accept me better. Thank you, mom. I love you and I'm your biggest fan.

My sister, mirror, and confidant, Julie Tolbert, has never wavered in her support of who I am. From the time I came out as lesbian and she said, "Duh," to the first time she saw me after I'd been on testosterone for about a year and she said, "Oh, you are a lot cuter as a man!" her hilarious, tender, honest, brilliant perspective on the world is one I would not know how to live without. I would choose you as my sister again and again, Julio. Thank you, I love you.

No one has been more involved in the behind the scenes process of this book than Samuel Ace, my witness, mentor, friend. I am constantly humbled by Sam's wisdom, clarity, vulnerability, and support. I have leaned heavily on him. Thank you, Sam, for teaching me both the courage to trouble the lines and the courage to let go. I dedicate this book to you.

It is no exaggeration to say that my understanding of love, family, and joy has been completely rearranged by Jennifer Hoefle, JC Olson, Molly Cooney, Anne Iverson, Courtney and Jennifer Jones-Vanderleest, Kristen Nelson, and KT Stefanski. I am a better person because I know each of you and because I let you know me. It is a gift to be found. For the rest of my life, thank you.

For talking with me and walking beside me: Stephanie Balzer. Lisa O'Neill, Noah Saterstrom, Ben Johnson. Rae Strozzo. Jenna Orzel. Ian Ellasante. Amy Shiner. You each remind me of the value of a good, honest word.

Some people calm me down by their very existence. By the way they live and love, by what they see and how they have a way of saying things, writing them down. Frankie Rollins, Julia Gordon, Arianne Zwartjes, Cara Benson, Rebecca Brown, Jen Hofer, and Dean Spade, thank you.

Katherine Ferrier, The Architects, Kimi Eisele, Vicki Brown, Greg Colburn, Katie Rutterer, and Lisa Bowden have changed the trajectory of my life simply through the practice of attention, collaboration, and composition. What you have done to my heart by practicing the things you say. *We don't get rid of fear, we work with it. Become more of who you are. Love something absolutely. We are composing together. Let it change. Openopenopenopenopen…*

My chosen family may be flung far and wide but you each comprise the cornerstone of my heart. Melisa Bailey. Kate Poland. Deb Crippen, Lynn Menefee, and Kieran Hixon. Leslie Ashford. Robin Eaton. Crystal Baldridge. Thank you. I love you.

To my dad, David Tolbert, it makes all the difference in the world to have you in my life again. And Tim McGinnis, your quiet strength and steady love for me and our family do not go unnoticed. They are such a gift. Thank you both, I love you.

For reading, editing, and being the kind of cheering section that makes me want to kick that poem's ass (in a good way): Deborah Poe, Hannah Ensor, Kristi Maxwell. For brainstorming and enduring more texts about a title than anyone should ever have to: Liz Latty and Dawn Lundy Martin.

I would like to gratefully acknowledge Byrdcliffe Arts Colony, where I was offered space to write the introduction. There I was also given camaraderie and a place among the sticks and leaves. To my fellow residents: as JP says, *I'll take you home, don't walk alone…*a special thank you to Renay Egami, JP Olsen, and Dolores Alfieri.

Stephen Motika, publisher of Nightboat Books, believed in this project from the moment we brought it to him. Thank you, Stephen, for your certainty and support.

And finally I want to extend my gratitude to my co-editor, Trace Peterson, without whom none of this could have come together as beautifully as it did. I don't think either of us knew when you said yes to co-editing this book with me that we were unofficially embarking on a platonic long distance intimate relationship with someone we'd never even met! I love you for your willingness, your courage.

Trace Peterson:

I offer my deepest gratitude to the following friends, colleagues, and comrades, without whom this book could not have been possible.

Thank you to Samuel Ace for being an unbelievably great friend and mentor. Sam, you are a vital connection that brought TC and me together so that this book could happen, but beyond this I feel that you are really the animating spirit of this book, and I dedicate it to you. Your encouragement, support, dedication, and sense of humor throughout this project helped give me the courage to always remember what is most important and to make it through an enormous amount of meticulous editorial work, challenging design problems, and complex communications with 53 authors, resulting in a book that we can all be proud of.

Thanks to Charles Alexander for allowing me to consult with him on the design of this book, and for helping me come up with useful solutions to several design challenges.

Thanks to the wonderful friends and readers who helped me hone the selection of poems for this book and get some perspective on the poetics statement, as well as offering essential feedback on my introduction: Charles, Sam, Andrew Levy, Barbara Cully, Brenda Iijima, Camille Roy, Filip Marinovich, Gregory Laynor, Joel Sloman, Paolo Javier, and Ruth Lepson. Thanks to Joel and Ruth also for participating in a writing group that inspired me to write some of the poems in this anthology.

Thanks to Fran Blau for permission to print kari edwards' poems in this anthology, and for her generous and enthusiastic spirit and friendship.

Thanks to Vincent Katz for introducing me to Raymond Foye, John Wieners' literary executor, and thanks to Raymond for his generous permission to print Wieners' poems in this anthology. Thanks to Robbie Dewhurst for recommending "Preface" as an appropriate poetics statement for Wieners given the context of this anthology's concerns. Thanks also to Gerrit Lansing and Jim Dunn for introducing me to John Wieners' poetry nearly a decade ago.

Thanks to Codie Leone for her friendship and consistently stunning wig styling throughout the years. I'm glad she got to hold a copy of this book in she hands before she passed away, even if she did not live to see me transition. I miss you a lot Codie.

Thanks to Joy Ladin and Trish Salah, both brilliant poet-critics & lovely people, for your tremendous inspiration and friendship. You make me want to live my life, write my poems, do my scholarly work, and pursue my dreams to the very fullest.

Thanks to the poet-friends who accept and support me whatever gender I am—you know who you are.

Thanks to my family (Mom, Dad, Pat P., Pat B., and the rest) for loving me and especially for loving my poetry. I am so grateful to all of you for finally coming around and embracing me once I became myself post-transition. Thank you for growing with me and turning into the most supportive family a trans gal could have.

Thanks to Danya Shneyer for the beautiful author photo.

Thanks to Stephen Motika for believing in this project, especially for his wisdom, support, and instincts that I absolutely trust.

Thanks especially to my co-editor TC Tolbert for his tireless energy and momentum, his enthusiasm for bringing people together, and his great taste in poetry.

Nightboat Books

Nightboat Books, a nonprofit organization, seeks to develop audiences for writers whose work resists convention and transcends boundaries. We publish books rich with poignancy, intelligence, and risk. Please visit our website, www.nightboat.org, to learn about our titles and how you can support our future publications.

This book has been made possible, in part, by grants from The Fund for Poetry and the New York State Council on the Arts Literature Program.

State of the Arts

NYSCA